U•X•L
Protests, Riots, and Rebellions
Civil Unrest in the Modern World

U•X•L
Protests, Riots, and Rebellions
Civil Unrest in the Modern World

VOLUME 3

Tracey Vasil Biscontini, Editor
Kathleen J. Edgar, Project Editor

U·X·L
A part of Gale, a Cengage Company

Farmington Hills, Mich • San Francisco • New York • Waterville, Maine
Meriden, Conn • Mason, Ohio • Chicago

Protests, Riots, and Rebellions: Civil Unrest in the Modern World

Tracey Vasil Biscontini, Editor

Project Editor: Kathleen J. Edgar
Acquisition Editor: Christine Slovey
Editorial: Elizabeth Manar, Mark Mikula
Rights Acquisition and Management: Carissa Poweleit, Ashley M. Maynard
Imaging: John L. Watkins
Product Design: Kristine A. Julien
Composition: Evi Abou-El-Seoud
Manufacturing: Wendy Blurton

© 2018 Gale, a Cengage Company

ALL RIGHTS RESERVED. No part of this work covered by the copyright herein may be reproduced, transmitted, stored, or used in any form or by any means graphic, electronic, or mechanical, including but not limited to photocopying, recording, scanning, digitizing, taping, Web distribution, information networks, or information storage and retrieval systems, except as permitted under Section 107 or 108 of the 1976 United States Copyright Act, without the prior written permission of the publisher.

For product information and technology assistance, contact us at
Gale Customer Support, 1-800-877-4253.
For permission to use material from this text or product, submit all requests online at **www.cengage.com/permissions**.
Further permissions questions can be emailed to **permissionrequest@cengage.com**

Cover art, front: Image of Umbrella Revolution, © Chris McGrath/Getty Images; Wounded Knee standoff, © Bettmann/Getty Images; Justice for All march against police violence, © Bill Clark/Getty Images; and child labor protest, courtesy of the Bain Collection/Library of Congress. Cover art, back: Image of sign held at immigration rally, © Jorge Salcedo/Shutterstock.com.

Inside art: Image of cheering crowd, © AlbertBuchatskyy/Shutterstock.com; document icon, © Colorlife/Shutterstock.com; and megaphone, © Gulnar Sarkhanl/Shutterstock.com.

While every effort has been made to ensure the reliability of the information presented in this publication, Gale, a Cengage Company, does not guarantee the accuracy of the data contained herein. Gale accepts no payment for listing; and inclusion in the publication of any organization, agency, institution, publication, service, or individual does not imply endorsement of the editors or publisher. Errors brought to the attention of the publisher and verified to the satisfaction of the publisher will be corrected in future editions.

Library of Congress Cataloging-in-Publication Data

Names: Biscontini, Tracey Vasil, editor. | Edgar, Kathleen J., editor.
Title: UXL protests, riots, and rebellions : civil unrest in the modern world / Tracey Vasil Biscontini, editor ; Kathleen J. Edgar, project editor.
Description: Farmington Hills, Mich. : UXL, a part of Gale, a Cengage Company, [2018] | Includes bibliographical references and index.
Identifiers: LCCN 2017045153 | ISBN 9781410339089 (set : alk. paper) | ISBN 9781410339102 (vol. 1 : alk. paper) | ISBN 9781410339119 (vol. 2 : alk. paper) | ISBN 9781410355874 (vol. 3 : alk. paper) | ISBN 9781410339096 (ebook : alk. paper)
Subjects: LCSH: Protest movements–History–Juvenile literature. | Civil rights movements–History–Juvenile literature. | Political participation–History–Juvenile literature.
Classification: LCC HM883 .U95 2018 | DDC 303.48/4–dc23
LC record available at https://lccn.loc.gov/2017045153

Gale
27500 Drake Rd.
Farmington Hills, MI 48331-3535

978-1-4103-3908-9 (set)   978-1-4103-3911-9 (vol. 2)
978-1-4103-3910-2 (vol. 1)   978-1-4103-5587-4 (vol. 3)

This title is also available as an e-book.
978-1-4103-3909-6
Contact your Gale sales representative for ordering information.

Printed in the United States of America
1 2 3 4 5 6 7 22 21 20 19 18

Table of Contents

Events by Topic of Protest (A Thematic Table of Contents) **ix**

Reader's Guide **xiii**

Chronology **xv**

Words to Know **xxxiii**

VOLUME 1

Chapter 1: Animal Rights **1**
    UCR Lab Raid to Protest Animal Testing **7**
    Bilbao Anti-bullfighting Protest **12**
    Global March for Elephants and Rhinos **18**
    Blackfish Documentary and SeaWorld Protests **25**

Chapter 2: Civil Rights, African American **35**
    Montgomery Bus Boycott **42**
    Little Rock Nine Crisis **47**
    Freedom Rides **54**
    Lunch Counter Protest, McCrory's **59**
    March on Washington for Jobs and Freedom **63**

Chapter 3: Civil Rights, Hispanic and Latino **71**
    East LA Blowouts **77**
    A Day without Immigrants **83**
    Mexican Indignados Movement **90**

Chapter 4: Economic Discontent **99**
    Secret Document of the Farmers of
        Xiaogang **105**

TABLE OF CONTENTS

    Porkulus Protests, Tea Party **111**
    15-M Movement **116**
    Brexit **122**

Chapter 5: Environment **133**
    Forward on Climate Rally **139**
    Copenhagen Protests **144**
    Global Frackdown **151**
    Pacific Climate Warriors Blockade **157**
    March for Science **163**

Chapter 6: Free Speech **171**
    Harry Potter Book Burning **177**
    Muslim Protests of Danish Cartoons **183**
    "Je Suis Charlie" Protests **189**
    Yale Student Protests on Free Speech **194**

Chapter 7: Globalization **203**
    Battle in Seattle: World Trade Organization Protests **209**
    Occupy Wall Street **216**
    March against Monsanto **223**

VOLUME 2

Chapter 8: Gun Control/Gun Rights **233**
    Black Panthers Carry Guns into California Legislative Building in Protest of Mulford Act **239**
    March on Washington for Gun Control **246**
    "I Will Not Comply" Rally **252**
    Democratic Congressional Representatives Sit-in for Gun Control Legislation **256**

Chapter 9: Human Rights **263**
    Attica Prison Riot **270**
    Capitol Crawl **276**
    March to Abolish the Death Penalty **284**
    Dalit Protests in India **290**
    Armenian Genocide Protests **297**

Chapter 10: Immigrant Rights **305**
    1844 Nativist Riots **311**

Pro-Migrant Rallies in Europe and Australia **318**

Protests against President Trump's Travel Ban **325**

Chapter 11: Independence Movements **335**

Grito de Lares **342**

Gandhi Leads Salt March **346**

The Velvet Revolution **352**

Chapter 12: Indigenous Peoples' Rights **361**

AIM Occupation of Wounded Knee **367**

Aboriginal Land Rights Protest **375**

Preservation of Amazon Rain Forest Awareness Campaign **379**

Dakota Access Pipeline Protest **384**

Chapter 13: Labor Rights **393**

Mother Jones's "Children's Crusade" **399**

Flint Sit-Down Strike against General Motors **407**

Delano Grape Strike and Boycott **414**

Fast-Food Workers' Strike **422**

Chapter 14: LGBTQ Rights **429**

Stonewall Riots **435**

White Night Riots **441**

Westboro Baptist Church Protests of Matthew Shepard **445**

Shanghai Pride Festival **452**

Protests of North Carolina House Bill 2 **458**

VOLUME 3

Chapter 15: Political/Government Uprisings **467**

Tiananmen Square Protests **473**

Fall of the Berlin Wall **478**

Arab Spring and the Syrian Civil Uprising **486**

Tahrir Square Protests (Egyptian Revolution) **493**

Umbrella Revolution **498**

Chapter 16: Racial Conflict **509**

Zoot Suit Riots **518**

Detroit Riots **524**

Soweto Uprising **530**

Justice for All March **539**

TABLE OF CONTENTS

Chapter 17: Reproductive Rights **549**
    March for Women's Lives **556**
    Operation Rescue **562**
    One-Child Policy Riots **568**
    Planned Parenthood Protests **574**

Chapter 18: Resistance to Nazis **585**
    White Rose Movement **592**
    Holocaust Resistance in Denmark **597**
    Warsaw Ghetto Uprising **602**
    Treblinka Death Camp Revolt **607**

Chapter 19: Slavery **617**
    Louisiana Rebellion (German Coast) **623**
    Nat Turner's Rebellion/Anti-slavery Petitions **628**
    Christmas Rebellion/Baptist War **634**
    Harpers Ferry Raid **638**
    Fight to Stop Human Trafficking **643**

Chapter 20: War **651**
    International Congress of Women **657**
    Student Armband Protest of Vietnam War **663**
    Student Protest at Kent State **669**
    Candlelight Vigils against Invasion of Iraq **676**
    Chelsea Manning and WikiLeaks **684**

Chapter 21: Women's Rights **693**
    Hunger Strikes by Suffragettes in Prison **701**
    Women's Suffrage Protest at the White House **707**
    Baladi Campaign **714**
    Malala Yousafzai All-Girls School **718**
    Women's March on Washington **724**

Research and Activities Ideas **xlv**

Where to Learn More **li**

General Index **lxix**

Events by Topic of Protest
(A Thematic Table of Contents)

The main entry events in *Protests, Riots, and Rebellions* are organized by theme and type in the list that follows. Entries may appear under more than one heading when numerous factors were involved. Boldface indicates volume numbers.

Animal Rights

Bilbao Anti-bullfighting Protest	**1:** 12
Blackfish Documentary and SeaWorld Protests	**1:** 25
Global March for Elephants and Rhinos	**1:** 18
UCR Lab Raid to Protest Animal Testing	**1:** 7

Children/Young Adult Issues

East LA Blowouts	**1:** 77
Harry Potter Book Burning	**1:** 177
Little Rock Nine Crisis	**1:** 47
Mother Jones's "Children's Crusade"	**2:** 399
Soweto Uprising	**3:** 530
Yale Student Protests on Free Speech	**1:** 194

Civil Rights

Baladi Campaign	**3:** 714
Day without Immigrants	**1:** 83
East LA Blowouts	**1:** 77
Freedom Rides	**1:** 54
Hunger Strikes by Suffragettes in Prison	**3:** 701
Little Rock Nine Crisis	**1:** 47
Lunch Counter Protest, McCrory's	**1:** 59
March on Washington for Jobs and Freedom	**1:** 63
Mexican Indignados Movement	**1:** 90
Montgomery Bus Boycott	**1:** 42
Women's Suffrage Protest at the White House	**3:** 707

Climate Change

Copenhagen Protests	**1:** 144
Forward on Climate Rally	**1:** 139
March for Science	**1:** 163
Pacific Climate Warriors Blockade	**1:** 157

Economic Issues

Battle in Seattle: World Trade Organization Protests	**1:** 209
Brexit	**1:** 122
Day without Immigrants	**1:** 83
Fast-Food Workers' Strike	**2:** 422
15-M Movement	**1:** 116
March on Washington for Jobs and Freedom	**1:** 63
Occupy Wall Street	**1:** 216
Porkulus Protests, Tea Party	**1:** 111
Secret Document of the Farmers of Xiaogang	**1:** 105

Education

East LA Blowouts	**1:** 77
Little Rock Nine Crisis	**1:** 47

ix

EVENTS BY TOPIC OF PROTEST (A THEMATIC TABLE OF CONTENTS)

Malala Yousafzai All-Girls School	**3:** 718
Soweto Uprising	**3:** 530
Yale Student Protests on Free Speech	**1:** 194

Energy, Power

Dakota Access Pipeline Protest	**2:** 384
Global Frackdown	**1:** 151
Pacific Climate Warriors Blockade	**1:** 157
Preservation of Amazon Rain Forest Awareness Campaign	**2:** 379

Environment

Battle in Seattle: World Trade Organization Protests	**1:** 209
Copenhagen Protests	**1:** 144
Dakota Access Pipeline Protest	**2:** 384
Forward on Climate Rally	**1:** 139
Global Frackdown	**1:** 151
March for Science	**1:** 163
Pacific Climate Warriors Blockade	**1:** 157
Preservation of Amazon Rain Forest Awareness Campaign	**2:** 379

Free Speech

Harry Potter Book Burning	**1:** 177
"Je Suis Charlie" Protests	**1:** 189
Muslim Protests of Danish Cartoons	**1:** 183
Yale Student Protests on Free Speech	**1:** 194

Globalization, Corporations

Battle in Seattle: World Trade Organization Protests	**1:** 209
March against Monsanto	**1:** 223
Occupy Wall Street	**1:** 216

Guns

Black Panthers Carry Guns into California Legislative Building in Protest of Mulford Act	**2:** 239
Democratic Congressional Representatives Sit-In for Gun Control Legislation	**2:** 256
"I Will Not Comply" Rally	**2:** 252
March on Washington for Gun Control	**2:** 246

Health Issues

Capitol Crawl	**2:** 276
March against Monsanto	**1:** 223
March for Women's Lives	**3:** 556
Planned Parenthood Protests	**3:** 574

Human Rights

Armenian Genocide Protests	**2:** 297
Attica Prison Riot	**2:** 270
Capitol Crawl	**2:** 276
Dalit Protests in India	**2:** 290
Gandhi Leads Salt March	**2:** 346
March to Abolish the Death Penalty	**2:** 284
Mexican Indignados Movement	**1:** 90

Immigration

Brexit	**1:** 122
Day without Immigrants	**1:** 83
1844 Nativist Riots	**2:** 311
Pro-Migrant Rallies in Europe and Australia	**2:** 318
Protests against President Trump's Travel Ban	**2:** 325

Income Inequality

Battle in Seattle: World Trade Organization Protests	**1:** 209
Delano Grape Strike and Boycott	**2:** 414
Fast-Food Workers' Strike	**2:** 422
Flint Sit-Down Strike against General Motors	**2:** 407
March on Washington for Jobs and Freedom	**1:** 63
Occupy Wall Street	**1:** 216

Independence Movements

Gandhi Leads Salt March	**2:** 346
Grito de Lares	**2:** 342
Velvet Revolution	**2:** 352

Indigenous Peoples' Rights

Aboriginal Land Rights Protest	**2:** 375
AIM Occupation of Wounded Knee	**2:** 367
Dakota Access Pipeline Protest	**2:** 384

Labor

Preservation of Amazon Rain Forest Awareness Campaign	2: 379
Battle in Seattle: World Trade Organization Protests	1: 209
Day without Immigrants	1: 83
Delano Grape Strike and Boycott	2: 414
Fast-Food Workers' Strike	2: 422
15-M Movement	1: 116
Flint Sit-Down Strike against General Motors	2: 407
March on Washington for Jobs and Freedom	1: 63
Mother Jones's "Children's Crusade"	2: 399
Secret Document of the Farmers of Xiaogang	1: 105

Land Rights

Aboriginal Land Rights Protest	2: 375
AIM Occupation of Wounded Knee	2: 367
Preservation of Amazon Rain Forest Awareness Campaign	2: 379

LGBTQ Issues

Protests of North Carolina House Bill 2	2: 458
Shanghai Pride Festival	2: 452
Stonewall Riots	2: 435
Westboro Baptist Church Protests of Matthew Shepard	2: 445
White Night Riots	2: 441

Police Brutality

Detroit Riots	3: 524
Justice for All March	3: 539
March on Washington for Jobs and Freedom	1: 63
Stonewall Riots	2: 435

Political Uprisings

Arab Spring and the Syrian Civil Uprising	3: 486
Fall of the Berlin Wall	3: 478
Tahrir Square Protests (Egyptian Revolution)	3: 493
Tiananmen Square Protests	3: 473
Umbrella Revolution	3: 498

Race Issues

Black Panthers Carry Guns into California Legislative Building in Protest of Mulford Act	2: 239
Detroit Riots	3: 524
East LA Blowouts	1: 77
Freedom Rides	1: 54
Justice for All March	3: 539
Little Rock Nine Crisis	1: 47
Lunch Counter Protest, McCrory's	1: 59
March on Washington for Jobs and Freedom	1: 63
Montgomery Bus Boycott	1: 42
Soweto Uprising	3: 530
Zoot Suit Riots	3: 518

Religion

"Je Suis Charlie" Protests	1: 189
Muslim Protests of Danish Cartoons	1: 183
Protests against President Trump's Travel Ban	2: 325

Reproductive Issues

March for Women's Lives	3: 556
One-Child Policy Riots	3: 568
Operation Rescue	3: 562
Planned Parenthood Protests	3: 574

Resistance to Nazis

Holocaust Resistance in Denmark	3: 597
Treblinka Death Camp Revolt	3: 607
Warsaw Ghetto Uprising (Poland)	3: 602
White Rose Movement	3: 592

Revolutions

Grito de Lares	2: 342
Tahrir Square Protests (Egyptian Revolution)	3: 493
Umbrella Revolution	3: 498
Velvet Revolution	2: 352

EVENTS BY TOPIC OF PROTEST (A THEMATIC TABLE OF CONTENTS)

Segregation/Desegregation

Freedom Rides	**1:** 54
Little Rock Nine Crisis	**1:** 47
Lunch Counter Protest, McCrory's	**1:** 59
March on Washington for Jobs and Freedom	**1:** 63
Montgomery Bus Boycott	**1:** 42

Slavery

Christmas Rebellion/Baptist War	**3:** 634
Fight to Stop Human Trafficking	**3:** 643
Harpers Ferry Raid	**3:** 638
Louisiana Rebellion (German Coast)	**3:** 623
Nat Turner's Rebellion/Anti-slavery Petitions	**3:** 628

Student Movements and Protests

East LA Blowouts	**1:** 77
15-M Movement	**1:** 116
Little Rock Nine Crisis	**1:** 47
Soweto Uprising	**3:** 530
Student Armband Protest of Vietnam War	**3:** 663
Student Protest at Kent State	**3:** 669
Tiananmen Square Protests	**3:** 473
Yale Student Protests on Free Speech	**1:** 194

Suffrage (Voting Rights)

Baladi Campaign	**3:** 714
Hunger Strikes by Suffragettes in Prison	**3:** 701
March on Washington for Jobs and Freedom	**1:** 63
Women's Suffrage Protest at the White House	**3:** 707

Violence

Bilbao Anti-bullfighting Protest	**1:** 12
Democratic Congressional Representatives Sit-In for Gun Control Legislation	**2:** 256
Global March for Elephants and Rhinos	**1:** 18
"Je Suis Charlie" Protests	**1:** 189
Justice for All March	**3:** 539
March on Washington for Gun Control	**2:** 246
March to Abolish the Death Penalty	**2:** 284
Mexican Indignados Movement	**1:** 90
White Night Riots	**2:** 441

War, Genocide, Ethnic Cleansing

Arab Spring and the Syrian Civil Uprising	**3:** 486
Armenian Genocide Protests	**2:** 297
Candlelight Vigils against Invasion of Iraq	**3:** 676
Chelsea Manning and WikiLeaks	**3:** 684
Holocaust Resistance in Denmark	**3:** 597
International Congress of Women	**3:** 657
Student Armband Protest of Vietnam War	**3:** 663
Student Protest at Kent State	**3:** 669
Treblinka Death Camp Revolt	**3:** 607
Warsaw Ghetto Uprising (Poland)	**3:** 602
White Rose Movement	**3:** 592

Women's Issues

Baladi Campaign	**3:** 714
Hunger Strikes by Suffragettes in Prison	**3:** 701
International Congress of Women	**3:** 657
Malala Yousafzai All-Girls School	**3:** 718
March for Women's Lives	**3:** 556
One-Child Policy Riots	**3:** 568
Operation Rescue	**3:** 562
Planned Parenthood Protests	**3:** 574
Women's March on Washington	**3:** 724
Women's Suffrage Protest at the White House	**3:** 707

Reader's Guide

The ancient Greek philosopher Heraclitus (535 BCE–475 BCE) once wrote that the only constant thing in life is change. Change is a natural part of human existence. It has driven everything from biological evolution to cultural advancement for thousands of years. Yet, despite the desire for change, accomplishing it can be difficult. Old ideas and prejudices are hard to overcome, and people often resist efforts to alter the current state of affairs.

For some, change involves the fight for human rights. Others seek to end war, to express ideas freely, or to live a lifestyle of their own choosing. Those who seek change use various forms of protest or civil unrest to make their voices heard. Although many protests are peaceful, some escalate into full-scale riots or rebellions. Nevertheless, the people involved in these movements strongly believe that their cause is worth fighting for.

U•X•L Protests, Riots, and Rebellions: Civil Unrest in the Modern World presents a detailed look at many of these efforts to enact change in the world. This 21-chapter work examines a wide range of diverse issues from the environment to free speech and racial conflict. Each chapter begins with a comprehensive overview designed to introduce readers to the topic. The text details 88 events as well as numerous sidebars that focus on various protests, conflicts, or social movements.

The entries are written in a style that makes complicated subjects easy for younger readers to understand. Each event is framed in the context of the historical period in which it occurred, examining not only the social forces that shaped the event but also the motivations of those who participated in it. Rather than solely focusing on what happened, each entry delves deeper into why it happened.

The chapters feature more than 200 photos and illustrations that help bring each event into sharper focus. In addition, each chapter includes a helpful

"Words to Know" box that defines key terms, and another box featuring questions designed to spark critical thinking. The set also includes 42 primary sources that provide additional information helpful in understanding the topic.

Additional Features

Protests, Riots, and Rebellions also contains a substantial and detailed chronology of events to help place each topic in its historical context. A "Where to Learn More" section lists books, periodicals, and websites to find additional information. The section "Research and Activity Ideas" provides students with ways to discuss and explore the topics further. Also included is a general glossary and a subject index.

Acknowledgments

The editors would like to acknowledge the following writers and editors at Northeast Editing, Inc. for their work on this volume: Tyler Biscontini, Eric Bullard, Cait Caffrey, Josephine Campbell, Mark Dziak, Angela Harmon, Jack Lasky, Elizabeth Mohn, Joanne Quaglia, Lindsay Rohland, Michael Ruth, Richard Sheposh, and Rebecca Zukauskas.

Special thanks to Susan Edgar, senior vocabulary editor at Cengage Learning, for sharing her expertise on historical events as we created the topic list. Additional thanks go to Justine Carson for her work on the index.

Suggestions Are Welcome

We welcome your comments on *U•X•L Protests, Riots, and Rebellions: Civil Unrest in the Modern World* and suggestions for other history topics to consider. Please write: Editors, *U•X•L Protests, Riots, and Rebellions* Gale, 27500 Drake Rd., Farmington Hills, MI 48331-3535; call toll free: 1-800-877-4253; fax to 248-699-8097; or send e-mail via http://www.gale.cengage.com.

Chronology

The chronology that follows contains a sampling of important events, protests, riots, and rebellions that occurred in the modern world.

c. 1760 to 1840	Period of transition beginning in Great Britain (and later spreading to Western Europe and North America) when manufacturing changed from hand to machine production. Some workers protested the loss of their jobs to machines during the Industrial Revolution.
1811	On January 8, several hundred slaves on Louisiana's German Coast near New Orleans stage an uprising that lasts for three days before military forces finally put it down.
1811	An anti-industrialization movement led by a group of angry textile workers and weavers called the Luddites begins in Great Britain.
1831–1832	A series of petitions sent to the Virginia General Assembly leads to a debate about the future of slavery in the state.
1835	On January 24, an uprising of Muslim slaves called the Malê revolt begins in Brazil.
1838	Author and poet Ralph Waldo Emerson (1803–1882) writes a letter to President Martin van Buren (1782–1862) in protest of the forced removal of the Cherokee in Georgia. The removal takes place and becomes known as the Trail of Tears.

McConnel & Company mills in England during the Industrial Revolution, c. 1820. PUBLIC DOMAIN

CHRONOLOGY

Ruins of the mission church destroyed during the Taos Revolt, 1847. © MATT RAGEN/SHUTTERSTOCK.COM

1844   In May and July, anti-immigrant mobs attack Irish immigrants in a series of riots that rock the city of Philadelphia, Pennsylvania.

1847   In January, a band of New Mexicans and Pueblo Indians revolt against the United States' occupation of northern New Mexico during the Mexican-American War (1846–1848). It becomes known as the Taos Revolt.

1848   The first women's rights convention in US history takes place in Seneca Falls, New York.

1859   Antislavery activist John Brown (1800–1859) leads an armed slave revolt at the US arsenal in Harpers Ferry, Virginia (now West Virginia).

1861   The US Civil War begins.

1863   In July, riots break out in New York City after Congress passes laws that allow the government to draft young men to serve in the US Civil War.

1865   The US Civil War ends.

1868   On September 23, Puerto Rican revolutionaries stage a brief uprising called the Grito de Lares in hopes of gaining their independence from Spain.

1880   Growing resentment of incoming Chinese immigrants leads to rioting in Denver, Colorado.

1886   On May 4, a labor rally near Haymarket Square in Chicago, Illinois, turns violent after someone throws a bomb at police.

1887   Pioneering female journalist Nellie Bly (Elizabeth Cochran Seaman, 1864–1922) goes undercover as an inmate in a New York mental hospital to expose the many abuses occurring there. Her report is published in the *New York World* newspaper and later in the book *Ten Days in a Mad-House*. Bly's type of investigation is the first of its kind.

1890   On December 29, tensions between the US Army and the Sioux on the Pine Ridge Reservation become intense. After a shot is fired, the army goes on to kill at least 150 Sioux men, women, and children in what becomes known as the Wounded Knee Massacre.

1898 The Spanish-American War begins in April after the USS *Maine* explodes in Havana Harbor, Cuba, in February. The war ends in August with the United States taking control of Guam, Puerto Rico, and the Philippines.

1903 In July, reformer Mary Harris "Mother" Jones (1837–1930) leads the Children's Crusade, also known as the March of the Mill Children, from Philadelphia, Pennsylvania, to Oyster Bay, New York, to bring attention to the problem of child labor.

1909 Women's rights activists imprisoned in Great Britain begin using hunger strikes to bring awareness to their cause.

1911 From September 14 to 22, El Primer Congreso Mexicanista, the first civil rights meeting for Mexican Americans, is held in Laredo, Texas.

1914 World War I begins in Europe.

1915 The International Congress of Women meets at The Hague in the Netherlands and creates several resolutions for peace.

1918 A group of National Women's Party members protest in front of the White House in Washington, DC, and call on the president to help women gain the right to vote.

1918 Between July and September, the anti-government Rice Riots break out in Japan in response to economic problems caused by low wages and high prices on goods such as rice.

1918 World War I ends.

1921 In August, thousands of frustrated West Virginian coal miners march on Blair Mountain and clash with coal company supporters and police for nearly a week in one of the largest labor uprisings in US history.

CHRONOLOGY

1929 — In November, women in Nigeria revolt against British colonial administrators in the Aba Women's War.

1930 — Indian independence movement leader Mohandas Gandhi (1869–1948) leads his famous Salt March in protest of the British Raj government's abuses of the Indian people.

1933 — On May 10, the Nazi Party holds a massive book burning in Germany, during which any books that do not support Nazi thinking or politics are destroyed.

1936 — General Motors employees in Flint, Michigan, go on a 44-day sit-down strike for better pay and improved working conditions.

1939 — World War II begins in Europe.

1942 — In February, President Franklin Roosevelt signs an executive order calling for people of Japanese ancestry on the West Coast to be relocated to internment camps. In March 1945 detainees at an internment camp near Santa Fe, New Mexico, rebel against guards in what becomes known as the Santa Fe Riot.

People of Japanese descent are sent to internment camps, 1942. COURTESY OF LIBRARY OF CONGRESS.

1942 — German medical student Hans Scholl (1918–1943) founds the White Rose movement, a resistance effort aimed at creating opposition to the Nazi Party.

1943 — People in Nazi-occupied Denmark begin resisting German rule and protecting Danish Jews from being sent to concentration camps.

1943 — On April 19, Jewish prisoners held in Poland's Warsaw Ghetto revolt against Nazi forces it what becomes known as the Warsaw Ghetto Uprising.

1943 — On June 3, chaos breaks out in Los Angeles, California, as angry American servicemen attack Mexican American and other minority youths in the Zoot Suit Riots.

1943 — In August, Jewish prisoners held by the Nazis at the Treblinka death camp in Poland revolt.

1945 — World War II ends.

CHRONOLOGY

1950 The Korean War begins.

1953 The Korean War ends.

1954 The Vietnam War begins.

1955 African Americans in Montgomery, Alabama, begin boycotting the public bus system after Rosa Parks (1913–2005) is arrested for refusing to give up her seat to a white passenger.

1957 In September, riots and other protests erupt in Little Rock, Arkansas, when nine African American students are admitted to the desegregated Little Rock Central High School.

1960 In April, a student uprising in South Korea known as the April Revolution leads to the overthrow of the First Republic of South Korea and the resignation of President Syngman Rhee (1875–1965).

1960 Chaos erupts in November when six-year-old Ruby Bridges (1954–) of Tylertown, Mississippi, becomes the first African American child to attend an all-white elementary school in the South.

Scene from the April Revolution in South Korea, 1960. © AP IMAGES.

1961 In January, nine African Americans stage a sit-in at a McCrory's lunch counter in Rock Hill, South Carolina, to protest the store's refusal to serve African American customers.

1961 Beginning In May, bus trips through the American South called the Freedom Rides are held in protest of Jim Crow laws and segregation at interstate bus stations.

1963 On August 28, about 250,000 people participate in the March on Washington for Jobs and Freedom in protest of racial segregation and other forms of discrimination. Civil rights icon the Rev. Dr. Martin Luther King Jr. (1929–1968) delivers his famous "I Have a Dream" speech.

1964 Between June and August, civil rights groups organize a voter registration drive called the Mississippi Summer Project in an effort to increase voter registration in that state.

CHRONOLOGY

Fannie Lou Hamer at Democratic National Convention. COURTESY OF LIBRARY OF CONGRESS.

1964 In August, voting rights and civil rights activist Fannie Lou Hamer shocks the nation during a speech at the Democratic National Convention in Atlantic City, New Jersey. She details the abuse she suffered at the hands of white citizens and police while trying to help register African American voters.

1964 The Free Speech Movement takes off at the University of California, Berkeley.

1965 On September 8, grape pickers in Delano, California, begin a labor strike with the help of the Agricultural Workers Organizing Committee and the United Farm Workers. The movement, which is led by César Chávez (1927–1993), continues until 1970.

1965 In December, students at several schools in Des Moines, Iowa, begin wearing black armbands to protest the Vietnam War.

1967 On May 2, members of the Black Panther Party stage a protest at the California State Capitol over a proposed gun control law that would prohibit them from conducting armed patrols of African American neighborhoods.

1967 On July 23, a race riot begins in Detroit, Michigan, after a police raid on an after-hours bar. The riot quickly becomes one of the worst of its kind in US history, resulting in 43 deaths, 7,200 arrests, and 2,000 damaged buildings.

1968 On March 1, Chicano students in Los Angeles, California, stage the first of a series of walkouts known as the East LA Blowouts in protest of unequal conditions at local high schools.

1968 On April 4, Martin Luther King Jr. is assassinated in Memphis, Tennessee.

May 1968 French student protest poster that reads "Be young and shut up." © ROGER VIOLLET/GETTY IMAGES.

1968 In May, civil unrest sweeps across France as student protests and widespread labor strikes temporarily disrupt the nation's government and economy.

CHRONOLOGY

1968 — On September 7, several hundred feminists stage a protest against the Miss America Pageant on the Atlantic City boardwalk in New Jersey.

1968 — In October, during the Olympic Games in Mexico City, Mexico, African American sprinters Tommie Smith (1944–) and John Carlos (1945–) raise their fists as they receive their medals in a gesture meant to promote human rights.

Protest of the Miss America Beauty Pageant, 1968.
© BETTMANN/GETTY IMAGES.

1969 — On June 28, a police raid on a New York City gay nightclub called the Stonewall Inn leads to a series of violent protests and riots.

1969 — On November 20, a group of 89 Native Americans go to Alcatraz Island in San Francisco Bay and claim it as their own "by right of discovery." Their occupation of the island continues until June of 1971.

1970 — On May 4, a protest against the Vietnam War at Kent State University turns deadly when members of the Ohio National Guard open fire on demonstrators and kill four students.

Bob Dylan and Joan Baez protested the Vietnam War through song. © TRINITY MIRROR/MIRRORPIX/ALAMY.

1971 — Whistle-blower Daniel Ellsberg (1931–) reveals details from a secret US government report about US involvement in the Vietnam War to the *New York Times*. The report comes to be known as the Pentagon Papers.

1971 — On September 9, prisoners demanding better living conditions and political rights at Attica Correctional Facility in upstate New York begin a violent four-day revolt. A total of 43 people are killed in the uprising.

1972 — On January 30, British soldiers shoot and kill 28 unarmed people participating in a peaceful protest over the arrest of more than 300 people accused of working with the Irish Republican Army (IRA). This event soon becomes known as Bloody Sunday.

1973 — On February 27, about 200 Native Americans led by members of the American Indian Movement (AIM) take control of Pine Ridge Reservation in South Dakota. Their occupation of the reservation continues until May 8.

The Pentagon Papers were released in 1971. © MPI/GETTY IMAGES.

U•X•L Protests, Riots, and Rebellions: Civil Unrest in the Modern World

CHRONOLOGY

1975   The Vietnam War ends.

1976   On June 16, hundreds are killed in Soweto, South Africa, when a student protest turns violent. The violence brings attention to the problem of racism in South Africa and plays an important role in eventually ending the apartheid system.

1977   Chicago-based neo-Nazis attempt to hold a march in Skokie, Illinois, but are blocked by local officials. The case eventually reaches the US Supreme Court, where it is decided that the neo-Nazis' right to march is protected by the 1st Amendment. The march in Skokie is never held.

1979   On May 21, the White Night Riots erupt in San Francisco, California, after convicted killer Dan White (1946–1985) is given a light sentence for the murders of Mayor George Moscone (1929–1978) and gay rights activist and politician Harvey Milk (1930–1978).

1979   On October 14, as many as 125,000 people participate in the National March on Washington for Lesbian and Gay Rights.

1980   On August 14, shipyard workers in Gdańsk, Poland, stage a successful strike that leads to a strong anti-communism movement in the country.

1985   On April 20, animal rights activists break into a laboratory at the University of California, Riverside, to free animals used in experiments.

1986   In March, a pair of reproductive rights rallies called the March for Women's Lives are held in Washington, DC, and Los Angeles, California.

1988   On January 26, thousands of Australian Aboriginals hold a peaceful equal rights rally in Sydney during the 200th anniversary of Australia Day.

1989   Kayapo chief Raoni Metuktire (c. 1930–) leads a campaign against the building of a dam in the Amazon rain forest with the help of rock star Sting (1951–).

CHRONOLOGY

1989 On November 9, the Berlin Wall falls.

1989 On November 17, a political movement called the Velvet Revolution begins in Czechoslovakia and ends just over a month later with the end of communism in that country.

1990 On March 12, disabled activists protest delays in passing the Americans with Disabilities Act (ADA) by crawling up the steps of the US Capitol in an event called the Capitol Crawl.

1990 In October, a Jewish group wants to lay a cornerstone for a temple at the site of the Al-Aqsa Mosque, a Muslim holy place in Jerusalem on a hill known as the Temple Mount. A group of Palestinians respond by throwing rocks and bottles at border police as well as at Jews, who are praying at the Western Wall just below the mosque on the hill. Israeli troops respond and kill 23 Palestinians; several hundred others are injured in the riots.

Temple Mount Riots, 1990.
© MENAHEM KAHANA/AFP/GETTY IMAGES.

1991 In December, the collapse of the Soviet Union is complete.

1992 The pro-life organization Operation Rescue holds an anti-abortion protest called the Spring of Life.

1992 On April 29, riots break out in Los Angeles, California, after several city police officers are found not guilty in a criminal case concerning the beating of an African American man named Rodney King (1965–2012) during an arrest.

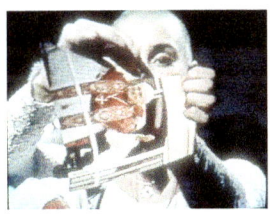

Sinead O'Connor causes a stir when she rips the pope's picture in 1992 on SNL. © YVONNE HEMSEY/HULTON ARCHIVE/GETTY IMAGES.

1992 In October, Irish singer Sinead O'Connor (1966–) appears on NBC's *Saturday Night Live* and sings Jamaican artist Bob Marley's (1945–1981) song "War." As she concludes her performance, she rips up a picture of Pope John Paul II (1920–2005), saying "fight the real enemy." She was protesting sexual abuse in the Catholic Church.

1994 Members of Greenpeace send two ships in an attempt to stop Norwegian ships from hunting whales.

1995 On October 16, Nation of Islam leader Louis Farrakhan (1933–) leads the Million Man March in Washington, DC, to raise awareness of the importance of American family values, unity, and civil rights.

Million Man March in Washington, DC, in 1995. © JAMES LEYNSE/GETTY IMAGES.

U•X•L Protests, Riots, and Rebellions: Civil Unrest in the Modern World xxiii

CHRONOLOGY

1998	On October 16, members of the Westboro Baptist Church protest at the funeral of Matthew Shepard (1976–1998), a young man who was murdered for being gay.
1999	On November 30, a series of protests known as the Battle for Seattle break out in Seattle, Washington, during the World Trade Organization (WTO) Ministerial Conference.
2000	On October 15, the first March to Abolish the Death Penalty is held in Austin, Texas. The inaugural event is called the March on the Mansion.
2001	On September 11, terrorists hijack airplanes that crash into the World Trade Center in New York City; the Pentagon in Washington, DC; and a field in western Pennsylvania. Almost 3,000 people are killed.
2001	In response to the September 11 attacks, the United States forms a coalition of nations and begins a war in Afghanistan on October 7.
2001	On December 30, Pastor Jack Brock of the Christ Community Church in Alamogordo, New Mexico, organizes a book burning at which copies of the Harry Potter series are destroyed.
2002	On November 30, various people in the United Kingdom protest the materialism rampant before the holidays by having a "Buy Nothing Day."
2002	Surfers against Sewage, a group in the United Kingdom, stages a protest to raise awareness about ocean pollutants, including plastics, and the need to keep the coasts clean.
2003	On March 16, thousands of candlelight vigils are held across the world in protest of the impending invasion of Iraq. The war begins on March 19.
2004	On August 29, a group called One Thousand Coffins participates in a march held in New York City to protest the Iraq War.

Organizer of Buy Nothing Day, Michael Smith, in 2002. © ROGER BAMBER/ALAMY.

Participant in the Surfers against Sewage protest, 2002. © SION TOUHIG/GETTY IMAGES.

CHRONOLOGY

2005	On September 30, the Danish newspaper *Jyllands-Posten* publishes several cartoons depicting the Muslim prophet Muhammad. Many Muslims voice concern over the portrayals and some protests turn violent.
2005	On December 3, the first Global Day of Action is held worldwide to protest climate change.
2006	On May 1, protests called a Day without Immigrants are held in cities across the United States. The event is also called the Great American Boycott.
2006	In late November and early December, damage to a statue of a Dalit hero triggers violent protests near Mumbai, India.
2007	In May, thousands of people riot in China against the government's controversial one-child policy.
2008	The women's rights group Soroptimist International of Great Britain and Ireland begins its Purple Teardrop campaign to combat human trafficking.
2008	In February, several Danish newspapers reprint the 2005 cartoon depicting the prophet Muhammad. At least 200 people are killed as protests flare in Denmark and several other nations.
2009	The conservative anti-tax Tea Party movement begins with protest rallies in cities across the United States.
2009	In June, the first Shanghai Pride Festival is held. The event is the first LGBTQ festival to take place on the Chinese mainland.
2009–2010	About 110 people are killed in ongoing protests in Iran over the election of President Mahmoud Ahmadinejad (1956–), which the protesters claim was fraudulent. The protests are known as the Iranian Green Movement.
2009	On October 11, thousands of members of the LGBTQ community and their supporters stage the National Equality March in Washington, DC.
2009	On December 16, about 1,700 people are arrested as thousands of protesters try to disrupt the United Nations Climate Change Conference in Copenhagen, Denmark.

Participants during the Global Day of Action, 2005, to fight climate change.
© PHOTOFUSION/GETTY IMAGES.

CHRONOLOGY

2010	Classified information stolen by US Army soldier Chelsea Manning (then Bradley Manning, 1987–) is first released on the website WikiLeaks.
2010	On August 21, protesters stage an anti-bullfighting rally in front of the Guggenheim Museum in Bilbao, Spain.
2010	In November in Nigeria, people march in conjunction with the Movement for the Survival of the Ogoni people. They are marking the 15th anniversary of the deaths of the Ogoni martyrs, who were executed by the government amid controversy.
2010	On December 17, a Tunisian street vendor named Mohamed Bouazizi (1984–2011) sets himself on fire in a protest against the government.
2011	In January, ongoing protests inspired by Mohamed Bouazizi's actions force Tunisia's president to resign. The protests spread to other nations in northern Africa and the Middle East, beginning a movement known as the Arab Spring.
2011	In January and February, massive anti-government demonstrations take place in Egypt's Tahrir Square.
2011	On March 11, a powerful earthquake strikes Japan, unleashing a massive tsunami. The earthquake and tsunami kill about 19,000 people and severely damage the Fukushima Daiichi Nuclear Power Station.
2011	In March, an uprising begins in Syria. It eventually turns into a brutal civil war that was still ongoing as of early 2018.
2011	The first "Slutwalk" is held after a police officer in Toronto, Canada, suggests women should stop dressing like "sluts" to avoid sexual assault. The protest took on rape culture, which includes blaming or shaming the victims of sexual assault.
2011	The March 28 killing of his son prompts Mexican poet Javier Sicilia (1956–) to organize several protest marches against drug violence in Mexico.
2011	On April 25, demonstrators hold several marches in France and Germany to protest the use of nuclear power.

March by the Movement for the Survival of the Ogoni People, 2010. © PIUS UTOMI EKPEI/ GETTY IMAGES.

Slutwalk, first held in 2011, is an annual event, shown here in 2014. © TYLER MCKAY/ SHUTTERSTOCK.COM.

CHRONOLOGY

2011 On May 15, more than 80,000 people take part in a series of economic protests known as the 15-M movement in Spain.

2011 On September 17, a global protest against economic inequality called Occupy Wall Street starts in New York City and spreads throughout the country and other parts of the world.

2011 The Iraq War ends.

2011 In December, residents of Wukan, China, protest illegal land grabs in their fishing village. Claiming that local officials sold communal land and provided no compensation to residents. the protesters become outraged when a local village leader is killed while in police custody.

Wukan, China, residents protest illegal communal land sales, 2011. © STR/GETTY IMAGES.

2012 Starting in March, protesters in Fukushima, Japan, begin to meet in front of the prime minister's house to protest the use of nuclear power.

2012 On November 29, fast-food workers at McDonald's and other restaurants begin going on strike to protest low wages.

2012 Students in Montreal, Canada, take to the streets to protest a tuition hike and other rising fees at the country's universities.

2013 On January 26, about 1,000 protesters take part in the March on Washington for Gun Control in honor of the 20 children and 6 staff members who were murdered in the Sandy Hook Elementary School shooting several weeks earlier.

Students protest tuition hikes in Montreal, 2012. © ROGERIO BARBOSA/AFP/GETTYIMAGES.

2013 On February 17, more than 40,000 environmentalists rally in front of the White House as part of the Forward on Climate rally in Washington, DC.

2013 On May 25, people in 436 cities around the world protest against Monsanto, a multinational corporation that produces and promotes genetically modified foods.

2013 In July, the Black Lives Matter movement forms.

2013 On November 21, protests called the Euromaidan demonstrations begin to sweep across Ukraine and eventually lead to the 2014 Ukrainian revolution.

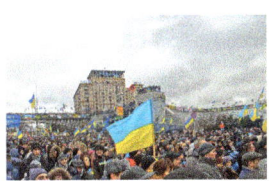

People participating in the Euromaiden protests in the Ukraine, 2013. © PROCESS/SHUTTERSTOCK.COM

CHRONOLOGY

2014	*Blackfish*, a documentary alleging the abuse of orca killer whales at SeaWorld, causes a significant number of animal rights activists to campaign against the parks.
2014	In February, activists around the world protest against the Russian government's harsh policies on homosexuality days before the start of the Sochi Olympic Games.
2014	On April 15, Islamist militants violently kidnap several hundred teenage girls from a boarding school in Nigeria. People around the world respond with the Bring Back Our Girls campaign.
2014	In September, thousands of protesters in Hong Kong clash with police when China announces it will still not allow Hong Kongers to freely select their own leaders. This event is known as the Umbrella Revolution.
2014	On October 3 and 4, animal rights activists around the world continue their annual protests against the poaching of elephants and rhinos in Africa.
2014	On October 11, thousands of environmental activists march in protest of expanded fracking practices.
2014	On October 17, Pacific Climate Warriors attempt to blockade Newcastle Harbor in Australia with kayaks, dinghies, and canoes to prevent coal ships from leaving the harbor.
2015	Saudi Arabia allows women to vote and run in municipal elections for the first time in the country's history.
2015	In January, tens of thousands of people attend rallies throughout France in response to a terrorist attack at the offices of the French magazine *Charlie Hebdo*.
2015	On April 4, people protest the passage of the Religious Freedom Restoration Act in Indiana. They are concerned that the act will allow people to legally discriminate against people based on their sexual orientation or their gender identity.

Participants at the Religious Freedom Restoration Act protest in Indiana, 2015.
© AP IMAGES/DOUG MCSCHOOLER.

CHRONOLOGY

2015 — On April 24, protesters around the world march to mark the 100th anniversary of the Armenian genocide. The protesters demand that Turkey acknowledge its role in the Armenian genocide.

2015 — Malala Yousafzai (1997–), who was shot by the Taliban for speaking out for girls' education, opens an all-girls school for Syrian refugees. A year earlier, she became one of the youngest people ever to win the Nobel Peace Prize.

2015 — On October 13, demonstrators in Turkey protest a double suicide bombing that occurred during a peace rally in Ankara several days earlier. The protesters hold signs of people killed by the blasts.

Anti-terrorism protest in Turkey, 2015. © ADEM ALTAN/GETTY IMAGES.

2015 — On November 21, following terror attacks in Paris, France, earlier that month, Muslims in Italy stage a rally to protest terrorism and violence. Many carry signs reading "Not in My Name."

2015 — In November, students at Yale University protest in response to racial issues at their school. The protests occur after the university issues advice on what types of Halloween costumes might be considered offensive to others.

Italian Muslims rally against terrorism, 2015. © EUGENIO MARONGIU/SHUTTERSTOCK.COM.

2016 — In January, armed anti-government militia members take over the Malheur National Wildlife Refuge near Burns, Oregon. They demand the federal government return the land to the people and release two local ranchers who were put in prison for committing arson on public land. Most of the protesters are not from Oregon but have traveled to the state from Arizona, Montana, and Idaho, among others.

Armed participants at the Malheur National Wildlife Refuge in Oregon, 2016. © ANADOLU AGENCY/GETTY IMAGES.

2016 — On January 24, activists in Greece hold a pro-migrant rally.

CHRONOLOGY

Participants protest lead in the water in Flint, Michigan, 2016. © BILL PUGLIANO/GETTY IMAGES.

Candelight vigil to protest deaths of Tibetans, 2016. © MANJUNATH KIRAN/AFP/GETTY IMAGES.

Counterprotesters urge people to reject hate at Stone Mountain protest, 2016. © AP IMAGES/BEN GRAY.

2016 On February 19, the Rev. Jesse Jackson (1941–) leads a national mile-long march in Flint, Michigan, to raise awareness and demand help to combat the water crisis in the city. A change in the city's water source had led to the corrosion of water pipes that began leaching harmful levels of lead into residents's tap water.

2016 In March, after the self-immolation of two Tibetans in Bangalore, India, a candlelight vigil is held. A schoolboy and a monk had set themselves on fire and died in protest of Chinese rule in the region of Tibet.

2016 Beginning in April, Native Americans and other protesters rally against the Dakota Access Pipeline in North Dakota.

2016 In April, dozens of pro-LGBTQ rights and anti-LGBTQ rights protesters demonstrate in Raleigh, North Carolina, after the passing of the state's Public Facilities Privacy and Security Act. The act pertains to which bathrooms transgender people can use.

2016 In April, white supremacists hold a protest at Stone Mountain, a monument to Confederate leaders, in Georgia. Their white power rally is interrupted by counterprotesters who urge people to reject hate and racism.

2016 On June 22, congressional Democrats stage a sit-in to protest the House of Representatives' refusal to vote on gun control.

2016 On June 23, the United Kingdom votes to leave the European Union. Thousands of people in London take to the streets to protest the decision.

2016 In the fall, San Francisco 49ers quarterback Colin Kaepernick (1987–) begins a protest against racial injustice and police brutality in the United States. He first sits and then later kneels when the national anthem is played at the team's games. Eventually, other athletes join his protest.

2016 In November, following the surprise victory of Republican candidate Donald Trump (1946–) in the US presidential

	election, protesters take to the streets in various cities to demonstrate against him. Many voice concerns about the negative remarks and promised policies that Trump made during the campaign that would impact women, Hispanics and Latinos, African Americans, Muslims, immigrants, gays, and others.
2017	On January 21, more than two million women march for women's rights and other issues in Washington, DC, on the first day of Donald Trump's (1946–) presidency.
2017	On January 28, protesters across the United States march against President Trump's immigration policy known as the travel ban.
2017	Protests erupt periodically at the University of California, Berkeley, in an attempt to stop controversial speakers from appearing at events on campus. Protests also erupt between pro-Trump supporters and counterprotesters.
2017	On February 11, antiabortion activists throughout the United States protest against Planned Parenthood. Counterprotests in support of Planned Parenthood funding are also held.
2017	On April 22, activists around the world gather in support of government funding for science. The event is known as the March for Science.
2017	On June 25, protesters march in Washington, DC, in support of traditional marriage.
2017	In August, white supremacist protesters and counterprotesters violently clash in Charlottesville, Virginia. The incident results in the death of counterprotester Heather Heyer (c. 1985–2017).
2017	In October, people use the hashtag #MeToo to raise awareness of sexual assault and harassment. Many people, especially women, document the various ways in which they have been victimized by sexual predators. The discussion prompts some of the accused people to resign from their jobs; others are fired.

2017 In December, protests erupt in the Middle East when President Donald Trump announces that the United States will recognize Jerusalem as the capital of Israel. The move stokes the Israeli-Palestinian conflict.

Words to Know

Ableism: Discrimination against disabled people.

Abolition: The act of ending or stopping something.

Abolitionist movement: A campaign held during the 19th century to end slavery in the United States.

Aboriginal: A member of the native people of region, such as Australia or Canada.

Accessibility: How easy or difficult it is for physically disabled individuals to navigate a building.

Activist: One who takes action to support or oppose an issue.

Advocate: One who defends a certain cause.

Allied powers: The group of nations that fought Nazi Germany and other Axis powers during World War II.

Amendment: A change in the wording of a law or bill.

Anarchist: A person who rebels against authority and believes governments should be overthrown.

Animal welfare: To assure the care and comfort of animals.

Apartheid: A series of laws in South Africa that legalized discrimination and ordered the separation of people by race.

Armory: A place where military weapons are made and stored.

Aryan: Adolf Hitler's idea of a master race of people who were tall and had blond hair and blue eyes.

WORDS TO KNOW

Ashram: A religious retreat.

Assassination: The killing of someone for political reasons.

Asylum: Protection given to refugees that grants them the right to stay in a new country.

Austerity: Conditions of extreme spending cuts at a national level.

Autonomy: Self-government.

Background check: The process that allows authorities to examine the history of a person before he or she can purchase a gun.

Bill: A draft of a law that is presented to lawmakers for a vote.

Bloc: A group of nations that work together toward a common interest.

Boycott: A refusal to buy or use certain items, products, or services as a form of protest.

Bribery: Offering someone a gift in return for a favor.

Candlelight vigil: An assembly of people who hold candles to show support or opposition for a cause or event.

Capital punishment: A death sentence issued by a court to an individual found guilty of committing a serious crime; also known as the death penalty.

Capitalism: An economic system in which land and wealth are mostly owned by private individuals.

Captivity: The state of being held under the control of someone and not allowed to leave.

Cartridge: A tube that contains a bullet that the user puts into a gun.

Caste system: A system that groups people into different social classes based on wealth, occupation, or other factors.

Censorship: The act of removing any content considered harmful or offensive from books, newspapers, or other media.

Census: Provides a count of a population for specific information about the people living in a country.

Chemical weapons: Weapons that use chemicals to kill or seriously injure people.

Chicano: A term used to describe a Mexican American individual.

Christianity: A religion based on the teachings of Jesus Christ.

Civil disobedience: A public refusal to follow certain laws as a peaceful form of protest.

Civil rights: Guarantees of equal political, social, and economic freedoms to all citizens of a country.

Civilian: A person who is not active in the military or a member of law enforcement.

Climate change: Long-term, significant, measured change in the climate as seen in temperature, wind patterns, precipitation, and other factors. The term is often used today to describe any changes to global weather patterns that result from human practices.

Climate refugee: Any person who has been forced to leave his or her home as a direct result of changes to the environment.

Colonialism: An economic system in which Western European nations controlled various underdeveloped countries located around the world.

Colony: A country or other area that is controlled by a more powerful country.

Communism: A political system in which private ownership of property is eliminated and government directs all economic production. The goods produced and accumulated wealth are, in theory, shared relatively equally by all.

Conception: The moment when a male's sperm fertilizes a female's ovum.

Conservative: A view that favors traditional beliefs concerning social issues and wants limited government spending.

Constitution: A country's document of laws.

Consumerism: An economic concept based on buying and using goods.

Contraceptive: A method or device used to prevent pregnancy.

Corporatism: Occurs when big businesses become powerful enough to take control of the state.

Crusade: An important mission, usually involving moral beliefs and often requiring a long journey.

WORDS TO KNOW

D

Dalit: A member of the lowest social class in India's caste system. They were previous known as Untouchables, a term that is considered derogatory.

Death camp: Prison camps where Nazis killed hundreds of thousands of Jews and other prisoners from across Europe during World War II.

Deforestation: The clear-cutting of forests for such human purposes as homes, businesses, and farms.

Delegate: A person at a meeting who represents others.

Democracy: A form of government in which people choose leaders by voting.

Deport: To remove immigrants from a nation and send them back to their home country.

Depression: A period in which economic activity is limited and joblessness is widespread.

Desegregate: To end the practice of keeping different groups of people separated by joining them together as one.

Desertification: A process in which land becomes increasingly dry and unusable due to climate change.

Developing countries: Poor nations that are looking to advance economically and socially.

Dictator: Ruler who has total power over a country.

Disability: A physical, developmental, or mental condition that limits a person's activities in certain areas of life.

Discrimination: Unfair treatment based on one's race, ethnicity, or other distinction.

Draft: A process by which young men are required to serve in the armed forces. Some countries also draft women.

Drug cartel: A group that produces and sells illegal drugs.

E

Economic inequality: A large difference in income between the poor and the wealthy.

Economy: The combined wealth and other resources of a country.

Electoral votes: Votes cast by a select group of people from each state to elect the president of the United States.

Embassy: The office in one country where a representative of another country lives and works.

Endangered: A plant or animal that is in danger of becoming extinct.

Environmentalism: The idea that people must actively take part in political and social movements to bring about positive changes that improve the health of the planet.

Ethnicity: A division of human beings by culture, language, or home country.

Etiquette: A social custom or skill that guides the way people behave in the presence of others.

Execution: The killing of a person who has been sentenced to die.

Extinct: A term to describe a species that has completely died out.

F

Factory farm: A farm where many animals are raised, often indoors, for food.

Fetus: An unborn, developing human.

Final Solution: A plan for killing all Jews in Nazi-controlled areas.

Fiscal responsibility: When the government taxes just enough to pay for necessary expenses.

Force-feed: To make a person eat by forcefully putting food down his or her throat.

Fossil fuels: Energy sources such as gas, oil, and coal that result from ancient natural processes, such as the decay of ancient plants and animals.

Fracking: A method of getting natural gas and oil from rock by injecting water at high pressure into the ground.

Free trade: The buying and selling of goods and services between nations without any special taxes or rules to limit trade.

G

Gender expression: Individuals' external presentation of gender, including how they dress, style their hair, and refer to themselves.

WORDS TO KNOW

Gender identity: Individuals' personal inner experience of their gender, which may not match the sex they were assigned at birth.

Genocide: The killing of many members of the same race, religion, ethnicity, or culture.

Ghetto: Poor area of a city where certain groups of people live.

Global warming: Rising temperature of Earth's atmosphere caused by an increase of greenhouse gases.

Globalization: Occurs when countries do business on an international level.

Greenhouse gases: Gases that collect in the upper atmosphere of Earth and are believed to be responsible for changes to the planet's climate and weather patterns.

Gun control: Any attempt to create policies that offer more protections from gun violence.

Gun rights: A term used to describe attempts to protect the ability of Americans to own and use guns.

H

Handgun: A firearm that can be held and fired with one hand.

Hate crime: A crime committed against a person because of his or her race, religion, national origin, gender, sexual orientation, or disability.

Hate group: A group that supports hatred, anger, or violence toward members of a certain race, religion, national origin, gender, or sexual orientation.

Hispanic: A person who is from or who has ancestors from a Spanish-speaking country.

Hitler Youth: Nazi Germany's children's organization that taught Nazi ideas to youths so they would grow up supporting the Nazi Party.

Holocaust: Nazi Germany's mass killing of European Jews and others during World War II.

Hostage: A person who is captured and held against his or her will until certain demands are met.

Housing bubble: An increase in housing prices caused by high demand that eventually decreases, causing values of properties to decline sharply.

WORDS TO KNOW

Human trafficking: The practice of forcing people to perform labor or participate in sex work.

Humane: Acting in a caring or considerate manner.

Hunger strike: The act of refusing to eat to bring about a desired change.

Hydroelectric energy: Energy that is generated from the force of moving water.

I

Idol worship: The worship of a false god.

Immigrant: A person who enters a new country after leaving his or her home country.

Impoverished: Extremely poor.

Indentured servant: A person who works for another person in exchange for travel, food, and housing for a specified amount of time.

Indigenous: Originating in or living naturally in a certain region.

Industry: The production of goods from raw materials in factories.

Integration: The practice of combining different groups in society to make them equal.

Islamization: A shift in a society's culture toward the religion of Islam.

Ivory: The hard, white substance that makes up the tusks and some teeth of certain animals.

J

Jim Crow laws: Laws created mostly in the American South in the late 19th and early 20th centuries that kept black citizens from enjoying the same rights as white Americans.

L

Labor union: An organization of workers that is formed to protect their rights and interests.

Latin America: A region south of the United States that includes Mexico, Central America, South America, and islands in the Caribbean.

Latino: A person who is from or who has ancestors from a Latin American country.

Legislature: A group of people responsible for making laws.

Liberal: A view that favors new ideas.

M

Market economy: An economic system of free competition in which prices are determined by supply and demand.

Maroons: Freed Spanish slaves who lived in the mountains of Jamaica.

Migrant: A person who moves from one place to another in search of work.

Militant: Using violent or aggressive means in support of a cause.

Militia: A group of citizens with military training who are called to service only in the event of emergencies.

Minimum wage: The lowest hourly rate that an employer can pay a worker.

Monopoly: When a single company or person is the sole provider of a product or service.

Mortgage: Payments made on a loan from a bank to help pay for the purchase of a home.

Multinational company: A company that does business in many countries around the world.

Muslim: A follower of Islam, a religion founded by the prophet Muhammad.

N

National Guard: A branch of the armed forces that usually deals with problems within the United States.

Nativism: A policy that protects the rights of a country's native people over immigrants' rights.

Natural resources: Water, soil, minerals, and other materials that are found in nature and are important to humans.

Nazi Party: A political party that controlled Germany from 1933 to 1945 under the leadership of Adolf Hitler.

Negotiate: To discuss something in hopes of making a deal.

North Atlantic Treaty Organization (NATO): A military partnership of the United States, Canada, and various European countries.

O

Occult: Matters that deal with the supernatural or magic.

Ovum: A female reproductive cell, sometimes called an egg.

P

Pacifist: Someone who is strongly opposed to war and fighting.

Parliament: A lawmaking body.

Partisans: Members of armed organizations that fight against forces that are controlling their country.

Pepper spray: A spray made from cayenne pepper that can cause a burning feeling in a person's eyes and throat when applied.

Petition: A written request made to an official person or organized body.

Picket: A protest that involves a group of people marching at a site with signs on posts or pointed sticks.

Pipeline: A system of connected pipes that are used to transport liquids and gases over a long distance.

Plantation: A large area of land that is usually worked by manual labor.

Poaching: The illegal hunting or killing of an animal.

Police brutality: The use of more force than necessary by police.

Political correctness: The act of avoiding certain language or activities that could offend a particular person or group.

Pork barrel spending: Funds attached to legislation for projects that benefit a lawmaker's home district.

Pro-choice: A term used to describe people who support a woman's right to choose whether or not to have an abortion.

Pro-life: A term used to describe people who are against abortion.

Prophet: A messenger of God.

WORDS TO KNOW

R

Racial diversity: To include people from various racial backgrounds.

Racial insensitivity: A lack of understanding of the experiences of people of other races.

Racism: The belief that one human being is better than another because of his or her race.

Radical: Someone who favors extreme measures to make a point or bring about change.

Recession: A period when trade and economic production slow.

Reformer: A person who tries to bring changes to society.

Refugee: A person who leaves his or her home country because of war or mistreatment based on race, religion, or political opinion.

Renewable energy: Sources of energy that can be naturally replaced by the environment and include solar, wind, and water sources.

Repeal: To cancel or withdraw something, especially a law.

Reservation: An area of land set aside for use by certain people.

Reservoir: A human-made lake created to store water for use by a community.

Resistance: The effort to fight against a powerful force.

Revolution: The overthrow of one type of government in favor of another.

S

Sanction: An official punishment usually imposed on a country by another nation or group of nations.

Sanctuary: A refuge for animals where they are protected from harm and able to roam freely.

Segregation: The separation of groups of people.

Semiautomatic weapon: A type of gun that allows the user to fire bullets quickly due to an automatic reloading process.

Sexual orientation: A person's sexual identity, which relates to whom a person is attracted. Sexual orientation includes gay, lesbian, bisexual, straight, and asexual.

Sexual reproduction: Occurs when two individuals have sex and produce an offspring.

Sharia: Islamic law based on the teachings of the Koran.

Sit-down strike: A protest in which a group of workers sit down on the job and refuse to complete any work.

Sit-in: A peaceful protest in which people occupy a place for long periods, often in a seated position, to call attention to a certain social issue.

Slave driver: A slave who is responsible for organizing and punishing other slaves.

Socialism: A political system in which the central government provides goods and services to all members of a society equally.

Sperm: A male reproductive cell.

Stimulus: An action that causes another action to take place.

Strike: An organized work stoppage to force employers to meet certain demands.

Suffocate: To die from not being able to breathe.

Suffrage: The right to vote.

Suffragist: A person who works to gain voting rights for people who are not allowed to vote.

Sustainable: A method of using natural resources without depleting them or damaging them permanently.

Sweatshop: A small factory where people work long hours for low pay.

T

Tactic: Something used to effect change.

Tariff: A tax or fee added to foreign products to make them more expensive.

Terrorism: The use of fear and violence to achieve political goals or social change and to create fear.

Terrorist: Someone who uses fear and violence to influence others.

Trafficking: The act of buying or selling an illegal product or service.

Traitor: Someone who has betrayed his or her country.

Transgender: A term used to describe a person whose gender identity differs from the sex he or she was assigned at birth.

WORDS TO KNOW

Tribunal: A decision-making body that has authority in a specific area.

Trimester: A period of pregnancy lasting about three months, during which the fetus develops.

U

Unconstitutional: Going against the US Constitution.

Undocumented or unauthorized immigrants: Immigrants who enter a country without permission or who stay longer than they are allowed.

Union: An organized group that protects workers' rights.

Universal Declaration of Human Rights: A document that defines the rights that the United Nations believes should belong to every person in the world.

US Supreme Court: The highest court of the federal government.

V

Visa: A government document that allows a person from another country to stay in the United States.

Voluntary manslaughter: A sentence for a crime in which a person has no previous intent or plans to kill another person, which usually happens in the moment.

W

Weapons of mass destruction (WMD): Powerful weapons that can destroy entire cities or regions.

Whistle-blower: A person who publicly reports the illegal or unethical activities of an organization or a government.

White supremacist: A person who believes the white race is superior to other races.

Z

Zoot suit: A flashy oversized suit that was popular in the 1940s.

15

Political/Government Uprisings

Tiananmen Square Protests 473

Fall of the Berlin Wall 478

Arab Spring and the Syrian Civil Uprising 486

Tahrir Square Protests (Egyptian Revolution) 493

Umbrella Revolution 498

People have protested governments for thousands of years and for many reasons. These reasons usually are specific to the countries where the protests occur. The political situations that lead people to protest in one country may not spark the same response in another country. Throughout history, however, the general goal of most political or government protests has been to secure freedom and fairness for all.

In many cases, a group's decision to protest the government is based on how strong its members think they are. If the people in the group see themselves as strong, they will likely allow themselves to become willing enough to protest. If they feel weak, they will probably be too afraid. Fearful people generally do not protest.

When the citizens of a nation become unhappy with their government or the condition of their society, they are likely to protest. The causes of this unhappiness vary. Unjust laws, mistreatment of certain groups, corrupt governments, and leaders who rule as dictators are just a few reasons why people protest.

Causes of protests

Dictators are rulers who have total power over a country. Dictators usually do not grant their people many rights. Rights are legal guarantees that a government will treat its people in certain ways. Citizens of countries with dictatorships have to do whatever the dictators say or face some sort of punishment. The people hold no power at all. Many people in nations with dictatorships have protested for democracy. Democracy is a type of government that allows all citizens to vote for officials to make laws for them. In democracies people have more rights and access to opportunities.

Political/Government Uprisings

> ## WORDS TO KNOW
>
> **Activist:** One who takes action to support or oppose an issue.
>
> **Assassination:** The killing of someone for political reasons.
>
> **Chemical weapons:** Weapons that use chemicals to kill or seriously injure people.
>
> **Communism:** A political system in which private ownership of property is eliminated and government directs all economic production. The goods produced and accumulated wealth are, in theory, shared relatively equally by all.
>
> **Democracy:** Government in which all people vote for officials to make laws for them.
>
> **Dictator:** Ruler who has total power over a country.
>
> **Economy:** The combined wealth and other resources of a country.
>
> **Muslim:** A follower of Islam, a religion founded by the prophet Muhammad.
>
> **North Atlantic Treaty Organization (NATO):** A military partnership of the United States, Canada, and various European countries.
>
> **Revolution:** The overthrow of one type of government in favor of another.
>
> **Terrorism:** The use of violence to achieve political goals or social change and to create fear.

Not all protests occur in countries ruled by dictators. People also protest other types of governments. For example, sometimes governments fail to include representatives of the people they serve when they make new laws. As a result, the unrepresented people have no way to voice their support for or opposition to these laws. Other times government officials fail to support the interests of the people who elected them. Officials may become corrupt and look out only for themselves. In some cases, governments pass laws that treat certain groups unequally. In response to all of these situations, people may become upset and revolt.

Protests can end in many ways. Sometimes protesters achieve their goals and convince their governments to change. Other times governments use force to stop protests. Several factors can affect the success of protests. One factor is how much the protests disturb daily life where they take place. A government may meet protesters' demands simply to end the disturbance. Public opinion also can help protests succeed. If most people in a country support the protesters' views, a powerful government may be more likely to change. Similarly, pressure from other nations may lead an existing government to change. History has shown that the success or failure of a protest often depends on the strength, emotions, and unity of the protesters.

Ancient political protests and revolutions

Political protests and revolutions started occurring in the ancient world. A revolution is the overthrow of one type of government in favor of another. Sometimes protesters succeeded in achieving their goals. Other times the protests or revolutions failed.

In the 370s BCE, the Spartans ruled over the Greek city of Thebes (pronounced THEEBZ). The Spartans came from a Greek city-state called Sparta. In 378 BCE the Theban people revolted. A small group of Thebans killed Spartan leaders after disguising themselves to gain access to their party. A revolution followed these murders. The Theban people defeated the Spartans in battle in 371 BCE. The victory allowed Thebes to become a democracy.

Another ancient revolution involved the assassination of Roman dictator Julius Caesar (pronounced JU-lee-us SEE-zer; 100–44 BCE) in 44 BCE. An assassination is the killing of someone for political reasons. Roman politicians stabbed Caesar to death because they believed he held too much power over Rome. Caesar's killers hoped to take over Rome after their revolt, but they failed. Other Romans defeated the assassins in battle. Rome later became the Roman Empire and was led by a dictator known as an emperor.

Julius Caesar was killed because Roman politicians believed he had too much power. © PSEUDOLONGINO/SHUTTERSTOCK.COM.

Political protests in the Middle Ages

The Middle Ages was a period in European history that lasted from the 5th century to the 15th century CE. During the Middle Ages, many European countries were feudal (pronounced FEW-del) societies. In a feudal society, wealthy officials owned land and poor farmers called serfs worked the land.

People in feudal societies were divided into classes. Monarchs, or kings and queens, gave land to a class called nobles. These nobles were known as lords or barons. The lords and barons took the land in exchange for remaining loyal to the monarch. The nobles employed serfs to farm the land. Serfs had little wealth and no place to live. The nobles allowed

Political/Government Uprisings

CRITICAL THINKING QUESTIONS

1. Were the Tiananmen Square protesters right to stop Mikhail Gorbachev from visiting the square? Was this a good way for the Chinese people to show their anger with the Chinese government? Explain.

2. Why do you think the Chinese government responded to the Tiananmen Square protests with violence? Why did the government try to hide the event from the world? What do these actions suggest about the government?

3. Why do you think some East Germans risked their lives trying to escape to West Berlin? What does this suggest about life in East Germany?

4. Why do you suppose the revolution in Tunisia during the Arab Spring succeeded while the protests that occurred in Syria turned into a civil war?

5. What do you think drove Mohamed Bouazizi to set himself on fire in Tunisia? What can you assume about the political and economic situations in Tunisia, based on Bouazizi's actions?

6. Why did the revolutions in Tunisia and Egypt inspire Arabs in other countries to protest their own governments? Do you think these revolutions were necessary to convince other Arabs to start voicing their opinions?

7. What do you think about the Umbrella Revolution protesters' decision to block main roads in Hong Kong? Was this an effective way to protest? Was it wrong for them to disrupt daily life in the city? Explain.

---

the serfs to live on the land, and the serfs paid the nobles with the food they harvested. Using this system, the nobles were able to keep the serfs constantly poor.

This feudal lifestyle made lower classes resent the upper classes who held power over them. The barons disliked that English monarchs could make any laws they wanted. The monarchs did not have to respect the rights of English citizens. In 1215 the barons revolted against King John (1166–1216) of England. They forced him to sign a document called the Magna Carta. The Magna Carta made English monarchs follow certain rules. In this case, the barons' protest against the king succeeded.

Other medieval political protests and revolts failed. During the Peasants' Revolt of 1381, English serfs were outraged that they had to pay high taxes to the government. They also disliked that the English people were divided into social classes. The peasants marched to the city of London to protest these matters to the English government. Royal forces killed hundreds of the protesters, which ended the revolt. Little changed in England because of this unsuccessful revolt.

Early modern rebellions

Political protests continued in the early modern period. Some of these protests brought about large-scale violent revolution. The Boston Tea Party of 1773 was one of these protests. It was one of the events that led to the start of the American Revolution (1775–1783) in 1775.

Great Britain ruled over the 13 colonies in what became the United States as a result of the war. Colonies are countries or areas controlled by more powerful nations. The British government made American colonists pay high taxes on certain goods, such as tea. The colonists had no representation in the British government, so they had no way to oppose these taxes. The colonists thought the taxes were unfair.

A group of colonists decided to protest the tea tax in December 1773. The group sneaked onto British ships in Boston, Massachusetts, and dumped hundreds of crates of tea into the water. The protest angered the British government. The conflict between the colonists and the British became more intense over the next year and a half. The American Revolution began in 1775. The American colonists banded together and fought the British to gain their freedom. They eventually defeated Britain in battle. The United States then became a free country and went on to become one of the most powerful nations in the world.

The French Revolution (1789–1799) began a few years later and achieved similar success. Kings had ruled France for centuries before the revolution began. However, the French believed that King Louis XVI (1754–1793) had become too powerful. His unpopular laws affected all the citizens of France. The French people wanted to become a democracy. After suffering under the king for many years, the people became furious and revolted. They came together to overthrow, and ultimately execute, the king in Paris. Ten years of violence followed the king's removal. However, France eventually became a full democracy.

Modern political protests

Political protests in the 20th and early 21st centuries were similar to protests of the past. Some aimed to reform unfair laws while others tried to replace entire governments. For example, in the early 20th century, women in several countries peacefully protested their governments to gain the right to vote in political elections. Women in the United Kingdom marched in public to show their frustration with their lack of suffrage (right to vote). The British government arrested the women, who only became more determined in response. They continued protesting for their right to vote. In 1928 the British government gave the right to vote to all women older than 21. Various other countries did the same.

The US civil rights movement of the 1950s and 1960s is another example of a nonviolent mass protest against a government. During this period, African Americans became angry about laws that treated them differently than white Americans. Many laws, especially in the South, made blacks use separate public areas from whites. Blacks had their own public restrooms, buses, and restaurants, which were inferior to those available to whites. Blacks wanted the government to treat them equally under the law.

In the 1950s a civil rights activist named the Rev. Dr. Martin Luther King Jr. (1929–1968) helped to start a peaceful protest movement against unfair and unequal treatment by the government. Activists are people who publicly support or oppose certain issues. King encouraged blacks to march in public to demand equal rights. He did not want anyone to be hurt during the protests. However, this did not make him any less outraged about the unfair treatment blacks received. In 1963, at a large protest called the March on Washington for Jobs and Freedom, King spoke about a day when all Americans would be treated equally and live peacefully together in the country. The civil rights movement succeeded for the most part. Laws passed in 1964 and 1965, especially, secured rights and opportunities for disadvantaged groups of US citizens.

In the spring of 2017, anti-government protests began in the South American country of Venezuela. Thousands of people started protesting after Venezuela's supreme court tried to take power away from the country's National Assembly. A supreme court is a country's most powerful legal court. The Venezuelan National Assembly makes laws for the country.

The Venezuelan people believed the supreme court wanted to make the president more powerful. Citizens protested the government in the streets of Venezuelan cities. Police fought with the protesters. The protests continued in Venezuela into the summer of 2017.

History has shown that political and government protests have achieved different levels of success. Some brought about impressive change, overthrowing leaders and replacing entire governments. Others achieved smaller successes, such as changes to unfair laws. Still others failed to make any real change.

> *History has shown that political and government protests have achieved different levels of success. Some brought about impressive change, overthrowing leaders and replacing entire governments. Others achieved smaller successes, such as changes to unfair laws.*

Tiananmen Square Protests

LOCATION: Beijing, China

DATE: 1989

The Tiananmen (pronounced TYEN-AHN-MUN) Square protests took place in Beijing, China, from April to June 1989. Tiananmen Square is a large public square in the center of Beijing. Hundreds of thousands of Chinese people filled the square during those months to protest the Chinese government. The protesters claimed the ruling Communist Party of China was too powerful. They wanted China to become more democratic.

The protests began in April 1989. They followed the death of a Chinese politician who had tried to reform the government. Large groups of Chinese students used his death as a reason to protest China's Communist leaders. Hundreds of thousands of other citizens later joined the student protesters. The Chinese government sent the military to Tiananmen Square to put down the protests. Chinese leaders tried to hide the events from the world by banning reporters from filming them. Police arrested thousands of protesters between April and June.

In early June 1989, Chinese soldiers started firing at the protesters. These shootings ended the protests. China never reported the official number of people killed during the event. Many nations around the world criticized China for its response to the Tiananmen Square protests.

Origins of the protests

The Tiananmen Square protests began as a response to the death of Chinese politician Hu Yaobang (pronounced WHO YOW-bahng; 1915–1989) on April 15, 1989. Hu had joined the Communist Party of China in his youth. He remained a member into the mid-1960s. In 1966 Chinese leader Mao Zedong (pronounced MAHoh DZEH-duhng; 1893–1976) started the Cultural Revolution (1966–1976). This was Mao's attempt to make China more Communist. Mao's government removed any officials from power who did not seem to support the Communist Party fully. The Cultural Revolution forced Hu from the party in 1966.

Political/Government Uprisings

> ### "What Tiananmen Taught Me"
>
> *In this primary source excerpt from CNN, Trini Leung of Amnesty International recalls how she joined a few activists on a trip to Tiananmen Square to witness the student protests. The article describes what she observed 25 years earlier.*
>
> I'll never forget the morning of June 2, 1989. I was living in Hong Kong and, together with a few fellow activists, we decided there was nowhere else to be but Beijing, near Tiananmen Square. It was a decision that changed my life....
>
> I remember seeing hundreds of people running along Chang'an Avenue after government forces moved in. Some were pushing carts carrying injured men and women, looking for a safe place, shouting for help. I saw blood—lots of blood, much of it from peaceful demonstrators who only the previous day had been in an almost festive mood.
>
> As the evening drew on, the chorus of cheers had been replaced by the sound of gunfire as the army moved towards Tiananmen Square. I remember the ground beneath our feet seemed to shake due to the sheer number of tanks approaching....
>
> "How can they do this to our students?" I heard some people cry. The mixture of panic, rage and fear among protesters was palpable in the night air. By midnight, as troops moved from the outskirts of Beijing into Tiananmen Square, we found ourselves among tens of thousands unarmed, ordinary citizens who were pushing towards the area where the students were in an

Hu lived in the Chinese countryside until 1976, the year Mao died. Two years later, the new Chinese government returned Hu to power in the Communist Party. He became the leader of the party in 1981. Hu wanted to reform Chinese society. He hoped to do this by making the country more democratic. A more democratic China would make the Chinese people more free.

Other members of the Communist Party opposed Hu because they did not want to reform Chinese society. Some Chinese people started protesting for democracy in the mid-1980s. Hu believed the party should listen to the protesters. Other Chinese leaders disagreed. They forced Hu to resign as leader of the Communist Party in 1987. He died in 1989.

Tiananmen Square protests begin

Hu's death upset many young Chinese people. They were sad that Hu was dead, and they were angry that the government still had not adopted democratic reforms. Students started gathering in Tiananmen Square on April 15, 1989, to mourn Hu's death. They also protested China's

Political/Government Uprisings

effort to shield them from the troops who were closing in.

Warnings circulated the crowd that those heading toward the square might be placing themselves in danger. Still, waves of people continued walking in the opposite direction from us, towards the approaching army in defiance of the warnings. As we headed away from the area, we could here automatic rifles being fired. As the night went on, we were greeted by images of wounded protesters, fired upon or crushed as armored vehicles and troops moved in.

I was deeply saddened by what I saw—the scenes that were to be seared into my memory to this day—and I felt awful guilt, guilt because I couldn't do anything to help stop the bloodshed.

I had never in my life witnessed violence on this scale, nor shots, and screams of pain and anguish.

As the sun rose on June 4, I sat on the balcony of the Beijing Hotel, in front of Tiananmen Square, surrounded by activists and journalists from Hong Kong who were as desperate as me to figure out what was happening. Yet confusion still reigned, as bullets continued to pierce the early morning air....

As one of those who witnessed firsthand the brutal crackdown, I'm often asked what I have learned from those events. And for me, there is really only one answer: We must continue the fight for justice and freedom. And the authorities must never be allowed to expunge the events of that day from the pages of history.

SOURCE: Leung, Trini. "What Tiananmen Taught Me." CNN, June 4, 2014. Available online at http://globalpublicsquare.blogs.cnn.com/2014/06/04/what-tiananmen-taught-me/ (accessed October 15, 2017). Courtesy of Cable Network News, Inc.

Communist government. Thousands of additional protesters assembled in the square over the next few days. By April 18 people in cities and universities across China were protesting against the Chinese government. They called the government a dictatorship. The people wanted greater democracy, a healthier economy, and better jobs.

The Chinese government soon warned protesters that they were participating in illegal activities and could face severe punishment. The demonstrators ignored this warning. On April 22 they attended a memorial service held for Hu in Tiananmen Square. The protesters then requested to meet with Li Peng (pronounced LEE PUHNG; 1928–) to discuss their demands. Li was the premier, or head of government, of China. The Chinese government refused to let protesters meet with Li.

Demonstrations grow

The protests in Tiananmen Square expanded in May 1989. Early that month, tens of thousands of people joined demonstrations in the square and in other cities throughout China. Communist Party leaders still

Political/Government Uprisings

Pro-democracy student protesters come face to face with police outside the Great Hall of the People in Tiananmen Square on April 22, 1989, in Beijing. They are taking part in the funeral ceremony of former Chinese Communist Party leader and liberal reformer Hu Yaobang during an unauthorized demonstration to mourn his death. His death triggered a wave of pro-democracy protests.
© CATHERINE HENRIETTE/AFP/GETTY IMAGES.

refused to take the protests seriously. They believed the demonstrations would end over time.

Student protesters in Tiananmen Square were angry that the Chinese government was not responding to their activities. Several hundred students began a hunger strike as a result. A hunger strike is a form of protest in which people refuse to eat. Still, the Chinese government did nothing. The demonstrators in the square next planned to disrupt Soviet leader Mikhail Gorbachev's official visit to China. Gorbachev was to arrive at Tiananmen Square on May 15, 1989. The large groups of protesters in the square forced Chinese leaders to greet Gorbachev elsewhere. This embarrassed the government.

About 1.2 million people attended demonstrations in Tiananmen Square on May 19. The leader of the Communist Party, Zhao Ziyang (pronounced JOW DZUH-yahng; 1919–2005), appeared in the square that day. He tried to convince the people to stop protesting. In exchange he said he would make some democratic reforms to China's government. Other Chinese leaders refused to make deals with the demonstrators. They forced Zhao out of his position.

Military force

The Chinese government then placed parts of Beijing under military control. Chinese soldiers in tanks and other vehicles tried to travel to the center of Beijing. Protesters blocked the vehicles' paths. This forced the soldiers to stop. The government had told the soldiers not to attack civilians. However, by early June, government leaders were mad that the demonstrations continued. On June 1 the Chinese government banned all news media from photographing or recording the Tiananmen Square protesters or the Chinese military. The next day the government officially decided to use military force to stop the demonstrations.

About 50 trucks and 10,000 troops began advancing toward Tiananmen Square in the early morning of June 4. The military got to the square at about 1 a.m. Protesters set up walls to try to stop the vehicles from advancing, but the trucks broke through the blockades. Soldiers then started firing on the civilians. Many students and other protesters died. Some people fought back against the military, throwing rocks and firebombs at the soldiers.

The Chinese military continued attacking the protesters throughout June 4. Thousands of people ran from Tiananmen Square to escape the violence. China never reported the actual number of people killed in the protests that day. Reporters at the scene later estimated the Chinese military had killed between several hundred and several thousand people. Government forces also arrested about 10,000 people. The violence that day effectively ended the Tiananmen Square demonstrations.

The Chinese military had full control of Beijing by June 5. The military wanted to make sure the city was peaceful again. That day, a line of army tanks drove down a busy city street. They were going to Tiananmen Square. At one point, a man entered the street and stood in front of the first tank. He blocked the line of tanks from moving forward. Several reporters photographed the man standing in front of the tanks. After a few minutes, other people in the street pulled the man away from the tanks. One particular image of the man standing in the street later became a famous symbol of the Tiananmen Square protests. People claimed it showed the man's nonviolent refusal to let the military control the Chinese people. The man's name remained unknown in the 21st century. He was referred to only as "Tank Man."

Aftermath

The Chinese government's response to the Tiananmen Square protests shocked other countries around the world. Gorbachev said the violence in China upset him. He hoped the Chinese government would soon become more democratic. Members of the US Congress, the lawmaking body of the United States, were angry about the event. They wanted President George H. W. Bush (1924–) to take action against China for killing demonstrators. Bush later passed economic sanctions, or punishments, against China. These sanctions were intended to hurt China's economy.

Chinese government leaders claimed the protesters in Tiananmen Square had been trying to overthrow the Communist government. The leaders said the military had to put down the demonstrations to save China's economy. The Chinese government still officially held this opinion years later.

On June 4, 2009, journalists from around the world tried to enter Tiananmen Square. They wanted to report stories on the 20th anniversary of the protests. The Chinese government banned journalists and foreign news agencies from entering the square though.

Various protesters arrested during the Tiananmen Square demonstrators were still in prison in the 21st century. China eventually started releasing some of these prisoners. In 2016 Chinese officials announced that they would release the last Tiananmen Square protester from prison. The Communist Party still controlled the Chinese government at this time.

Fall of the Berlin Wall

LOCATION: Berlin, Germany
DATE: 1989

From 1961 to 1989, the Berlin Wall divided Germany's capital city, Berlin, into West Berlin and East Berlin. It also separated West Berlin

Political/Government Uprisings

from the territory of East Germany that surrounded it. The division of Berlin and Germany resulted from the Cold War (1945–1991) between the Soviet Union and the West. A cold war is a war of ideas rather than violent fighting. When discussing the Cold War, "the West" usually refers to the United States and the countries of Western Europe, such as the United Kingdom and France.

The West and the Soviet Union did not always oppose each other. They fought together against Germany during World War II (1939–1945). However, the Soviet Union and the West had conflicting ideas about running governments and economies. An economy is the combined wealth and other resources of a country.

After World War II ended in 1945, the Cold War began. One of the first disagreements between the Soviet Union and the West was how to manage Germany's affairs after Germany had been defeated in the war. The countries decided to split Germany, and its capital city, in half. The Soviet Union controlled East Germany, and the West controlled West Germany.

To keep people from leaving, the East German government began building the Berlin Wall in 1961. The wall remained in place until 1989, when people began to tear it down. The fall of the Berlin Wall was a major cultural event of 20th-century Europe.

Division of Germany

The Berlin Wall was one result of the Cold War. The Cold War was a time of great distrust between the Soviet Union and the West. Soviets and Westerners disagreed on many matters. The Soviet government was Communist. Communism is a political system in which property is owned collectively and all people are paid according to what they need. In reality, the Soviet government ruled the Soviet Union with total power. At the same time, most Western nations were democracies. People in these countries were free and had many rights.

The Soviet Union and the West each distrusted the other's political ideas. Each side wanted to stay separated from the other so the ideas would not mix. This forced separation resulted in the division of Germany after World War II.

The United States, the Soviet Union, the United Kingdom, France, and other nations all had been part of the Allied powers, or Allies, during World War II. The Allies were the nations that fought against Germany. Germany, led by Adolf Hitler (1889–1945), tried to take over Europe.

To keep people from leaving, the East German government began building the Berlin Wall in 1961. The wall remained in place until 1989, when people began to tear it down. The fall of the Berlin Wall was a major cultural event of 20th-century Europe.

Political/Government Uprisings

Easter Rebellion, Ireland, 1916

East Germans were not the only people to protest a controlling government during the 20th century. Another example of this kind of political protest is the Easter Rebellion of 1916. During this rebellion, Irish nationalists revolted against the rule of the larger United Kingdom of Great Britain and Ireland. Nationalists believe that countries should be totally politically independent.

By 1916 the United Kingdom had legally controlled Ireland for more than 100 years. England, the most powerful country in the United Kingdom, had ruled over Ireland in various ways for centuries. Many of the Irish people did not like that Ireland was part of the United Kingdom. They wanted Ireland to be a free nation.

In the mid-1910s, an Irish organization called the Irish Republican Brotherhood (IRB) started planning to revolt against British authorities in Ireland. The group wanted Ireland to become a republic. In a republic, the nation's people, not kings and queens, hold power.

Irish nationalist Patrick Pearse (1879–1916) led the IRB. He and other leaders planned to revolt in April 1916. About 1,600 people joined the rebellion.

The rebellion began in the Irish capital of Dublin on April 24, 1916, the day after Easter Sunday. The event later became known as the Easter Rebellion for this reason. It was also called the Easter Rising. Pearse and his fellow fighters attacked British forces across Dublin. They took control of the city's post office and various other buildings. Later on April 24, Pearse announced that Ireland was a republic.

The Allies defeated Germany in 1945. Later that year the Allies met to discuss what to do with Germany. They decided to split the country in two. The Soviet Union took control of eastern Germany. The United States, the United Kingdom, and France oversaw western Germany.

The parties divided Germany's capital city, Berlin, the same way. However, Berlin was located completely inside the Soviet Union's part of Germany. The Soviet government in eastern Germany disliked having Western powers so near. The Soviets wanted to make the Western countries leave Berlin. They tried stopping food and other supplies from entering West Berlin, but this plan failed. The Western countries simply dropped supplies to West Berlin from airplanes.

At the same time, the two halves of Germany formed their own countries in 1949. West Germany officially became the Federal Republic of Germany and Bonn was chosen as its capital. West Germany's government was democratic like the governments of Western nations. East

Political/Government Uprisings

The IRB's success did not last long. The British government sent soldiers to take back Dublin the next day. British and Irish forces fought each other over the next few days. The violence destroyed large parts of Dublin. About 450 people died in the conflict. More than 2,000 were wounded. The British government defeated the uprising on April 29.

The Easter Rebellion failed. The British government arrested, tried, and executed the leaders of the IRB. However, the Irish War of Independence (1919–1921) began in 1919 to free Ireland from British control. The war ended with a cease-fire in 1921. A cease-fire occurs when both sides in a war agree to stop fighting.

The British government allowed Ireland to become the Irish Free State in 1922. This was an independent nation that the United Kingdom still officially owned. Ireland became the Republic of Ireland in 1949. The country was finally free from British rule.

During the Easter Rebellion, Irish citizens sought to end British rule in Ireland. © UNIVERSAL HISTORY ARCHIVE/UIG VIA GETTY IMAGES.

Germany became the German Democratic Republic. The government of East Germany was Communist. It was similar to the Soviet government.

Rising tensions

At first, German citizens could easily travel between East Berlin and West Berlin. They crossed the Soviet-Western border to go to work or for other reasons. Germans could do the same at the border of East Germany and West Germany.

Life in East Germany was often difficult. East Germany was generally poorer than West Germany. Many people had no food and no place to live. The East German government held total power. The people could not change their government. West Germany was a democracy. Its people were free. Many East Germans envied this freedom and moved to West Germany to make better lives for themselves. More than 3 million people had left East Germany for West Germany by the early 1960s.

In response to so many people leaving, East Germany began to build up the inner German border in 1952. The government set up a series of barriers to stop people from traveling between East Germany and West Germany and to prevent people from leaving East Germany. The barriers made it difficult for East Germans to cross into West Germany at the inner German border. However, they had another option.

Control of Berlin was still divided between East Germany and West Germany. East Germans could enter the western half of Berlin and enjoy the same freedoms that they would have enjoyed in West Germany. However, East Germans would not be able to travel any farther than West Berlin because Berlin was located entirely within East Germany. The distance from West Berlin to the border of West Germany was about 100 miles (161 kilometers). By the early 1960s, tens of thousands of East Germans were entering West Berlin every month.

Building the Berlin Wall

The loss of so many people to West Berlin embarrassed East Germany. Its leaders realized that the world would begin to think that life in East Germany was difficult and unhappy. The East German government wanted to stop people from leaving. Its solution was to block off West Berlin entirely. Physical structures would stop all East Germans from leaving their country and entering West Berlin.

The East German government started building the Berlin Wall in August 1961. The wall began as simple barbed-wire fencing placed along the border of East Berlin and West Berlin. Over the next several months, East Germany built two large concrete walls along the border. One wall was closer to West Berlin. The other was closer to East Berlin. An empty section of land was in the middle. The walls were about 12 feet (3.6 meters) high and 4 feet (1.2 meters) thick. The walls ran about 27 miles (43 kilometers) through the center of Berlin. East Germany eventually built the walls to surround West Berlin entirely. They stretched for a total of 96 miles (154 kilometers). The Berlin Wall completely separated West Berlin from East Germany. It was common for the Berlin Wall to separate family members from one another.

Resistance attempts

East Germany added more defenses to the Berlin Wall over time. Guards with guns watched the concrete wall at all times. More than 300 guard

Political/Government Uprisings

People stand and sit on the Berlin Wall at the Brandenburg Gate in November 1989. Many hit the wall with hammers to knock pieces of it down. The wall had separated East and West Berlin since 1961 and kept people apart. © INTERFOTO/ALAMY.

towers lined the wall. The guards immediately shot anyone they saw trying to climb the wall.

The area between the two concrete walls became known as the "death strip." It contained many hazards meant to keep East Germans from entering West Berlin. One part of the strip was sand. Its purpose was to show guards the footprints of people who climbed and jumped over the walls. Other death strip dangers included guard dogs, ditches to stop vehicles, and trip wires. Trip wires are wires attached to devices that activate when the wires move. In the death strip, the trip wires were attached to machine guns that fired at people who accidentally touched a wire.

Still, about 5,000 East Germans successfully escaped to West Berlin between the early 1960s and the late 1980s. Some people jumped out of building windows that were near the Berlin Wall. Others climbed over barbed-wire fences. Still others crawled through sewers to cross into West Berlin. Some people even flew over the wall in hot-air balloons. With all of these acts of escape, East German people protested the government and the difficult living conditions in East Germany.

The Cold War continued into the late 1980s. The Berlin Wall remained in place during this time.

Political/Government Uprisings

President Reagan's Remarks on the Berlin Wall

This primary source excerpt contains portions of US President Ronald Reagan's speech that he gave at the Brandenburg Gate in West Berlin, Germany, on June 12, 1987. This speech is often quoted, especially Reagan's infamous words to Soviet leader Mikhail Gorbachev: "Mr. Gorbachev, open this gate! Mr. Gorbachev, tear down this wall!"

We come to Berlin, we American Presidents, because it's our duty to speak, in this place, of freedom....

To those listening in East Berlin, a special word: Although I cannot be with you, I address my remarks to you just as surely as to those standing here before me. For I join you, as I join your fellow countrymen in the West, in this firm, this unalterable belief: Es gibt nur ein Berlin. [There is only one Berlin.]

Behind me stands a wall that encircles the free sectors of this city, part of a vast system of barriers that divides the entire continent of Europe. From the Baltic, south, those barriers cut across Germany in a gash of barbed wire, concrete, dog runs, and guardtowers. Farther south, there may be no visible, no obvious wall. But there remain armed guards and checkpoints all the same—still a restriction on the right to travel, still an instrument to impose upon ordinary men and women the will of a totalitarian state. Yet it is here in Berlin where the wall emerges most clearly; here, cutting across your city, where the news photo and the television screen have imprinted this brutal division of a continent upon the mind of the world. Standing before the Brandenburg Gate, every man is a German, separated from his fellow men. Every man is a Berliner, forced to look upon a scar....

In the West today, we see a free world that has achieved a level of prosperity and well-being unprecedented in all human history. In the Communist world, we see failure, technological backwardness, declining standards of health,

Protests against the Berlin Wall

The Cold War approached its end in the mid-1980s. Mikhail Gorbachev (pronounced meek-ha-EEL gor-ba-CHOFF; 1931–) became leader of the Soviet Union in 1985. He reformed the country with new ideas. These ideas encouraged the country to pursue friendly diplomatic relations with other nations.

People in East Germany also started protesting against their government around this time. The people wanted the government to give them more freedoms. They wanted to be free to go anywhere they wanted, including West Berlin and West Germany.

In 1987 US President Ronald Reagan (1911–2004) traveled to West Berlin to give a speech. During the speech, he challenged Gorbachev to tear down the Berlin Wall. Gorbachev worked to change the Soviet Union over the next few years. He called for the country to stop interfering in Eastern European matters. This meant giving up control of East Germany.

even want of the most basic kind—too little food.... After these four decades, then, there stands before the entire world one great and inescapable conclusion: Freedom leads to prosperity.... Freedom is the victor....

We hear much from Moscow about a new policy of reform and openness.... Are these the beginnings of profound changes in the Soviet state? Or are they token gestures...?

There is one sign the Soviets can make that would be unmistakable, ... General Secretary Gorbachev, if you seek peace, if you seek prosperity for the Soviet Union and Eastern Europe, if you seek liberalization: Come here to this gate! Mr. Gorbachev, open this gate! Mr. Gorbachev, tear down this wall!...

The totalitarian world produces backwardness because it does such violence to the spirit, thwarting the human impulse to create, to enjoy, to worship. The totalitarian world finds even symbols of love and of worship an affront....

Even today when the Sun strikes that sphere [the television tower at Alexander Platz]—that sphere that towers over all Berlin—the light makes the sign of the cross. There in Berlin, like the city itself, symbols of love, symbols of worship, cannot be suppressed.

As I looked out a moment ago from the Reichstag, ... I noticed words crudely spray-painted upon the wall, perhaps by a young Berliner, "This wall will fall. Beliefs become reality." Yes, across Europe, this wall will fall. For it cannot withstand faith; it cannot withstand truth. The wall cannot withstand freedom.

SOURCE: "US President Reagan's Remarks on East-West Relations at the Brandenburg Gate in West Berlin," Reagan Library Archives, June 12, 1987. Available online at https://reaganlibrary.archives.gov/archives/speeches/1987/061287d.htm (accessed October 15, 2017). Courtesy of Ronald Reagan Presidential Foundation and Institute.

Germans in East Berlin continued protesting the Berlin Wall into late 1989. They wanted the wall to be destroyed. On November 9, 1989, East Germany announced that it would allow people to travel to West Germany. East Germans immediately began crowding around the Berlin Wall. They wanted to cross into West Berlin.

The people gathered at the wall so quickly after the announcement that guards at the wall had not heard about the new policy. They eventually called other officials and learned that Germans could enter both halves of Berlin. The guards slowly started letting East Germans through the wall's gate. The crowd became too large for the guards to handle. They later opened the gate and let people freely cross into West Berlin.

The fall of the Berlin Wall

Germans from both sides of the Berlin Wall rejoiced on the night of November 9. They helped one another climb on top of the wall to celebrate. Many people started breaking down the wall themselves. They broke off pieces of the wall with hammers and other tools. The people wanted to keep the pieces as reminders of the wall. Thousands of other East Germans passed through the Berlin Wall's gates the next day. Germans from West Berlin cheered their arrival.

Germans continued breaking down the Berlin Wall over the next few weeks. The German government began truly destroying the wall in 1990. East Germany and West Germany reunited into the single nation of Germany, or the Federal Republic of Germany, on October 3, 1990. Berlin remained the German capital.

The reunion of East Germany and West Germany helped other countries affected by the Cold War. Other Eastern European countries that the Soviet Union controlled protested in favor of democracy in the late 1980s. The Soviet Union finally broke apart in 1991. The Cold War ended that year. Countries once under Soviet control were able to create their own governments.

The fall of the Berlin Wall was an important event in European history. The wall was one of the most famous symbols of the Cold War between the Soviet Union and the West. Its fall announced to Germans and the rest of the world that the conflict had ended. Eastern European nations were finally free from Soviet rule.

Some parts of the Berlin Wall remain standing in Berlin. They remind visitors of Germany's history during the Cold War.

Arab Spring and the Syrian Civil Uprising

LOCATION: Syria; other Middle Eastern and northern African nations
DATE: 2011

The Syrian civil uprising was part of the Arab Spring, A series of political protests and revolutions, the Arab Spring occurred in many countries across northern Africa and the Middle East in 2010 and 2011. The term *Arab* is based on the historic use of the Arabic language by people from these countries. Anti-government protests started in Tunisia in late 2010.

Similar protests then began in nearby countries such as Egypt, Libya, Yemen, Bahrain, and Syria. Most of the protests called for dictators in these countries to leave office. People wanted their governments to become democracies instead.

In some countries the Arab Spring protests forced dictators to give up their power. These countries then created new governments. Some of them remained mostly peaceful after the Arab Spring. In other nations the demonstrations failed to change anything. The protests led to civil war and other violence. Civil wars are conflicts fought between people from the same country.

The Arab Spring caused major unrest in Syria. People in Syria began peacefully protesting the government of President Bashar al-Assad (pronounced bah-SHAR al-a-SOD; 1965–). They believed al-Assad was a dictator. The Syrian government tried to stop the protests with force. Some protesters began fighting back against the government. They became an organized rebel group. The violence between the two sides began the Syrian Civil War. The war was still ongoing in the fall of 2017.

Origins of the Arab Spring

Mohamed Bouazizi (pronounced boo-a-ZEE-zee; 1984–2011) was a 26-year-old vegetable seller in Tunisia. Bouazizi had struggled to find a steady job for several years. He needed to earn money to support his family, which included his mother and six brothers and sisters. In about 2003 Bouazizi became a vegetable seller on the streets of Sidi Bouzid (pronounced SEH-dee boo-ZEED), a city in central Tunisia.

In December 2010 police officers told Bouazizi that he could not sell vegetables from his cart because he did not have a permit from the government. Bouazizi refused to give up his cart. A police officer struck him. She forced Bouazizi to stop selling food from the cart.

Bouazizi was embarrassed about what had happened. He was angry that the Tunisian government had obstructed his only means to make money for his family. He immediately tried to complain to the local government. No one listened to him. Less than an hour after the police took his cart, Bouazizi went to the street outside the local government building. He covered himself in gasoline. Then he lit himself on fire. Bouazizi's extreme measures were meant to show the Tunisian government how angry people were about policies that kept people like him poor. This event began the Arab Spring.

The protest grows

At first Bouazizi survived the fire. He was taken to a hospital to have his burns treated. People in Sidi Bouzid soon heard about what Bouazizi had done. They became outraged that President Zine El-Abidine Ben Ali's government did so little to help Tunisian citizens. The people began protesting Ben Ali. They wanted him to leave office after 23 years in power. Ben Ali visited Bouazizi in the hospital to try to calm the people. Tunisians continued to protest.

News of Bouazizi's action quickly spread to other parts of Tunisia. People across the country joined in the protests against Ben Ali. They wanted his entire government to give up power so Tunisia could become a democracy. Protesters fought with police. About 300 people died in conflicts that stretched into January 2011. On January 4, Bouazizi died in the hospital.

Ben Ali told the people he would meet their demands by making his government more democratic. He said he would hold new political elections. The people refused to accept his proposals. They kept calling for Ben Ali to leave office.

Ben Ali finally resigned on January 14, 2011. He left Tunisia for safety in Saudi Arabia. The Tunisian people were then free to create a government that would truly help Tunisians. The country elected members of the parliament later in 2011. Tunisia eventually became a republic.

Arab Spring spreads

The protests that forced Ben Ali to leave office were part of what became known as the Tunisian Revolution. People in nearby Arab nations heard about the events in Tunisia. These nations included Algeria, Egypt, and Morocco in northern Africa and Bahrain, Saudi Arabia, Syria, and Yemen in the Middle East. Powerful politicians or kings controlled these countries. However, citizens in these nations believed they could do what the Tunisian people had done. They thought mass protests might force dictators in their nations to leave office, too.

The Tunisian Revolution first spread to Egypt. Mass protests began in Tahrir Square in Cairo on January 25, 2011. Egyptians wanted President Hosni Mubarak to leave office after almost 30 years in power. He finally resigned on February 11. The Tahrir Square protests began the Egyptian Revolution.

People in Yemen also began protesting their president, Ali Abdullah Saleh (pronounced AH-lee ahb-DUHL-ah SAH-leh; 1942–), in late

January 2011. Saleh had been ruling Yemen for 33 years by that time. Many Yemenis were living in poverty. Terrorism had been destroying the country for years. Terrorism is the use of violence and fear to achieve political goals.

Saleh tried to calm the protesters. He promised not to run for reelection as president of Yemen, but the protesters wanted him to leave office immediately. They refused to stop protesting. About 2,000 Yemeni protesters died in battles with government forces in early 2011.

Violence continued in Yemen into late 2011. In November Saleh agreed to give power to his vice president. Saleh officially resigned as president of Yemen in February 2012. In the following years, however, more terrorism and war overtook Yemen. The country remained troubled into the late 2010s.

Arab Spring continues

Protests in the Arab island country of Bahrain started on February 14, 2011. The revolutions in Tunisia and Egypt inspired the Bahrainis to protest. Demonstrators gathered in the Bahraini capital city of Manama. The Bahraini government was a monarchy. The protesters did not want King Hamad bin Isa Al Khalifa (pronounced HAH-mahd bihn EE-sah al kah-LEE-fah; 1950–) to give up power. Instead they wanted the king's government to become more democratic and give Bahrainis more rights.

In March, soldiers from Saudi Arabia arrived in Bahrain to crush the protests. About 30 Bahrainis and several police officers died in the conflicts. Hamad told Bahrainis he would change the government to meet some of their demands. He said he planned to release government prisoners. He promised to punish government officials who killed or injured Bahrainis who had been arrested. After the protests, Bahrainis, for the most part, felt that the government had not changed at all.

The Egyptian Revolution influenced people in nearby Libya to start protesting their own leader, Mu'ammar al-Qaddafi (pronounced moo-AH-mahr al-gah-DAF-ee; 1942–2011). Qaddafi was a former military officer. He took control of Libya from the Libyan king in 1969. Qaddafi ruled Libya with total power over the next 42 years. His government arrested or killed anyone who publicly disagreed with him.

Libyans began protesting against Qaddafi and his government in mid-February 2011. Government forces responded by shooting at protesters.

Saleh tried to calm the protesters. He promised not to run for reelection as president of Yemen, but the protesters wanted him to leave office immediately. They refused to stop protesting. About 2,000 Yemeni protesters died in battles with government forces in early 2011.

Political/Government Uprisings

Iranian Green Movement, Iran, 2009

People in the Middle Eastern country of Iran protested their government about a year and a half before the Arab Spring began. In June 2009 Iranian President Mahmoud Ahmadinejad (pronounced mah-MOOD ah-mad-in-uh-ZHAHD; 1956–) was reelected. However, the people believed the election was unfair, and they protested. Their protests became known as the Iranian Green Movement.

More than 39 million people voted in the June 12, 2009, election. Ahmadinejad was declared the winner. The Iranian government claimed that he had received more than 62 percent of the votes.

The government said Ahmadinejad's main opponent in the election had received about 34 percent of the votes. Many Iranian people disputed these figures and were unhappy with the results. They thought the numbers were too far apart to be accurate. The people believed Ahmadinejad had won the election unfairly by changing the results of the vote.

In the weeks after the election, people became angry about the results. So hundreds of thousands of Iranians gathered in the streets of Tehran (pronounced tay-RAN), the capital of Iran. The protesters demanded to know where their votes were. Iranian religious leaders ordered an immediate stop to the demonstrations. The protesters refused. Government forces then started violently stopping the protests.

In late June, a government sniper shot 26-year-old musician Neda Agha-Soltan (pronounced NAY-da AHG-ah SOL-tan; c. 1983–2009) as she was standing near a Green Movement demonstration. Soltan died from her injuries. Protesters used their cell phones to record her death in the street. They managed to get the video of Agha-Soltan's death posted on the Internet, and it eventually became world news.

The Iranian protesters had to use the Internet to report such news because the government had already shut down newspapers, magazines, and certain websites that the protesters had been using. The lack of media there to cover the story meant that the

---

The response made even more Libyans across the country want to join the protests. Some groups of Libyans opposed to Qaddafi armed themselves with weapons. They started fighting government forces to control the capital of Tripoli (pronounced TREH-puh-lee). The North Atlantic Treaty Organization (NATO) bombed government targets to help the rebels. NATO is a military partnership of the United States, Canada, and various European countries. Thousands of people died in the battles.

Qaddafi managed to escape from Tripoli. He tried to run from the rebels. The rebels captured and killed him in October 2011. The Libyan part of the Arab Spring became known as the Libyan Civil War. Numerous groups continued fighting for control of the country in the late 2010s.

Political/Government Uprisings

protesters had to become journalists themselves to circulate information about the Green Movement. Ordinary citizens who do this are called citizen journalists. The news they provide is not professionally produced, but its purpose is to inform others of events that governments try to keep secret. The Green Movement is regarded as an important event in the history of citizen journalism.

More than 100 people were killed in battles between government forces and protesters. Police arrested about 10,000 people. The government mistreated many of those arrested. In the months following the protests, officials conducted mass round-ups of the protesters. Some were made to stand trial. Punishments ranged from lengthy prison sentences to execution.

The Iranian government was not able to silence the Iranian Green Movement until early 2010. The Tunisian and Egyptian Revolutions in early 2011 inspired some Iranians to begin protesting again. About 1 million Iranians protested their government in February 2011. In the end, the government stopped these protests too.

An Iranian protester holds up a picture of Neda Agha-Soltan, who was shot and killed during post-presidential election riots in 2009. People managed to get a video of her death out to let the world know what was happening in Iran. Agha-Soltan became a symbol of the opposition movement. The release of the video taken by a witness to the death marked an important event in the history of citizen journalists.
© AFP/GETTY IMAGES.

Arab Spring in Syria

Citizens of Syria became involved in the Arab Spring in March 2011. In Daraa (pronounced dar-AH), a city in southern Syria, a group of children wrote anti-government messages on a school wall. More than a dozen children were arrested in response. As a result, people in Daraa began protesting the government of President Assad.

Assad became president of Syria in 2000, succeeding his father. As president, he kept Syria in a state of emergency, which meant the Syrian people did not have the right to speak their opinions freely. Assad's government was able to arrest anyone at any time. Protesters in Daraa wanted Assad to leave office. Government forces fired weapons at the protesters.

Political/Government Uprisings

Syrians shout "Freedom!" at a protest near the city of Daraa on March 25, 2011. The protests spread across Syria as people demonstrated against the Assad family after government forces killed dozens of demonstrators. Bashar al-Assad became president of Syria in 2000. © REUTERS/KHALED AL-HARIR/ALAMY.

The violence angered Syrians in other parts of the country. They also began protesting Assad. Hundreds of thousands of Syrians had joined the protests by July 2011.

In an effort to please the protesters, Assad ended Syria's state of emergency. He also made it legal for Syrians to protest peacefully. However, Syrians continued to push Assad to give up his power.

From protest to civil war

Assad sent tanks into Syrian cities to stop the protests. Syrians who opposed Assad united to form the Free Syrian Army. The army fought Assad's forces. The rebels hoped to destroy Assad and his government. What began as a civil uprising turned into the Syrian Civil War.

The civil war continued over the next few years. Rebels captured large parts of northern and eastern Syria in 2012. Assad's forces tried to regain control of these areas from the rebels. The civil war destroyed many Syrian cities. Hundreds of thousands of innocent people died. Assad created great international controversy in mid-2013 for using chemical weapons against the rebels. Such weapons use chemicals to kill or seriously injure people. The 2013 attack killed more than 1,400 Syrian citizens. The United States and other countries later demanded that Syria destroy its chemical weapons. The use of chemical weapons is against various international agreements.

The Syrian Civil War was ongoing in the late 2010s. Numerous militant Islamist groups had joined the war. Assad remained in power. The rebels continued trying to destroy his government.

As of early 2017, according to some estimates, about 465,000 people had died or were missing due to the Syrian Civil War. More than 5 million Syrians had left the country. They became refugees in Europe and elsewhere. Refugees are people who leave a country to escape violence. More than 1.5 million people from Syria and elsewhere in the Middle East fled by sea to Europe starting in 2015. Many people drowned trying to reach safety in Europe. Refugees who did survive were soon part of a growing migrant crisis in Europe, as countries tried to deal with the arrival of so many new people to their lands.

Results of the Arab Spring

The Arab Spring had different results in different countries. Most critics agree that Tunisia was the only Arab nation that truly became a democracy after the Arab Spring. Tunisia eventually created a new constitution. It held national elections for its parliament and president.

No other Arab countries where protests took place became democracies like Tunisia. War and other violence continued in Yemen, Libya, and Syria. In Egypt, leaders who took control after Mubarak resigned continued to silence their political opponents.

At the same time, some critics believe that the Arab Spring was good overall for the Arab people. The protests allowed people to oppose leaders who had ruled them for a long time. The Arab Spring encouraged people in a number of Middle East and northern African countries to discuss, debate, and fight for a better future.

Tahrir Square Protests (Egyptian Revolution)

LOCATION: Egypt

DATE: 2011

In January and February 2011, Egyptians gathered to protest against their president and government. Thousands assembled in Tahrir (pronounced

Political/Government Uprisings

TAH-hreer) Square, a large public square in Egypt's capital city of Cairo. The protesters had grown weary of Egyptian President Hosni Mubarak (pronounced HOZ-nee mu-BAR-ek; 1928–). Mubarak had been in power for 30 years. The protesters claimed that Mubarak ruled like a dictator. They thought Mubarak should be doing more to create jobs, help the poor, and end government corruption. The people wanted better jobs with wages that would allow them to live decent lives.

The Tahrir Square protests continued for about two weeks. During that time, Egyptians pushed Mubarak to resign, or leave office. Police violently fought the protesters. Hundreds of people were killed, and thousands were injured. In the end, Mubarak resigned as president of Egypt on February 11, 2011.

After the Tahrir Square protests, also known as the Egyptian Revolution, the Egyptian people were able to vote for their leaders. They elected new government officials in late 2011 and early 2012. However, the newly elected presidents also held great power and silenced those who opposed them. As a result, some critics argue that the Egyptian Revolution failed to create a true democracy.

Origins of protests

The Egyptian people began protesting Mubarak's government in January 2011. The people had many complaints. Under Mubarak's rule, the Egyptian people had few rights. Mubarak also gave his government great power. The Egyptian government could arrest almost anyone.

Mubarak had been in power for a long time. He became president of Egypt in 1981. He was reelected to office numerous times, mainly because no one opposed him in presidential elections. As a result, he remained in power for several decades. He ruled as a dictator during this time.

In 2005 the United States convinced Mubarak to let someone run against him in the presidential election. However, Mubarak won this election, too. Critics said he won because his government interfered to stop the other candidate from winning.

By that time few Egyptians felt comfortable commenting publicly on Mubarak's dictatorship. Egyptians knew Mubarak was getting older. They felt unsafe wondering who would replace Mubarak as president. At the same time, the people were angry that Mubarak remained in power while many were poor and had very few rights. The people also disliked that many of them were living in poverty while Mubarak remained extremely wealthy.

> *In 2005 the United States convinced Mubarak to let someone run against him in the presidential election. However, Mubarak won this election, too. Critics said he won because his government interfered to stop the other candidate from winning.*

Then, in December 2010, protests in the nearby northern African nation of Tunisia (pronounced too-NEE-zhe) began. A vegetable seller set himself on fire to protest the dictatorship of Tunisian President Zine El-Abidine Ben Ali (pronounced ZAYN el AH-beh-deen ben AH-lee; 1936–). Ben Ali had been in power since the late 1980s. The Tunisian people blamed Ben Ali for the vegetable seller's death and protested his long rule. They said Ben Ali gave no rights to his people. The protests forced Ben Ali to resign as president on January 14, 2011. The protests in Tunisia became known as the Tunisian Revolution. The revolution was the start of the Arab Spring, to which protesters in Egypt would soon contribute.

The Tunisian Revolution inspired Egyptians to protest their own president. It showed the Egyptian people that anti-government protests could bring about real political change. Egyptians wanted Mubarak to give up his power. They were tired of being unemployed and living in poverty. They wanted a new government that would give them basic rights. The people began to protest.

The Tahrir Square protests begin

The Egyptian Revolution began on January 25, 2011. Egyptians were already out in the streets to observe a national holiday in honor of police. Thousands of Egyptians in Cairo instead called the public gathering a "day of rage." They intended to unite and begin protesting the government together.

The people gathered in downtown Cairo near the offices of Mubarak's political party, the National Democratic Party. The offices were located near Tahrir Square, which was often crowded with people and vehicles. Thousands of protesters started calling for Mubarak to leave office.

Egyptian police tried to make the protesters leave the square after a few hours. The police used water cannons and tear gas to fight the protesters. Tear gas is a chemical that causes severe burning of the eyes. News of the Cairo protests quickly spread throughout Egypt. Egyptians then began protesting Mubarak in other cities across the country.

The protests became more violent over the next few days. Protesters threw rocks and firebombs at police. Numerous protesters and police officers had died in the violence by January 26. Police arrested hundreds of people. Protesters and police continued to fight each other in many Egyptian cities.

Political/Government Uprisings

Anti-government protesters in Egypt wave flags in Tahrir Square during a protest in Cairo on February 4, 2011. Tens of thousands of Egyptians protested for the nation's president to quit. © MOHAMMED ABED/AFP/GETTY IMAGES.

The Tahrir Square protests continue

Early in the morning on January 29, Mubarak announced to the nation that he had dismissed his entire cabinet. A cabinet is a group of advisers who helps a president or other official lead a country. Mubarak did not say he would leave office as president, though, so the protests continued.

Thousands of people remained in Tahrir Square on January 29. They would not leave even after Egyptian soldiers began firing their guns into the air. Later that day Mubarak named a vice president. Mubarak had never had a vice president during his 30 years in power. He believed a vice president might calm the protesters.

By January 31 about 250,000 people had assembled in Tahrir Square. They wanted Mubarak to leave office. They would not accept any other solution. Mubarak still refused to give up power. Instead, he publicly named a new cabinet. His vice president then said the government would work with opposing parties to reform, or improve, the country's laws.

Mubarak resigns

On February 1 Mubarak partly gave in to one of the protesters' demands. He announced that he would not run for reelection as president in September 2011. He also said he would reform Egypt's laws and repair the national economy. The protesters claimed this was not enough. They wanted Mubarak to leave office immediately. Critics of Egypt said Mubarak was trying to trick the people into letting him stay in power.

Violence continued in Cairo and other Egyptian cities. Fights between protesters and Mubarak supporters injured about 1,500 people in Tahrir Square. The Egyptian military tried to scare protesters out of the square. Soldiers drove tanks near the square and fired guns into the air. Mubarak supporters encouraged the protesters to leave because he had agreed to meet some of their demands. The protesters refused. They camped there in tents for days. They claimed they would stay until Mubarak left office.

On February 10, Mubarak again told the Egyptian people that he would stay in power until the September 2011 election. The announcement further outraged the protesters. Finally, on February 11, Mubarak resigned as president of Egypt. He gave control of the country to the Egyptian military.

The protesters celebrated in Tahrir Square until the next day. They then started clearing the square while they waited to see what would happen next. About 850 people died in violent conflicts with Egyptian government forces during the protests. Thousands were injured.

Egypt after the revolution

On February 14, 2011, the Egyptian military presented a six-month plan for the future of Egypt. The plan called for a new constitution for the country. A constitution is a country's document of laws. The military promised that the government would hold new elections for the parliament and the presidency. A parliament is a group of lawmakers. The military said that civilians, or non-military individuals, would make up the new government.

Egypt's shift from Mubarak's rule to a new government was not smooth. More people protested over the next few months. They wanted the military to create a democratic government more quickly. This time, the military responded to protests with direct violence. Government forces arrested many people for protesting in Tahrir Square. The military later beat, jailed, and killed many protesters.

Political/Government Uprisings

Electing a new government

Egypt held parliamentary elections from late 2011 until early 2012. Politicians from the Muslim Brotherhood and other Islamic political groups won most of the seats. Muslims are followers of the religion of Islam. Muslims respect the prophet Muhammad (c. 570–632) and follow the teachings of the Koran, the holy book they believe Muhammad wrote. Prophets are individuals whom people believe are messengers of God. The Muslim Brotherhood wanted to create Islam-based laws for Egypt.

The Egyptian people elected Mohamed Morsi (pronounced MOR-see; 1951–) of the Muslim Brotherhood as president of Egypt in June 2012. He was the first president the Egyptian people ever elected themselves. However, Morsi was similar to Mubarak. He gave himself almost unlimited power. People protested his rule over the next year. The Egyptian military forced Morsi from office in July 2013. The Egyptian people then elected former military general Abdel Fattah el-Sisi (pronounced AHB-del FAH-tah el SEE-see; 1954–) as president in 2014. Critics felt that Sisi was a dictator like Morsi and Mubarak.

In the end the 2011 Tahrir Square protests achieved only some of their goals. The protests drove Mubarak to resign the presidency of Egypt after three decades. Egyptian protesters had risked arrest, injury, and death to make this happen. The Egyptian Revolution also brought a new government and new laws to Egypt.

However, not all Egyptians were satisfied with the governments that followed Mubarak's rule. Some people protested Morsi for being too powerful, like Mubarak. Sisi's government also silenced critics and protesters. Journalists and others outside Egypt have claimed that the country only seems like a democracy under Sisi but it is not.

Umbrella Revolution

LOCATION: Hong Kong, China

DATE: 2014

The Umbrella Revolution, or Umbrella Movement, was a mass protest movement that took place in Hong Kong from September to December 2014. Hong Kong is a territory of China. It is located on China's

Political/Government Uprisings

southern coast. China allows Hong Kong to self-govern to a great degree but still holds final authority over policies and practices in the territory. The Umbrella Revolution protests were a response to a Chinese government ruling in August 2014. That month China decided that it would not allow Hong Kong to choose its own leaders freely by the year 2017.

In 1997 China had claimed that it would permit Hong Kongers to select their own rulers in 20 years. Instead, as that deadline approached, China decided it wanted to continue to choose the candidates for whom the people of Hong Kong could vote. This was an effort to prevent Hong Kong citizens from electing leaders who might call for the region's independence from China. Hong Kongers started protesting China's decision in September 2014. At first, the protesters were mostly students. Tens of thousands of others later joined them. The protesters wanted China to give Hong Kong the freedom to choose their own leaders in a democratic fashion.

Hong Kong and China

Hong Kong had been part of China since ancient times. The United Kingdom made the area a British colony in the mid-19th century. A colony is a country or region that another country controls politically. The United Kingdom returned Hong Kong to China in 1997. From that point, China controlled Hong Kong through a process called "one country, two systems." Hong Kong was officially China's territory, but it could still mostly govern itself.

The region had its own courts and a free press. A free press refers to news media that the government does not censor, control, or limit. In the capital of Beijing, the Chinese government managed other important matters concerning Hong Kong. For instance, the Chinese army would defend Hong Kong from attack in the event of a military conflict. The Chinese government oversaw the region's relations with foreign countries as well. China also chose the leaders of the Hong Kong government. Hong Kong's main leader is the chief executive. Over the years, China used a committee of 1,200 people to choose candidates for chief executive. Most of the committee members politically supported the Chinese government. By using this selection committee, China made sure the candidates for chief executive agreed with Chinese politics.

In 1997 China claimed that it would allow the people of Hong Kong to elect their own leaders by 2017. Political activists in Hong Kong

At first, the protesters were mostly students. Tens of thousands of others later joined them. The protesters wanted China to give Hong Kong the freedom to choose their own leaders in a democratic fashion.

Political/Government Uprisings

Activists during the Umbrella Revolution in Hong Kong block streets in October 2014.
© COLOURSINMYLIFE/
SHUTTERSTOCK.COM.

watched the Chinese government carefully as the mid-2010s drew near. They wanted to make sure China would follow through on its promise. In 2013 some activists set up a protest group called Occupy Central with Love and Peace. Central referred to the Central District of Hong Kong, the downtown area of the city. The activists would start protesting if China did not keep its word.

In August 2014 China passed a new law relating to Hong Kong's elections. The law stated that China would continue to choose candidates to run for Hong Kong's chief executive. These candidates would have to revere both China and Hong Kong. Political activists in Hong Kong began protesting against China's decision in September 2014.

Umbrella Revolution begins

The anti-China protests started when students refused to go to class. Many Hong Kong citizens supported the students. The students gathered outside the Hong Kong city government building. They protested China's decision to continue controlling Hong Kong's government. The Occupy Central protest group started publicly protesting a few days later. All protesters called for China to allow Hong Kongers greater freedom in political elections. They also wanted Hong Kong chief executive Leung Chun-ying (pronounced lee-yoong Chuhn Yeeng;

1954–) to resign. The protesters believed he was more loyal to China than Hong Kong.

Hong Kong police tried to stop the protests. Police officers formed lines to block the protesters from getting close to the city government building. On September 26, 2014, about 150 protesters pushed past police and entered the building. Officers arrested many of these citizens.

Tens of thousands of protesters remained outside the building over the following days. Police tried to break up the crowds using tear gas and pepper spray. Tear gas and pepper spray are substances that cause tearing and burning of the eyes. Still, the leaders of Occupy Central and other protest groups called for demonstrators to remain nonviolent in their activities. At the same time, the protesters promised they would not stop until China gave Hong Kong free elections. Protesters started carrying umbrellas in the streets with them. They used the umbrellas to defend themselves against the police's pepper spray. The protesters' umbrellas inspired the name Umbrella Revolution. Yellow umbrellas and ribbons became the defining symbols of the revolution.

Umbrella Revolution grows

The number of protesters in Hong Kong grew over the next few weeks. Thousands of protesters eventually occupied numerous spaces across the city. These included various downtown areas and several shopping districts. In many cases, the protesters blocked main streets in the city. Their presence stopped many buses, trams, and cars from traveling across downtown Hong Kong.

Meanwhile, Hong Kong police continued to oppose the protesters. Numerous protesters and police officers were injured in violent conflicts. The police also arrested many protesters for gathering in public places illegally.

Despite conflicts with police, the pro-democracy protesters remained in the streets of Hong Kong into late 2014. During this time, the protests did more than just block traffic. They interfered with the Hong Kong economy. The protests forced many stores and banks to close. The unrest in the city also made the Hong Kong dollar drop in value. This meant Hong Kong's currency was now worth less in international business dealings. The Hong Kong dollar's value decreased because the protests made the region seem unstable to the rest of the world.

Political/Government Uprisings

8888 Uprising, Myanmar, 1988

The 8888 Uprising took place in Myanmar (pronounced ME'YAN-mar; also known as Burma) in 1988. Protesters in the 8888 Uprising (so named because it began on August 8, 1988) opposed the dictator Ne Win (1911–2002). He had ruled Myanmar since 1962. Protesters wanted Myanmar to become a democracy.

Ne Win's government was socialist. Socialism is a political system in which a central government is expected to distribute goods and services to all members of a society equally. Ne Win's bad policies and decisions soon ruined Myanmar's economy. Many of the country's residents became poor.

Ne Win made the economy worse in the mid-1980s. His policies contributed to many families losing their savings, including savings for college. In response, students started protesting against Ne Win's government. The protests spread around the country. Government authorities violently put down the protests.

Students, doctors, children, and others later planned even bigger protests against Ne Win. They chose August 8, 1988, as their starting date. That day the protesters demanded that Ne Win give up control of Myanmar. They wanted the country to become a democracy. This way, the people could vote for their own leaders.

The 8888 Uprising saw Aung San Suu Kyi (pronounced AUNG sahn su chee; 1945–) become a kind of national hero. Suu Kyi was the daughter of General Aung San (1915–1947), who had helped Myanmar become an independent country in the 1940s. Suu Kyi was living in the United Kingdom at the beginning of the 8888 Uprising. She returned to Myanmar in August 1988 to care for her sick mother. Soon, Suu Kyi realized she could not ignore the protests occurring around her. She felt she had to assist the protesters because of what her father had done for the country.

Suu Kyi planned peaceful demonstrations throughout Myanmar. She encouraged people to call for democratic changes, including fair elections. Ne Win responded to the protests violently. He ordered his military to arrest and kill the protesters. Suu Kyi herself was placed under house arrest in 1989 and spent much of the next 15 years in custody. The protesters fought the military with rocks and knives. In the end, Ne Win's forces killed about 3,000 people during the protests. Most of these protesters were students.

Public support for protests

The Chinese government refused to meet the protesters' demands during the Umbrella Revolution. Some news agencies around the world claimed this was because the Communist Party of China would not allow an opponent of the party to govern Hong Kong. The Communist Party of China is the main political party in China. It controls the entire country. According to the news agencies, the Chinese government would always oppose any pro-democracy politician becoming chief executive of Hong

Political/Government Uprisings

Ne Win resigned from office in 1988. Another dictatorship took power in Myanmar that year. In the 21st century, the country made some new laws with a more democratic spirit. Still, Myanmar was not a full democracy. Suu Kyi won the Nobel Peace Prize in 1991 and became state counselor, a kind of prime minister, of Myanmar in 2016. In 2017, however, some people called for her prize to be revoked following her silence regarding the brutal treatment and persecution of a Muslim minority group, the Rohingya, in Myanmar.

Women from Myanmar shout anti-military government slogans during a protest in New Delhi, India, on August 8, 2006. They are protesting on the 18th anniversary of the historic 8888 Uprising when the Myanmar government suppressed a pro-democracy movement. Some of their signs refer to Aung San Suu Kyi, a pro-democracy leader who was put under house arrest on and off for 15 years between 1989 and 2010. © RAVEENDRAN/AFP/GETTY IMAGES.

Kong. This could lead to Hong Kong becoming independent. Independence in Hong Kong could inspire people in other areas of China to want to become more democratic as well.

Hong Kong citizens were divided on supporting the Umbrella Revolution protests. Most of the demonstrators were students and other young people. Their supporters were mostly young too. Many older Hong Kongers opposed the protests. To them, the protesters could never win because the Chinese government was too strong.

A pro-democracy activist holds a yellow umbrella in front of a line of police on a street in Hong Kong in November 2014. They are near one of the protest sites that police will start to clear out that week. Police have been authorized by Hong Kong's high court to arrest any protesters who try to obstruct their efforts. © CHRIS MCGRATH/GETTY IMAGES.

Older people were afraid that the Umbrella Revolution protests would cause China to take away some of the freedoms that Hong Kong already had. Additionally, older Hong Kong citizens worried about the region's economy. They said living in the city was expensive. The demonstrations had caused the growth of Hong Kong's economy to slow. The older people did not like this. They felt very strongly about this since they believed China would never meet the protesters' demands.

End of the protests

The Umbrella Revolution protests lasted into late 2014. The demonstrators had set up camps at their various protest locations. They planned to protest at the camps until China gave Hong Kong more democracy. The demonstrations had often become violent. Protesters fought with the police who tried to clear the streets. The demonstrators also fought with other Hong Kong citizens who opposed their activities. These citizens tried to take down the protester camps.

Hong Kong police started taking down the camps in late November 2014. Sometimes the protesters accepted these actions peacefully. Other demonstrators fought with officers. Police cleared the last of the protesters' camps by mid-December. Throughout the demonstrations, Leung refused to leave office as Hong Kong chief executive. Nevertheless, he did not seek reelection for a second term. In early 2017 he was succeeded by Carrie Lam (1957–), the first woman elected chief executive of Hong Kong.

Most of the Umbrella Revolution protesters returned to school or work following the end of the demonstrations. Many activists later reported they still hoped Hong Kong would become a democracy one day. Some noted that Hong Kong's powers of self-government were set to run out in 2047. The former protesters were unsure of what would happen to Hong Kong after that.

Not everyone was able to return easily to their old lives. In 2014 Hong Kong authorities had arrested some protest leaders and charged them with illegally assembling in public places. In August 2017 a Hong Kong court sentenced three young protest leaders to serve between six and eight months in prison. Tens of thousands of Hong Kongers publicly protested the court's decision on August 20, 2017.

For More Information

BOOKS

Bingham, Jane. *Tiananmen Square: June 4, 1989*. Chicago: Raintree, 2004.

Kelly, Nigel. *The Fall of the Berlin Wall: The Cold War Ends*. Rev. ed. Chicago: Heinemann Library, 2006.

Lusted, Marcia Amidon. *Tiananmen Square Protests*. Edina, MN: ABDO, 2011.

PERIODICALS

Abouzeid, Rania. "Bouazizi: The Man Who Set Himself and Tunisia on Fire." *Time* (January 21, 2011). Available online at http://content.time.com/time/magazine/article/0,9171,2044723,00.html (accessed August 18, 2017).

Dearden, Lizzie. "Berlin Wall: What You Need to Know about the Barrier That Divided East and West." *Independent* (November 7, 2014). Available online at http://www.independent.co.uk/life-style/history/berlin-wall-what-you-need-to-know-about-the-barrier-that-divided-east-and-west-9847347.html (accessed August 14, 2017).

Iyengar, Rishi. "6 Questions You Might Have about Hong Kong's Umbrella Revolution." *Time* (October 5, 2014). Available online at http://time.com/3471366/hong-kong-umbrella-revolution-occupy-central-democracy-explainer-6-questions/ (accessed August 21, 2017).

Kaiman, Jonathan. "Hong Kong's Umbrella Revolution—the Guardian Briefing." *Guardian* (September 30, 2014). Available online at https://www.theguardian.com/world/2014/sep/30/-sp-hong-kong-umbrella-revolution-pro-democracy-protests (accessed August 21, 2017).

McCarthy, Tom. "Under the Umbrellas: What Do Hong Kong's Protesters Want from China?" *Guardian* (September 29, 2014). Available online at https://www.theguardian.com/world/2014/sep/29/hong-kong-democracy-protests-china-umbrellas-police (accessed August 21, 2017).

Rayman, Noah. "6 Things You Should Know about the Tiananmen Square Massacre." *Time* (June 4, 2014). Available online at http://time.com/2822290/tiananmen-square-massacre-facts-time/ (accessed August 23, 2017).

Schiavenza, Matt. "China's Forgotten Liberal Hero." *Atlantic* (April 16, 2014). Available online at https://www.theatlantic.com/international/archive/2014/04/chinas-forgotten-liberal-hero/360722/ (accessed August 23, 2017).

WEBSITES

"The Arab Spring: A Year of Revolution." National Public Radio, December 17, 2011. http://www.npr.org/2011/12/17/143897126/the-arab-spring-a-year-of-revolution (accessed August 18, 2017).

"Arab Uprising: Country by Country—Egypt." BBC News. http://www.bbc.com/news/world-12482291 (accessed August 18, 2017).

"The Berlin Wall Falls and USSR Dissolves." US Department of State, Office of the Historian. https://history.state.gov/departmenthistory/short-history/berlinwall (accessed August 14, 2017).

Childress, Sarah. "Timeline: What's Happened since Egypt's Revolution?" Public Broadcasting Service, September 17, 2013. http://www.pbs.org/wgbh/frontline/article/timeline-whats-happened-since-egypts-revolution/ (accessed August 15, 2017).

"Hong Kong Protests: Timeline of the Occupation." BBC News, December 11, 2014. http://www.bbc.com/news/world-asia-china-30390820 (accessed August 21, 2017).

Keating, Joshua. "Why Was Tunisia the Only Arab Spring Country That Turned Out Well?" *Slate*, January 28, 2015. http://www.slate.com/blogs/the_slatest/2015/01/28/why_was_tunisia_the_only_arab_spring_country_that_turned_out_well.html (accessed August 18, 2017).

Kennedy, Merrit. "A Look at Egypt's Uprising, 5 Years Later." National Public Radio, January 25, 2016. http://www.npr.org/sections/thetwo-way/2016/01/25/464290769/a-look-at-egypts-uprising-5-years-later (accessed August 15, 2017).

McKirdy, Euan. "Tens of Thousands Protest Jailing of Hong Kong Pro-Democracy Leaders." CNN, August 21, 2017. http://www.cnn.com/2017/08/20/asia/hong-kong-protests-joshua-wong/index.html (accessed August 21, 2017).

"Tiananmen Square Fast Facts" CNN, May 28, 2017. http://www.cnn.com/2013/09/15/world/asia/tiananmen-square-fast-facts/index.html (accessed August 23, 2017).

"Timeline—Arab Spring: A Year That Shook the Arab World." Reuters, January 13, 2012. http://in.reuters.com/article/tunisia-revolution-anniversary-idINDEE80C0IT20120113 (accessed August 18, 2017).

"Timeline: Egypt's Revolution." Al Jazeera, February 14, 2011. http://www.aljazeera.com/news/middleeast/2011/01/201112515334871490.html (accessed August 15, 2017).

"Timeline: Tiananmen Protests." BBC News, June 2, 2014. http://www.bbc.com/news/world-asia-china-27404764 (accessed August 23, 2017).

"Tunisian Revolution." Al Jazeera, December 17, 2015. http://www.aljazeera.com/indepth/inpictures/2015/12/tunisian-revolution-151215102459580.html (accessed August 18, 2017).

van Stekelenburg, Jacquelien. "People Protest for Many Reasons, Yet We Don't Know How Effective Protests Are." London School of Economics and Political Science, November 30, 2015. http://blogs.lse.ac.uk/politicsandpolicy/how-effective-are-protests/ (accessed August 23, 2017).

16

Racial Conflict

Zoot Suit Riots **518**

Detroit Riots **524**

Soweto Uprising **530**

Justice for All March **539**

All human beings are part of the same species. That means every person in the world shares the same basic human characteristics. Human beings often divide themselves into smaller groups based on ethnicity or race. Ethnicity is defined by a person's culture, language, or home country. Race is based on differences in physical appearance, such as skin color. Racism is the idea that one human being is better than another simply because of his or her race.

According to experts who study history, some ancient cultures believed they were superior to others, but not because of race. For example, the ancient Greeks felt their society was better because they lived in a "perfect" climate. The Greeks thought people who lived where it was too hot or too cold were less intelligent because of the weather. The Romans believed their way of life was superior and referred to all outsiders as "barbarians." Both cultures welcomed people of different races if the outsiders accepted the ways of Greek and Roman societies.

An excuse for racism

In the late 1400s and early 1500s, European explorers began sailing to different regions around the world. In many places, they encountered people with a different skin color and a different way of life. These explorers brought news of their discoveries back to Europe. At the time, people in Europe were beginning to look at the world in a more scientific light—investigating new ideas, gathering data, and basing conclusions on evidence. Scientists of the era began to examine the issue of race.

In the 1600s and 1700s, some medical experts divided human beings along racial lines. They placed people into groups similar to how plants and animals were divided. They felt that people with different skin colors were members of a different species of human. In addition to physical

Racial Conflict

WORDS TO KNOW

Apartheid: A series of laws in South Africa that legalized discrimination and ordered the separation of people by race.

Civil rights: Guarantees of political, social, and economic freedoms to all citizens of a country equally.

Discrimination: Unfair treatment based on one's race, ethnicity, or other distinction.

Ethnicity: A division of human beings by culture, language, or home country.

Jim Crow laws: Laws created mostly in the American South in the late 19th and early 20th centuries that kept black citizens from enjoying the same rights as white Americans.

Migrant: A person who moves from his or her home area to a different region.

Police brutality: The use of more force than necessary by police.

Racism: Unfair treatment of people of different races, usually based on the idea that one's own race or culture is better.

Sanction: An official punishment usually imposed on a country by another nation or group of nations.

Suffocate: To die from not being able to breathe.

White supremacist: A person who believes the white race is superior to other races.

Zoot suit: A flashy oversized suit popular in the 1940s.

differences, these people had customs and traditions that seemed strange to the European scientists. Because they did not understand the diverse cultures, the Europeans began to judge these differences based on their worldview, or what they knew at the time, which were European traditions. This led them to believe some races were better than others and that Europeans were superior to all.

This idea of superiority made Europeans feel they had the right to take control over people of other races. They took land away from people in Africa, Asia, and North and South America, and they established settlements in those regions. They enslaved people from Africa and forced them to work in colonies such as those in the Caribbean islands and North and South America. In many places, people of other races had fewer rights and less freedom than European people.

The issue of slavery

In the early 1600s, British colonists brought indentured servants with them when they settled in Virginia. An indentured servant was someone who agreed to work for a specified length of time in order to gain passage

CRITICAL THINKING QUESTIONS

1. Why did many Europeans in the 1600s and 1700s think it was acceptable to treat people of other races unfairly?

2. Why do many African Americans think they are treated unfairly by police officers?

3. How did the uprising in Soweto help bring an end to apartheid in South Africa?

4. Why were students angry about having to learn in Afrikaans?

5. Do you think Black Lives Matter should concentrate on gaining equal rights for all people, not just African Americans? Why or why not?

6. What do you think was the reason for the Unite the Right rally in August 2017?

7. Do you think it was necessary during the Detroit riots of 1967 for demonstrators to break into businesses and set fires to buildings to show their anger over their mistreatment? What, if anything, could they have done differently to express their anger? Explain.

8. Should people be drafted to fight in wars for their country? Should all races be drafted equally? Should women be drafted? Explain.

9. Do you think there was anything wrong with zoot suits? Why or why not? How did zoot suits lead to a riot?

10. What lessons do you think can be learned from the Zoot Suit Riots? Explain.

---

to the New World. Many of these indentured servants came from Ireland, Germany, and Scotland. After working for several years, they would earn their freedom and start a new life. Some of the first African slaves brought to Virginia were treated as indentured servants. By the late 1600s, however, slavery was legalized in the British colonies and servants could no longer work toward their freedom.

Explorers from Spain and Portugal were the first Europeans to bring African slaves to their colonies in the Americas. For nearly two centuries, millions of Africans were brought to the Americas as slaves; about 600,000 of those slaves were transported to what became the United States. Even after the United States won its independence from Great Britain, slavery continued in the southern states until 1865. Slave owners did not see slaves as human beings. They were thought of as property and could be bought and sold. Even in northern states where slavery was illegal, people of African descent were often seen as inferior to white people.

Most of the world's nations declared slavery illegal during the 1800s. People who had lived their entire lives as slaves now had their freedom, but unfair treatment based on race continued. In some places, white-run governments passed laws that limited the rights of people of other races.

Racial Conflict

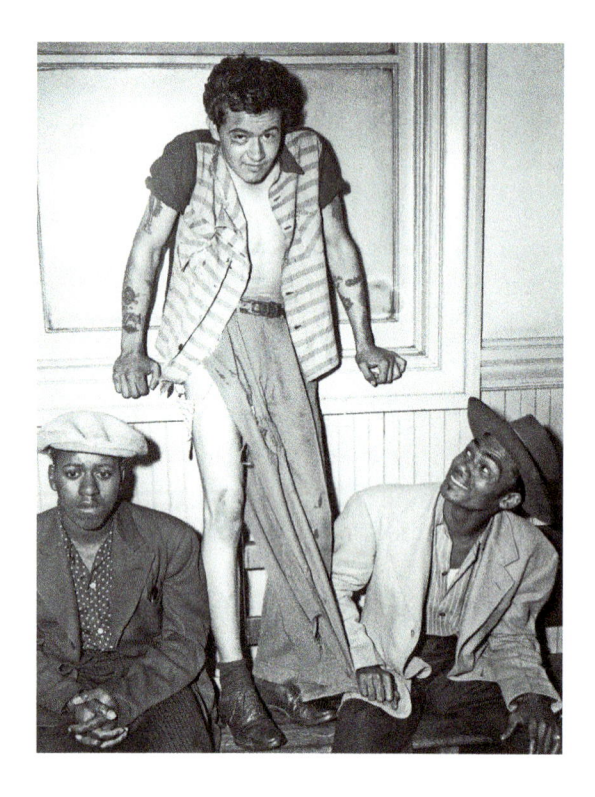

A young man named Paul Acevedo stands in his tattered clothing, flanked by two men in zoot suits, following a major clash in Los Angeles. As tensions grew high, servicemen not only targeted Mexican Americans but other minorities wearing zoot suits or fancy clothes.
© BETTMANN/GETTY IMAGES.

In the United States, many places made it difficult for African Americans to vote. Some laws forced whites and blacks to go to different schools or sit in different areas in restaurants and other public places. Many African Americans were angry with these laws, but it was difficult to change them.

Examples of violence

Disputes between races sometimes led to violent conflict. In 1863 racist attitudes and anger about the American Civil War (1861–1865) sparked the New York City draft riots. Many poor white people believed they were being forced to fight in the war. They also thought it was unfair that the city's African Americans did not have to serve in the military and go to war. Over several days of rioting, African Americans were the targets of much of the violence.

In 1943, during the height of World War II (1939–1945), white servicemen attacked groups of Mexican Americans and other minorities in Los Angeles, California. The violence was called the Zoot Suit Riots after the baggy style of clothes worn by many of those who were attacked. The riots began over an argument that people should not be allowed to wear the expensive suits during a time of war. However, after several days of violence, it became apparent that racism was the cause of many of the attacks.

Across the United States in the late 19th and early 20th centuries, violence against people of different races was common. In the American South, some people organized groups that promoted the idea that the white race was superior. These groups primarily targeted African Americans. They sought to bully African Americans who tried to stand up for their rights. In some cases, people were beaten or even killed simply because of the color of their skin.

Fighting back

Ideas about race began to change in the 20th century. Scientists who study the human body and human behavior discovered that the old ideas about race were wrong. People with different skin colors are not different species of human beings. All humans belong to the same species. Dividing people based on race was an idea created by humans. This new information, however, did not change the minds of many people.

In the nation of South Africa, many white people had long believed that they were the superior race. In 1948 white government leaders passed a series of laws that separated people according to race. Black South Africans could not live, work, or go to school with white South Africans. There were more black people living in the nation, but they had fewer rights than white people.

Many black people were angry at the system. When the blacks tried to stand up for their rights, however, the government punished them or put them in jail. In 1976 anger over the language taught in South African schools grew into a nationwide uprising. The government's violent response to the rioters shocked many people around the world. It also helped unite South Africa's black population. International pressure and efforts from within South Africa eventually brought positive change to the nation.

New laws, old problems

In the United States, African Americans achieved a large victory in the 1960s. The US government ended many of the laws that treated African Americans unfairly. African Americans were given the same rights as all other Americans. The new laws made it illegal to treat people differently because of their skin color.

Despite the new laws, racism continued to be a problem in the United States. Many African Americans believed they were still being treated unfairly and were not receiving all the rights they were promised by the government. They also felt that they did not get the same opportunities that white Americans did.

Anger at police

Many African Americans were especially angry at the justice system in the United States. They pointed to statistics that showed African Americans were more likely to be charged with a crime and jailed than white Americans were. They also believed that police officers in many cities were unfairly targeting them because they were black.

Racial Conflict

Many race riots occurred in the 1960s in the United States. Here, police are shown frisking a black man and woman during the Watts riots in Los Angeles in 1965. © ROLLS PRESS/POPPERFOTO/GETTY IMAGES.

In the mid-20th century, tensions between police and African Americans resulted in several major conflicts in the United States. A police raid at an African American bar in Detroit, Michigan, turned violent in 1967. The raid was seen by many in the black community as an example of police mistreatment of African Americans. Five days of rioting led to more than 40 deaths and thousands of arrests.

In Los Angeles in the 1980s and early 1990s, many African American residents saw the police as an unjust force. In 1991 Los Angeles police officers were filmed beating a black motorist who tried to flee on foot after a high-speed car chase. The motorist was suspected of being drunk. The officers were charged with a crime, but they were found not guilty in April 1992. The decision angered many people in the black community. Thousands of people rioted for three days in Los Angeles. More than 60 people died and more than 2,000 were injured.

Shootings lead to protests

Even into the early 21st century, many black citizens continued to feel the American justice system was working against them. In 2012 an unarmed black teenager was shot and killed during a confrontation with a neighborhood watch volunteer in Florida. The incident angered many African Americans. When a jury found the volunteer not guilty in July 2013, that anger grew.

The court decision prompted several activists in California to organize a campaign against what they saw as injustice and police violence. The movement was called Black Lives Matter. In 2014 members of Black Lives Matter protested the police shooting of an unarmed black man in Ferguson, Missouri. The group discovered that its slogan and message were becoming popular with African Americans across the country.

Members of Black Lives Matter joined other protests. In December 2014, some members participated in a large demonstration called the Justice for All march in Washington, DC. It was held to raise awareness of police violence against African Americans. It also called on the US government to change how the justice system treats black citizens.

Continued conflict

Issues of race seemed to divide many Americans in the early 21st century. African Americans believed that racism and injustice continued to be major problems in the United States. Groups like Black Lives Matter inspired others to speak out against possible mistreatment of African Americans by police. These groups organized several protests in cities where officers were accused of shooting unarmed African Americans.

Others found different ways to protest. In a peaceful protest of police brutality and the deaths of unarmed black citizens, San Francisco 49ers quarterback Colin Kaepernick decided to sit when the national anthem was played at National Football League (NFL) games, beginning in 2016. Eventually, Kaepernick chose to kneel, which either drew praise or anger from fans. A few other players began to kneel during the anthem, too.

In September 2017, President Donald Trump (1946–) strongly criticized Kaepernick and other players who knelt, saying they were disrespecting the flag. The NFL responded at the next set of games. Many players, owners, and coaches came on to the field together, some then knelt and others locked arms as they united to acknowledge racial injustice.

The focus on race in the United States also prompted Americans to examine the country's past. Some people believed that statues and flags representing the side of the Southern states during the US Civil War were racist symbols. Some viewed them as a symbol of hate. They saw these

Racial Conflict

Protests and Sports

Many people have taken a stand against racial injustice by joining in marches and protests. Sometimes, well-known figures such as athletes can use their fame to make a statement about a cause.

During the 1968 Olympic Games in Mexico City, Mexico, African American sprinters Tommie Smith (1944–) and John Carlos (1945–) wanted to make a statement about racial discrimination in the United States. After Smith won the gold medal and Carlos won the bronze medal in the 200-meter dash, they saw an opportunity to make their point.

Before they received their medals, the athletes took off their shoes as a protest against poverty. As the US national anthem played, they lowered their heads and raised one fist covered in a black glove. Smith raised his right hand to represent black power; Carlos raised his left hand as a sign of black unity. The silver medalist, Peter Norman of Australia, supported the protest by wearing a badge from the organization Olympic Project for Human Rights, which was against racism in sports.

At the time, many people were angry at the athletes. The crowd booed, and Smith and Carlos were later kicked out of the Olympics and suspended from the US track team. However, as time went on, many people saw Smith and Carlos as heroes who stood up for the rights of African Americans.

In a similar form of protest, Colin Kaepernick (1987–), while a quarterback with the San Francisco 49ers of the National Football League (NFL), refused to stand during the national anthem during his team's first three preseason games in 2016. Of mixed race, Kaepernick said he did it to protest police brutality against African Americans, which had resulted in several high-profile deaths in recent years. Kaepernick's reasons for his protest appeared on NFL.com. "I am not going to stand up to show pride in a flag for a country that oppresses black people and people of color.... To me, this is bigger than football and it would be selfish on my part to look the other way. There are bodies in the street and people getting paid leave and getting away with murder."

Kaepernick continued his protest by kneeling for the anthem during games. Other NFL players joined the protest by kneeling, sitting, or raising their fists as the anthem played. While many people thought the gestures were disrespectful, the players said they did it to protest racial injustice.

In September 2017 US President Donald Trump said that players should be fired if they continued to protest during the anthem. In response, NFL players knelt, locked arms, or refused to take the field for the anthem during the third week of the regular season. They said their actions were meant to show unity and take a stand against racial injustice. Kaepernick could no longer take part in the protests

objects as representing a war fought to continue the practice of slavery. Some saw them as symbols of intimidation that were used during the Jim Crow era when blacks were segregated from whites in the South. Some hate group members carried Confederate flags in protests and demonstrations. In some places, people organized protests and community campaigns to push for the removal of these symbols from their

Racial Conflict

because no NFL team would hire him, which many people attributed to his form of protest.

Some Americans supported the players and their right to speak out. Others were angry the players chose to protest during the anthem. An October 2017 poll by the Associated Press found that a majority of Americans did not support protests during the anthem but also did not agree with the president's comments. Kaepernick's efforts pertaining to racial injustice earned him the 2017 Sports Illustrated Muhammad Ali Legacy Award.

Two protests about racial injustice made major headlines nearly 50 years apart. Left: At the 1968 Olympic Games in Mexico City, USA gold medalist Tommie Smith (center) and bronze medalist John Carlos raise their fists in a black power salute as an anti-racism protest. They are standing on the podium where they received their medals along with Australian silver medalist Peter Norman. Right: San Francisco 49ers Eric Reid (35) and Colin Kaepernick (7) take a knee during the national anthem prior to their season opener against the Los Angeles Rams during an NFL football game in September 2016. OLYMPICS: © ROLLS PRESS/POPPERFOTO/GETTY IMAGES; NFL: © AP IMAGES/DANIEL GLUSKOTER.

communities. Others saw the symbols of the Southern past as representing history rather than racism, as a way to honor their ancestors who fought in the war. They organized protests to protect these symbols.

Despite differences of opinion, most Americans stand together and do not approve of racism itself. However, some never stop believing in the idea that white people are superior to other races. These people are called

Racial Conflict

Hate in the United States

917 The number of hate groups active in the United States in 2017 (SPLC)	**About 40** The number of organized and active Ku Klux Klan groups, representing about 3,000 members in 2017 (ADL)	**86** The percentage growth of anti-Semitic incidents in the first three months of 2017 (ADL)
56.9 The percentage of reported single-bias hate incidents that were motivated by race, ethnicity or ancestry in 2015 (FBI)	**5,850** The number of hate crime incidents reported to the FBI in 2015 (FBI)	**Most** The proportion of white supremacists who do not belong to an organized group (ADL)

SOURCE: SPLC (Southern Poverty Law Center); ADL (Anti-Defamation League); and FBI (Federal Bureau of Investigation).

© 2018 CENGAGE®.

white supremacists. Some white supremacists held protests of their own to promote their way of thinking. At one of those protests in August 2017, a young white woman was killed and several others injured when a white supremacist drove his car into a crowd of people. The injured people were part of a group of counterprotesters who opposed white supremacists' views.

Zoot Suit Riots

LOCATION: Los Angeles, California

DATE: June 1943

Racism has often been a cause for violence in American history. The United States consists of people from many different backgrounds. This frequently leads to conflicts between different groups of people who misunderstand one another. Such conflicts can easily become violent as things spiral out of control over time. Most of these conflicts have been between white Americans and groups such as African Americans and Mexican Americans. Fear and anger between different cultural groups often leads to violence.

In 1943 the United States was heavily involved in World War II (1939–1945), fighting against Germany and Japan. People up and down the West Coast were worried about the possibility of another Japanese attack on American soil. People were on edge; many became very distrusting of those who were different. As is often the case, fear turns into anger, and anger turns into violence. Such is the case of Los Angeles, California, and the Zoot Suit Riots.

Mexican Americans were among the groups of people who became the target of hate and racism in Los Angeles in the early 1940s. Thousands of Mexicans moved to Southern California at the time to help with the war effort. Many white residents viewed their Mexican and Mexican American neighbors with unease and even hate. This was especially true after young men of Mexican descent began wearing fancy outfits called zoot suits. These oversized suits quickly became a symbol of the conflict between white residents and Mexican Americans, and led to a series of violent clashes called the Zoot Suit Riots. The Zoot Suit Riots demonstrated the depth of Los Angeles's race problems and the broader issue of racism in mid-20th-century America.

A growing problem

Race issues between white Americans and Mexican Americans existed long before the 1940s. This was especially true in the western United States. Mexicans actually lived in the region many years before the first white settlers arrived. Even so, most whites did not understand Mexican culture and saw Mexican Americans as simple migrants, or people who move from place to place to find work. As a result, whites often mistreated Mexican Americans and kept them from getting better-paying jobs. This made life difficult for Mexican Americans and led to hard feelings between them and the white community.

The race problem in Los Angeles began to reach a boiling point in the early 1940s. The onset of World War II forced many Americans to give up their jobs to serve their country in the military. As a result, much help was needed to fill the jobs they left behind. This led many Mexicans to enter the United States to take the service and agriculture jobs that were suddenly available. As the number of Mexicans in Los Angeles grew, so too did feelings of fear and hate among white residents.

Many young Mexican American men wore flashy outfits called zoot suits. Zoot suits were oversized suits featuring broad-shouldered jackets and balloon-leg pants. Most people who wore zoot suits also wore large showy

Racial Conflict

hats and pocket watches with dangling chains. So many young Mexican Americans wore zoot suits that some people began to believe that they were all gang members or street thugs. The media encouraged these beliefs by portraying Mexican American zoot suiters as dangerous criminals.

Zoot suits also caused problems in another important way. The US War Production Board put a limit on how much fabric people could use during the war to make sure there was enough material for the military to use. Because zoot suits used so much fabric, people thought that Mexican Americans were being wasteful and unpatriotic. This made the hate and distrust between Mexican Americans and white citizens even worse.

Sleepy Lagoon murder The zoot suit situation took a major turn for the worse on August 1, 1942. That night, a brawl broke out between two groups of young Mexican Americans who gathered at an East Los Angeles swimming hole called Sleepy Lagoon. The next day a young man named Jose Diaz (c. 1919–1942) was found dead on a roadside near the swimming hole. Police responded by arresting hundreds of Mexican American youths. Twenty-two were eventually accused of the murder.

Things only got worse when the case went to trial. Even though there was little to no real evidence, five Mexican American youths were found guilty of assault and another 12 were found guilty of murder. Two were sentenced to life in prison. All of these decisions were later overturned, and all of the youths were released. This served only to increase the hatred between Mexican Americans and white residents. By early 1943, Los Angeles was brimming with racial tension that was ready to explode.

Zoot Suit Riots

The simmering anger over zoot suiters finally boiled over during the summer of 1943. A large number of sailors, soldiers, and other military men were stationed in the Los Angeles area at the time. Many disliked the Mexican American zoot suiters because of their flashy clothes, which seemed disrespectful to them. Some also thought that the zoot suiters were draft dodgers who were wrongly avoiding military service. In fact, many zoot suiters were actually too young to serve. Regardless, things were getting very heated and dangerous in Los Angeles.

The turning point came on May 31. That day, a fight broke out between a group of US service members and a group of young Mexican Americans. One sailor was severely beaten in the fight. Several days later, on June 3, a group of 50 angry navy service members looking for revenge

Two victims, one stripped and another badly beaten, of a gang of US servicemen at a cinema in Los Angeles, California, during the Zoot Suit Riots in June 1943. The riots broke out as tensions rose between servicemen stationed in the city and Latino youths, among whom zoot suits were the latest fashion. © ANTHONY POTTER COLLECTION/HULTON ARCHIVE/GETTY IMAGES.

took to the streets of Los Angeles armed with clubs and attacked anyone they saw wearing a zoot suit. Before long, the city erupted into chaos.

For the next several days, riots broke out in downtown Los Angeles as gangs of sailors and soldiers ran through the streets attacking Mexican Americans and stripping them of their zoot suits. Many zoot suiters were left bloodied and beaten on the street. Instead of stopping the servicemen, police arrested the injured zoot suiters.

The rioting got worse as time passed. Off-duty police officers and other people soon joined servicemen in attacking zoot suiters. Eventually, the fighting even spilled off the streets and into restaurants and movie theaters. In time, the riots even spread out of downtown Los Angeles and into other neighborhoods. Some service members from San Diego and

Racial Conflict

Los Angeles Riots, 1992

One of the worst race riots in US history took place in Los Angeles, California, in April 1992. The problem that triggered these riots began more than a year earlier. On March 3, 1991, an African American man named Rodney King (1965–2012) led police on a high-speed chase through Los Angeles County. When he eventually gave himself up, the uncooperative King was arrested by several white police officers who brutally beat him. When the public learned of the beating, which was captured on video, outraged people around the country demanded justice.

The officers involved in the King beating were arrested and charged with assault a few weeks later. When their case was finally heard in April 1992, all of the officers, except one, were cleared of any wrongdoing. African Americans and other people across Los Angeles were furious with this outcome and violence broke out immediately after the court's decision was announced on April 29.

The violence started at the intersection of Florence Boulevard and Normandie Avenue in South Central Los Angeles. Rioters there blocked traffic and attacked motorists. One white truck driver was nearly beaten to death in the riot. Before long, the violence spread into other parts of the city. Hundreds of fires were set, and many people were hurt. The chaos continued until military troops and riot police arrived. On May 1 Rodney King spoke out against the violence, asking for everyone to please get along. By May 4 things had calmed down. The violence resulted in more than 60 deaths, about 7,000 arrests, and almost $1 billion worth of property damage.

The following year, two of the officers involved in the King beating were convicted of violating King's rights by using unreasonable force. Most civil rights activists saw this

---

other places started traveling to Los Angeles to join the fight. Mexican Americans and others were attacked and beaten, even if they were not wearing zoot suits.

The riots continued until military officials finally confined all servicemen to their barracks, which are buildings in which soldiers live. By the time the fighting ended, hundreds of young Mexican Americans and African Americans were arrested. Although no one was killed, the damage was done. Local newspapers claimed the riots were a response to immigrant crime, but it was obvious to most that they were really about racial hate.

Aftermath

The Los Angeles City Council banned zoot suits immediately after the riots. Weeks later, a committee put together by California Governor Earl

decision as a victory. In any event, the Los Angeles riots taught Americans an important lesson about the potentially deadly results of racism.

A young man on a bike observes buildings burning and smoke clouds filling the skies as a result of the 1992 Los Angeles riots. © PETER TURNLEY/CORBIS/VCG VIA GETTY IMAGES.

Warren (1891–1974) found that the riots were motivated by racism and that the focus on zoot suits was little more than an excuse for violence. The committee also reported that teenage misbehavior was a problem among all American youths, not just those who happened to be of Mexican descent.

Reaction to the Zoot Suit Riots was swift. People across the country recognized the role that race played in the riots. They condemned the military for allowing servicemen to so violently attack American citizens. Many people also condemned the Los Angeles media for contributing to the problem by unfairly depicting young Mexican Americans as dangerous thugs.

After the Zoot Suit Riots, racial protests were held in a number of American cities, including New York, Philadelphia, and Detroit.

Racial Conflict

These protests helped bring attention to America's serious racism problem. In addition, the riots did much to inspire the civil rights movement that would achieve a great deal of change in the years to come.

Detroit Riots

LOCATION: Detroit, Michigan
DATE: July 1967

The Detroit riots are also known as the 12th Street riot and the Uprising of 1967. They were violent, race-based protests that took place in Detroit, Michigan, for five days in July 1967. The riots began after Detroit police raided an illegal after-hours bar in the city. The raid angered witnesses, especially African Americans. For years, blacks in Detroit had felt that the city's mostly white police force was targeting them specifically. The police raid on the illegal bar greatly angered African Americans and others who felt the police had been mistreating them. The raid released the tensions that had been building in Detroit for years.

Existing racial tensions made the Detroit riots all the more intense when they erupted following the police raid. For five days, Detroit citizens rioted. Local and state police, the National Guard, and US Army soldiers tried to stop them. The rioters destroyed some 2,000 buildings in the city. US troops eventually put down the riots and restored order to Detroit. The violence caused 43 deaths, hundreds of injuries, and more than 7,000 arrests. Historians later judged the Detroit riots of 1967 as one of the worst riots in US history. This was due to the number of deaths during the riots and the amount of damage to city property.

1960s Detroit

Before the 1960s, Detroit was a booming employment center. Numerous automobile factories employed many Detroit citizens. Thousands of people traveled from the southern United States to Detroit and other northern cities to find jobs. Black and white Americans were part of this movement north. The mixing of the races sometimes created tensions between blacks and whites. Race-based riots broke out in Detroit in 1943. However, Detroit remained financially strong.

Detroit's economy and racial populations started to change in the 1960s. An economy is all the wealth and other resources of a country, city, or other region. Some parts of Detroit became overcrowded with low-income citizens, mostly African Americans. For example, 60,000 African Americans were forced to live in a series of small apartments in the Detroit neighborhood of Virginia Park. The apartments were too small to house this amount of people, but the residents had nowhere else to go.

Around the same time, Detroit's automobile factories started moving away from the city, eliminating jobs. Many white people moved out of Detroit's center to quiet nearby suburbs; others moved to follow the jobs. With so many people suddenly gone from the city, Detroit started to suffer economically. Businesses closed, unemployment rose, and poverty spread. Most of those left behind in the inner city were African Americans.

Relations between these black residents and Detroit's mostly white police force became tense as the 1960s continued. Police officers regularly acted aggressively toward African Americans. They targeted blacks for arrest and some police acted violently toward them. Police mistreatment of citizens is called police brutality. African Americans in Detroit were angry that the city's white police officers treated them in these ways. The relationship between Detroit police and black residents continued to worsen into the late 1960s.

Origins of the riots

The Detroit police often targeted the African American nightlife that occurred in the city. Twelfth Street was a busy area of primarily African American businesses and clubs. Many of the clubs and bars on 12th Street engaged in illegal activity. "Blind pigs," as they were known, were bars that sold alcohol without having legal permission to do so. Due to this, the busiest times for the bars were often late at night or early in the morning hours. Police were less likely to notice the activities at these times. However, Detroit police found out about such places and often raided them to stop their illegal activities.

One of these blind pigs was secretly located in the offices of a local civil rights organization at the intersection of 12th and Clairmount

Relations between these black residents and Detroit's mostly white police force became tense as the 1960s continued. Police officers regularly acted aggressively toward African Americans. They targeted blacks for arrest and some police acted violently toward them.

Racial Conflict

New York City Draft Riots, July 13–16, 1863

Racial conflicts have occurred in the United States for centuries. More than 100 years before the Detroit riots of 1967, mobs of white Americans started the New York City draft riots of 1863. During the US Civil War (1861–1865), Americans were angry that the US government had recently passed a military draft. A draft is a legal order to make citizens serve in a country's military. African Americans were excluded from the draft because they were not considered US citizens at that time. Also, the plan allowed men to avoid the draft by paying a large fee to hire someone to take their place.

Many Americans in the North already opposed the war before the passing of the draft in March 1863. This was especially true of immigrants and other poor Americans. Immigrants are people who move to another country to live permanently. These people could not afford to pay the fee to avoid being drafted into the military. They disliked the war and the draft because they had to fight while the wealthy paid to escape it.

Racial tensions added to this anger, especially in New York City. Most poor immigrants in the city in the 1860s were white Irishmen. They did not like that they had to compete with African Americans for jobs. Many whites at the time thought they were better than blacks. They did not think they should have to fight in the war and risk their lives when African Americans did not. They worried that blacks would take their jobs.

Tensions exploded on July 13 in New York City at a government building where drafting was to take place. A group of white firefighters broke into the building and began destroying it. More people started rioting against the draft later that day. They set buildings on fire and stole weapons from storehouses.

The mob eventually came upon an orphanage for black children. After destroying everything inside, they set it on fire. The crowds did this because they were angry with African Americans. They also attacked the homes of wealthy businessmen.

More racial violence followed on July 14 and 15. Members of the mob killed individual African Americans. Neither city nor state leaders could control the disorder. Finally, thousands of US troops arrived in New York on July 16 to stop the riots. They fought the rioters and eventually restored order. The draft was put on hold. In all, about 120 people died in the riots, including 12 African Americans whom the mobs had beaten and killed. Historians estimate that nearly 2,000

Streets. The club was crowded in the early morning of Sunday, July 23, 1967. Detroit was experiencing especially hot, humid weather at the time. Many people had entered the club to enjoy the air-conditioning on the warm night.

At about 3:35 a.m. on July 23, Detroit police raided this blind pig. They arrested more than 80 people inside and brought them out to wait for police cars that would take them to the police station. While the police were waiting, a few hundred people gathered in the street to watch the activity. Someone eventually threw a bottle into the street. More bottles

people were injured. On August 19, the draft was reinstated.

Following the draft riots, thousands of African Americans left New York City to live safely elsewhere. Many politicians and business owners fought to have the draft declared unconstitutional because it was unfair to working-class citizens. After the Civil War, the draft was not put into play again until 1917 and the start of US involvement in World War I (1914–1918). The New York City draft riots are still considered one of the most violent protests ever to occur in the United States.

The New York City draft rioters burned an African American orphanage after police rescued its young inhabitants.
© EVERETT HISTORICAL/SHUTTERSTOCK.COM.

and other objects followed. The people were angry that the police had forcefully disturbed their nightlife.

At first the police did not respond to the thrown objects. They simply continued placing the people they had arrested in police vehicles. Someone then threw an object through the window of a police car, smashing it. This inspired the crowd of people in the street to start rioting against the police. The police officers themselves left the scene, but the chaos continued. Some people broke into nearby stores and stole items. This was the start of the Detroit riots.

Racial Conflict

A Michigan National Guard armored personnel carrier stands guard along with five tanks and a small fleet of helicopters in an attempt to quell the rioting on Detroit's west side on July 24, 1967.
© BETTMANN/GETTY IMAGES.

Rioting spreads

At about 6:30 a.m., the rioters also started numerous fires in buildings on 12th Street. Firefighters arrived to control the fires, but the rioters attacked them, too. Only about 200 police officers of Detroit's total force of 4,700 were on duty on this early Sunday morning. More than 1,000 additional officers arrived on the streets by mid-morning. However, even this number of officers could not stop the rioters from breaking into stores and setting fires. The riots quickly spread beyond 12th Street to other parts of Detroit.

Detroit Mayor Jerome Cavanagh (1928–1979) struggled to control the riots. He thought it would help if he publicly ordered police not to shoot rioters. The break-ins, looting, and fires only spread. By early afternoon on Sunday, July 23, about 10,000 people were rioting in the streets.

The mayor then requested that Michigan Governor George Romney (1907–1995) send officers of the Michigan State Police to Detroit to help stop the riots. Romney sent 300 state troopers to the city, but this was still not enough to stop the spread of violence. The riots spread and covered an area of 100 city blocks.

The Michigan National Guard arrived in Detroit on Sunday night. The National Guard is part of the US military. None of these groups could stop the riots by Sunday night, but they arrested more than 1,000 people. Five people died in violence with police on Sunday.

The riots end

Rioting became more intense on Monday, July 24. Some rioters stole guns and started shooting at firefighters and police officers. They also cut fire hoses that firefighters had been using to put out the fires. An additional 16 rioters were killed in the violence on Monday.

The ongoing chaos encouraged Romney to request assistance from the US government. He asked President Lyndon B. Johnson (1908–1973) to send the US military to Detroit. Johnson ordered several thousand US Army troops to the city on Tuesday, July 25. The soldiers drove through the streets of Detroit in tanks, which are large troop transport vehicles. Ten more people died on Tuesday in clashes with law enforcement.

Still the riots continued into Wednesday, July 26. Another 12 people died. However, the thousands of law enforcement officers in the city, as well as the thousands of US troops, eventually silenced the disorder. By Thursday, July 27, Detroit was relatively calm, although some scattered violence was reported. The army began to withdraw from the city on Friday, July 28.

Aftermath

Although the violent protests in Detroit are considered race riots, it is important to note that some of the rioters were white. This is one of the reasons why some historians believe the riots were about poverty and social inequality not just race. In total, 43 people died during the rioting. More than 7,000 people were arrested, and nearly 350 were injured. The violence had also significantly damaged Detroit itself. Rioters had broken into and looted about 1,700 stores. They burned 1,400 buildings and other structures, leaving about 5,000 city residents without homes. The total damage to the city was valued around $50 million.

After the riots had ended, President Johnson created the National Advisory Commission on Civil Disorders, also known as the Kerner Commission, to investigate the numerous race riots that had taken place in the United States in the mid- to late 1960s. Riots also occurred in Harlem in New York City, Watts in Los Angeles, and Newark, New Jersey. The commission was made up of politicians and others. Its main purpose was to identify the cause of racial violence throughout the United States.

The Kerner Commission released a 400-plus page report on the subject in February 1968. The report claimed that more than 150 violent riots had occurred in the United States between 1965 and 1968. Most of the people involved were African Americans. The report said

Racial Conflict

Governor George Romney on the Detroit Riots

In this primary source excerpt, Sheila C. Bernard interviews former Michigan Governor George Romney in 1988 about the Detroit riots that occurred in 1967. Part of the "Eyes on the Prize II" Interviews at Washington University, the discussion centers on Romney's recollection of the violent riots that shook the city while he governor of the state.

INTERVIEWER [SHEILA C. BERNARD]: In 1967 Watts had erupted, Newark had just burned, um, did you think a riot would happen in Detroit? . . .

GEORGE ROMNEY: No, I didn't and most other people didn't. Ah, as a matter of fact it was quite a surprise to people in Detroit because Detroit had been treated very favorably, uh, by the Johnson administration, had been given a lot of, uh, special help in meeting urban problems. So it was a surprise. . . .

INTERVIEWER: When did you first hear about the rioting?

GEORGE ROMNEY: Well they called me . . . the Sunday morning it started, to tell me that, uh, there was a riot. [My] counsel had called me . . . and he said that, uh, the mayor and the other city officials thought they were going to be able to handle it, uh, so unless I was called back, well I didn't need to be concerned about it. . . .

INTERVIEWER: And when did it become something . . . ?

GEORGE ROMNEY: About the middle of the afternoon they called back to indicate that it was out of control, that the city officials felt they needed state help. And that's the first time I knew that the situation was as serious as it was. . . .

white racism and discrimination against black individuals had been causing the tension and violence between black and white Americans. Furthermore, the report argued that the African American rioters only wanted to be treated equally in American society. Based on the violence and damage done during the riots, historians later named the Detroit riots of 1967 as one of the worst in US history.

Soweto Uprising

LOCATION: Soweto, South Africa

DATE: June 16, 1976

In the late 1940s, the white-run government of South Africa passed several laws that made it legal to discriminate against black and mixed-race people.

INTERVIEWER: That night, on Sunday night you toured the city by helicopter. Can you describe to me what you saw and what was going through your mind?

GEORGE ROMNEY: Well there were fires all over a good part of city, particularly along Grand Boulevard and 12th Street and it looked like a battlefield. . . . There were about three square miles that had huge fires, dozens of them. They weren't small fires, they were huge fires. And it was a terrifying sight because it was obvious that there was a terrible disaster taking place. So it was very distressing to see the scope of it and the . . . destructiveness of it. . . .

INTERVIEWER: When and how was it decided that federal troops were needed.

GEORGE ROMNEY: . . . after midnight when it was clear that the riot was increasing in magnitude, it wasn't being reduced. And furthermore, it was clear that the, uh, National Guard plus the state police plus the local police would probably not be able to handle it. It wasn't certain that they couldn't handle it, but after all we had a group of uh, people out there trying to deal with it who were . . . not trained to deal with riots. The National Guard had arrived late anyway because the National Guard had been on encampment up in northern Michigan, so they had to be brought all the way down. Of course the situation grew worse as they were being transported down to the riot area. Ah, so it was in the early morning of, uh, Monday that we decided that we . . . might need federal assistance.

SOURCE: Bernard, Sheila C. "Interview with George Romney." Eyes on the Prize II Interviews, Washington University Digital Gateway Text, October 31, 1988. Available online at http://digital.wustl.edu/e/eii/eiiweb/rom5427.0379.138georgeromney.html (accessed October 15, 2017). Courtesy of Washington University Digital Gateway Text.

To discriminate against means to treat someone unfairly because he or she is different. The laws divided South Africans along racial lines and forced black and white people to live and work separately. The laws were called apartheid (pronounced uh-PAR-tait), a word that means "separateness" in Afrikaans (pronounced ah-free-KAWNTZ), one of the languages of South Africa.

Black and mixed-race South Africans suffered under apartheid for many years. Even though black people made up most of the population, they had fewer rights than white people. By the 1970s, anger was growing among black South Africans. The government fought efforts to change its laws and often punished people who tried to protest apartheid.

In 1976 thousands of black students in Soweto (pronounced suh-WAY-toh) gathered to protest new government rules that forced them to learn in Afrikaans. Soweto was a black township near Johannesburg, South Africa's largest city. As the students marched to a local stadium for what was meant to be a peaceful demonstration, armed police stopped

Racial Conflict

Steve Biko and the Black Consciousness Movement

Steve Biko (1946–1977) was a nonviolent political activist who led the Black Consciousness Movement (BCM). Biko and the BCM resisted apartheid (pronounced uh-PAR-tait), the discriminatory government in South Africa. The BMC believed in civil rights, freedom of speech, and equality for people of color. Biko was imprisoned by the South African government. His death at the hands of the authorities made him a symbol for the anti-apartheid struggle.

Bantu Steve Biko was born in the homeland of the Xhosa (pronounced KOH-suh) people. His given name, "Bantu," means "people." Biko became aware of racial inequality when he was young. He was expelled from high school because of his political ideas. Eventually, he took his political activism to a higher level and a much larger audience—the people of South Africa.

Biko witnessed the injustice of apartheid first-hand. Race relations between blacks and whites deteriorated as apartheid took hold. Apartheid was the government system of discrimination against blacks and other people of color in South Africa. These policies included segregation in public places, low wages, poor education, and inadequate housing. Plus, blacks were denied from participating in the government.

Biko believed that blacks should be the leaders of South African society and should control the government. After all, he reasoned, the majority of people in South Africa were black. He did not believe in the white-dominated apartheid government. Biko hoped to abolish it.

In 1968 the BCM formed in resistance to apartheid. At that time, people of color were referred to as "non-white." Biko believed that by referring to themselves as "black," they would not have to define themselves in terms of "white" society. The BCM sought to raise self-awareness among blacks, giving them a sense of pride. They

them. Fights broke out and police began firing into the crowd of children and teenagers. Several students were killed. Hundreds more died in the violence that followed.

News of the deaths spread across South Africa, and soon people in other parts of the country began to protest and riot. Eventually the government was able to get the rioting under control. However, the uprisings captured the attention of the world. People began to see how black South Africans were being treated under apartheid. Other nations responded by punishing South Africa. The country eventually decided to end apartheid in the 1990s.

A brief history of South Africa

Modern South Africa is made up of many different ethnic groups. The first people to live in the region were known as the Khoikhoi (pronounced

Racial Conflict

said blacks should believe they are equal human beings, worthy of freedom. "Black is beautiful" became their slogan.

The BCM united struggling people by sponsoring community programs. The group supported medical clinics and built schools and day-care facilities, as well as aided small business owners.

Biko and the BCM also supported protests against apartheid such as the Soweto Uprising. The South African government considered Biko to be a threat and placed him under a "banning order" in March 1973. The banning order restricted his movements. He could not talk with more than one person at a time. He could not speak in public. He could not be quoted by the media. He could not travel without permission.

The banning order was the government's way to keep Biko from spreading the word of BCM. However, it didn't stop Biko. He met with his friend, journalist Donald Woods (1933–2001), who wrote down Biko's ideas and later published *Biko* in 1977. Also, Biko sneaked out, traveling to speak at rallies and meet with political leaders.

On August 18, 1977, Biko met with black leaders in Cape Town, about 625 miles (1,000 kilometers) from his home. While on his way home, Biko was stopped at a roadblock by the police. He was put in the Port Elizabeth jail for breaking the banning order. Several weeks later, on September 11, 1977, Biko was found in Pretoria, nearly 700 miles (1,130 kilometers) from the Port Elizabeth jail. He was badly beaten, tied up, and naked. He died the next day.

Protests sprang up as news of Biko's death reached the public. Many believed he was beaten while in police custody for going against the government. Biko became the symbol of the abuses of apartheid. His funeral was held on September 25, 1977. An estimated 20,000 people attended.

Steve Biko inspired people to stand up for their rights and to believe in themselves. After his death, others continued the fight against apartheid.

KOY-koy) and the San. Other groups such as the Zulu (pronounced ZOO-loo), Xhosa (pronounced KOH-suh), and Sotho (pronounced SOO-toh) arrived later. In 1652 Dutch settlers from the Netherlands began arriving in southern Africa. Most were farmers who needed land to grow their crops. They fought with the native people of the area and forced many of them off their land.

In the 1700s, more Dutch settlers arrived. They were joined by farmers from Germany and France. The foreign settlers formed a unique culture and developed their own language called Afrikaans. Afrikaans was based on Dutch, but it also mixed in elements from local African languages. People who spoke Afrikaans were called Afrikaners.

In 1806 the British took control of southern Africa. The Afrikaners and the English did not get along at first. The Afrikaners were very religious and believed that people of different races should be kept separate. Many Afrikaners moved inland to establish their own territories away from the British. In 1910 the territories of the British and Afrikaners joined together to form the nation of South Africa.

Most of the population of South Africa was made up of the Zulu, Xhosa, Sotho, and other native groups of the area. South Africa's government, however, was run by the white descendants of the European settlers. In 1948 an Afrikaner-led group called the National Party won control of the government. That same year, they began passing the apartheid laws.

Life under apartheid

Black South Africans were already treated poorly by the white government before apartheid. After the laws were passed, black citizens were forced from their homes and ordered to live in separate areas called districts. Black citizens were even separated from people of mixed-race descent. In some cases, families were broken up and forced to live in separate districts.

Most of the nation's land was set aside for white use only. If black or mixed-race people wanted to enter a "white" area, they would have to carry documents giving them permission to be there. People of different races were not allowed to go to the same schools or restaurants, use the same bathrooms, or marry people of another race. Black South Africans were also not allowed to work in many of the same jobs as white people.

Several groups tried to lead efforts to fight apartheid, but the government often arrested anyone who spoke out against it. In some cases, anti-apartheid activists spent many years in jail. The government also cracked down on public demonstrations. In 1960 police began firing on a crowd of unarmed protesters in the black township of Sharpeville. Known as the Sharpeville Massacre, 69 people were killed and 180 wounded on March 21, 1960. As a result, more than 10,000 people were arrested in protests following the incident.

Decision sparks anger

In 1974 the South African government announced a new rule that required schools to teach many of their subjects in Afrikaans. Half of all classes were to be taught in English and half in Afrikaans. Some subjects, such as math and social studies, were to be taught only in Afrikaans. Black students were very angry at the rule. Many of them did not understand

Racial Conflict

Afrikaans. Most spoke English or their native languages such as Zulu or Xhosa. They also saw Afrikaans as the language of apartheid and a symbol of discrimination. Discrimination is unfair treatment based on race or other personal qualities.

School officials and teacher groups spoke out against the rule. The government, however, refused to change its plans. South African officials said that because the government gave money to help run schools for black students, it had the right to choose the language used by those schools. A South African education official said that if black students did not like the rule, they should just "stay away from school."

The rule took effect in 1975. Many black students struggled to learn the new language and could not focus on the lessons themselves. As anger grew, students in some schools organized protests and rallies against the rule. At first, the protests were small. In early 1976, students from the township of Soweto wanted to organize a larger rally to make their voices heard. They planned the demonstration for June 16, 1976.

Rally turns violent

On the morning of June 16, between 10,000 and 20,000 black students from Soweto left their classrooms and gathered to begin the rally. The

Black students protested after learning that their school classes would be taught in the Afrikaan language, a language most of them did not know. Here, they are seen running during the riots in Soweto. Police opened fire after tear gas failed to stop them.
© BETTMANN/GETTY IMAGES.

Racial Conflict

"I Saw a Nightmare"

This primary source excerpt features testimony by reporter Sophie Topsie Tema before the Cillié Commission of Inquiry that investigated the riots in Soweto. As a journalist for The World, *Tema was a witness to the riot. In this part of the inquiry transcript, she is being interviewed by Mr. Hlungwani about what she saw of the confrontation between students and police. Tema is explaining what was happening when she arrived at the scene.*

Hlungwani: Did the [police] seem to be watching the movement of the students or did it appear that they were going to act against the students?

Tema: At that time it did not look like they were going to act against the students. In my opinion I thought that they were first going to talk to the students to find out from them what they want there or rather to disperse them....

Hlungwani: You are behind the police and the police are marching towards the students and then you got out of the car and then?

Tema: I followed [the police].... Some of the [students] were singing [a Sotho traditional song].... Others were whistling and screaming to the police, "Go away, we do not want the police here" and others were waving their placards....

The police first threw teargas into the midst of the students. Then some of the students in the front line hurled stones at them in retaliation, it was then that this policeman pulled out the revolver, aimed at the students and fired. It was after this policeman had fired and more shots followed, that most of the students attacked the police. I remember at one stage I had to run....

plan was for them to march to a nearby soccer stadium for a peaceful demonstration. Some of the students believed the rally was going to be a fun event and looked forward to it. Many carried signs that read "Down with Afrikaans!"

South African police knew about the rally and took up positions along the planned route. As the students began to march toward the stadium, some police officers began to challenge them. Students began to hear rumors that police were using violence to stop the march. At one point near Orlando West High School, a group of about 50 police officers blocked a large group of marching students.

The students stood in place, singing and whistling at police. The police tried to break up the crowd and force the students to turn back. Small fights began to break out between police and students. Police began to shoot over the heads of the students as a warning to turn back. They also threw tear gas into the crowd. Tear gas is a chemical that causes a burning feeling in a person's eyes and throat.

Racial Conflict

As we were trying to get away from the scene, me and Stanley [her driver] ... met four students carrying a fifth. The fifth was hit on the left chest and they were running with him towards the Pheferi Clinic, which was not very far away from the scene....

While we were in the next [street] with Stanley, a boy came to us. He did not seem to be a student because he did not have a uniform on, and he asked us for a lift. I could see that this boy was limping. I asked him what was wrong. He told me that he had been shot in his leg. He was bleeding from behind his right thigh....

I actually asked him if he was with the students. He said no, I had gone to my aunt's place and I was trying to make my way home.

We took him to the Pheferi Clinic, I and Stanley.... We dropped him off at the door and we drove right back to the scene....

We could see that the situation was dangerous, we saw a boy who had an overall on, carrying another boy in his arms and a girl next to him. She was crying, weeping, and they were coming towards us. I then asked Stanley to stop the car and I ordered these people to get into our car so that we could rush him to the clinic. Stanley, the girl and the injured boy and the one who was carrying the injured boy, went to the clinic. I followed them on foot to the clinic, which was not very far. When I got there, the doctors had tried to examine the boy, but they told us that he was dead already.

SOURCE: Pohlandt-McCormick, Helena. "Testimony before the Cillié Commission: Sophie Topsie Tema." *"I Saw a Nightmare—": Doing Violence to Memory: The Soweto Uprising, June 16, 1976.* New York: Columbia University Press, 2010. Available online at http://www.gutenberg-e.org/pohlandt-mccormick/pmh02u.html (accessed October 15, 2017). Courtesy of Project Gutenberg.

Witnesses at the scene say police suddenly started to fire their guns into the crowd. Many students ran for safety while others began to throw rocks at the police. Two students were killed when police first opened fire. One of those students was 12-year-old Hector Pieterson (1963–1976). A photograph of Pieterson's body being carried away from the fighting by an older boy became a famous symbol of the uprising. Many people outside of South Africa saw the picture and became angry at the actions of South Africa's government.

Uprising spreads

Violence soon spread across Soweto. As police tried to break up the crowds, more and more students began to fight back. They attacked the police with rocks and sticks, and set fire to a local post office and a government building. Some students filled glass bottles with gasoline and rags, set them on fire, and threw them at police. The police had more powerful weapons, but many of the students had grown up in Soweto and

Racial Conflict

knew the streets. They were able to attack the police, and then run and hide before they could be caught.

The fighting continued in Soweto for a week. Other members of the community joined the students in their protest. At first, police said that 23 people were killed in the Soweto riot, but they later admitted the death toll was about 575. Many people who lived in the township claimed the actual number was much higher. Some estimates say thousands of people were killed by police.

The events in Soweto inspired black students in other parts of South Africa to rise up and demonstrate against the government. Many of these protests also turned violent as students clashed with police who tried to stop them. Within a month after the incident in Soweto, many black townships in South Africa were openly defying the South African government. In July 1976 the South African government decided to end the rule that forced students to learn in Afrikaans.

The authorities were eventually able to get most of the rioting under control, but scattered fighting continued into 1977. Many black citizens across the country began to protest actively against the government. Workers staged strikes and refused to work. Some people refused to buy South African products in an effort to hurt the government economically. Members of black communities held rallies and symbolic mass funerals to represent those killed in the violence.

The effects of the uprising

Images of the violence in South Africa caught the attention of people around the world. The United Nations (UN) called a special meeting to condemn the government of South Africa for using violence against its own people. The UN is an organization of 193 world nations that tries to promote cooperation and peace between countries. The UN decided to punish South Africa by stopping the sale of weapons to the country. In 1985 both the United States and United Kingdom placed economic sanctions on South Africa. A sanction is an official punishment usually imposed by a nation or several nations on another country.

In South Africa, the uprising united many people in the country's black communities. They formed groups and organizations that worked to change the nation's laws. The South African government faced a united opposition at home. It also felt international pressure to end apartheid. Its leaders attempted to reform some of its laws, but it was not seen as enough.

The fighting continued in Soweto for a week. Other members of the community joined the students in their protest. At first, police said that 23 people were killed in the Soweto riot, but they later admitted the death toll was about 575.

In 1989 a new government led by F. W. de Klerk (1936–) took control in South Africa. De Klerk began the process of ending the apartheid system in 1990. By 1994 all the apartheid laws were overturned, and black and white South African leaders worked together to create new laws to run the country. That same year, South Africa elected Nelson Mandela (1918–2013) as its first black president. Mandela was a leader in the fight against apartheid in the 1960s. He had been jailed for 27 years before being freed in 1990.

Justice for All March

LOCATION: Washington, DC

DATE: December 13, 2014

The Justice for All march was held on December 13, 2014, in Washington, DC. More than 10,000 people gathered to march to the Capitol building. Other similar rallies were held throughout the country. Organizers wanted to bring attention to the killings of black individuals by white police officers throughout the United States. The peaceful protests were held in response to several cases in which police officers were seen as not being held responsible for their actions.

Organizers of the marches wanted police officers to end the practice of racial profiling. Racial profiling occurs when certain individuals are targeted based on their race instead of an actual offense or crime. Many people felt that race was a main factor in several cases in which the black suspect died at the hands of a white police officer. In these cases, the officers were not punished, and this angered many people.

Some individuals held violent riots and protests, while others formed organizations to raise awareness of racism experienced across the country. Black Lives Matter was one of the movements organized to campaign against racism in the United States. Members from Black Lives Matter joined civil rights activist the Reverend Al Sharpton (1954–), the National Action Network (NAN), and other groups to take part in the Justice for All march and other rallies held across the country.

Racial Conflict

Origins of Black Lives Matter

The Black Lives Matter movement formed in 2013. It was established in response to George Zimmerman (1983–) being cleared of any wrongdoing in the death of Trayvon Martin (1995–2012). Zimmerman, a Hispanic American man who was 29 at the time, was a volunteer for a crime watch group in his Sanford, Florida, neighborhood. In February 2012, Martin, a 17-year-old African American male, was visiting his father, who lived in the neighborhood.

Martin was walking through his father's neighborhood on the night of February 26, when Zimmerman spotted him. Zimmerman called police to report a suspicious person. Operators on the phone told Zimmerman not to approach Martin, but he ignored the request. A few minutes later, Zimmerman shot Martin. Police arrived on the scene, and Zimmerman admitted that he had shot Martin. He said that Martin attacked him when he confronted the teenager, and he showed them wounds that he said were from Martin.

As details about the incident were released to the public, many people questioned whether Zimmerman was telling the truth about what happened that night. Some people called for Zimmerman to be arrested and charged for murdering Martin. Others defended Zimmerman.

In April 2012, Zimmerman was charged with second-degree murder, which is the killing of another person on purpose but without a plan to

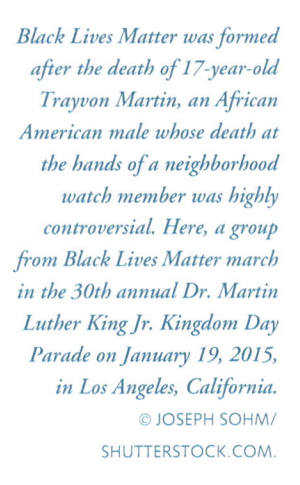

Black Lives Matter was formed after the death of 17-year-old Trayvon Martin, an African American male whose death at the hands of a neighborhood watch member was highly controversial. Here, a group from Black Lives Matter march in the 30th annual Dr. Martin Luther King Jr. Kingdom Day Parade on January 19, 2015, in Los Angeles, California.
© JOSEPH SOHM/SHUTTERSTOCK.COM.

kill. The trial began in June 2013, and Zimmerman pleaded not guilty to the charges. On July 13, 2013, a jury found Zimmerman not guilty.

Several protests across the United States began after the verdict, or decision, of the case. Many people were angry that Zimmerman was not found guilty of the murder of Martin. A woman named Alicia Garza (c. 1981–) was very upset after learning the outcome of the case.

Garza posted a message on her Facebook page expressing her feelings about the ways African Americans are treated in the United States. She ended the message by saying that all black lives matter. Her friend Patrisse Cullors (c. 1983–) shared Garza's message and used the tagline #blacklivesmatter with it on several social media sites. The two women then discussed ways they could help. Activist Opal Tometi (1984–) joined them in their efforts.

The three women posted messages on social media sites. They asked others to share their views on why black lives matter to them, and thus began the Black Lives Matter movement. The women advertised the organization and led a protest march in Beverly Hills, California. The movement did not gain much notice until 2014. It received further recognition following other incidents involving police officers and African American victims.

In July 2014, African American Eric Garner (1970–2014) was killed by white police officer Daniel Pantaleo (c. 1985–) in Staten Island, New York. Pantaleo arrested Garner for supposedly selling cigarettes. During the arrest, Pantaleo placed Garner in a chokehold, which caused Garner to suffocate. When someone suffocates, he or she dies from being unable to breathe. Pantaleo was not held responsible for the death, which led to

How have highly publicized fatal police shootings of black citizens impacted police officers? Pew Research reports the following:

86%	93%	76%
The percentage of police officers surveyed who believe their jobs are harder	The percentage of police officers surveyed who are more concerned about safety	The percentage of police officers surveyed who say they are more hesitant to use force when appropriate

SOURCE: Morin, Rich, Kim Parker, Renee Stepler, and Andrew Mercer. *Behind the Badge: Amid Protests and Calls for Reform, How Police View Their Jobs, Key Issues and Recent Fatal Encounters Between Blacks and Police*. Pew Research Center, January 11, 2017. http://www.pewsocialtrends. org/2017/01/11/behind-the-badge/.

Racial Conflict

Charlottesville Protests, August 11–12, 2017

Racism exploded in Charlottesville, Virginia, over August 11 and August 12, 2017. Groups of white supremacists, including the Ku Klux Klan (KKK), neo-Nazis, and members of the "Alt-Right," planned a Unite the Right rally. White supremacists believe that the white race is superior to other races. Often times, they target minorities and others who hold different views. White supremacists use insults or threaten to harm those they have targeted. For these reasons, these groups are known as hate groups. Before this event, many members of these groups existed mostly in online communities. They decided to hold a public rally to oppose the removal of a monument to General Robert E. Lee (1807–1870), a leader of the Confederate army during the US Civil War (1861–1865). Many people felt that the statue of Lee was not the real reason for the rally. They believed that the groups wanted to make their presence known in the country. As Americans, they have the right to protest peacefully; this is afforded to them by the 1st Amendment to the US Constitution—the right to free speech.

On the evening of August 11, participants holding torches marched two by two, across the campus of the University of Virginia. The marchers chanted, "You will not replace us!," "Jews will not replace us!" To many people, these chants are racist. The marchers stopped at the statue of US founding father Thomas Jefferson (1743–1826) on campus, where they were met by a group of student counterprotesters and members of the Antifa. The Antifa, or anti-fascists, protest against racism, corporate wealth, and social oppression. Police held back as the two groups clashed; the police later put down the fighting.

The rally for the next day was supposed to start at 5 p.m., but groups on both sides had gathered by the morning. Although Virginia State Police and Charlottesville police were there to keep the peace, fighting broke out between the Antifa and the white supremacists by mid-morning. The police officers eventually stepped in to end the chaos and ordered everyone to leave. Virginia Governor Terry McAuliffe (1957–) declared a state of emergency.

A short time later a man attending the rally as part of the white supremacist groups drove his car into a group of counterprotesters. Heather Heyer (1985–2017), a white woman, was killed, and several others were injured. Police later caught and arrested James Alex Fields Jr. (c. 1997–) and charged him with second-degree murder, among other charges.

Later that evening, a helicopter carrying two state troopers, Lieutenant H. Jay Cullen (c. 1969–2017)

protests in New York. Supporters carried signs with taglines "black lives matter" and "I can't breathe."

The Black Lives Matter movement received more attention the following month after an incident in Ferguson, Missouri. Police officer Darren Wilson (1986–) shot and killed 18-year-old African American Michael Brown (1996–2014). Brown was not armed. After the killing, anti-police protests and riots occurred in the city. Garza, Cullors, and Tometi traveled

Racial Conflict

and Berke M. M. Bates (1976–2017), crashed not far from Charlottesville. They were in the air monitoring the events of the day. The cause of the crash remained under investigation as of September 2017.

When discussing the events in Charlottesville, US President Donald Trump did not initially condemn the actions of the white supremacists, stating that people on both sides were to blame for the violence. His statement was widely criticized by other politicians, civil rights leaders, and people from around the globe. Many average citizens have called on the president to denounce the KKK, Alt-Right, and neo-Nazis because they believe that white supremacy is not an American value.

Neo-Nazis, Alt-Right members, and white supremacists encircle and chant at counterprotesters at the base of a statue of Thomas Jefferson after marching through the University of Virginia campus with torches in Charlottesville. The protest shocked the nation. © SAMUEL CORUM/ANADOLU AGENCY/GETTY IMAGES.

to Ferguson and met with protesters. They saw many people holding "black lives matter" banners. Wilson was not made to stand trial for Brown's death, which upset many people. After this, numerous people joined Black Lives Matter. Members called for equality for all black people, including men, women, members of the LGBTQ (lesbian, gay, bisexual, transgender, and questioning/queer) community, and disabled individuals, in areas such as education, employment, and the justice system.

U•X•L *Protests, Riots, and Rebellions: Civil Unrest in the Modern World*

Similar incidents involving police officers and black victims continued into the following year. In another case, African American Freddie Gray (d. 2015) died following his arrest in Baltimore, Maryland. He died from spinal injuries he received while being transported in a police van, in which he was not properly secured. Black Lives Matter protests erupted in Baltimore. Although six police officers were arrested, and some stood trial, none was found guilty of Gray's death.

The incidents and the outcomes left many people upset and angry. The Black Lives Matter movement continued to ensure that these and similar incidents were not overlooked or forgotten. Members planned protests and posted messages on social media sites.

Justice for All March

The killing of unarmed black individuals by police officers led to an organized march known as the Justice for All march on December 13, 2014, in Washington, DC. Smaller rallies were held that day in other cities, including New York City; Boston, Massachusetts; Chicago, Illinois; and Oakland, California. The NAN, a nonprofit civil rights organization, along with the organization's founder, Sharpton, organized the main Justice for All march in Washington, DC. Other participating groups included the National Urban League, the American Civil Liberties Union (ACLU), the League of United Latin American Citizens, the National LGBTQ Task Force, and the United Federation of Teachers. Demonstrators also included members of other organizations, such as the Black Lives Matter movement, and families of those impacted by police violence.

Sharpton is a civil rights activist, minister, and host of the television talk show *PoliticsNation* on MSNBC. He founded NAN in 1991. The main purpose of the organization is to protect the civil rights of all US citizens regardless of race, religion, ethnicity, or gender. It was modeled after the spirit of the Rev. Dr. Martin Luther King Jr. (1929–1968), who fought for civil rights during the 1950s and 1960s. NAN's mission is similar to that of the Black Lives Matter movement, but it includes all races, not just black individuals. NAN works for all citizens to have equality in areas such as criminal justice, voting, employment, and education.

Sharpton organized the peaceful event after New York police officer Pantaleo was not charged in the chokehold death of Garner in early December 2014. A few weeks prior to this decision, Ferguson police

Racial Conflict

Thousands of protesters participate in the Justice for All march against police violence on Pennsylvania Avenue in Washington, DC, on December 13, 2014. Protesters held a rally at Freedom Plaza before marching to the US Capitol. © BILL CLARK/CQ ROLL CALL/GETTY IMAGES.

officer Wilson was not held responsible in the Brown case. These decisions and others like them were the main reasons for the Justice for All march.

The Justice for All event began in the morning, with crowds gathering at Freedom Plaza in the nation's capital. People of all races from all over the United States showed up to demonstrate and voice their concerns. Many called out, "Black lives matter," "Hands up, don't shoot," and "I can't breathe," as they marched toward the US Capitol building. The latter phrase was in response to the suffocation of Garner. They chanted the names of the victims killed by police, beat drums, and played music as they marched.

Many family members of the victims attended the event. Lesley McSpadden (c. 1980–), the mother of Brown, and Sybrina Fulton, the mother of Martin, spoke at the event. Esaw Garner, Eric Garner's widow, led a crowd of supporters. Other family members of those killed were also in attendance. A wide range of Americans, including African Americans, Latinos, Asians, whites, young adults, the elderly, the wealthy, and the poor joined the march.

The event was supposed to be a peaceful protest, but some Ferguson activists who opposed Sharpton's involvement in the movement tried to take over the stage and grab the microphone from event organizers. Some of these protesters believed Sharpton was too old to have a say in the modern movement and that only black lives should be represented at the march. They were stopped. Sharpton spoke at the event, telling supporters that while black lives mattered, all lives mattered. He asked everyone to remain united in the fight for civil rights in the wake of the events unfolding in the nation.

In addition, some smaller demonstrations were held in other cities across the country. In New York, a Millions March gathered on Fifth Avenue, and participants chanted "black lives matter." A hike to promote healing was held in Oakland, California. Rallies elsewhere remained mostly peaceful, although police intervened in some areas to arrest a few people for disruptive behavior. March organizers hoped to draw attention to race relations in the United States and to raise awareness of needed reforms to police practices nationally.

For More Information

BOOKS

Brown, Julian. *The Road to Soweto: Resistance and the Uprising of 16 June 1976.* Woodbridge, UK: James Currey, 2016.

Bruns, Roger A. *Zoot Suit Riots.* Santa Barbara, CA: Greenwood, 2014.

Fredrickson, George M. *Racism: A Short History.* Princeton, NJ: Princeton University Press, 2002.

Peiss, Kathy. *Zoot Suit: The Enigmatic Career of an Extreme Style.* Philadelphia: University of Pennsylvania Press, 2011.

Sussman, Robert Wald. *The Myth of Race: The Troubling Persistence of an Unscientific Idea.* Cambridge, MA: Harvard University Press, 2014.

PERIODICALS

Baeder, Ben. "Zoot Suit Riots: The Sleepy Lagoon Murder Case That Helped Spur the WWII Era Los Angeles Race Riots." *San Gabriel Valley Tribune* (May 31, 2013). Available online at http://www.sgvtribune.com/article/ZZ/20130531/NEWS/130539861 (accessed September 15, 2017).

Burke, Jason. "Soweto Uprising 40 Years On: The Image That Shocked the World." *Guardian* (June 16, 2016). Available online at https://www.theguardian.com/world/2016/jun/16/soweto-uprising-40-years-on-hector-pieterson-image-shocked-the-world (accessed September 15, 2017).

Day, Elizabeth. "#BlackLivesMatter: The Birth of a New Civil Rights Movement." *Guardian* (July 19, 2015). Available online at https://www.theguardian.com/world/2015/jul/19/blacklivesmatter-birth-civil-rights-movement (accessed September 15, 2017).

Fears, Darryl. "Thousands Join Al Sharpton in 'Justice for All' March in D.C." *Washington Post* (December 13, 2014). Available online at https://www.washingtonpost.com/national/health-science/sharpton-to-lead-justice-for-all-march-in-dc/2014/12/13/36ce8a68-824f-11e4-9f38-95a187e4c1f7_story.html (accessed September 15, 2017).

Gaffey, Conor. "South Africa: What You Need to Know about the Soweto Uprising 40 Years Later." *Newsweek* (June 16, 2016). Available online at http://www.newsweek.com/soweto-uprising-hector-pieterson-memorial-471090 (accessed September 15, 2017).

Gregory, Alice. "A Brief History of the Zoot Suit: Unraveling the Jazzy Life of a Snazzy Style." *Smithsonian* (April 2016). Available online at http://www.smithsonianmag.com/arts-culture/brief-history-zoot-suit-180958507 (accessed September 15, 2017).

Hoglund, Andy. "Flashback: Detroit Erupts into Race Riots in 1967." *Rolling Stone* (July 28, 2017). Available online at http://www.rollingstone.com/culture/news/flashback-detroit-erupts-into-race-riots-in-1967-w494702 (accessed September 15, 2017).

McGraw, Bill. "Detroit '67: 'We've Got Trouble'—Routine Police Raid Ignites 5 Days of Rioting." *Detroit Free Press* (July 22, 2017). Available online at http://www.freep.com/story/news/local/michigan/detroit/2017/07/23/detroit-riots-blind-pig/487920001/ (accessed September 15, 2017).

Orlov, Rick. "Riots Exposed Long-Lingering Racial Tensions in Los Angeles." *Long Beach Press-Telegram* (April 27, 2012). Available online at http://www.presstelegram.com/article/zz/20120427/NEWS/120429273 (accessed September 15, 2017).

Rothman, Lily. "What We Still Get Wrong about What Happened in Detroit in 1967." *Time* (August 3, 2017). Available online at http://time.com/4879062/detroit-1967-real-history/ (accessed September 15, 2017).

Wheeler, Linda. "The New York City Draft Riots of 1863." *Washington Post* (April 29, 2013). Available online at https://www.washingtonpost.com/lifestyle/style/the-new-york-draft-riots-of-1863/2013/04/26/a1aacf52-a620-11e2-a8e2-5b98cb59187f_story.html?utm_term=.fdb9796f03ab (accessed October 8, 2017).

"Zoot Suit Riots: Sailors vs. Pachucos a Turning Point for Latino Culture in California." *Mercury News* (June 4, 2013). Available online at http://www.mercurynews.com/2013/06/04/zoot-suit-riots-sailors-vs-pachucos-a-turning-point-for-latino-culture-in-california (accessed September 15, 2017).

WEBSITES

Heim, Joe. "Recounting a Day of Rage, Hate, Violence and Death." *Washington Post*, August 14, 2017. https://www.washingtonpost.com/graphics/2017/local/charlottesville-timeline (September 15, 2017).

Lee, Trymaine. "Justice for All: Thousands March against Police Violence." MSNBC, July 21, 2015. http://www.msnbc.com/msnbc/justice-all-thousands-expected-march-washington-against-police-violence (accessed September 15, 2017).

"1943: Zoot Suit Riots." *National Geographic*. https://www.nationalgeographic.org/thisday/jun3/zoot-suit-riots (accessed September 15, 2017).

"Soweto Student Uprising." South Africa: Overcoming Apartheid, Building Democracy. http://overcomingapartheid.msu.edu/sidebar.php?id=65-258-3 (accessed September 15, 2017).

"Uprising of 1967." Detroit Historical Society. https://detroithistorical.org/learn/encyclopedia-of-detroit/uprising-1967 (accessed September 15, 2017).

Whack, Errin Haines, and Emily Swanson. "AP-NORC Poll: Disapproval for Anthem Protest, Trump Response." Associated Press, October 6, 2017. https://www.apnews.com/bfe9374818bc49e3a82c451e4c611905 (accessed October 16, 2017).

Wyche, Steve. "Colin Kaepernick Explains Why He Sat during National Anthem." NFL.com, August 27, 2016. http://www.nfl.com/news/story/0ap3000000691077/article/colin-kaepernick-explains-protest-of-national-anthem (accessed October 16, 2017).

17

Reproductive Rights

March for Women's Lives **556**

Operation Rescue **562**

One-Child Policy Riots **568**

Planned Parenthood Protests **574**

Reproductive rights is a broad topic that includes issues relating to sexual reproduction, including people's right to determine whether and when they want to have children and how many children they will have. Reproductive rights also include a person's access to sexual education and reproductive health-care services, including contraceptives and abortions. Contraceptives, also called birth control, are the various methods or devices used to prevent pregnancy. These include condoms, birth control pills or hormonal implants, and intrauterine devices (IUDs). Abortion is the ending of a pregnancy by medical methods. Some women can take medication to end a pregnancy, while others undergo a surgical procedure performed by a doctor.

Other reproductive rights issues include forced sterilization and forced abortion. Sterilization involves a surgery that makes an individual unable to produce a baby. Over the years, some governments have forced sterilization on citizens considered unfit to be parents due to their income, race, mental health, or intelligence. In a similar manner, some governments have forced women to have abortions in an effort to control the population.

Two sides at odds

Many people believe that government agencies and other individuals should not be allowed to interfere with individuals' reproductive rights. They feel that these decisions should be personal and private. Despite this, countries around the world have a long history of regulating reproductive rights, especially for women. Women are the ones who carry, give birth to, and, oftentimes, rear children. Because of this, many people believe that women should have the right to make decisions about their reproductive health and have control of their own bodies.

WORDS TO KNOW

Abortion: The ending of a pregnancy through medical methods.

Conception: The moment when a male's sperm fertilizes a female's ovum.

Contraceptive: A method or device used to prevent pregnancy.

Embryo: A stage of development after an ovum is fertilized by a sperm, typically lasting about eight weeks.

Fetus: An unborn, developing human more than eight weeks past fertilization.

Ovum: A female reproductive cell, sometimes called an egg.

Pro-choice: A term used to describe people who support a woman's right to choose to have an abortion.

Pro-life: A term used to describe people who are against abortion.

Radical: Someone who favors extreme measures to make a point or bring about change.

Sexual reproduction: Occurs when two individuals have sex and produce an offspring.

Sperm: A male reproductive cell.

Trimester: A period of pregnancy lasting about three months, during which the embryo or fetus develops.

The World Health Organization (WHO) states that information about family planning and access to reproductive health services, including the use of modern contraceptives, is a human right. It allows women to space out the birth of children, which has multiple positive health benefits for mothers and children. These include preventing unintended pregnancies, reducing maternal and infant deaths, reducing the numbers of premature births and low birth weight infants, reducing rates of sexually transmitted diseases, and allowing adolescents and women to achieve their full potential by focusing on their education and careers. Many feel that in addition to family planning information and birth control, access to safe, legal abortion is necessary for women to achieve reproductive freedom. People who are considered pro-choice support legal abortion and reproductive rights.

Many people who are pro-choice are concerned about the health of the mother. They believe women and girls should be able to have an abortion if the pregnancy puts their health in danger. Complications from pregnancy and childbirth can be life-threatening. Pro-choicers are also concerned about the health of the baby. Some developing embryos or fetuses may have abnormalities or genetic conditions that would make it hard to survive after they are born. It is difficult for some pregnant women to consider giving birth to a baby they know might die or have a poor quality of life. In addition, those supporting choice believe that women and girls should be able to have an abortion in cases of rape or incest. Incest is when close relatives have sex and often involves rape.

In contrast, some people believe that the use of contraceptives or abortion to prevent or end a pregnancy is wrong. Such people have moral or religious objections to birth control or abortion or both. Some believe that life begins at conception, which is when a man's sperm fertilizes a woman' ovum. They see abortion as not just the ending of a pregnancy but also the ending of a life. They believe it is wrong to abort an embryo or fetus even if it may have a life-threatening condition or disability.

Not all people who oppose abortion are against birth control. Some who oppose abortion believe birth control is one way to reduce the number of abortions. However, others feel that birth control is wrong because they believe that anything that interferes with conception is against "God's plan." This is often because they believe that sex is strictly for reproduction purposes. People on this side of the reproductive rights issue are considered pro-life.

Although reproductive rights have been a concern for centuries, the fight for these rights truly developed during the mid-20th century. This was when laws restricting the discussion of birth control in the United States ended and when the first hormonal birth control pills were introduced. In 1973 the US Supreme Court legalized abortion through its decision in *Roe v. Wade*. This particular case divided the nation. From that point on, pro-choice and pro-life supporters have fought a sometimes violent battle over women's reproductive rights.

Reproductive rights history

Humans have been using various methods to control reproduction for thousands of years. Ancient Egyptians, Greeks, and Romans used various herbs, plant extracts, and other ingredients as spermicides, which are substances that kill sperm. People used condoms made from animal parts or fabric in the 17th century. For hundreds of years, women took mixtures of various herbs to prevent pregnancy or cause an abortion.

Most scholars agree that abortion was not a crime in the United Kingdom or the United States for many years. Women could take various measures to have an abortion, as long as it was done before the woman could feel the fetus move. This movement usually occurs in the second

CRITICAL THINKING QUESTIONS

1. Do you think that protests such as the March for Women's Lives have any effect on how people feel about abortion? Why or why not?

2. What effect do you think the March for Women's Lives has had on presidential elections?

3. Do you think the government should be able to limit abortions for women? Why or why not?

4. Do you think the government should cut funding to Planned Parenthood? Explain your answer.

5. How did the Spring of Life protest in Buffalo, New York, differ from the Summer of Mercy protest in Wichita, Kansas? What effects did these differences have on the results of the protests?

6. The Spring of Life protest was one factor that led to the passage of the FACE Act. Do you think the FACE Act is necessary? Why or why not?

7. Do you think China's one-child policy was a good idea? Why or why not?

8. Do you think governments in general have a right to monitor their citizens' reproductive choices? Explain your answer.

---

trimester of pregnancy. Human pregnancy is divided into three trimesters (each usually lasts about three months) that mark the development of the embryo or fetus. Before the 19th century, merchants would travel to various towns, selling herbs and drugs that could bring on an abortion. Some of these merchants even advertised their services in newspapers.

19th-century limitations Feelings toward abortion and contraceptives started to change in the 19th century. The United Kingdom passed laws against abortion in the early 1800s. Regulation of abortion then began in the United States around the 1850s. American professor and author Leslie J. Reagan argued in her 1997 book *When Abortion Was a Crime* that there may have been several reasons for the shift in attitudes regarding abortion. Around the mid-19th century, some American women had begun to fight for the right to vote. Others were trying to gain entrance to colleges and universities and begin working in careers outside the home. Limiting access to abortion was one way to prevent women from taking jobs, particularly in professions previously only held by men.

Reagan argues that another reason for the change had to do with who was having abortions. In the United States, wealthy white women were having the most abortions in the latter half of the century. At the same time, immigrants from around the world were coming to the country.

Reagan believes that limiting abortion was done to encourage white women to have more children. The hope among the country's white leaders was to raise the birth rates among white people. That way, they reasoned, immigrants and blacks would not outnumber whites. In 1873 Congress passed the Comstock Act, which banned access to information regarding abortion and contraceptives. By 1890 there were laws in place that banned abortions except in cases where a woman's life would be in danger by continuing a pregnancy. States soon followed with their own laws against abortion.

Early 20th century Although new laws had been put into place, women continued to use birth control and have abortions in the United States. Wealthy women who wanted abortions had an easier time than women from lower economic classes did. The rich could pay doctors to perform procedures in their homes, or they could travel to countries where abortion was legal. Outlawing abortion forced many poorer women to find another way to terminate a pregnancy. They would sometimes try to abort the embryo or fetus themselves using unsafe chemicals or devices. Other times, women would have abortions performed by untrained individuals. Many women were seriously hurt or died as a result of these illegal abortions.

Several organizations formed to try to help women access birth control and safe abortions. Activist Margaret Sanger (1879–1966) founded one of these organizations. An activist is someone who fights for a specific cause or issue. Sanger opened the first birth control clinic in the United States in 1916. Due to her actions, she spent a month in jail. However, Sanger continued her efforts. The organization she founded would become the Planned Parenthood Federation of America in the 1940s. Planned Parenthood continued to provide women with access to reproductive health services into the 21st century.

Mid-century changes After women gained the right to vote in 1920 and as they continued to fight for equal rights, attitudes about sex and sexual reproduction were changing. In 1960 American women had access to hormonal birth control pills for the first time. The pill was very effective at preventing pregnancy. Some birth control pills were found to be effective for reducing symptoms of premenstrual syndrome (PMS) and menstrual cramps. For many women, the pill also separated sex from reproduction and allowed them more freedom in their lives. They could

Reproductive Rights

have more control over the timing and size of their families or even whether or not to have children. By 1973, 70 percent of married women between ages 15 and 44 used contraception. Of course, the pill did not eliminate the need for abortion entirely.

During the 1960s, several women's organizations formed. One such organization was the National Organization for Women (NOW), which started in 1966. NOW and other women's rights groups worked together to challenge laws on abortion. Eventually, one case made it all the way to the US Supreme Court. The Supreme Court is the highest court in the United States. The justices on the court decide if laws are in keeping with the US Constitution, which is the set of principles on which the US government is based.

Roe v. Wade was a case that challenged a Texas law against abortion on the basis that it denied women their constitutional rights. The court decided that several amendments in the Constitution protect a person's right to privacy. The justices felt that a woman's right to choose to have an abortion was included in this right to privacy. This decision made it so states could not outlaw abortion in the first trimester of pregnancy. It also said that state laws regulating abortion in the second and third trimesters had to be reasonable and include an exception for protecting the life of the woman.

The case of *Roe v. Wade* divided the nation. People formed pro-life groups to try to reverse the decision. The two sides eventually gained support from the two major political parties. Pro-choice activists had support from most Democrats, while Republicans usually supported pro-life advocates. The effects from the decision in *Roe* would be felt for years to come.

Roe v. Wade was a case that challenged a Texas law against abortion on the basis that it denied women their constitutional rights. The court decided that several amendments in the Constitution protect a person's right to privacy. The justices felt that a woman's right to choose to have an abortion was included in this right to privacy.

Modern fight for reproductive rights The debate over reproductive rights grew more heated over the years. In the 1980s and 1990s, both sides in the abortion argument protested and marched to make their voices heard. In some cases, the fight for reproductive rights grew violent and even deadly. Across the country, pro-life radicals bombed and set fire to women's health-care clinics where doctors provided abortions. A radical is someone who goes to extreme measures to make a point about an issue or cause. An antiabortion group kidnapped a doctor who performed abortions and his wife in the early 1980s. In 1993 an abortion opponent shot and killed Dr. David Gunn (1946–1993) outside his clinic, which provided abortions. This event marked the first murder by pro-life advocates in the battle over abortion; however, it was not the last.

As activists on both sides continued to speak out into the 21st century, the abortion debate continued to play out in the courts. Some states passed laws that limited access to abortion. These laws sometimes made it difficult for women to find abortion providers in their own states.

Modern laws also sought to regulate contraceptives. In 2014 the US Supreme Court ruled in the case *Burwell v. Hobby Lobby* that "closely-held corporations," such as family-owned companies, did not have to provide insurance coverage for contraceptives for employees. The decision was based on the idea that being required to provide contraceptive coverage could harm the owners' freedom of religion. A Christian family owns Hobby Lobby, the company named in the case.

Some women's rights groups worried about how this decision would affect access to birth control in the future. Critics also noted that employees might not share the business owner's religious beliefs or beliefs about contraception. In addition, women who were on the pill for a variety of other health reasons, such as controlling PMS symptoms, regulating heavy or irregular periods, reducing menstrual cramps, hormonal imbalances such as polycystic ovary syndrome and primary ovarian insufficiency, or treating acne, would lose coverage, as well.

Another reproductive rights case in the 2010s that received a great deal of attention was *Whole Woman's Health v. Hellerstedt*. This case involved Texas laws that forced abortion providers to have surgical-grade facilities. Doctors at these clinics also had to have admitting privileges at local hospitals. This meant the doctors could admit clinic patients to the hospital. Women's rights activists argued that the Texas laws forced many clinics to close, leaving women without access to safe and legal abortions. The court agreed, noting that these laws put an unnecessary burden on women seeking abortions in Texas.

The fight continues

The debate over reproductive rights continues. Both sides remain firm in their beliefs regarding contraceptives and abortion. New state laws continue to try to limit access to abortion. At the same time, women's rights organizations voice concern about such laws. Many activists worry that stricter laws against abortion would force women to seek out illegal and dangerous methods to end unwanted pregnancies, just as they had in the past. Some of this concern is supported by data. A 2016 report by the *New York Times* found that Internet searches on how to induce, or cause, an abortion were higher in states with greater limits on access to the procedure.

In October 2017 the administration of US President Donald Trump (1946–) announced that it was rolling back a health insurance requirement on birth control. This new rule allowed exemptions for any employer to refuse coverage for no-cost birth control for their employees based on religious or moral objections. This decision had the potential to impact the lives of many women.

The Centers for Disease Control and Prevention reports that from 2011 to 2013, approximately 62 percent of women aged 15 to 44 were currently using contraception. Critics noted that once women, especially teenagers, lost access to no-cost birth control, the number of pregnancies would increase and so would abortions. According to Maggie Fox for NBC News, "A 2012 study of more than 9,000 women found that when women got no-cost birth control, the number of unplanned pregnancies and abortions fell by between 62 and 78 percent."

The Guttmacher Institute, a nonprofit organization that advocates for reproductive rights, estimated in 2016 that globally, if all adolescents ages 15–19 in developing regions who did not have access to contraceptives were given access, it would mean there were 6 million fewer unintended pregnancies every year, preventing 2.1 million unplanned births, 3.2 million abortions (many of them unsafe), and 5,600 maternal deaths. Several state attorneys general sued the Trump administration over the birth control decision.

March for Women's Lives

LOCATION: Washington, DC; Los Angeles, California

DATE: March 9 and 16, 1986

The 1973 US Supreme Court decision in *Roe v. Wade* legalized abortion in the first trimester of pregnancy in the United States. It also divided the nation. Even in the 21st century, abortion continues to be a heated topic. Some people believe that women should have the right to make their own decisions about when or if they have children. People often refer to supporters of reproductive rights as pro-choice activists. Other people

Reproductive Rights

Demonstrators hold signs and banners outside the Capitol in Washington, DC, on March 9, 1986, as they wait for speeches by the organizers of the March for Women's Lives. Thousands participated in the demonstration for women's rights to birth control and legal abortion. © AP IMAGES/TOM REED.

feel that abortion is wrong. These people usually have strong religious and moral objections to abortion. They believe that life begins at conception, so they view abortion as the taking of a life. These people are pro-life advocates.

In the years following the Supreme Court decision, the two sides participated in various campaigns to try to make their voices on this subject heard. One of the most successful protests in the fight for reproductive rights was the March for Women's Lives held in Washington, DC, and Los Angeles, California, in March 1986. This march was a response to the violence used by pro-life radicals against women's health clinics where abortions were performed. The March for Women's Lives was also a counterprotest to an annual pro-life march that had been held in Washington in January 1986.

Political climate in the 1980s

Abortion was legalized by the Supreme Court's decision in 1973's *Roe v. Wade*. Although abortion was legal, accessing reproductive health care was still difficult in the 1980s. For many years, pro-life activists often stood outside of women's health clinics. They would attempt to talk women out of getting abortions.

In the mid-1980s, some radical pro-lifers used violent methods to try to prevent people from obtaining abortions while also gaining attention for their cause. For instance, in 1982 members of an antiabortion group called Army of God kidnapped a doctor who ran a women's health clinic that provided abortions. They also kidnapped the doctor's wife. The members released the couple after a week. Pro-life radicals were also responsible for about 25 bombings and arson attacks on women's health clinics in 1984. The following year there were more bombings and attacks.

On January 1, 1985, the bombing of a women's health clinic in Washington, DC, drew the attention of US President Ronald Reagan (1911–2004), a Republican. Reagan condemned the violence against the clinic, even though he supported pro-life activists in general.

Over the years, pro-choice activists found ways to counter the pro-lifers' actions. They helped escort women to and from health clinics to keep them safe. They went to court to try to create buffers around women's health clinics. They also protested and marched to protect women's reproductive rights.

The National Organization for Women

On January 23, 1986, antiabortion protesters held their annual March for Life rally in Washington, DC. The march attracted about 40,000 pro-lifers from across the country. The demonstrators called on politicians to find ways to overturn, or reverse, the decision in *Roe v. Wade*. President Reagan even addressed the marchers from the White House, marking the second year in a row he had shown his support for the antiabortion activists.

The many attacks on women's health-care clinics and the annual March for Life protest encouraged several women's organizations to speak out for reproductive rights in a big way. One such organization was the National Organization for Women (NOW), which was first established in 1966. One of NOW's founders was the famed feminist writer Betty Friedan (1921–2006). Feminists believe that men and women should have equal rights and opportunities. NOW and other women's rights groups had worked to help legalize abortion through the Supreme Court decision in *Roe v. Wade*.

Following that decision, the group spent much of the 1970s and early 1980s focused on attempting to pass the Equal Rights Amendment (ERA). This amendment would grant equality under the law and prevent

Competing Marches

The March for Life is an annual protest against abortion held in Washington, DC. The first March for Life was held on the one-year anniversary of the US Supreme Court's decision in *Roe v. Wade*. Antiabortion activist Nellie Gray (1924–2012) organized the March for Life from her home in Washington. About 20,000 people attended the first march on January 22, 1974. Gray then turned the march into an annual event. The March for Life Education and Defense Fund became a nonprofit organization, and Gray became its leader. One of the group's purposes was to try to influence government officials to support overturning the ruling in *Roe*. The stated goal of the group is to pass a Mandatory Human Life Amendment to the US Constitution. Such an amendment would protect all human life beginning at conception.

Thousands of pro-life supporters attend the march each year. In 1981 the crowd's numbers reached an estimated 60,000. That year President Reagan agreed to meet with a group of antiabortion activists at the White House. In 1985 and 1986 Reagan addressed the pro-life marchers from the White House through an electronic hookup. The march continues to bring anti-abortion activists to Washington, DC, each year.

On January 27, 2017, thousands of pro-life supporters flocked to Washington for the annual March for Life. Pro-life supporters at the march had allies in the White House again. Vice President Mike Pence (1959–) became the highest-ranking White House official to ever address the March for Life crowd in person at the 2017 protest. The *Washington Post* quoted Pence as telling the protesters, "We will not rest until we restore a culture of life in America."

However, the March for Life occurred just days after the Women's March on Washington. Held on January 21, 2017, the Women's March was the largest organized protest march in US history. An estimated 3 million to 4 million marchers demonstrated in cities across the United States. An estimated 500,000 marched in Washington, DC, alone. The Women's March was a worldwide reaction to the election of President Donald Trump (1946–), whom many women worried would set the fight for reproductive rights back 50 years.

One of the stated goals of the Women's March was preserving the "ability to access quality reproductive healthcare services, birth control, HIV/AIDS care and prevention, or medically accurate sexuality education" as well as "open access to safe, legal, affordable abortion and birth control for all people, regardless of income, location or education."

---

states or the federal government from denying equal rights based on a person's sex. However, the ERA was three states shy of ratification in 1982. For an amendment to the US Constitution to become law, a certain number of states must give their approval, or ratify the amendment. The ERA never received support from enough states.

After the failure of the ERA, NOW had to refocus its efforts in the fight for women's rights. From 1977 to 1982, Eleanor Smeal (1939–)

served as NOW's president. Smeal lost her position when the ERA failed to pass, and Judy Goldsmith (1938–) took over. Goldsmith did not stay in office long, though. In 1985 Smeal won the presidency back at the organization's national conference, and she had big plans for NOW's next steps.

March for Women's Lives

NOW wanted to counter the annual March for Life and send a clear message to President Reagan. The group wanted Reagan to know that they would protest any effort his administration put forth to overturn *Roe v. Wade*. With the help of 350 organizations and nearly 300 college groups, NOW organized the first March for Women's Lives in 1986. The organizers planned for the march to take place on both the East and West Coasts.

The first march was held in Washington, DC, on March 9, 1986. Women and men from various backgrounds came from across the country to march along a 3-mile (4.8-kilometer) route from the White House to the Capitol building. They showed their support for safe and legal access to abortion by holding signs and chanting, "Not the church, not the state, women must decide their fate."

Famous feminist Gloria Steinem (1934–) and former congresswoman Bella Abzug (1920–1998) participated in the march. Between 80,000 and 125,000 people took part in the Washington event, making it one of the largest reproductive rights marches at the time. This was more than double the size of the March for Life rally held in January of that year. Only one person was arrested during the march. A pro-life minister named Jerry Horn moved through the crowds holding what he said was a human fetus. Police arrested Horn and investigated how he had obtained the fetus.

The West Coast march was held in Los Angeles on March 16. Actors Jane Fonda (1937–), Morgan Fairchild (1950–), and Ed Asner (1929–) participated in the march. Despite a thunderstorm and pouring rain, about 30,000 people marched to show their support for reproductive rights. Several pro-life counterprotesters also attended the rally, but their shouts were drowned out by the mostly upbeat crowd of pro-choice activists.

Continued protests

NOW continued to organize marches focused on reproductive rights throughout the late 1980s. In 1992 NOW joined with other women's rights organizations to fight against new challenges to *Roe v. Wade* in the

Supreme Court. *Planned Parenthood of Southeastern Pennsylvania v. Casey* was a case that could redefine abortion laws. In 1988 and 1989, Pennsylvania set new limits on access to abortion. These limits included requiring married women to get their husband's consent to obtain an abortion. In addition, underage women had to receive consent from their parents to have an abortion. Pro-choice supporters felt that these limits would weaken reproductive rights.

Many pro-choice groups and advocates also believed that support for abortion access had decreased after more than a decade of Republican control of the White House. They hoped that a large demonstration would help bring attention to the threat to women's reproductive rights. On April 5, 1992, about 750,000 demonstrators from across the country attended another March for Women's Lives in Washington. Several months later, Bill Clinton (1946–), who supported reproductive rights, won the presidential election. This marked the first time a Democrat was in the White House in 12 years. However, the Supreme Court case did not go in the pro-choicers' favor. Although the court defended the decision in *Roe v. Wade*, the justices also upheld many of Pennsylvania's new abortion rules. The only exception was the measure regarding married women obtaining their husband's consent to have an abortion.

New threats to reproductive rights surfaced in the early 21st century. Republican George W. Bush (1946–), who was firmly pro-life, became president in 2001. About two years after becoming president, Bush signed the Partial-Birth Abortion Ban Act. This law banned a particular type of abortion performed in the third trimester of pregnancy. This type of procedure was very rare, but it had become a key issue in the debate over abortion.

Pro-choice advocates worried that such laws could lead to additional limits on legal abortion in the future. They felt it was once again time to rally massive support for reproductive rights. In April 2004, NOW and other organizations came together to prepare for another March for Women's Lives in Washington. This event was bigger than all of the previous marches. More than 1 million people protested to protect legal abortion, access to birth control, and other reproductive rights. The march showed that the pro-choice movement had many supporters. Nevertheless, the demonstration did not prevent Bush from winning reelection months later. The pro-choicers faced another loss in 2007, when the Supreme Court upheld the president's Partial-Birth Abortion Ban Act.

More than 1 million people protested to protect legal abortion, access to birth control, and other reproductive rights. The march showed that the pro-choice movement had many supporters.

Operation Rescue

LOCATION: Buffalo and Amherst, New York

DATE: Spring 1992

In the spring of 1992, pro-life organization Operation Rescue held an antiabortion protest in the cities of Buffalo and Amherst, New York. Organizers called the protest the Spring of Life. The main goal of the protest was to force health clinics to close, at least for a short time. If the clinics were closed, women would be unable to have abortions during that time.

Hundreds of pro-life supporters gathered in Buffalo for the protest. Just as many pro-choice supporters arrived for a counterprotest. The counterprotesters were able to prevent the Spring of Life event from closing any clinics. All the clinics in Buffalo and Amherst continued to perform their normal activities without interruption during the protest. In the end, the Spring of Life protest did not achieve many of the goals that Operation Rescue organizers had set. However, the protest did help lead to a new federal law designed to protect patients at reproductive health clinics of any kind.

Background on Operation Rescue

Operation Rescue is a pro-life organization that seeks to end abortion in the United States. Activist Randall Terry (1959–) started Operation Rescue in 1986. The organization's name refers to its goal of "rescuing" the unborn. The organization works to achieve this goal by trying to stop women from having abortions and stop doctors from performing them.

Like many pro-life groups, Operation Rescue believes that human life begins at conception. Conception is the moment when sperm fertilizes an egg and a woman becomes pregnant. During a pregnancy, the fertilized egg, or embryo, begins to grow into a fetus (usually considered to be about eight weeks after fertilization), or a developing human. Abortion effectively ends a pregnancy. For this reason, pro-lifers think of abortion as ending human life. They believe that doctors who perform abortions are committing murder.

In its early days, Operation Rescue staged peaceful, nonviolent protests to spread its pro-life message. Many members still participate in these types of protests. Some branches use more extreme measures to spread their message. They may try to scare women or doctors who are entering women's health clinics where abortions are performed. Some Operation Rescue members have been suspected or accused of promoting violence against doctors who perform abortions. Other members have committed violent acts. As a result, Operation Rescue is sometimes considered an extremist group.

Operation Rescue has changed its name several times throughout its history. In 1998 the original Operation Rescue group changed its name to Operation Save America. A different branch of the group then began using the name Operation Rescue. As of 2017, both organizations continued to work to end abortion in the United States.

Operation Rescue's methods

Operation Rescue uses several methods to achieve its goals. The group's first "rescue" in 1986 was similar to a sit-in. A sit-in is the act of sitting in a particular place as a form of protest. To protest abortion, Terry and several other group members barred themselves inside a women's health clinic in Binghamton, New York, and refused to leave. All the people involved in the protest were arrested and jailed for several days. In the past, Operation Rescue members blocked entrances to clinics or tried to prevent clinic workers and patients from entering the building. Since 1994, laws have banned the blocking of clinic entrances.

Other activities Operation Rescue uses to achieve its goals are picketing and sidewalk counseling. Picketing is standing or marching, often while holding signs, to protest something. Operation Rescue members sometimes hold signs showing graphic, or disturbing, images of aborted fetuses. Sidewalk counseling involves members of Operation Rescue trying to convince women not to enter a clinic. The purpose of sidewalk counseling is to get women to change their minds about abortion. Members of Operation Rescue may arrive before a clinic opens to verbally abuse doctors and nurses who work there.

The most extreme members of Operation Rescue have used violence to protest abortion. In 1998 pro-life protester James C. Kopp (1954–), a well-known associate of Terry, followed a doctor home from a women's health clinic in Buffalo, New York. Kopp hid outside the

In the past, Operation Rescue members blocked entrances to clinics or tried to prevent clinic workers and patients from entering the building. Since 1994, laws have banned the blocking of clinic entrances.

Reproductive Rights

doctor's house. He then shot through the window of the house and killed the doctor. Kopp later fled the country but was eventually arrested, tried, and found guilty of murder.

Planning a protest

In late 1991 Operation Rescue leaders announced plans to protest women's health clinics in Buffalo, New York. The group had held a successful protest in Wichita, Kansas, the previous summer. That protest, called the Summer of Mercy, lasted 46 days and caused at least one clinic to shut down for a week. Operation Rescue leaders hoped to build on their success in Wichita with the Buffalo protest, which they named the Spring of Life.

Organizers chose Buffalo for the Spring of Life protest for several reasons. First, the city's mayor, James Griffin (1929–2008), welcomed the organization to the city. Second, a large portion of Buffalo's population was Catholic. The Catholic Church teaches that abortion is a sin, so many Catholics are pro-life. Finally, Buffalo had a large population of people who opposed abortion for political reasons. Protest organizers thought they would receive much support from Buffalo's local residents.

Operation Rescue leaders intended the Spring of Life protest to serve as practice for larger protests later that year. The organization planned to protest at the Democratic National Convention (DNC) in New York City and the Republican National Convention (RNC) in Houston, Texas. The DNC is an event at which members of the Democratic Party select a candidate to run for president. The RNC is a similar event for the Republican Party. Operation Rescue wanted to hold large protests at both conventions in hopes of bringing its pro-life message to a national audience.

Anti-abortion demonstrators stage a protest outside of a Houston Planned Parenthood clinic during the 1992 Republican National Convention. The demonstrators are from Operation Rescue, a Christian pro-life organization. © GREG SMITH/CORBIS/CORBIS VIA GETTY IMAGES.

Spring of Life protest begins

Operation Rescue's Spring of Life protest began in late April 1992. Hundreds of pro-life supporters traveled to Buffalo to join the protest. They planned to protest outside six clinics there and in nearby Amherst, New York. The protesters hoped to force the clinics to close, so women would be unable to have abortions there. In this way, Operation Rescue would achieve its goal of rescuing the unborn.

During the protests, pro-lifers gathered outside clinics. Some held signs with pro-life messages or disturbing images. Some sang hymns and quietly prayed. Others yelled phrases such as "It's not a fetus! It's a baby!" or "Murder!"

As the Spring of Life event continued, the protesters became more forceful. On the morning of April 23, nearly 200 people were arrested for marching outside a clinic in Amherst. Police officers formed a blockade in front of the clinic to protect patients and prevent protesters from entering. Some protesters tried to push past the officers. Others tried to run around the line of officers. Although officers arrested all of these protesters, some demonstrators struggled with police. Those protesters faced more serious charges than the ones who cooperated with police.

The protests in Buffalo continued for several more days. Operation Rescue's leaders originally planned the Spring of Life protest to last for two weeks. After 10 days, between 400 and 600 protesters had been arrested. In addition, the protests had failed to shut down a single clinic. On April 30, organizers stopped their planned activities. They instead held a day of prayer and fasting, which involves not eating food.

Countering the Spring of Life

As soon as Operation Rescue announced its plan for a protest in Buffalo, several pro-choice groups in the area united. They formed a new group called Buffalo United for Choice (BUC). BUC quickly began planning a counterprotest against Operation Rescue's Spring of Life.

The counterprotest to the Spring of Life was very effective. Each morning, pro-choice volunteers gathered outside the women's health clinics in Buffalo and Amherst. They linked arms and formed blockades to prevent pro-lifers from getting too close to the clinics. Other volunteers guided patients and workers into clinics to protect them from the pro-life protesters.

BUC's counterprotest allowed women's health clinics in Buffalo and Amherst to remain open. All the clinics were able to provide health services for their patients without interruption. At one point during the Spring of Life, a worker at a clinic in Amherst reported that no patients had canceled their appointments.

Reproductive Rights

Summer of Mercy Protest, 1991

Operation Rescue staged a successful protest in Wichita, Kansas, in the summer of 1991. The pro-life group called the protest the Summer of Mercy. Organizers planned the event to last for one week, but it ended up lasting six times longer than they expected..

Operation Rescue chose Wichita because Dr. George Tiller (1941–2009), one of the few US doctors who performed late-term abortions, had a clinic there. A late-term abortion is performed during the last three months of pregnancy. These types of abortions usually are rare.

Doctors usually perform late-term abortions only when continuing a pregnancy is dangerous for the mother or the fetus. Sometimes late-term abortions are allowed for other serious reasons. About 10 to 12 of the 2,000 abortions Tiller performed at his clinic each year were late-term abortions.

When Dr. Tiller heard about the Summer of Mercy protest, he agreed to close his clinic for one week. His clinic had been targeted in the past. In 1986 it had been firebombed. He wanted to avoid conflict with the protesters. During the first week, hundreds of protesters flooded the streets of Wichita. They gathered outside Tiller's clinic to protest. They held signs with slogans such as "Babies Killed Here" and "Tiller's Slaughter House." Others prayed, sang hymns, and read passages from the Bible.

Operation Rescue leaders were pleased with the protest's success after the first week. They decided to extend the protest. The decision angered Tiller. He had patients who needed health services. He could not keep his clinic closed any longer.

When Tiller reopened his clinic, protesters became more forceful. Hundreds sat outside the clinic's doors to block the entrance. Some chained themselves to the fence around the clinic. Others laid down, refusing to move, even when instructed to do so by police. Staff inside the clinic were afraid to leave, not knowing if the protesters

Results of the protest

Operation Rescue leaders had set several goals for the Spring of Life protest. They wanted to shut down clinics and prevent abortions. They wanted to encourage support for the pro-life movement. They wanted to gain more followers to participate in future protests. The protest did not accomplish many of these goals.

A few factors contributed to the Spring of Life protest's failure. First, pro-life protesters faced a large and effective pro-choice counterprotest. When members of Operation Rescue protested in Wichita in the summer of 1991, they met with very little resistance. In Buffalo the counterprotest was strong. It succeeded in preventing pro-lifers from getting too close to clinics, clinic patients, and clinic staff.

Reproductive Rights

would become violent.. About 25 percent of Wichita's police force had to be sent to control the protesters. Even then, some protesters managed to slip past officers.

In the end, about 30,000 people participated in the Summer of Mercy. The protest lasted six weeks, from July 15 to August 25. Police officers arrested more than 2,700 people during that time. Operation Rescue leaders considered the protest a huge success. They soon began planning similar protests in other cities in the United States.

Tiller continued to practice at his clinic in Wichita, but he faced constant danger. In 1993 a pro-life supporter shot him in both arms. His injuries were not serious, and he was able to return to work. However, on May 31, 2009, pro-life supporter Scott Roeder (1958–) walked into the church where Tiller was attending services with his wife. Roeder shot and killed Tiller.

Roeder was convicted of first-degree murder in 2010 and sentenced to 50 years without parole. His sentence was reduced in 2013 to 25 years without parole.

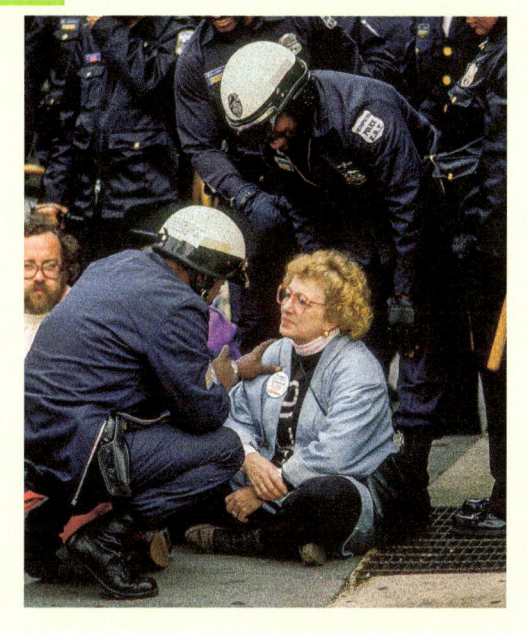

Operation Rescue activists stage protests in various cities in the country. Here, Washington, DC, police arrest some of the 350 members of Operation Rescue for blocking the entrance to an abortion clinic on Georgia Avenue NW, on November 17, 1990. © BY MARK REINSTEIN/SHUTTERSTOCK.COM.

Second, two months before the start of the protest, the courts issued an injunction, or order. The injunction barred protesters from going within 15 feet (4.5 meters) of patients entering or leaving a clinic. It also made it difficult for Operation Rescue members to practice sidewalk counseling on patients.

Third, Operation Rescue's methods did not appeal to many of Buffalo's pro-life residents. Although they opposed abortion, they thought Operation Rescue's graphic signs and marches attracted too much bad publicity. As a result, they distanced themselves from Operation Rescue.

Aftermath

A few days after Operation Rescue ended its protests in Buffalo, the US House of Representatives began discussing a bill related to women's health clinics. A bill is a proposed law. If passed, the proposed law would make it illegal to block people from entering a women's health clinic.

The bill was originally proposed in 1991. It gained more support after Operation Rescue's protests in Buffalo in 1992. During hearings for the bill, the House heard from women who were patients at reproductive health clinics across the United States. Protesters had blocked all the women from entering the clinics where they received care.

More than a year later, the bill passed into law. On May 26, 1994, President Bill Clinton signed the Freedom of Access to Clinic Entrances Act, or FACE Act. The federal law bans the use of force or the threat of force against people trying to enter any type of reproductive health clinic. It also bans blocking the entrance to any such clinic. The law protects both clinics where abortions are performed and crisis pregnancy centers where people usually counsel women against abortion.

One-Child Policy Riots

LOCATION: China

DATE: May 2007

In 1979 the government of China created a policy to help slow the growth of its population. The policy allowed most Chinese couples to have just one child. Sometimes government officials firmly enforced the policy. Other times they were more relaxed about the rules. Still, the policy was not always popular among the people, especially in rural areas.

Early 2007 was one period when officials enforced the policy very strictly. They sent teams into Chinese villages to collect fines from people who had more than one child. If people could not afford to pay, they faced other forms of punishment. In response, many farmers began a riot to protest these punishments in late May. Over a period of several days, farmers destroyed government buildings and cars. They fought with police and government officials.

In the end, the riot had little effect on China's one-child policy. In the mid-2010s, however, Chinese officials changed the policy. The new policy allowed Chinese couples to have two children.

A growing nation

In 1949 the nation known as the People's Republic of China, or just China, formed. The new government, led by Chairman Mao Zedong (pronounced MAHoh DZEH-duhng; 1893–1976), immediately began to work to make the quality of life in China better. The government improved sanitation. Sanitation is the process of keeping communities clean and healthy. It involves removing trash, cleaning streets, and building systems to carry away and treat human waste. Medicine improved, too.

At the same time, Mao encouraged people to have children. Mao believed that more children meant more people to join the workforce someday. He believed that more workers would help China's economy grow. An economy is the system in a country through which goods are produced, distributed, and purchased. A country with a growing economy generally has a strong workforce and more wealth. These factors benefit the people who live in that country.

In 1949 China had a population of about 550 million people. According to the website Asia for Educators, China's population increased rapidly, adding another 112 million people by 1964. The population grew fast and more workers were becoming involved in industry rather than agriculture. A famine occurred between 1959 and 1961. A famine is an extreme shortage of food. The country's food supply could not keep up with the growing population. Between 30 million to 45 million people died.

The country's leaders realized that China had a population problem. They knew that the birth rate had to slow down if the country were to continue to grow and develop its economy. The birth rate is the number of live births per 1,000 people in a population in one year. During the 1970s, leaders introduced a policy known as "late, long, few." The policy encouraged couples to wait until later in life to have children, to wait longer between children, and to have fewer children. The policy did help slow China's birth rate. Still, Chinese leaders believed that more had to be done.

During the 1970s, leaders introduced a policy known as "late, long, few." The policy encouraged couples to wait until later in life to have children, to wait longer between children, and to have fewer children. The policy did help slow China's birth rate.

Introducing the one-child policy

Between 1949 and 1979 China's population swelled from about 550 million people to about 975 million people. The "late, long, few" policy helped slow the birth rate in the 1970s. However, government leaders wanted to slow the birth rate even more. The growing population was becoming a problem. It threatened the plans that Chinese leaders had for improving their nation. As a result, leaders introduced a one-child policy.

China's one-child policy basically set a limit of one child per couple. Chinese officials did not apply the policy evenly across the population. They were very stern about the policy for couples in cities but less firm about it for people in rural areas. Even so, people who lived in rural areas resisted the policy. Some had two or even three children. Over time, the Chinese government added certain exceptions to the rule. Males are valued over females in China because males are viewed as being stronger and more responsible with a greater earning potential. If a first child was a girl, a couple was sometimes allowed to have a second child. If a first child had a disability, a couple could have a second child. Ethnic minorities were allowed to have more than one child. An ethnic minority is a group of people with a shared culture or background who make up a small portion of a country's total population.

Enforcement of China's one-child policy varied over time. Officials were stricter at some times than at others. Enforcement of the policy could be quite harsh. Some couples with multiple children had to pay fines. Sometimes officials forced women to have abortions if they had not received approval for a second child. Other times officials forced couples to have medical procedures that made it impossible for them to have more children. Some workplaces posted notices that identified the women who were allowed to become pregnant. The idea behind the notices was to pressure other women to avoid becoming pregnant.

Some couples made difficult decisions to avoid breaking the rules of the one-child policy. If couples were going to have only one child, they wanted a son. As a result, some couples who learned that they were going to have a girl chose to have an abortion instead. In rural areas, couples sometimes abandoned, or even killed, female babies.

The road to riots

Families in rural areas often resisted the one-child policy. Families who lived on farms depended on children to help with the work. Since farmers provided food for the Chinese population, the government did not always firmly enforce the one-child policy for rural families. Other times, however, the government treated rural families harshly.

In 2007 the government sent work teams to southern China to enforce the one-child policy. Among the places the work teams visited were Guangxi (pronounced GWONG-SHE) and Guangdong (pronounced GWONG-DUNG). From February to May, work teams carrying sledgehammers (large, heavy hammers) visited many villages in the

Reproductive Rights

Forced Abortions and Sterilization in China

This primary source excerpt was taken from an interview given by Chen Guangcheng, a blind Chinese activist who advocates for people with disabilities. In the early 21st century Chen looked into reports of women being forced to have abortions during a government crackdown of the one-child policy. Due to his activism, he encountered difficulties with the government and fled China for the United States. China ended its one-child policy in 2016, allowing couples two children.

As soon as someone reports to the government that someone is pregnant or is having a second child, the workers of the family planning department will use any means necessary to come to your home, put you in their car and take you to the hospital for a forced abortion and sterilization operation.

Many times these teams would come at night, with weapons such as clubs. They will jump over the walls around your home, open your front gate, and drag pregnant women off their beds without giving them a chance to put on decent clothes, and force them into the car and to the hospital for an abortion. Forced to not just abort, but also be sterilized.

They also force you to sign, under coercion, an agreement with them. Of course, in reality no one signs of free will but if you don't then they will force you to sign, because once you've signed it then it absolves them of any possible legal ramifications from what they have done to you.

What I have just described is occurring very commonly in China.

If they don't catch the pregnant woman then they will arrest her relatives such as her spouse, siblings, parents, even her uncles and aunts are all possible targets to be captured by them and be taken back to the family planning department and locked up for a few days to even months at a time, and beaten every day. Some places there will even be ridiculous rules, for example if in this area one family has violated the one-child policy they [authorities] will arrest everyone within 50 meters [50 yards] of that house and lock them up.

The people [in China] live very close to one another, most of the homes are built together so we are easily talking about up to twenty families being arrested, and beaten up while they are locked away. This has been done for decades, and has severely destroyed any chance for China to have rule of law. They [authorities] will lock you up in the family planning department and beat you everyday and then will use a cover story and say that they are merely "educating" them and "teaching" them about the one-child policy.

SOURCE: Chen Guangcheng. "Chen Guangchen: The One-Child Policy." The Freedom Collection, George W. Bush Institute. Available online at http://freedomcollection.org/interviews/chen_guangcheng/?vidid=1052 (accessed October 15, 2017). Courtesy of George W. Bush Institute.

region. The work teams forced families with more than one child to pay fines. The fines ranged from $65 to $9,000. According to reports, some families who already had paid fines for second or third children were forced to pay again.

Reproductive Rights

Villagers shared stories online about families who could not afford to pay. Work teams sometimes took personal property from these families. People in the region reported that work teams took cattle, electronic equipment, dishes, household items, and motorcycles. The work teams froze some families' bank accounts. As a result, the families could not access money they had saved in banks. Sometimes the work teams used their sledgehammers to destroy families' homes and property.

Some newspapers reported that work teams used a machine to knock down a man's house when he could not afford to pay the fines. Other reports stated that work teams forced women to have abortions if they did not have approval to have another child. Many residents of Guangxi and Guangdong became angry as a result of these events.

One-child policy riots

As news of the work teams' punishments spread, thousands of farmers began to riot in May 2007. Some of the worst rioting occurred in Shapi (pronounced SHAY-PEE) Township in Guangdong. Rioters broke down the wall of a government building. They raided the building's offices and damaged computers and documents. They then set fire to the building.

Elsewhere rioters chased government officials and members of work teams and beat them. Some rioters fought with police. Others overturned cars and lit the vehicles on fire.

Angry residents tell foreign journalists how government work teams carried out the enforcement of China's one-child policy in the country in May 2007. Thousands of citizens clashed with police in a riot over an official campaign that residents said included forced abortions, property destruction, and arrests. Residents were demanding that authorities make amends for the brutal three-month campaign to enforce family-planning rules. © GOH CHAI HIN/AFP/GETTY IMAGES.

Chinese government officials refused to comment on or provide information about the riots. Chinese media were not allowed to report on the riots either. American newspapers gathered information from online accounts from villagers and other sources. They reported that the rioting took place over a period of three to four days. About 3,000 people participated in the riots. Reports suggested that two to five people died during the riots, but those numbers could not be proven. Many people were arrested.

The one-child policy riots did not result in any immediate changes. The policy remained in place in China until the mid-2010s.

Results of the one-child policy

China's one-child policy had mixed results. The policy succeeded in slowing China's birth rate. According to the *Encyclopedia of Environmental Issues*, China's population would have had about 300 million more people by 2010 if the one-child policy had not been created.

China managed to grow its economy at the same time that it slowed its birth rate. As a result, people enjoyed many benefits. Their living standards improved. They had access to better education. They received better health care and lived longer.

The one-child policy had some negative results, however. By the mid-2010s, the number of people of working age in China was getting smaller. Government officials worried that this could hurt China's economy. At the same time, the population of older people in China was growing. According to Will Worley of the *Independent*, more than 15 percent of China's people were older than 60 in 2014. Because so many female fetuses were aborted or baby girls abandoned or killed, fewer females exist to take care of aging parents.

In addition, China was expected to have about 24 million "extra" males by 2020, according to the *Encyclopedia of Environmental Issues*. China also had many "invisible" children. These were children whose births were never registered with the government. The government had no official record of these children. It is as if they did not exist.

Revised family-planning policy

In 2009 rumors spread that the Chinese government planned to end the one-child policy. No changes were made to the policy that year, though.

Six years later, in 2015, the government announced that the one-child policy would end on December 31.

As of January 1, 2016, China began to allow two children per couple throughout the country. The Xinhua (pronounced SHEEN-HWAH) News Agency, the official news agency of China's government, explained that the change was meant to balance the population of China and help with the problem of China's aging population.

Planned Parenthood Protests

LOCATION: United States

DATE: February 11, 2017

Planned Parenthood is one of the largest providers of reproductive health services in the United States. According to Planned Parenthood, it serves more than 2.5 million people per year at centers across the country. Many of those who get health services at Planned Parenthood are low income. However, Planned Parenthood is often the target of protests. In addition to a variety of health services, the organization provides abortions. Many people who think that abortion is wrong, such as pro-life groups, oppose the organization because it offers the medical procedure to women. They also feel that the US government should cut funding to Planned Parenthood because it offers abortion services, even though by law federal funds cannot be used for abortions. Pro-choice supporters believe that Planned Parenthood should continue to receive funding because it provides essential health services to people across the country.

Pro-life groups have organized numerous protests against Planned Parenthood. The demonstrations mostly focused on the issue of abortion itself. The focus of these protests has changed over time. Pro-lifers began to protest the government funding of Planned Parenthood. A movement called #ProtestPP organized rallies to take place on February 11, 2017, in cities across the United States to protest the government funding of Planned Parenthood.

Pro-choice advocates organized their own counterprotests for the same day. They showed up at the sites of numerous #ProtestPP demonstrations to show their support not only for a woman's right to choose but also for Planned Parenthood and the many services it provides to women.

Planned Parenthood

Planned Parenthood Federation of America, commonly known as Planned Parenthood, is a nonprofit organization that provides health services to women, men, and children. As a nonprofit, Planned Parenthood does not operate to make money. It offers reproductive health services such as birth control, pregnancy testing, tests and treatment for sexually transmitted diseases, and cancer screenings. It provides sexual education and works to protect reproductive rights. Planned Parenthood also participates in medical research projects.

As the largest provider of reproductive health services in the United States, Planned Parenthood has more than 600 health centers across the country. These centers offer a variety of services. The organization receives money from the government, from private citizens' donations, and from patients who receive services.

History of the organization An activist and nurse named Margaret Sanger founded what would become Planned Parenthood in 1916. She opened the first clinic in Brooklyn, New York, to give women advice about family planning and to distribute birth control information, which was illegal in the United States at the time. The Comstock Act banned the distribution of birth control information and devices. Police arrested Sanger, but she continued her efforts.

More women's health clinics opened throughout the United States. In 1938 a US judge lifted the federal ban on the distribution of birth control information and devices. After this time, clinics around the United States could legally distribute contraceptives. In 1942 some of the clinics organized to officially become the Planned Parenthood Federation of America. At this time, more than 400 clinics were providing contraceptives to people in the United States.

Abortion was illegal in the United States at this time. Many women sought illegal abortions to end unwanted pregnancies. At times, untrained individuals performed these illegal procedures. Many women were seriously injured or died from unsafe abortions.

In 1970 several states legalized abortion. These included New York, Hawaii, Alaska, and Washington. That same year, Planned Parenthood of Syracuse, New York, began providing abortions. This was the first Planned Parenthood clinic in the country to provide abortion services. In 1971 two lawyers filed a lawsuit, *Roe v. Wade*, against the state of Texas to make abortion legal there. The case eventually made its way to the US

An activist and nurse named Margaret Sanger founded what would become Planned Parenthood in 1916. She opened the first clinic in Brooklyn, New York, to give women advice about family planning and to distribute birth control information, which was illegal in the United States at the time.

Reproductive Rights

Norma McCorvey

Norma McCorvey (1947–2017) was the plaintiff, or the person who files a lawsuit, in the US Supreme Court case *Roe v. Wade*. The decision in *Roe* legalized abortion in the United States in 1973. McCorvey was known as Jane Roe in court to keep her identity a secret. At the time, she was pregnant and seeking an abortion in Texas, but the procedure was illegal there.

McCorvey had a troubled childhood and lived on her own from a young age. She married an older man but left him when she was pregnant. She gave birth to a daughter, and her mother raised the child. She later had another daughter but put her up for adoption. When McCorvey became pregnant a third time, she decided that she wanted to have an abortion, but it was not legal in Texas. She did not have enough money to travel to another state where the procedure was legal to obtain an abortion.

She met two lawyers, Linda Coffee (1942–) and Sarah Weddington (1945–), who convinced her to become the plaintiff in their case, which they filed to challenge Texas's strict abortion law. The defendant was Henry Wade (1914–2001), who was a lawyer representing the state of Texas. The case, *Roe v. Wade*, made its way through the court system. The Supreme Court eventually heard the case.

By the time the decision was made in 1973, McCorvey had given birth and put her child up for adoption. She lived a quiet life in the years that followed the *Roe v. Wade* decision. McCorvey eventually changed her mind about abortion and became a pro-life supporter. She wrote two books about her life and her new views on abortion. She worked to educate others and led efforts to overturn, or reverse, the *Roe* decision. She wanted to make abortion illegal again. McCorvey died in February 2017.

Supreme Court, which legalized abortion in the United States in 1973 through its decision in *Roe*. Planned Parenthood then began offering abortion services at many of its clinics across the country.

Debate over abortion

The legalization of abortion began a heated debate between those on both sides of the issue. Pro-life supporters worked to convince others that abortion was wrong. They protested against *Roe v. Wade* and those who defended abortion. Pro-lifers tried to overturn *Roe v. Wade*. They put pressure on lawmakers to make abortion illegal again.

Pro-choice advocates focused on making sure that women had reproductive health rights and access to quality care. They believed that women should have a choice about what happens to their bodies. They wanted to protect a woman's right to have an abortion, obtain birth control, and access sexual education materials.

Reproductive Rights

Attorney Gloria Allred and Norma McCorvey (right), also known as Jane Roe, the plaintiff from the landmark court case Roe vs. Wade during Pro Choice Rally, July 4, 1989, in Burbank, California. © BOB RIHA, JR./GETTY IMAGES.

Pro-life groups launched protests against Planned Parenthood and other health centers that performed abortions. They held demonstrations outside of clinics to scare patients who were there to obtain abortions. They carried signs with disturbing images of aborted fetuses and called patients seeking abortions "murderers." They also threatened violence against Planned Parenthood staff. The violent acts against Planned Parenthood increased. Abortion opponents set clinics on fire, committed acid attacks, planted bombs at the facilities, planned and carried out the murders of doctors who performed abortions, and killed several people at abortion-provider facilities.

Government funding and Planned Parenthood

Planned Parenthood began receiving government funds in 1970. These funds are from Title X, which is also known as the National Family Planning Program. Title X is a grant that provides family planning services to those who cannot afford them. Money in the form of a grant does not have to be paid back. Planned Parenthood also receives federal money from Medicaid. Medicaid is government health-care coverage for people who cannot afford to buy health insurance. Medicaid pays Planned Parenthood for services provided to people who are covered by it.

Opponents of abortion asked members of Congress to pass laws limiting funding to Planned Parenthood because the organization performed abortions. In 1976 Congress passed the Hyde Amendment. This amendment banned the use of federal funds to pay for abortions unless the woman's life was in danger or in cases of sexual assault or abuse. This meant that women who received health-care coverage from the government through Medicaid could not use this insurance to cover abortion services. Many people felt that the passage of the Hyde Amendment hurt many women who could not afford abortion services on their own.

The use of government funds continued to be an important issue in the years that followed for Planned Parenthood. Planned Parenthood states that abortions account for only 3 percent of its services. And, after the Hyde Amendment, government funds cannot be used for abortion services. However, government funding of Planned Parenthood was questioned again in 2011 and 2015, when some Republican members of Congress pushed for a plan to take government funds away from Planned Parenthood. Funding for government organizations was set to run out, and some members of Congress proposed letting this happen as a way to stop giving money to Planned Parenthood. Other members of Congress did not support this plan because it would shut down the government. Both times the plan did not pass. The government did not shut down, and Planned Parenthood kept its federal funds.

Funding Planned Parenthood once again became an important issue during and after the 2016 presidential election. Candidates differed on their views of abortion. As the first female candidate for a major national party, Hillary Clinton was in favor of reproductive rights, including access to abortion. She supported funding for Planned Parenthood and the organization endorsed her candidacy. She stated in her political platform that she would "defend access to affordable contraception, preventive care, and safe and legal abortion." She also noted her belief that "personal health decisions should be made by a woman, her family, and her faith, with the counsel of her doctor." Candidate Donald Trump expressed very different opinions. After the election, President Trump (whose views on the issue have varied over time) and Vice President Mike Pence, both pro-life Republicans, vowed to limit abortion access. Pence was

Reproductive Rights

Several hundred Planned Parenthood supporters rallied in Washington Square Park in New York City to protest against proposed cuts to the service. Similar rallies were held around the country on February 11, 2017, to counter pro-life rallies held that day calling on Congress to defund Planned Parenthood. © A KATZ/SHUTTERSTOCK.COM.

a pro-life supporter who spoke at the March for Life in January 2017. The appointment of conservative Neil Gorsuch (1967–), another opponent of abortion, to the US Supreme Court also helped to strengthen the pro-life movement. A conservative view favors traditional ideas or policies. Planned Parenthood president Cecile Richards noted that within days of President Trump's election in November 2016, that it had experienced an "unprecedented outpouring of support" in donations and volunteers. By March 2017, National Public Radio reported that Planned Parenthood had gained over 600,000 new donors and 36,000 new volunteers.

Planned Parenthood protests

An organization known as #ProtestPP, which is made up of state and national pro-life groups, formed in 2015 to protest Planned Parenthood because it offered abortions to women. It scheduled protests for August 22, 2015, and October 10, 2015, at various Planned Parenthood clinics throughout the United States. Tens of thousands of supporters joined more than 600 individual protests on those days. It followed with a nationwide protest of Planned Parenthood in April 2016 that it intended to hold each year after. #ProtestPP then held several prayer gatherings outside of more than 100 Planned Parenthood locations in October 2016 during the organization's 100th-year anniversary.

The focus of the #ProtestPP shifted to the funding of Planned Parenthood in early 2017. Supporters believed that the government should take the funds from Planned Parenthood and give them to health organizations that do not offer abortion services. #ProtestPP planned rallies for February 11, 2017. Pro-life supporters gathered outside of more than 200 Planned Parenthood locations in cities across the United States. The purpose of the demonstrations was to protest the organization because it provides abortions and to urge Congress and the president to take away its government funding. It wanted to take away that funding even though the money cannot be used for abortions but is instead used to provide vital health services for low-income women. The protesters carried signs that read, "Pray to End Abortion" and "Defend Life."

Counterprotesters showed up at many of the #ProtestPP demonstrations to voice their side. Some Planned Parenthood supporters tried to block the #ProtestPP supporters. Others organized rallies outside of politicians' offices and government buildings to avoid conflict with the #ProtestPP demonstrators. Some of the pro-choice protests were larger than the pro-life ones. At a rally in Washington, DC, pro-choicers yelled, "Women must decide their fate." Pro-choice advocates believed that Planned Parenthood should continue to receive government funds so that they could continue to offer health services such as breast and cervical cancer screenings, tests and treatment for sexually transmitted diseases, birth control, and sex education. The demonstrations in February 2017 were mostly peaceful.

Future of funding

As of mid-2017, the government continued to fund Planned Parenthood. However, in January of that year, the House of Representatives passed the No Taxpayer Funding for Abortion and Abortion Insurance Full Disclosure Act, also known as HR 7. The bill, if fully passed, would not allow insurance companies to cover abortion procedures. Some states already ban insurance companies from paying for abortions. HR 7 would prevent all insurance companies in the United States from providing funds for abortions. The bill still has to be voted on by the Senate and signed by the president for it to become a law.

For More Information

BOOKS

Ford, Lynne E., ed. "March for Women's Lives (1992, 2004)." In *Encyclopedia of Women and American Politics*. New York: Facts on File, 2008, 299–300.

Hoffman, Steve G. "Operation Rescue." In *Culture Wars in America: An Encyclopedia of Issues, Viewpoints, and Voices*. 2nd ed. Edited by Roger Chapman and James Ciment. New York: M.E. Sharpe, 2014, 696–697.

Reagan, Leslie J. *When Abortion Was a Crime: Women, Medicine, and Law in the United States, 1867–1973*. Berkeley: University of California Press, 1998.

Weldon, Lynn L., and Karen N. Kähler. "Population-Control and One-Child Policies." In *Encyclopedia of Environmental Issues*. Rev. ed. Vol. 3. Edited by Craig W. Allin. Pasadena, CA: Salem Press, 2011, 987–989.

PERIODICALS

Beech, Hannah. "China Abandons One-Child Rule as Its Population Ages and Men Outnumber Women." *Time* (October 29, 2015). Available online at http://time.com/4092453/china-one-child-rule/ (accessed August 30, 2017).

Fitzpatrick, Laura. "China's One-Child Policy." *Time* (July 27, 2009). Available online at http://content.time.com/time/world/article/0,8599,1912861,00.html (accessed August 30, 2017).

Hirsch, Arthur. "Operation Rescue to Halt Abortion Clinics Blockade but Group Says It May Resume Efforts." *Baltimore Sun* (April 30, 1992). Available online at http://articles.baltimoresun.com/1992-04-30/news/1992121047_1_operation-rescue-abortion-clinics-abortion-rights (accessed August 28, 2017).

Kahn, Joseph. "Chinese Villagers Riot over Stricter Population-Control." *New York Times* (May 21, 2007). Available online at http://www.nytimes.com/2007/05/21/world/asia/21iht-china.3.5808227.html?mcubz=0 (accessed August 30, 2017).

Khazan, Olga. "Bringing Down the Flowers: The Controversial History of Abortion." *Atlantic* (March 2, 2016). Available online at https://www.theatlantic.com/health/archive/2016/03/bringing-down-the-flowers-the-controversial-history-of-abortion/471762/ (accessed August 31, 2017).

Langer, Emily. "Norma McCorvey, Jane Roe of Roe v. Wade Decision Legalizing Abortion Nationwide, Dies at 69." *Washington Post* (February 18, 2017). Available online at https://www.washingtonpost.com/national/norma-mccorvey-jane-roe-of-roe-v-wade-decision-legalizing-abortion-dies-at-69/2017/02/18/24b83108-396e-11e6-8f7c-d4c723a2becb_story.html (accessed August 31, 2017).

Manegold, Catherine S. "Abortion War, Buffalo Front: Top Guns Use Battle Tactics." *New York Times* (April 25, 1992). Available online at http://www.nytimes.com/1992/04/25/nyregion/abortion-war-buffalo-front-top-guns-use-battle-tactics.html?pagewanted=all&mcubz=3 (accessed August 28, 2017).

Stumpe, Joe, and Monica Davey. "Abortion Doctor Shot to Death in Kansas Church." *New York Times* (June 1, 2009). Available online at http://www.nytimes.com/2009/06/01/us/01tiller.html?pagewanted=all&mcubz=3 (accessed August 30, 2017).

Wheeler, Linda, and Lyle V. Harris. "80,000 March on Washington." *Washington Post* (March 10, 1986). Available online at https://www.washingtonpost.com/archive/local/1986/03/10/80000-march-on-washington/fc5fb1b2-c6c7-4ab5-95fa-21c3ac305341/?utm_term=.f7225b69c9b2 (accessed August 30, 2017).

Worley, Will. "China Ditches One-Child Policy—Launches Two-Child Policy." *Independent* (December 28, 2015). Available online at http://www.independent.co.uk/news/world/asia/china-ditches-one-child-policy-and-launches-two-child-policy-a6788246.html (accessed August 30, 2017).

Zauzmer, Julie, and Sarah Pulliam Bailey. "March for Life: Pence Speaks as Thousands Assemble at Washington Monument." *Washington Post* (January 27, 2017). Available online at https://www.washingtonpost.com/local/march-for-life-thousands-assemble-at-washington-monument/2017/01/27/7d880d52-e40a-11e6-ba11-63c4b4fb5a63_story.html?utm_term=.3dd582a252c8 (accessed October 13, 2017).

WEBSITES

"Accelerating Uptake of Voluntary, Rights-Based Family Planning in Developing Countries: Evidence Brief." World Health Organization, February 11, 2017. http://apps.who.int/iris/bitstream/10665/255859/1/WHO-RHR-17.07-eng.pdf?ua=1 (accessed October 18, 2017).

"China's Leaders to Nix 1-Child Policy after 35 Years." CBS News, October 29, 2015. https://www.cbsnews.com/news/china-communist-party-to-abolish-one-child-policy/ (accessed August 30, 2017).

Darroch, Jacqueline E., Vanessa Woog, Akinrinola Bankole, and Lori S. Ashford. "Adding It Up: Costs and Benefits of Meeting the Contraceptive Needs of Adolescents" Guttmacher Institute, 2016. https://www.guttmacher.org/sites/default/files/report_pdf/adding-it-up-adolescents-report.pdf (accessed October 18, 2017).

Dwyer, Colin. "Protests against Planned Parenthood Rouse Dueling Rallies Nationwide." National Public Radio, February 11, 2017. http://www.npr.org/sections/thetwo-way/2017/02/11/514717975/protests-against-planned-parenthood-rouse-dueling-rallies-nationwide (accessed August 31, 2017).

Fox, Maggie. "Trump Contraceptive Move Could Lead to More Abortions." NBC News, October 8, 2017. https://www.nbcnews.com/health/health-care/trump-contraceptive-move-could-lead-more-abortions-n808581 (accessed October 8, 2017).

"History of Abortion." National Abortion Federation. https://prochoice.org/education-and-advocacy/about-abortion/history-of-abortion/ (accessed August 31, 2017).

"History of the March for Life." March for Life Education and Defense Fund. http://marchforlife.org/history-of-the-march-for-life/ (accessed August 30, 2017).

"Issues and Trends in China's Demographic History." Asia for Educators, 2009. http://afe.easia.columbia.edu/special/china_1950_population.htm (accessed August 31, 2017).

McBride, Alex. "Expanding Civil Rights: Landmark Cases Roe v. Wade." Public Broadcasting Service, December 2006. https://www.pbs.org/wnet/supremecourt/rights/landmark_roe.html (accessed August 31, 2017).

"Planned Parenthood at a Glance." Planned Parenthood. https://www.plannedparenthood.org/about-us/who-we-are/planned-parenthood-at-a-glance (accessed October 3, 2017).

Ravitz, Jessica. "The Surprising History of Abortion in the United States." CNN, June 27, 2016. http://www.cnn.com/2016/06/23/health/abortion-history-in-united-states/index.html (accessed August 31, 2017).

"Why Defund Planned Parenthood?" #ProtestPP. http://protestpp.com/about (accessed August 31, 2017).

18

Resistance to Nazis

White Rose Movement
(Germany) **592**

Holocaust Resistance
in Denmark **597**

Warsaw Ghetto Uprising
(Poland) **602**

Treblinka Death Camp
Revolt (Poland) **607**

People across Europe began to resist Adolf Hitler (1889–1945) and the National Socialist German Workers' Party, also known as the Nazi (pronounced NOT-see) Party, soon after they took control of Germany in 1933. Born in Austria, Hitler became the leader of Germany. He served as chancellor, or head of the government, of Germany from 1933 until 1945. Hitler wanted to make Germany a powerful country. He wanted Germany's territory to expand across Europe.

Hitler started this expansion by ordering the invasion of Poland in 1939. In response to the invasion, several European countries joined together as the Allied powers, or Allies, and declared war on Germany and the Nazis. World War II (1939–1945) had begun. By the end of the war, many other countries were involved in the fighting. The Allies included Australia, Belgium, Brazil, Canada, France, Greece, Poland the Soviet Union, the United Kingdom, and the United States. The Nazis in Germany joined with several other countries to form the Axis powers. Some of these countries were Bulgaria, Finland, Hungary, Italy, and Japan.

Germany eventually invaded and took control of large parts of Europe. Nazi rule stretched across the continent. At first no one was powerful enough to resist the Nazis. As a result, the Nazis were able to carry out Hitler's plan to expand Germany. Part of this plan involved removing Jews from German life. Jews are people who follow the religion of Judaism (pronounced JEW-da-i-zem). Hitler thought Jews were inferior to, or not as good as, other German citizens.

To separate Jews from the rest of German society, Hitler first ordered all Jews to be placed in ghettos. Ghettos are poor areas of cities where certain groups of people are forced to live. Then, in the early 1940s Hitler ordered the killing of the Jews in Europe. The Nazis tried to carry out Hitler's orders by sending Jews to death camps. These were prison camps

WORDS TO KNOW

Allied powers: The group of nations that fought Nazi Germany and other Axis powers during World War II.

Aryans: The Nazis' idea of a master race of people who were tall and had blond hair and blue eyes.

Communism: A political system in which private ownership of property is eliminated and government directs all economic production. The goods produced and accumulated wealth are, in theory, shared relatively equally by all.

Concentration camp: Prison center where Jews and other prisoners of the Nazis were forced to work under extremely harsh conditions.

Death camp: Also known as extermination camps; camps where Nazis murdered millions of Jews and other prisoners, many in gas chambers, from across Europe during World War II.

Deport: To send to another country or area, as the Nazis deported Jews and others to prison and death camps.

Final Solution: The Nazis' plan for killing all Jews in Nazi-controlled areas.

Ghetto: Poor area of a city where certain groups of people are forced to live.

Hitler Youth: Organization that taught Nazi ideas to children.

Holocaust: Nazi Germany's mass killing of European Jews and others from groups they persecuted during World War II.

Partisans: Members of armed organizations that fight against forces that are controlling their country.

Socialism: A political system in which the central government provides goods and services to all members of a society equally.

---

that held Jewish prisoners from across Europe. The Nazis killed millions of Jews in the camps' gas chambers, which were rooms the Nazis filled with poison gas. Nazi Germany's mass killing of European Jews during World War II is called the Holocaust (pronounced HO-luh-kost).

Not all Europeans simply accepted Nazi Germany's practices. In the early 1940s people in various European countries united to resist Nazi rule. Resistance groups formed within Germany and in countries controlled by Germany. These countries included Denmark, France, Lithuania, the Netherlands, and Poland.

Resistance groups sprang up throughout Europe. These groups were formed by people who wanted to take a stand against, or resist, Nazi tactics. The resistance included both Jews and non-Jews. Some groups resisted the Nazis peacefully. They secretly passed out advertisements that criticized the Nazi Party. Other resistance groups used violence. They attacked German supply lines and killed Nazi spies. Many Jews openly resisted the Nazis in the ghettos and death camps. In these cases, Jewish prisoners stole weapons and tried to kill their Nazi guards. The Nazis killed most people who tried to resist their rule.

All of these resistance movements continued working against the Nazis throughout Europe into the mid-1940s. The Allies defeated Germany in 1945. Germany's defeat freed Europe from Nazi rule.

Start of the Nazi resistance

The Nazis ruled most of Europe with total power during much of World War II. They removed Jews from their homes and put them in concentration camps or death camps. Concentration camps were Nazi prison centers where Jews and other prisoners were forced to work. Many were worked to death. The Nazis arrested, and often killed, anyone who publicly disagreed with Nazi laws.

Different groups of Europeans responded differently to the Nazis' harsh treatment of Jews and others. Some non-Jewish Europeans did nothing as the Nazis rounded up and arrested Jews. They believed it was better not to get involved. Other Europeans were simply too afraid to help the Jews. They knew the Nazis killed those who helped Jews hide from arrest.

Some Europeans resisted Nazi rule any way they could. Many used peaceful methods of resistance, though some used violence. Resistance movements formed in numerous countries throughout Europe. Even some citizens within Germany tried to resist Nazi power.

German Socialists and Communists were among the first groups to resist the Nazis in Germany. Socialists are followers of socialism. Socialism is a political system in which a central government provides goods and services to all members of a society equally. Communists are followers of Communism. Communism is a political system in which property is owned collectively and people are paid according to what they need.

Despite their name, the Nazis opposed socialism. They opposed Communism, too. They tried to silence those throughout Germany who believed in these ideas. Some Socialists and Communists resisted the Nazis by secretly attacking Nazi ideas in writing. The groups then made copies of their writings and quietly passed them out to the German people. The Socialists and Communists hoped their writings would convince Germans not to support the Nazi government. However, Nazi forces soon found those responsible for the writings. The Nazis arrested

Resistance to Nazis

CRITICAL THINKING QUESTIONS

1. How were the Treblinka prisoners most likely feeling as they prepared to revolt and escape? Why do you think they decided to carry out such a dangerous plan?

2. How do you think the prisoners who escaped from Treblinka survived outside the prison?

3. What do you think of Hitler's intention to make the Danes allies of the Germans? Should the Danes have done whatever the Nazis asked simply to stay safe? Explain.

4. What do you think of the Danes' willingness to live under Nazi control to protect Danish Jews? What does this suggest about Danish society and values?

5. Why did members of the White Rose risk their lives to resist the Nazis? What values do you think drove them to care more about freedom than their own safety?

6. Why do you think so many Germans did not resist the Nazis? Is it possible for that many people to agree with the Nazis' ideas?

7. Why do you suppose the Warsaw Ghetto Uprising inspired other Jewish prisoners in Nazi camps to revolt even though that uprising failed? How do you think the uprising made other Jews feel about their own situations?

---

the Socialists and Communists and sent them to concentration camps. Many of these prisoners died in the camps.

Peaceful resistance

European resistance to Nazis grew into the 1940s. Like the Socialists and Communists in Germany, some Europeans resisted peacefully. An example of peaceful Nazi resistance inside Germany was the White Rose movement. College students in Munich (pronounced MYU-nik), Germany, started this secret resistance group in 1942. Two of these students were brother and sister Hans (1918–1943) and Sophie (1921–1943) Scholl.

The White Rose movement focused on resisting Nazis with ideas. The Scholls made pamphlets that spoke out against Nazi policies. The siblings wanted to convince the German people not to support the Nazi government. Members of the White Rose movement also painted anti-Nazi messages on walls. The Nazis caught the Scholls and other White Rose members in 1943 and quickly executed them.

Other groups peacefully resisted the Nazis by helping Jews avoid arrest. Some non-Jewish Europeans hid Jews in their homes. Others gave Jews the supplies they needed to survive. These supplies included clothing, food, weapons, money, and false papers. Papers identified people in

Nazi territories. The papers revealed who was Jewish and who was not. Jews who received false papers could present themselves to Nazis as non-Jews. This could help them survive.

Some forms of peaceful resistance to Nazis were meant to show defiance, or disobedience. For instance, some German citizens refused to serve in the German military. Others listened to messages from the Allies on their radios, which the Nazis did not allow. Some prisoners in concentration camps formed religious study groups. The Nazis did not permit this, either. These actions did not hurt the Nazis directly. Sometimes they simply made people feel better about living under Nazi control.

Violent resistance

Armed resistance movements formed throughout Europe as Nazis took over more and more of the continent. The French resistance was a network of fighters who opposed the Nazi government in France. A similar resistance movement organized in Denmark after Germany invaded that country in April 1940. The Danish resistance attacked Nazi military areas. It destroyed Nazi railroads and killed people who spied on the Danes and reported back to the Nazis. These and other resistance groups in Europe helped Jews and others escape the Nazis. Sometimes they provided false papers. Other times they hid Jews and others from the Nazis.

Armed resistance groups in some countries fought the Nazis directly. This kind of organized resistance formed in countries such as Czechoslovakia (pronounced check-o-slo-VAH-key-uh), Greece, Poland, the Soviet Union, and Yugoslavia. People who fought in these groups were called partisans. Partisans are members of armed organizations that fight against forces that are controlling their country. Partisans planned dangerous missions against the Nazis. For instance, the Czech (pronounced CHECK) resistance killed Nazi officer Reinhard Heydrich (pronounced RINE-hart HI-drek; 1904–1942) in Prague (pronounced PRAWG), Czechoslovakia, in 1942.

The Polish resistance was one of the largest in Europe during World War II. It included more than 300 separate organizations throughout Poland. These were both military and political groups. The non-military resistance groups ran secret schools because the Nazis had closed many of Poland's schools.

The armed Polish resistance was called the Home Army. Officers of the Polish Army directed it. The officers trained fighters and collected

Resistance to Nazis

Polish resistance fighters in a fight with Nazi soldiers on the streets of war-torn Warsaw, 1944. © SOVFOTO/ UIG VIA GETTY.

weapons for the resistance. They planned attacks on the Nazis in Poland. The Home Army's most famous attack on Nazi forces was the Warsaw Ghetto Uprising of 1944. The Home Army attempted to free the Polish city of Warsaw from Nazi control during this conflict. Fighting in the city lasted from August 1 to October 2, 1944. The Nazis eventually defeated the Home Army. The uprising destroyed Warsaw and left hundreds of thousands of Polish citizens dead. The Nazis sent hundreds of thousands of survivors to concentration camps.

Armed resistance against Hitler

Violent resistance against the Nazis included attempts to kill Hitler. Numerous people tried to kill Hitler throughout World War II. Some attackers were individuals working alone. Others were German Army officers who secretly opposed Hitler's policies.

A Swiss student named Maurice Bavaud (pronounced buh-VOD; 1916–1941) tried to kill Hitler in 1938. Bavaud thought Hitler was the physical form of Satan, the devil of the Christian religion. Believing that Hitler might destroy the Roman Catholic Church, a major branch of Christianity, Bavaud wanted to kill Hitler to stop this from happening. He tried to shoot Hitler at a Nazi parade in Munich in November 1938, but he could not see him clearly enough. Bavaud then tried to leave

Germany, but the Nazis caught him. He confessed to trying to kill Hitler, and the Nazis later killed him.

German carpenter Johann Georg (pronounced YO-hawn GAY-org) Elser (1903–1945) tried to kill Hitler in 1939. Elser thought Hitler's policies would destroy Germany by forcing the nation into war. He wanted to kill Hitler to save Germany. Elser built a bomb and planted it in a brewery in Munich. Hitler planned to speak at the brewery on November 8, 1939. Elser timed his bomb to explode near Hitler while he was speaking. However, Hitler began speaking an hour early. As a result, the bomb exploded 13 minutes after Hitler had finished speaking and left the stage. The Nazis arrested Elser later that night. They killed him in 1945.

Several high-ranking German Army officers tried to kill Hitler in the early 1940s for various reasons. Most believed Hitler's policies were cruel and dangerous. They wanted to kill Hitler and end World War II. For example, in 1943 German Army officer Henning von Tresckow (pronounced TRESS-cow; 1901–1944) attempted to kill Hitler with a bomb planted inside a case of brandy, a type of alcohol. Tresckow asked a member of Hitler's staff to take the brandy with him on Hitler's plane to Berlin, Germany, and deliver it to a friend there. Tresckow later heard that Hitler had arrived safely in Berlin. Confused, Tresckow sent his partner to Berlin to get the bomb back. Tresckow discovered that the bomb's fuse had stopped working, which prevented the bomb from exploding.

One of the most famous plans to kill Hitler became known as the July 20 Plot. German Army officer Claus von Stauffenberg (pronounced CLOWSE von STOW-fen-berg; 1907–1944) was to take a briefcase with a bomb in it to Hitler's "Wolf's Lair" headquarters in Poland on July 20, 1944. Hitler would be at a meeting in a conference room there. Stauffenberg traveled to the headquarters and set down the briefcase near Hitler. However, another officer later moved the briefcase to the other side of a table leg. The bomb exploded, but the table leg protected Hitler from most of the explosion. As a result, Hitler survived. The Nazis soon arrested and killed Stauffenberg and his partners.

The Allied powers finally defeated Germany in the spring of 1945. Hitler killed himself that April. Throughout World War II, the Nazis crushed most attempts to resist them. Still, some groups, such as the Polish resistance, truly challenged Nazi rule. At the same time, every attempt to kill Hitler failed. Germany's defeat in 1945 freed Europe after six years of Nazi control.

White Rose Movement

LOCATION: Germany

DATE: June 1942–February 1943

The White Rose movement was a German resistance group that formed in Munich, Germany, in 1942 to oppose Adolf Hitler and the Nazi Party. Hitler and the Nazis rose to power in the 1930s. They wanted to expand Germany's territory and increase German power in Europe. Hitler started World War II when he ordered the invasion of Poland in 1939. Although many Germans supported Hitler and the Nazi Party, some opposed them. Those who opposed Nazi rule formed resistance groups to fight against the Nazis.

Brother and sister Hans and Sophie Scholl founded the White Rose in Munich, Germany, in 1942 to resist Hitler and the Nazis. The White Rose was a peaceful organization. Its members resisted Nazi rule by trying to convince Germans not to support Hitler. The Scholls disliked that the Nazis ruled Germany with total power. They also opposed the Nazis' mass killings of Jews.

White Rose members knew that they could not actually defeat the Nazis with their ideas. Instead they claimed that they wanted to save the spirit of Germany from Nazi influence. The Scholls and others created small paper advertisements called leaflets and left them for people in Munich and other cities to find. The leaflets contained writings that criticized the Nazis. White Rose members wanted educated Germans to read the leaflets and revolt against the Nazis.

The White Rose movement continued until early 1943. In February of that year someone informed the Gestapo (pronounced geh-STAW-po) of the Scholls' identities. The Gestapo was the Nazis' secret police force. Gestapo officers soon arrested the Scholls and another member of the group. The Nazis quickly executed members of the White Rose movement for their actions against Nazi Germany. The Nazis destroyed other attempts to resist them during World War II. In later decades Germans praised members of the White Rose for their actions against the Nazis.

Origins of the White Rose movement

The White Rose movement was one example of resistance to Nazis within Germany. Many Germans supported Hitler and the Nazi Party. They believed the Nazis would make Germany a powerful country.

Other Germans opposed the Nazis. They disliked how the Nazis used force to make all Germans follow Nazi laws. The Gestapo closely watched the German people to make sure they obeyed the Nazis. The Gestapo could arrest and kill anyone they caught criticizing the Nazis. Later in the 1930s and early 1940s, the Nazis started arresting Jews in Germany and other countries and making them prisoners in ghettos or concentration camps. Some Germans opposed this. Many others did not object for fear they would be sent to prison, too.

The idea that Nazis had total control of Germany angered university student Hans Scholl. Hans had once supported Hitler and the Nazis. He joined the Hitler Youth as a teenager in the early 1930s. The Hitler Youth was a group that taught Nazi ideas to children so they would grow up supporting the Nazi Party. Hans began to dislike the Hitler Youth as he got older. He realized that it was turning children into Nazis.

Sophie Scholl was featured on a postage stamp in Germany in the 1990s. © NEFTALI/ SHUTTERSTOCK.COM.

Hans served briefly in the German Army. While serving, he saw some of the Nazis' actions against Jews in Poland. The Nazis sent Polish Jews to concentration camps, where they were forced to work, or death camps, where they were killed. These actions deeply upset Hans.

Hans began studying medicine at the University of Munich in the early 1940s. There, he expressed his anti-Nazi ideas to others. His younger sister, Sophie, also opposed the Nazis. She also became a student at the University of Munich. The Scholls shared their thoughts on the Nazi Party with their friends at the university, including Alexander Schmorell (pronounced shmuh-RELL; 1917–1943) and Christoph Probst (1919–1943). The students agreed that Hitler was turning the German people into slaves of the Nazi Party. In 1942 the Scholls and their friends formed the White Rose movement to oppose the Nazis.

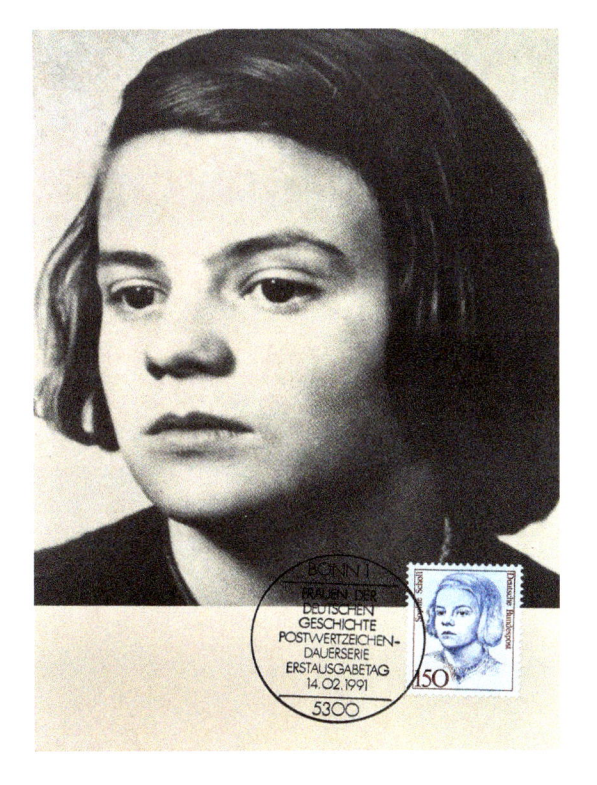

White Rose activities

Members of the White Rose knew they could not openly attack the Nazis. The Nazis would arrest and kill them for doing so. Instead, Hans and a fellow White Rose member began writing leaflets in the summer of 1942. The leaflets described the Nazis' secret actions. These actions included the killing of Jews and Polish citizens. The leaflets encouraged Germans to protest the Nazi Party. Members of the White Rose hoped the leaflets would convince educated Germans that Nazis were destroying Germany.

The Scholls and their friends secretly delivered their leaflets all over Munich. They left the first leaflet they wrote at the University of Munich. It stated that Nazis were evil and that the German people should resist them. The leaflet encouraged readers to make copies and pass them on to the German people.

The White Rose continued making leaflets throughout 1942. Group members soon expanded their activities. They sent leaflets to people in the mail. They had White Rose members deliver leaflets to other cities in Germany. Later the group turned to writing anti-Nazi messages on walls throughout Munich. First they traced outlines of the messages they wanted to write. Then they took the outlines out to the streets at night and wrote the messages in large letters on buildings and walls. Some of these graffiti messages read "Down with Hitler!" or "Hitler the Mass Murderer!" Others simply read "Freedom!"

Hiding from the Gestapo

The Scholls and their friends performed all of their activities in secret. However, they knew their leaflets and messages had attracted the Gestapo's attention. They also knew they were risking their lives by continuing to make the leaflets.

The Gestapo began searching for those responsible for the leaflets. Gestapo officers tried to trace the leaflets back to their starting point. They looked for possible sources of paper, envelopes, and postage needed to make and send the leaflets. The Gestapo tried to find the machines that White Rose members used to copy the leaflets. None of the Gestapo's methods worked. The Gestapo could not find the members of the White Rose.

End of the White Rose

In early 1943, the Soviet Union defeated Germany at the Battle of Stalingrad in the southwestern region of the Soviet Union. This defeat

Resistance to Nazis

Effects of the Battle of Stalingrad

Many modern historians refer to the Battle of Stalingrad as the turning point of World War II. The German defeat there convinced many Europeans that Nazi Germany was not as strong as it seemed. The battle inspired Europeans in many countries, including the members of the White Rose in Germany, to become more daring in resisting Nazi rule.

Nazi forces fought the Battle of Stalingrad against the Soviet Army from July 1942 to February 1943. The battle consisted of the Soviet Army's defense of the southwestern Soviet city of Stalingrad (later Volgograd) in Russia against the Nazis. Adolf Hitler wanted to control Stalingrad so he could use it as a base from which to capture more Soviet territory.

The Nazis attacked Stalingrad for many months. The Soviets fiercely defended the city. Any Soviet who could hold a weapon fought against the Nazis. Both sides lost many soldiers in the fighting. The Nazis advanced far into the city, but the Soviets eventually pushed them back. By early February 1943, the Soviets had killed or captured every German soldier in Stalingrad. A total of about 2 million people died in the battle.

The German defeat at the Battle of Stalingrad had enormous effects on Europeans. Hitler was embarrassed by his army's defeat. Europeans living under Nazi control started to doubt whether Germany was as powerful as Hitler had led the world to believe. After the Battle of Stalingrad, Danish people under Nazi rule started actively resisting their occupiers. The battle also encouraged the Scholls to print another White Rose pamphlet, which encouraged Germans in Munich to rebel against the Nazis.

The Battle of Stalingrad marked the point at which Germany lost its advantage in World War II. The Soviets attacked the Nazis from the east, while other Allied powers attacked from the west. Members of resistance groups such as the White Rose sensed the Nazis' newly revealed weaknesses. Individuals soon became bolder in their approaches to Nazi resistance. However, in the case of the White Rose, the Nazis still crushed all civilian attempts to resist them.

made many people realize that Nazi forces were not as strong as they claimed to be. Members of the White Rose felt this way, too. The Scholls decided to print another leaflet.

In February 1943, the Scholls created their sixth White Rose leaflet. It stated that Hitler had tricked Germans into giving away their freedom. It demanded that Hitler return freedom to the German people. It encouraged students in Munich to revolt against the Nazis.

On February 18, 1943, the Scholls left copies of the leaflet in the University of Munich's main stairwell. Sophie still had many copies left when she reached the top of the stairs. She threw them over the railing so they would fall to the bottom of the stairs. A university janitor saw Sophie

Resistance to Nazis

Leaflets, like those distributed by the White Rose, are part of a monument at the Univesity of Munich. © ANAHTIRIS / SHUTTERSTOCK.COM.

do this. He quickly called the Gestapo and told them about the Scholls. The Gestapo arrived and arrested the Scholls and then quickly found and arrested Probst.

The Scholls and Probst were taken to court on February 22, 1943. The judge in the trial wondered why the three young people would want to do so much harm to Germany. He noted that they all had gone to German schools and joined the Hitler Youth. Sophie responded, saying that many Germans believed what the White Rose movement believed. The difference was that members of the White Rose were brave enough to express those beliefs. In the end, the judge ruled that the Scholls and Probst were guilty of treason, or committing crimes against one's own country. The judge sentenced the three to death.

The Scholls were allowed to meet with their parents in prison later that day. Then they met with Probst one last time. The Nazis executed the Scholls and Probst a few hours after the trial. The Gestapo continued to search for more members of the White Rose movement. They eventually found Schmorell and various others. The Nazis tried and executed them, too.

The White Rose movement became well-known among Germans after World War II. Many Germans honored White Rose members as resistance heroes of Germany's Nazi era. The University of Munich later named one of its public squares after the Scholls. The names of other White Rose members appeared on schools and streets throughout Germany.

Holocaust Resistance in Denmark

LOCATION: Denmark
DATE: 1943

Beginning in 1939, Nazis under the leadership of German leader Adolf Hitler invaded many European nations. After taking control of the government, they arrested Jews who lived in these countries and sent them to concentration camps or death camps. The Nazis repeated this process in nearly every country they invaded from the late 1930s to the early 1940s. However, the Nazis treated Denmark differently.

The Nazis did not want to destroy Denmark or kill Danes (the people of Denmark). They considered Danes to be similar to the German people. Although the Nazis invaded Denmark in 1940, they let the Danish government continue to oversee the country. At first the Nazis did not even send Denmark's Jews to concentration camps. Relations between Germany and Denmark were mostly friendly.

The relationship between the two countries changed in 1943. The Allied powers, a group of nations that formed to fight the Nazis, started to defeat Germany on the battlefield that year. As a result of the Allied powers' success, the Danes began to resist Nazi control over Denmark. They stopped working for the Nazis. They attacked Nazi equipment and secretly destroyed Nazi property. They publicly protested the Nazis. In response the Nazis took control over the Danish government. They started searching for Jews to arrest and send to concentration camps.

Members of the Danish resistance stopped this from happening. They hid Jews from the Nazis; sometimes they took them to Sweden on boats. Sweden was neutral in World War II, which means that it did not take sides in the war. Almost all of Denmark's 7,500 Jews lived safely in Sweden for the rest of the war. Historians claim that the Danish resistance to the Nazis was responsible for protecting these people from being killed in the death camps.

Resistance to Nazis

Bent Melchior

Bent Melchior (pronounced MEL-key-or; 1929–) was 14 years old when Nazi violence made him flee his home country of Denmark in 1943. Before leaving, Melchior lived with his family in Copenhagen. His father was a rabbi, or Jewish teacher, at a synagogue (pronounced SIH-nuh-gog) in Copenhagen. Synagogues are Jewish prayer temples.

In September 1943 the Danish government warned the country's Jews that Nazis planned to arrest them and send them to concentration camps. The arrests were slated for Friday, October 1. The Nazis knew many Jews would gather that night to begin celebrating their holy Sabbath day.

The Melchiors decided to leave Denmark. First, the Melchiors took a train to the Danish coast. They hid there until they could take a fishing boat to Sweden. Jews had to pay thousands of dollars each to take the boats.

The trip was difficult. Many people around the Melchiors became seasick. The Jews had to hide below the deck. Nazi planes flew overhead, looking for Jews who were trying to escape Denmark. The Melchiors' boat reached Sweden after about 18 hours of sailing.

Danish Jews quickly settled in Sweden. They understood the Swedish language fairly easily. Melchior even attended a Danish school. However, the Swedish people did not always treat Danish Jews kindly. The Swedish people gave the Danes only secondhand goods. Secondhand items have been used previously by someone else. For example, Danish Jews received only secondhand clothing in Sweden. Many Danish Jews felt unwelcome there.

The Allied powers defeated Nazi Germany in May 1945. The Melchior family and the rest of the Danish Jews were then able to return home. The Melchiors moved back into their apartment in Copenhagen.

Melchior felt like a different person after living in Sweden. He later joined numerous groups that helped Danish Jews and refugees. Refugees are people who are forced to leave

Nazi opinion of Denmark

Denmark had a small Jewish community of about 6,000 people in the 1930s. Most lived in the Danish capital of Copenhagen (pronounced ko-pen-HAY-gen). Danish Jews made up just a small part of the overall Danish population.

After Hitler invaded Poland, many Jews in Europe left their homes to escape the Nazis. Some Jews from Germany and Eastern Europe traveled to safety in Denmark. About 1,500 Jews from these regions had moved to Denmark by 1940.

Hitler and the Nazis believed Jews were inferior to the Germans. Hitler thought the German people were part of the "Aryan race" (pronounced Air-ee-an) and considered them to be the master race.

Resistance to Nazis

their homes due to war or other violence. Melchior later became the chief rabbi of Denmark, as his father had been. In the 2010s, when he was in his late 80s, Melchior could still remember details of his family's escape to Sweden.

Rabbi Bent Melchior (left), the former chief rabbi of Denmark. © FREYA INGRID MORALES/ANADOLU AGENCY/GETTY IMAGES.

To Hitler the perfect Aryan was tall and had blond hair and blue eyes. The Nazis thought it was dangerous for Jews to live near Aryans. The Nazis believed Jews would make Aryans "impure." This is why the Nazis separated Jews from the rest of the German population.

The Nazis believed Danes were Aryans, too. Many Danes were tall and blond. They looked like the Aryan people that Hitler viewed as perfect. Therefore, Hitler did not want to take complete control of Denmark during his expansion across Europe. He wanted the Danes to become Germany's allies. For this reason, the Nazis occupied, or took control of, Denmark in April 1940 with friendlier policies than they had used in other European countries they had invaded.

Early occupation

The German Army invaded Denmark on April 9, 1940. Danish soldiers fought the Nazis but they were too powerful. The Danish Army surrendered and the Nazis then took control of Copenhagen. Christian X (1870–1947), the Danish king, quickly surrendered Denmark to the Nazis.

The Nazi occupation of Denmark was different from most other Nazi occupations in Europe during World War II. The Nazis did not want to destroy Denmark. The Danish government also was unwilling to put its people in danger by violently resisting the Nazis. Therefore, the Nazis took control of Denmark somewhat peacefully. They allowed the Danish government to stay in place. The government could still make laws on all matters relating to Denmark itself. The Danes kept control of their court system and army.

The Nazis, however, controlled Denmark's foreign policy, or relations with other countries. The Nazis also made Denmark produce food and other goods on a schedule. Most Danes disliked Nazi control, but they knew the Nazis would become violent if they resisted. Non-Jewish Danes also wanted to discourage the Nazis from arresting and killing Denmark's Jews. The Danes, therefore, lived peacefully under Nazi rule at first.

Resistance begins

The Allies defeated Germany in numerous battles in early 1943. Many Europeans in occupied countries saw these defeats as proof that the German Army was not as strong as it had once seemed. Some Danes began to resist the Nazis in their country. They refused to produce the goods the Nazis needed. They destroyed Nazi equipment. These acts angered the Nazis.

Later in 1943 the Nazis demanded that the Danish government allow Nazi courts to judge members of the Danish resistance. The Danish government refused. Soon the Nazis took full control of Denmark. They took over the Danish military and police. They started arresting Jewish and non-Jewish Danes. These actions inspired Danes to start publicly protesting Nazi rule.

In early September 1943 Hitler began sending Danish Jews to ghettos elsewhere in Europe. A Nazi secretary in Denmark wondered whether sending Danish Jews to the ghettos would hurt Germany's relationship with Denmark. He told German diplomat Georg Ferdinand Duckwitz (pronounced GAY-org FER-din-and DUCK-vitz; 1904–1973), who was assigned to Copenhagen, that the Jews were about to be sent out of the country.

This 1943 photo shows a boat carrying Danish Jews to safety in neighboring Sweden three years after the Nazi invasion. © AFP/GETTY IMAGES.

Duckwitz did not think sending Danish Jews to the ghettos was a good idea. He warned the Danish government of what was about to happen. The government then warned Jews about the plan. Christian X and his government began secretly working with the Danish people to rescue Jews from the Nazis. They planned to send them on boats to Sweden, where they would be safe.

Denmark's 7,500 Jews first left their homes in Danish cities by walking or riding in cars or on trains. Non-Jewish Danes hid Jews in their homes or in churches or hospitals. Members of the Danish resistance helped Jews find safe hiding places until they could leave Denmark. The Danish police helped, too. They refused to allow Nazis to search Jewish homes. The Nazis forced some Danish police officers to look for hiding Jews. The officers simply ignored any Jews they found.

Danish fishermen waited for Jews on Denmark's coast. They took Jews across the strait to Sweden in their fishing boats. A strait is a narrow body of water between two landmasses. Throughout September 1943, the fishermen took about 7,200 Jews and almost 700 of their non-Jewish family members to Sweden. Once these people were safe, the fishermen took members of the Danish resistance to Sweden.

Resistance to Nazis

The Danish people's secret rescue saved most Jews in the country from the Nazis. The Nazis eventually arrested more than 470 Jews in Denmark. Most were German or Eastern European Jews. The Nazis sent them to a ghetto in Czechoslovakia.

In the following months the Danish people protested against the Nazis sending Jews to the ghetto. The Danish government asked the Nazis many times about what was happening to the Jews. Historians believe the Danish government's repeated questioning of the Nazis to get information about the Jews saved most of their lives as the Nazis did not want the Danish people to riot against them. In April 1945, the Nazis released Danish Jews from the ghetto; they went to Sweden.

Occupation ends

In 1944 relations between Germany and Denmark worsened. The Danes continued to protest the Nazis. The Nazis broke up the Danish police force. They sent thousands of police officers to concentration camps. The Danes also had little access to food or other goods. Crime increased throughout Denmark.

By this point Germany was losing the war against the Allies. The Allies defeated Germany in May 1945. Denmark was freed from Nazi control that month. About 120 Danish Jews died during the Holocaust. Most deaths had taken place during the escape to Sweden or in the ghetto in Czechoslovakia. Historians credit the Danish resistance with saving most of Denmark's Jews from Nazi death camps. As a result, more Jews in Denmark survived the Holocaust than in almost any other Nazi-controlled European country during World War II.

Warsaw Ghetto Uprising

LOCATION: Warsaw, Poland
DATE: April 19–May 16, 1943

On April 19, 1943, Jewish prisoners of the Warsaw ghetto in Nazi-controlled Poland staged an armed revolt against the Nazis. A ghetto is a poor area of a city where certain groups of people are forced to live. About 750 Jewish fighters in the ghetto attacked Nazis with guns and explosives. The strength of the Jews' resistance surprised the Nazis. The Nazis slowly burned down the ghetto over the next month in response. They finally defeated the uprising on May 16, 1943. The event became known as the Warsaw Ghetto Uprising.

The Warsaw ghetto was the largest of its kind in Europe during the Holocaust. The ghetto was created soon after the Nazi invasion of Poland in 1939, which started World War II (1939–1945). The Nazis eventually forced more than 400,000 Jews to live in the ghetto. The area was much too small to hold that many people. Thousands of Jews died from disease every month. Many others starved to death.

In late 1942 the Nazis ordered Jews in the Warsaw ghetto to be deported, or sent away, to death camps. In January 1943, some Jews in the ghetto responded to the news by banding together to resist the Nazis. They used weapons they had obtained to attack the Nazi guards. This violence stopped the deportations for a short time.

The Nazis returned to the Warsaw ghetto in April, planning to start up the deportations again. The Jewish resistance fighters had become stronger by this time. They used guns and grenades to fight off the Nazis for more than a month. The Nazis defeated the fighters in May by burning down the ghetto. About 7,000 Jews died in the uprising and 56,000 were captured. The Nazis sent thousands to concentration camps or death camps. Most of the Jews died in the camps. The Warsaw Ghetto Uprising was the largest revolt the Jewish people carried out against the Nazis during the Holocaust.

The Warsaw ghetto

Warsaw, the capital of Poland, was the largest Jewish community in Europe before World War II. About 350,000 Jews lived there in the 1930s. Jewish culture in Warsaw was thriving.

Germany invaded Poland on September 1, 1939. Over the next few weeks, the German Army bombed Warsaw heavily. The army marched into the city at the end of the month. Soon after the invasion, the Nazis created rules for Warsaw's Jewish population. The Nazis made Jews sew stars on their clothing, representing the six-pointed Star of David, a symbol of the Jewish religion. The Nazis took Jewish property and closed Jewish schools. All of these actions were part of the Nazis' plan to remove Jews from Europe.

The Nazis eventually forced more than 400,000 Jews to live in the ghetto. The area was much too small to hold that many people. Thousands of Jews died from disease every month. Many others starved to death.

The Nazis created the Warsaw ghetto in October 1940. The ghetto was a walled-off area of the city. The wall was about 10 feet (3 meters) high and topped with barbed wire. The Nazis made all Jews in Warsaw live in this ghetto. The Nazis then brought more Jews from nearby towns to live there. The total population of the Warsaw ghetto rose to about 400,000. In terms of population, it was the largest ghetto in Nazi-occupied Europe.

Jews could not escape from the ghetto. Nazis closely guarded the walls. The Warsaw ghetto covered about 1.3 square miles (3.4 square kilometers). This was a small space for 400,000 people. Often as many as seven people were forced to live in a single room. The Nazis did not give the Jews enough food. Thousands of Jews starved to death. Thousands of others died of diseases, which spread quickly in the tight living spaces.

Ghetto deportations

In July 1942 the Nazis started deporting Jews from the ghettos. The Nazis told the Jews they were going to concentration camps, where they would be forced to work. However, they sent many to death camps instead. The Nazis deported about 300,000 Jews from the Warsaw ghetto to the death camp at Treblinka. They sent thousands of other Jews to concentration camps. The Jews who remained in the ghetto eventually learned that the Nazis intended to kill them all.

Some young Jews in the Warsaw ghetto responded to this news by resisting. They formed groups such as the Jewish Combat Organization. The group was known as the ZOB, after its Polish name. A few hundred people belonged to the group.

ZOB members wanted to fight the Nazis who tried to take them to the death camps. The group contacted the Polish Home Army, a large Polish resistance movement. In the fall of 1942, the Home Army secretly sent guns and grenades into the Warsaw ghetto for the ZOB to use.

That October Nazi official Heinrich Himmler (pronounced HINE-rick HIM-ler; 1900–1945) ordered the Nazis to continue deporting Jews from the Warsaw ghetto. The Nazis planned to send Jews who could work to the concentration camps. The rest, the majority, would be sent to death camps.

Nazis entered the Warsaw ghetto in January 1943 to start deporting the Jews. The ZOB had been planning to resist the Nazis since receiving weapons from the Home Army. Members of the ZOB attacked the Nazis as they collected Jews for deportation. The fighters were armed only with

Often as many as seven people were forced to live in a single room. The Nazis did not give the Jews enough food. Thousands of Jews starved to death. Thousands of others died of diseases, which spread quickly in the tight living spaces.

pistols, but their attack surprised the Nazis. The Nazis eventually killed most of the fighters. Then they took revenge on Jews in the ghetto by quickly killing 1,000 of them. The Nazis deported about 6,000 Jews from the Warsaw ghetto that January. They temporarily stopped the deportations several days later.

The uprising

ZOB members who remained in the Warsaw ghetto felt good about the attack on the Nazis. They thought the revolt had forced the Nazis to stop deporting people from the ghetto to the death camps. The Jews wanted to continue resisting the Nazis, so they started building hideouts in the ghetto. They planned to hide in these areas with their weapons. The ZOB members would attack the Nazis from these hideouts if they tried to deport Jews again.

The Jews trained with their weapons over the next few months. They believed the Nazis would return for them. The Jews planned to protect themselves from being sent to death camps.

On April 19, 1943, Himmler ordered the Nazis to start deporting the rest of the Jews in the Warsaw ghetto. The Nazis entered the ghetto that day with tanks and artillery weapons. An artillery weapon is a large gun, similar to a cannon, that fires over long distances. The Jews had heard about the Nazis' plan before April 19. They were hiding as the Nazis marched into the ghetto.

About 750 Jewish resistance fighters from the ZOB attacked the Nazis. The fighters had pistols, grenades, and rifles. A young Polish fighter, Mordechai Anielewicz (pronounced MORE-deh-kai an-YELL-eh-vitch; 1919–1943), led the ZOB in battle. The fighters' attack on April 19 was so fierce that the Nazis retreated outside the ghetto.

The fighting continued as the Nazis struggled to defeat the uprising. On the third day Nazi commander Jürgen (pronounced YER-gen) Stroop (1895–1952) ordered the Nazis to burn down the entire Warsaw ghetto. Stroop believed this would force the Jews to leave their hideouts.

The method was effective. Many Jews left their hiding places due to the burning buildings and the firing of the artillery guns. The Nazis killed and captured thousands of Jews throughout April and into May. The Jews continued to surprise the Nazis with more attacks, though. The fight continued for nearly a month.

Resistance to Nazis

End of the uprising

Eventually the Nazi attacks became too much for the resistance fighters to handle. By May 1943 the ghetto's buildings had been reduced to piles of stone and brick. The Nazis captured the ZOB headquarters on May 8, while killing Anielewicz and many other fighters in the process.

Stroop announced that he had destroyed the Warsaw ghetto on May 16, 1943. He wanted to show survivors of the uprising that the Nazis totally controlled them. He did this by destroying the Great Synagogue near the ghetto.

Stroop kept a record of his and his soldiers' activities during and after the uprising. He claimed he had captured more than 56,000 Jews during the uprising. He also reported that his soldiers had killed about 7,000 Jews. The Jewish prisoners had killed about 300 Nazis.

Stroop sent about 7,000 Jews to the Treblinka death camp. In addition he sent more than 40,000 to various concentration camps throughout Poland. Small numbers of Jews successfully escaped from the Warsaw Ghetto after the Nazis defeated the uprising. They traveled through the ghetto's sewers to escape. Several months later the Nazis killed thousands more Jews from the Warsaw Ghetto in a mass shooting.

Forcibly pulled out of their hiding places during the Warsaw Ghetto Uprising, people stand with their hands raised as German soldiers with guns direct them out. © UNIVERSAL HISTORY ARCHIVE/UIG VIA GETTY IMAGES.

Historians later named the Warsaw Ghetto Uprising as one of the most important events of the Holocaust. It was the largest attack the Jews carried out against the Nazis during World War II. It was the first attack of its kind to occur in a city controlled by the Nazis. No previous Jewish attack on the Nazis had been as organized as the ghetto uprising in Warsaw.

This uprising was important for another reason, too. Jewish prisoners in other parts of Europe heard about it and were inspired to resist the Nazis, too. For instance, Jewish prisoners in the Treblinka death camp revolted against their Nazi guards in August 1943. Jews in the Białystok (pronounced bee-AW-li-stok) Ghetto in Poland attacked their guards the same month. Even though the Nazis put down all revolts against them, the resistance continued. The Warsaw Ghetto Uprising remained the most successful Jewish attempt to resist Nazi power.

Treblinka Death Camp Revolt

LOCATION: Poland

DATE: August 1943

In 1933 Nazi leader Adolf Hitler became the chancellor, or head of the government, of Germany. A year later, he named himself the führer (pronounced FYUR-er), which means "leader," of Germany. Hitler wanted to extend Germany's borders and expand German power in Europe. He started this expansion by ordering the invasion of Poland in 1939. Great Britain, France, and a few other Allied nations quickly responded to the invasion by declaring war on Germany. This marked the start of World War II, which lasted until 1945.

Hitler led Germany's Nazi Party. The Nazis did not want Jews in Germany. They thought Jews were inferior to other German people. With Hitler in power, the Nazis began to carry out a plan to remove Jews from Germany. The Nazis eventually moved Jews into concentration camps or death camps to separate them from non-Jews. At concentration camps, the Nazis imprisoned Jews and others and forced them to work. At death camps, the Nazis killed Jewish prisoners by the thousands. The United States Holocaust Memorial Museum estimates the number at 2.7 million total.

Resistance to Nazis

Treblinka Facts

- Located in northeastern Poland in remote wooded area
- In operation from July 1942 to November 1943
- Site included a labor camp and killing center, connected by a train line
- Guards manned watchtowers that were 26 feet high
- Between 800,000 to 925,000 Jews were killed at the camp
- About 50,000 others were killed at the camp (including men, women, and children)
- Guards shot prisoners and destroyed evidence at the camp before Soviet troops arrived
- Mass graves uncovered in 2012

SOURCES: Jewish Virtual Library and the United States Holocaust Memorial Museum.

© 2018 CENGAGE®.

The Nazis opened the Treblinka death camp in Poland in 1942. That same year a group of Jewish prisoners in the camp began planning to revolt and escape. The prisoners planned the escape for many months.

The Treblinka death camp revolt began on August 2, 1943. Several hundred of the camp's prisoners used stolen weapons to attack their Nazi guards. About 200 prisoners climbed over the camp's barbed-wire fences and escaped into nearby forests. Barbed-wire fences have sharp metal points meant to prevent people from climbing over them. Nazis chased and eventually killed about 100 escaped prisoners. The other 100 successfully escaped Treblinka during the revolt.

Some of the prisoners who escaped later joined resistance groups in Europe to fight against the Nazis. The Treblinka death camp closed in November 1943. The Treblinka death camp revolt later became a well-known event in the history of the Holocaust.

The Nazi death camps

From the start of his rule in 1933, Hitler claimed that certain groups of people were enemies of Germany. At first these groups included only members of certain political groups, such as Communists. In the mid-1930s, however, the Nazis began to treat Jews as enemies of Germany, too.

The Nazis started building concentration camps in the 1930s to house German enemies. These camps were for holding prisoners. The Nazis made the prisoners perform hard work. Many prisoners died from exhaustion and lack of food in the prison camps.

By 1942 the Nazis had developed the Final Solution—the plan to kill all Jews in Europe. To do this, the Nazis started opening death camps. These were similar to concentration camps or work camps, but they had large gas chambers. The Nazis forced groups of prisoners into these chambers and locked the doors. Then they filled the rooms with poison gas. The gas killed everyone inside.

The Nazis opened Treblinka and several other death camps in Poland in 1942. The Nazis chose Poland as the primary site of the death camps because that country had the largest Jewish population in Europe. At some of the death camps, Nazis killed thousands of Jewish prisoners a day.

Early planning at Treblinka

Treblinka was located in an area of Poland with thick forests. The Nazis planted trees alongside the prison's barbed-wire fences to hide the camp from outside view. They wanted to keep their death camps secret. Treblinka was open from July 1942 to November 1943. During that time, more than 850,000 prisoners, most of whom were Jews, were killed at Treblinka.

In 1942 the prisoners began planning a revolt against the camp guards. The prisoners knew they would need weapons to help them escape. To get weapons, the prisoners tried to bribe guards who worked at the camp. To bribe someone is to pay him or her to perform a certain, usually illegal, action. The prisoners bribed the guards with money they collected from the clothes of dead prisoners. Sometimes the guards gave the prisoners extra food in exchange for the money. However, the guards refused to give the prisoners weapons. Plans for the rebellion then stalled.

A new plan

In early 1943 Germany had one of its first battlefield defeats at the Battle of Stalingrad (pronounced STAW-len-grad) in the Soviet Union. The Soviet Union proved to be a powerful enemy as the battle lasted several months. The Soviets finally defeated the Germans. The loss proved to the world that the Nazis could be defeated.

The prisoners at Treblinka learned of the defeat from newspapers that new prisoners had secretly brought into the camp. The news encouraged the prisoners to continue their plans for a revolt. In addition, the number of new prisoners arriving at Treblinka had decreased. The prisoners took this as a sign that the Nazis were planning to close Treblinka soon and kill its remaining prisoners. This further inspired the prisoners to carry out their rebellion.

Ten Jewish prisoners started planning the revolt in the summer of 1943. More than 50 others soon joined them. The group temporarily kept the plans a secret from the other 800 prisoners of the camp.

The prisoners' plan was to steal weapons from the storage area. They would use the weapons to kill the guards and then escape. One of the prisoners was a locksmith, or a person who makes and repairs locks and keys. The locksmith secretly made a copy of the key to the storage area.

Resistance to Nazis

"The World Cannot Forget"

In this primary source excerpt from Associated Press reporter Aron Heller, published on October 31, 2010, the only two remaining survivors of the Treblinka death camp discuss their memories. (Both have since passed away.)

Samuel Willenberg and Kalman Taigman, 87-year-old Israelis, are devoting their final years to trying to preserve the memory of the 875,000 people systematically murdered [at Treblinka] in a one-year killing spree at the height of World War II. Almost all of them were Jews.

Only 67 people are known to have survived the camp, fleeing in a brazen revolt shortly before Treblinka was destroyed. Following the recent death of a prominent chronicler, Israel's national Holocaust memorial says the two Israeli men are now the final living link to one of the most notorious death camps in human history.

"The world cannot forget Treblinka," said Willenberg.

"Soon there will be no one left to tell," added Taigman....

[During his escape from Treblinka] Willenberg said he was shot in the leg as he climbed over bodies piled at the barbed wire fence and catapulted over. He kept running, ignoring dead friends in his path. He said his blue eyes and "non-Jewish" look allowed him to survive in the countryside before arriving in Warsaw and joining the Polish underground.

Later in life, he took to sculpturing to describe his experiences. His bronze statues reflect what he saw—Jews standing on a train platform, a father removing his son's shoes before entering the gas chambers, a young girl having her head shaved, prisoners removing bodies.

"I live two lives, one is here and now and the other is what happened there," Willenberg said in an interview at his Tel Aviv apartment. "It never leaves me. It stays in my head. It goes with me always."

His two sisters were murdered there. He described his survival as "chance, sheer chance," choking back tears. "It wasn't because of God. He wasn't there. He was on vacation...."

Taigman said he recalls the uprising vividly, and that resisting the Germans was a "dream" for the prisoners.

He entered Treblinka holding the hand of his mother, who was quickly pulled away from him and murdered. He left watching a Nazi flag burning in the distance from a blaze they had set—a small piece of revenge after nearly a year of torment.

"It was hell, absolutely hell," said Taigman.... "A normal man cannot imagine how a living person could have lived through it—killers, natural-born killers, who without a trace of remorse just murdered every little thing."

Taigman, who wandered in the Polish countryside for nearly a year after his escape, said his most lasting memory of Treblinka is fellow prisoners who had to remove bodies—often their own relatives—from gas chambers.

SOURCE: Heller, Aron. "Treblinka Death Camp Survivors: 'There Are Only 2 of Us Left.'" Associated Press, October 31, 2010. Available online at http://www.cleveland.com/world/index.ssf/2010/10/treblinka_death_camp_survivors.html (accessed October 15, 2017). Courtesy of Associated Press.

Resistance to Nazis

The prisoners eventually overheard their Nazi guards celebrating the upcoming closing of the Treblinka death camp. The prisoners knew that if they did not revolt before the closing, they would all be killed. They scheduled the revolt for August 2, 1943.

The revolt

The prisoners set the revolt to begin at 4:30 p.m. They chose this time so those who escaped the camp could hide from Nazi guards in the darkness of night. On August 2 a number of guards left the camp to swim in a nearby river. This meant fewer guards were at the camp to stop the revolt.

At about 2 p.m. on August 2, two camp prisoners used the copied key to enter the weapon storage room. The two prisoners passed several guns and grenades, small explosives thrown by hand, to other prisoners who were waiting outside the room's window. The prisoners outside the storage room hid the weapons in garbage bins. They planned to give them to other prisoners.

The plan soon went wrong. A Nazi guard stopped a prisoner for a random search. The guard discovered that the prisoner had a great deal of money. The prisoner, like many others, had collected money to pay for travel expenses after escaping from Treblinka. The other prisoners feared that the guard would make the prisoner reveal the escape plan. In a panic, one of the

Samuel Willenberg (center), who was then the only living survivor of an August 1943 prisoner rebellion at the Treblinka death camp, lights a candle at a ceremony honoring the victims on October 2, 2013.
© JANEK SKARZYNSKI/AFP/GETTY IMAGES.

Resistance to Nazis

Samuel Willenberg

Samuel Willenberg (pronounced VILL-in-berg; 1923–2016) was one of the few prisoners who successfully escaped from the Treblinka death camp during the 1943 revolt. Before his death in 2016, he was the last survivor of the camp.

Willenberg was born in Czestochowa (pronounced chest-uh-KO-vuh), Poland, in 1923. His family was Jewish. The Nazis broke up the Willenberg family when the Germans invaded Poland in 1939. They arrested Willenberg's two sisters in 1941.

Willenberg, along with thousands of other Polish Jews, was sent to a ghetto in Poland. In 1943 the Jews were transferred to Treblinka. The Nazis immediately killed most of the Jews who were with Willenberg.

He was able to survive the interrogation because he told the Nazis he was a bricklayer, or builder. The Nazis forced Willenberg to perform work throughout the camp. Since he was young and strong, Willenberg was able to do the work and survive the brutal conditions in the camp. But some others who were sent to Treblinka and kept on to work found the conditions too much to overcome.

Willenberg participated in the prisoner revolt in August 1943. He struggled to climb over the fence at Treblinka's main gate. A Nazi guard shot Willenberg in the leg, but he still managed to escape. Willenberg then traveled to the nearby Polish city of Warsaw. There, he joined the Polish resistance. In 1944 Willenberg fought the Nazis in the Warsaw Ghetto Uprising.

After World War II, Willenberg moved to Israel with his wife, Ada, who was a survivor of the Warsaw Ghetto. He became a surveyor for the Israeli government. A surveyor measures distances between points on a section of land to determine land area and boundary lines.

---

prisoners killed the Nazi guard. The rest of the prisoners then decided to start the revolt immediately.

The prisoners used the grenades to destroy the main buildings in the camp. The buildings included the guards' sleeping areas and the vehicle garage. The buildings caught on fire from the grenade explosions. Additionally, the prisoners used the stolen guns to kill as many guards as they could. The guards quickly recovered from their surprise. Guards in the camp's watchtowers began shooting at the prisoners on the ground. They killed many prisoners this way.

To escape Treblinka the prisoners had to climb over the barbed-wire fences near the camp's main entrance. They threw blankets over the sharp barbed-wire to prevent themselves from getting cut as they climbed over. Many prisoners died at the fences because guards in the watchtowers continued

Resistance to Nazis

Willenberg also started teaching people about the Holocaust. As a survivor of the Holocaust, he wanted people to know what had happened so it was never forgotten. He drew maps of Treblinka and wrote about his time in the camp. Willenberg later taught Israeli youth about Treblinka on trips to the former death camp in Poland. Additionally, he gave public talks about the Holocaust in Poland, Germany, Israel, and the United States.

Willenberg also became a sculptor, whose works were displayed in Poland, Germany, and Israel. His work depicted scenes from the Trelinka death camp. In old age Willenberg said he had been living two lives since being in Treblinka. One life was in the camp. The other life was made up of present events. He said the memory of Treblinka followed him always.

Willenberg died at his home in Israel on February 19, 2016. He was 93 years old. His wife, daughter, and three grandchildren survived him. During his lifetime, Willenberg received various awards. Those honors included the Virtuti Militari medal, which is Poland's highest military commendation.

Portrait of Polish sculptor Samuel Willenberg. At the time of his death, he was the last survivor of the Treblinka death camp. © CHUCK FISHMAN/GETTY IMAGES.

shooting at them. In the end about 200 prisoners escaped from Treblinka that day. The camp they left behind was on fire and partially destroyed.

After the revolt

The escaped prisoners ran into the forests outside the camp. Nazi guards quickly began chasing the prisoners on horses or in cars. The guards shot at some prisoners. They captured others and returned them to Treblinka. Of the 200 prisoners who escaped, about 100 got away from the guards. Some of the escaped prisoners eventually joined the Polish resistance against the Nazis.

Back at Treblinka, the Nazi guards made all recaptured prisoners take down the buildings that remained in the camp. The Nazis were closing Treblinka and wanted no signs of the camp left behind. The guards killed the prisoners after they finished the work.

Treblinka closed in November 1943. Between 800,000 and 925,000 Jewish prisoners had died there since July 1942. Fewer than 70 of the 100 prisoners who escaped from Treblinka lived to see the end of World War II. Some later published stories of the revolt. Historians consider the Treblinka death camp revolt an important example of Jewish resistance to the Nazis during World War II.

For More Information

BOOKS

Byers, Ann. *Rescuing the Danish Jews: A Heroic Story from the Holocaust*. Berkeley Heights, NJ: Enslow, 2012.

Scholl, Inge. *The White Rose: Munich, 1942–1943*. Middletown, CT: Wesleyan University Press, 1983.

Shuter, Jane. *Resistance to the Nazis*. Chicago: Heinemann Library, 2003.

PERIODICALS

Evans, Richard J. "Why Hitler's Plan during the Second World War Collapsed." *Guardian* (September 8, 2009). Available online at https://www.theguardian.com/world/2009/sep/08/hitler-germany-campaign-collapsed (accessed October 12, 2017).

Green, David B. "1943: Treblinka Inmates Rise Up against Nazi Captors." *Haaretz* (August 2, 2015). Available online at http://www.haaretz.com/jewish/features/.premium-1.668758 (accessed July 31, 2017).

Kopel, David. "The Warsaw Ghetto Uprising: Armed Jews vs. Nazis." *Washington Post* (October 10, 2015). Available online at https://www.washingtonpost.com/news/volokh-conspiracy/wp/2015/10/10/the-warsaw-ghetto-uprising-armed-jews-vs-nazis/?utm_term=.914e605236fd (accessed August 8, 2017).

Omer-Man, Michael. "This Week in History: Prisoners Revolt at Treblinka." *Jerusalem Post* (August 5, 2011). Available online at http://www.jpost.com/Features/In-Thespotlight/This-Week-in-History-Prisoners-revolt-at-Treblinka (accessed July 31, 2017).

WEBSITES

Burns, Lucy. "White Rose: The Germans Who Tried to Topple Hitler." BBC News, February 22, 2013. http://www.bbc.com/news/magazine-21521060 (accessed August 4, 2017).

"Denmark." United States Holocaust Memorial Museum. https://www.ushmm.org/wlc/en/article.php?ModuleId=10005209 (accessed August 3, 2017).

"German Resistance to Hitler." United States Holocaust Memorial Museum. https://www.ushmm.org/wlc/en/article.php?ModuleId=10005208 (accessed August 2, 2017).

"Holocaust Resistance: The Warsaw Ghetto Uprising." Jewish Virtual Library. http://www.jewishvirtuallibrary.org/the-warsaw-ghetto-uprising (accessed August 8, 2017).

Hornberger, Jacob G. "Holocaust Resistance: The White Rose—A Lesson in Dissent." Jewish Virtual Library. http://www.jewishvirtuallibrary.org/the-white-rose-a-lesson-in-dissent (accessed August 4, 2017).

"Jewish Resistance." United States Holocaust Memorial Museum. https://www.ushmm.org/wlc/en/article.php?ModuleId=10005213 (accessed August 2, 2017).

"The Occupation of Denmark." Denmark.dk. http://denmark.dk/en/society/history/occupation (accessed August 3, 2017).

Otzen, Ellen. "The Mass Escape of Jews from Nazi-Occupied Denmark." BBC News, October 8, 2013. http://www.bbc.com/news/magazine-24427637 (accessed August 3, 2017).

"Polish Resistance and Conclusions." United States Holocaust Memorial Museum. https://www.ushmm.org/learn/students/learning-materials-and-resources/poles-victims-of-the-nazi-era/polish-resistance-and-conclusions (accessed August 2, 2017).

Spörl, Gerhard. "How Denmark Saved Its Jews from the Nazis." Spiegel Online, October 17, 2013. http://www.spiegel.de/international/zeitgeist/book-examines-how-jews-of-denmark-were-saved-from-the-holocaust-a-928116.html (accessed August 3, 2017).

"Treblinka." United States Holocaust Memorial Museum. https://www.ushmm.org/wlc/en/article.php?ModuleId=10005193 (accessed July 31, 2017).

"Treblinka Concentration Camp: History & Overview." Jewish Virtual Library. http://www.jewishvirtuallibrary.org/history-and-overview-of-treblinka (accessed July 31, 2017).

"Warsaw Ghetto Uprising." United States Holocaust Memorial Museum. https://www.ushmm.org/wlc/en/article.php?ModuleId=10005188 (accessed August 8, 2017).

"White Rose." United States Holocaust Memorial Museum. https://www.ushmm.org/wlc/en/article.php?ModuleId=10007188 (accessed August 4, 2017).

"World War II: The Battle of Stalingrad." Jewish Virtual Library. http://www.jewishvirtuallibrary.org/the-battle-of-stalingrad (accessed October 12, 2017).

19

Slavery

Louisiana Rebellion (German Coast) **623**

Nat Turner's Rebellion/ Anti-slavery Petitions **628**

Christmas Rebellion/ Baptist War **634**

Harpers Ferry Raid **638**

Fight to Stop Human Trafficking **643**

Slavery is the practice of owning people. Throughout history, slaves have been considered the property of their owners. Most slave owners have treated their slaves like objects. Opponents of slavery have argued that treating human beings like property is wrong and immoral.

Slavery has existed in the world since ancient times. The most common purpose of slaves throughout human history has been to work for their owners. This work earned slave owners great fortunes. For this reason, slave owners have always considered slaves valuable.

Slavery has been based in the idea that certain groups of people are better than other groups. This is what has allowed slave owners to believe they have the right to own other humans and use them for whatever purposes they want. For instance, slaves in ancient Rome were usually foreigners the Romans captured in war. Slaves brought to the United States in the 17th through 19th centuries were African or of African descent. Their owners were white. White slave owners felt they could own African slaves because they believed white people were better than black people. Owners treated their slaves however they wanted. Many violently abused their slaves.

In the past, small groups of people have opposed slavery due to morality, or beliefs about what behaviors are right or wrong. Opponents of slavery argued that the practice was evil because it likened human beings to objects. Until about the 19th century, these opponents were few. However, in that century, both the United Kingdom and the United States made slavery illegal. Many other countries did this, too, both before and after the United Kingdom and the United States did.

Ancient slavery

Slavery is as old as human society itself. People in ancient Sumer and Egypt (in the Middle East) and Rome and Greece (in Europe) used slaves.

Slavery

WORDS TO KNOW

Abolition: The act of ending or stopping something.

Abolitionist movement: A movement to end slavery.

Armory: A place where military weapons are made and stored.

Colony: A country or other area that more powerful countries rule politically.

Human trafficking: The practice of forcing people to perform labor or participate in sex work.

Legislature: A group of people responsible for making laws.

Maroons: Freed Spanish slaves who lived in the mountains of Jamaica.

Militia: A group of citizens with military training who are called to service only in the event of emergencies.

Petition: A written request made to an official person or organized body.

Plantation: A large area of land that is usually worked by manual labor.

Slave driver: A person who is responsible for organizing and punishing slaves.

Trafficking: The act of buying or selling an illegal product or service.

In the ancient era, slavery was not a race-based practice. Slaves in Rome and Greece were usually prisoners captured in foreign wars. Poor families sometimes sold their own children as slaves just to make money.

Slaves in Rome and Greece were the same as any other property. Owners could do as they liked with their slaves. They bought and sold them or rented them to others. Many owners treated their slaves violently. They whipped them, branded them with hot metal, or killed them. No laws protected slaves. Therefore, it was accepted in society to treat slaves in these ways.

In both Rome and Greece, slaves were important parts of the workforce. Slaves worked in homes, on farms, or in mines. Many of them also worked on various public projects, such as the construction of roads, buildings, and waterways. These slave tasks were similar to jobs held by free people. Some citizens of both Rome and Greece disliked that slaves and free people appeared so similarly to each other. The Roman government rejected calls to make slaves wear clothing that would identify them as slaves. The government was afraid the slaves would then be able to tell if there was enough of them to unite and revolt against their owners.

Roman slave owners sometimes freed their slaves or let them pay for their freedom. The slaves could go on to get jobs and appear as any other Roman citizens. However, this could create more problems for the former

Carvings depicting bound slaves are found near the entrance to the temple complex of Abu Simbel, built c. 1250 BCE, in Egypt. © LEXYK/SHUTTERSTOCK.COM.

slaves. Romans considered slaves to be the lowest social class. Some people could not simply forget that someone had once been a slave. This meant that some former slaves continued to struggle for success and respect even after being freed.

Slavery in medieval Europe

Europe's ancient period ended in the late 5th century CE with the fall of the Roman Empire. Rome had controlled much of the Middle East and Europe during its most powerful years. This meant Roman laws and traditions were part of everyday life in these regions for centuries. One of these traditions was slavery. The practice existed nearly everywhere Rome had controlled in western Asia and Europe. However, foreign attackers destroyed Rome in the late 5th century. Roman culture gradually stopped influencing daily life in the areas of the old empire.

Slavery was part of the Roman culture that mostly disappeared from Western Europe starting around the 6th century. This era began the Middle Ages in Europe. The Middle Ages was a period of European history lasting from the 5th to the 15th century. Many European societies in the Middle Ages were feudal (pronounced FEW-dal). In feudal societies, wealthy officials owned land, and poor farmers called serfs farmed the land. Serfs were allowed to live on the land in exchange for giving the officials most of the food they grew. In this way, serfs remained mostly poor for their entire lives.

Slavery

CRITICAL THINKING QUESTIONS

1. Were slave owners who viewed their slaves as objects wrong and immoral? Or were they just ignorant about the idea of basic human rights? Would trying to educate slave owners about human rights make a difference? Why or why not?

2. What made Charles Deslondes a good leader?

3. What do you think the German Coast slave rebellion accomplished?

4. How did Nat Turner's rebellion lead to Virginia's slavery debate? Why do you think it moved people so much?

5. What do you think was most important about Virginia's slavery debate? Explain.

6. Why do you think Samuel Sharpe believed his planned strike could earn the Jamaican slaves their freedom?

7. Do you think Samuel Sharpe knew the strike would eventually turn violent? Why or why not?

8. What do you think John Brown wanted to accomplish with his raid? Explain.

9. Why do you think the Harpers Ferry raid was an important moment in American history? What did it accomplish?

10. Why do you think some victims of human trafficking would be afraid to seek help?

11. How can raising awareness about the issue help fight human trafficking?

The system of serfdom replaced slavery in Europe in the Middle Ages. People's views of serfs in the Middle Ages differed from the ancient view of slaves in one important way. In ancient times, slaves were considered objects. In the Middle Ages, serfs were seen as individuals. Unlike slaves, serfs controlled their own lives. They chose to work on wealthy people's land. They knew they would have a place to live if they did this. The wealthy officials did not own the laborers as ancient peoples had. Serfs could marry and have families. Slaves in ancient Rome could not legally marry but could pair with other slaves with their master's permission. Any children of slaves would also be slaves. Masters could sell any member of a slave family away from the other family members.

Serfdom started to disappear in Europe in the late 12th century. England and Scotland were the first European countries to replace feudalism with a new government in which all people had basic rights. However, slavery returned to Western Europe after several more centuries.

African slave trade

Some African cultures practiced slavery before the arrival of western European explorers in the late 15th century. They enslaved people as punishment for committing a crime or to pay off a debt. They also enslaved members of neighboring cultures they had captured in war. Europeans became involved in the African slave trade in the 15th century. They did this mostly as part of their settling of the Americas. The Americas consisted of South America and North America (which also includes Central America and the islands in the Caribbean Sea).

Countries such as Spain and Portugal started forming colonies in the Americas in the late 15th and early 16th centuries. Colonies are countries or other areas that more powerful countries rule politically. Europeans wanted to make money in the Americas by growing and selling crops. They thought using slaves to farm the land was the best way to do this. By using this system, slaves would complete the work and would not have to be paid.

Portuguese and Spanish settlers brought the first African slaves to the Americas around 1502. English and Dutch settlers later began exploring the Americas themselves. Slaves became valuable tools for farming American land. As a result, a complex slave trade arose among England, the Netherlands, Spain, and Portugal. Slave traders took Africans mostly from the West African coast. They shipped them to colonies in the future United States, South America, or to islands in the Caribbean Sea to sell. The traders then returned to Europe to resell goods they had obtained in America. This system was called the triangular trade, since it involved the three locations of Europe, Africa, and the Americas. Many slaves died of disease or starvation due to a lack of food and harsh conditions on the ships crossing the Atlantic Ocean.

The slave deck of the ship Wildfire, *transporating captured slaves from Africa to the Caribbean.* © EVERETT HISTORICAL/SHUTTERSTOCK.COM.

The African slave trade grew throughout the 17th and 18th centuries in the Americas. From the 16th to the late 19th century, about 12.5 million people were transported from Africa to the Americas as slaves; about 10.7 million survived the ocean voyage. Of those, about 600,000 slaves were brought to the United States. The European settlers used the slaves mostly for farm labor. As in ancient Greece and Rome, Europeans saw slaves as objects, not as human beings with rights.

End of the African slave trade

The early 19th century saw Europeans and Americans begin to change their opinions of slavery overall. Some people wanted to end slavery entirely. Others wanted to ban the slave trade, making it illegal for anyone to bring new African slaves to Europe or the United States. This change had come about as a result of developing views on human freedom and rights in the late 18th and early 19th centuries. The United States, Denmark, and Great Britain banned the transatlantic slave trade in the early 19th century. Spain, Portugal, and France followed later. Despite the bans, the illegal trade of African slaves continued until later in the century.

The end of the transatlantic slave trade did not yet mean the end of slavery, especially in the United States. The slave population in the nation grew during the first half of the 19th century. About 4 million blacks were slaves in the United States in 1860. Most of these people worked in the southern part of the country, where many slave owners were farmers. Life as a slave in the United States was difficult. Some slave owners brutally beat their slaves. Because children born to slaves were also considered slaves, many owners separated families to make money by selling family members to other slave owners. Owners also prevented their slaves from learning to read or write. African slaves in the United States had no legal rights.

However, at the same time, the abolitionist movement, which wanted to end slavery, had been growing in the United States. Opponents of slavery, called abolitionists, believed enslaving people was wrong. Most American abolitionists lived in the northern part of the United States. In 1861 the North and South went to war over their disagreement on the future of slavery in the country. This war was the US Civil War (1861–1865). It ended in a Northern victory in 1865. The United States made slavery illegal throughout the country later that year by passing the 13th Amendment to the US Constitution.

Life for freed blacks after the war remained difficult. The problems they faced were similar to those of Roman slaves who had been freed. Romans never forgot that someone had once been a slave. The same was true of freed African American slaves in the United States. Individual US states, mostly in the South, continued to treat African Americans poorly. They made laws that separated black Americans from white citizens. African Americans demanded that the US government give them equal rights well into the mid-20th century. The US government finally did this in the 1960s. From that point, the laws of the United States could not discriminate against black Americans. To discriminate against someone is to treat that person unfairly based on race or other personal differences.

Modern slavery

In the 21st century, slavery is banned in most parts of the world. Yet the practice continues to exist in different forms in almost every country. In the modern era, slavery is also referred to as human trafficking. Human trafficking is the practice of forcing people to perform labor or participate in sex work. Sex work involves engaging in sexual activity for money.

The Global Slavery Index claimed in 2016 that nearly 46 million people worldwide were slaves. The Walk Free Foundation publishes the Global Slavery Index every year to inform the public about slave conditions around the world. India had the most slaves, at more than 18 million in 2016. China and Pakistan also had several million slaves each. More than 1 million slaves lived in Europe. Sometimes people become slaves against their will. Other times, poverty forces people to sell themselves or their children into slavery so they will receive at least enough food to survive.

Most countries around the world have made slavery and human trafficking illegal. Many countries offer various support services to help victims of any forms of forced labor.

Louisiana Rebellion (German Coast)

LOCATION: Territory of Orleans, Louisiana
DATE: January 8–10, 1811

Revolts and rebellions were a common part of the Western slave experience. Many slaves who grew tired of the suffering they had to endure eventually fought back in some way. Some chose to carry out simple acts of resistance like doing poor work or pretending to be sick. Others struck back at their masters with violence or ran away in the hope of escaping the slave system altogether. In a few cases, large groups of slaves banded together in organized rebellions. This was often the most violent type of slave resistance.

Slave rebellions were less common in the United States than in other parts of the Americas because the plantations in the United States were much smaller than those in other places. Smaller plantations had fewer slaves and more white people to control them. Still, a number of slave rebellions did take place during and after the colonial period. A 1712 slave rebellion in New York City led to the death of 9 whites and 18 slaves. In 1739 a group of about 80 slaves rebelled in South Carolina and tried unsuccessfully to reach freedom in Spanish Florida.

One of the least known slave rebellions in US history occurred near New Orleans, Louisiana, in January 1811. The German Coast slave rebellion was a two-day revolt during which as many as 500 slaves rose up and attacked a number of nearby plantations. The slaves set their sights on taking New Orleans but were stopped by soldiers before they could reach the city. Although it was mostly forgotten by history, the German Coast slave rebellion was an important act of resistance that helped turn the tide in the fight against slavery in the United States.

Slavery in Louisiana

Slavery was common in Louisiana throughout its colonial history and into 1812, when it became a state. French Louisiana's slavery system differed from those in other North American colonies, however. Slave owners in Louisiana had to follow a special set of rules called the Code Noir, or slave code. The Code Noir forbade slave owners from torturing their slaves and required them to instruct their slaves in the Catholic faith. This meant that slavery in Louisiana was somewhat less harsh than in other colonies. However, it was still a brutal and cruel practice.

The growth of slavery in French Louisiana was slower than it was in British North America. In fact, only about 10 blacks were in the entire colony in 1712. Many of Louisiana's earliest slaves were Native Americans. Eventually slave traders imported many African slaves into Louisiana. Nearly 6,000 African slaves arrived in the colony before it fell to Spanish control in 1762. After that slave traders brought many more slaves to Louisiana. By 1795 more than 19,000 slaves and 16,000 free blacks were in the colony, some having been born there. Around 2,700 of the slaves worked on plantations along the German Coast near New Orleans.

The German Coast slave plantations were among the most important in all of Louisiana. They supplied New Orleans with most of its food. The slaves who worked on these plantations also built levees to protect the area from flooding. They worked hard all day to make their owners' lives easier. Slaves who tried to escape from the German Coast often hid in the nearby swamps. If caught, they were usually punished severely and even killed. Life for slaves along the German Coast was not easy.

Charles Deslondes Charles Deslondes (d. 1811) was one of the many slaves who toiled on Louisiana's German Coast. He worked on a plantation that belonged to Colonel Manuel Andry (c. 1758–1839). Deslondes was different than most other slaves. Because he was mixed race, whites treated him better and gave him more opportunities than black slaves. He eventually became a slave driver on the Andry plantation. This meant that he was in charge of keeping the other slaves in order and punishing them when necessary. Most other slaves feared him as a result.

Deslondes grew up while the French Revolution (1789–1799) was unfolding in Europe. As a child, he heard many stories about the revolution. These stories introduced Deslondes to ideas like liberty and brotherhood. While such ideas were quite foreign to most slaves, they were inspiring to Deslondes. He also eventually came to learn about the Haitian Revolution (1791–1804), which was a successful slave rebellion in the Caribbean. This revolution led to the birth of Haiti as an independent nation. Deslondes saw this success and was again inspired. Sometime later he decided to use his position of power as a slave driver to bring the German Coast slaves together in a revolution of their own.

German Coast slave rebellion

Deslondes worked for some time to convince his fellow slaves to take part in a rebellion. This was not an easy task. Many of the slaves hated him for being friendly with the plantation owner and working as a slave driver. Deslondes eventually managed to get through to them, however. With their help he planned one of the largest slave uprisings in US history.

The rebellion began on January 8, 1811. That night Deslondes and several other slaves entered the main house of the Andry plantation and attacked those inside. Deslondes managed only to wound Andry, but Andry's son was killed. The slaves then prepared to begin their march out of the plantation by gathering horses and arming themselves with farm tools and the few weapons they could find.

Deslondes quickly led the slaves off the Andry plantation. Their plan was to march to New Orleans, take over the city, and establish a new black republic there. Deslondes and the other slaves stopped at other plantations and set buildings on fire as they marched toward the city. More

Slaves who tried to escape from the German Coast often hid in the nearby swamps. If caught, they were usually punished severely and even killed. Life for slaves along the German Coast was not easy.

Slavery

Malê Revolt of 1835

The Malê Revolt was one of the most important slave rebellions in history and one of the most successful in South America. Even though it did not turn out the way its organizers had planned, it played a key role in the downfall of slavery in Brazil.

Brazil was a Portuguese colony until it became independent in 1822. Slavery continued to be practiced there even after the colonial period came to an end, however. The eastern state of Bahia had one of the country's largest slave populations. Slaves accounted for about one-third of the workforce there. Most of the slaves in Bahia were originally from different parts of Africa where Islam was the main religion. This meant Bahia's slave population was almost entirely Muslim. Sharing the same faith brought the slaves together and gave them strength.

The Muslim slaves of Bahia tried unsuccessfully to revolt in both 1814 and 1816. Although they were forced to practice their faith in secret after this, they continued to seek freedom. Years of preparation led to the Malê Revolt of 1835. The Muslim slaves planned to begin their revolt at dawn on January 25, but a police raid forced them to begin their attack several hours early. About 300 slaves and free Muslims marched through Bahia in hopes of taking several ships and sailing back to Africa. Government officials put together an armed response that quickly put an end to the uprising, however. More than 100 Africans and 14 Brazilian soldiers were killed in the fighting. The leaders of the revolt were put to death, and many of the slaves who took part were jailed.

The slaves involved in the Malê Revolt did not manage to win their freedom but did achieve some measure of success. The Malê Revolt led to more anti-slavery activity throughout Brazil and helped lead to the eventual end of slavery in the country in 1888.

slaves joined the march as it moved along. Some accounts suggest that their numbers grew to as many as 500. Others suggest that there were a total of somewhere between 150 to 200 slaves involved in the rebellion.

Word of the rebellion spread to other nearby plantations and New Orleans by noon the next day. A militia (pronounced muh-LIH-shuh), or volunteer military force, of about 80 local soldiers quickly formed in response. Deslondes realized he could not take the city if it was protected by the white soldiers, so he came up with a way to draw them out. He led the slaves toward the city until they were close enough to be seen by the defense force. Then Deslondes turned the slaves around and marched them back to a plantation in the opposite direction. The defense force took the bait and followed the slaves to the plantation. By the time they arrived there, however, the slaves had left and were already working their way back to New Orleans. Fearing the worst, local officials called for a second group of troops from Baton Rouge to help put down the rebellion.

Oral history helps preserve the past. Here, a martial artist talks to foreign and Brazilian students about the Malê slave rebellion. The revolt was one of the largest and best-organized slave rebellions in Brazil's long history of slavery. © AP IMAGES/SILVIA IZQUIERDO.

Deslondes and the slaves began fighting with the two defense forces and a third force put together by the wounded Andry on the morning of January 11. The fight did not last long. More than 60 slaves were killed and many more were injured. Some of those who survived the battle fled into the swamps. About 16 slaves, including Deslondes, were arrested. With that the rebellion finally came to an end.

Results

The slaves who were arrested were put on trial on January 13. They were all found guilty and put to death. Deslondes was also put to death after being tortured for at least a day. He died on January 15.

The German Coast slave rebellion was a failure in the end but had a lasting effect. The rebellion demonstrated the potential dangers of future slave revolts and left many people across the country worried about what would happen if slaves rose up again. The local white community in

Louisiana tried to prevent future violence by doing everything possible to erase the German Coast rebellion from history. This led to it being mostly forgotten in comparison to many other rebellions of its kind. The memory of Deslondes and his slave army managed to survive, however, and his brave attempt to found a black republic in New Orleans remains one of the region's most untold stories.

Nat Turner's Rebellion/Anti-slavery Petitions

LOCATION: Virginia

DATE: 1831–1832

The United States became divided over the issue of slavery in the 19th century. The debate became especially heated by the 1830s. People across the country began calling for the abolition, or end, of slavery. Even some people in southern states, where slavery was more common, thought that it was time to end the practice. Virginia was one southern state where a major debate over slavery arose in the 1830s.

Virginia's slavery debate was connected directly to a deadly slave revolt that shocked many people throughout the state. Lifelong slave Nat Turner (1800–1831) led a two-day slave rebellion in August 1831 that caused the deaths of as many as 65 whites. In the end it was the bloodiest slave revolt of its kind in US history. The uprising terrified people. It convinced many that they had to do something to address the problem of slavery in one way or another. Few could agree on exactly what to do, however.

Many Virginians asked their state government to take action on slavery. In the months that followed Nat Turner's rebellion, people sent petitions, or written requests, to state lawmakers. They asked members of the state legislature, or lawmaking body, to do something to help. Some sent anti-slavery petitions in support of abolition. Others wanted to keep slavery but called for free blacks to be removed from the state. The petitions led to an important debate in the Virginia legislature over the future of slavery. In addition to deciding the fate of slavery in Virginia, the debate showed that the South would continue to defend slavery and brought the nation closer to civil war.

Nat Turner's rebellion

A number of slave rebellions took place during the period when slavery was permitted in the United States. The rebellion that Nat Turner led in 1831 is often considered one of the most important in history. Turner was born into slavery. He spent most of his life working on a plantation in Southampton County, Virginia. Turner was deeply religious. He believed from an early age that he was meant to do something great. He claimed that he had a vision of a fierce battle between blacks and whites that was to occur in the near future. He eventually led this battle himself.

Turner first decided to start a slave revolt in February 1831, but he was unable to act on his plans until months later. He finally launched his attack on August 21. That night he and a group of about 75 fellow slaves traveled to several local farms and killed between 55 and 65 men, women, and children over two days. Military forces finally stopped the uprising on August 23. More than 100 slaves were killed in the final battle. Turner escaped capture at first and remained on the run for two months. He was finally caught on October 30.

Illustration shows the discovery of Nat Turner by Benjamin Phipps on October 30, 1831.
© EVERETT HISTORICAL/SHUTTERSTOCK.COM.

Turner was put on trial the following month. The court found him guilty of leading the rebellion. He was hanged along with 16 others on November 11. Both the rebellion and Turner's death had a major effect on the slavery debate. The violence of the rebellion terrified people across the South. It caused many to respond even more harshly to slaves' pleas for freedom. In the North, people who opposed slavery saw Turner as a victim of southern cruelty. They used his rebellion as a rallying point in the fight for abolition.

The immediate effects of Turner's rebellion were felt most strongly in Virginia. Many were concerned that more rebellions might occur. Newspapers published letters from readers who were worried about the dangers of living alongside both slaves and free blacks. Others responded angrily to anyone who dared to speak out in support of ending slavery. In short, Turner's rebellion left Virginia a very unsettled and divided state.

Petitions and debate on slavery

People across Virginia contacted the state legislature about slavery after the rebellion. Concerned citizens sent about 40 petitions asking the legislature to take action. The petitions proposed several solutions to the slavery problem. All of them showed just how divided Virginians were on the subject of slavery.

Some of the petitions called for all slaves to be freed. One petition sent from the Virginia Yearly Meeting of the Society of Friends (Quakers) argued that slavery was an evil practice. The petition stated that slavery unfairly denied Africans their most basic human rights. Another petition called for an end to slavery on the basis of the slave population's rapid growth. This petition's writers worried that it would be dangerous for Virginia to allow the slave population to outgrow the white population.

Other groups who submitted petitions asked the legislature to take even stronger measures. These groups wanted the legislature to both end slavery and remove all blacks from Virginia. They argued that removal was the best way to handle the slavery problem and make sure that the white population remained safe from further attacks.

Not everyone supported the idea of freeing slaves. Many wanted slavery to continue and instead focused their attention on free blacks. A number of pro-slavery groups wrote petitions arguing that free blacks were a dangerous influence on the slave population. These groups asked

Slavery

Uncle Tom's Cabin as Protest Literature

Author Harriet Beecher Stowe's (1811–1896) *Uncle Tom's Cabin* (1852) is among the most important American novels ever written. It exposed countless readers to the horrors of life as a slave and forever changed the way Americans thought about the practice of slavery. The novel is also an example of protest literature. Protest literature is stories or poems that call attention to social problems and express opinions against these problems. *Uncle Tom's Cabin* called on the United States to extend the rights and freedoms guaranteed by the US Constitution to all people, without regard to race.

Stowe's own experiences with slavery inspired her to write the novel. She lived in Cincinnati, Ohio, a city that was just across the Ohio River from the slave state of Kentucky. Stowe met many escaped slaves and learned much about the suffering they endured. She became an opponent of slavery and wanted to do something to help end its practice. She became even more determined after the US Congress passed the Compromise of 1850. This compromise ended the slave trade in the District of Columbia but also created the Fugitive Slave Law.

The Fugitive Slave Law required all people to help catch escaped slaves. Stowe disliked that the law forced her to participate in the slavery system, and she vowed to do something about it. Because she was a talented writer, Stowe decided to write an anti-slavery book.

Harriet Beecher Stowe was an abolitionist who wrote the popular anti-slavery novel Uncle Tom's Cabin *in the 1850s.* © EVERETT HISTORICAL/SHUTTERSTOCK.COM.

Uncle Tom's Cabin follows the story of a slave named Tom. He relies on his strong faith to cope with the harsh realities of slavery. Tom helps other slaves reach freedom. He eventually chooses to die rather than to deny his faith or provide information about the other slaves he is trying to protect.

Uncle Tom's Cabin was very popular among readers. It convinced many to support the anti-slavery movement.

---

the legislature to remove the state's free blacks and send them to the African colony of Liberia.

Some looked for a less extreme response to the slavery problem that was fairer to free blacks. At least one petition asked the legislature to consider banning free blacks and slaves from learning any trades or arts. The petition's authors thought the ban would prevent blacks from becoming widely accepted in white society and would protect white citizens' jobs.

The debate The debate over slavery in Virginia began well before the state legislature returned to session in December 1831. People across the state argued about whether slavery should be allowed to continue. These arguments showed just how divided Virginians really were. Most people in the western part of the state opposed slavery. People in eastern Virginia, who depended more on slavery to maintain their way of life, supported the practice.

Virginia Governor John Floyd (1783–1837) was the first person to speak when the legislature finally met to discuss slavery. Floyd was one of many who worried that allowing people to speak out against slavery in public might lead others to violence and could threaten slavery's survival. Floyd, like many government officials, wanted to avoid this risk. He warned lawmakers that black preachers and others who spoke out against slavery were dangerous. He recommended changing the laws to make it easier to keep slaves in order. He encouraged the idea of removing free blacks from the state.

The Virginia legislature was made up of two bodies called the House of Delegates and the Senate. Most of the slavery debate occurred in the House. Representatives in the House formed a special committee to address slavery. The committee discussed the possibility of removing free blacks or ending slavery but made little progress on actually doing either.

Leaders in the House of Delegates eventually decided to allow an open debate on slavery. In January the House heard arguments for and against the idea of ending slavery. Near the end of the month, House leaders decided that it was unwise to take an immediate action on the issue. The legislature passed just one bill related to slavery. The bill led to a law that limited the activities of both slaves and free blacks.

Results

The Virginia slave debate was the closest any southern state ever came to abolishing slavery. Many considered it a major accomplishment that a southern legislature gave serious consideration to a number of anti-slavery measures. In the end, however, the debate failed to achieve any significant changes to slavery in Virginia.

DC Compensated Emancipation Act

This primary source photo shows a document that was used in Washington, DC, to free slaves during the US Civil War. In April 1862, eight months before President Abraham Lincoln's Emancipation Proclamation went into effect, he signed the District of Columbia Compensated Emancipation Act and ended slavery in Washington, DC. Some 3,100 slaves were given their freedom. In exchange for that freedom, the government reimbursed slave owners for the cost of their slaves.

In honor of the 150th anniversary of the District of Columbia Compensated Emancipation Act in 2012, the National Archives displayed this rarely seen document. A review of the document shows the names of the slaves being released as well as how much money is being paid to the slave owner. When Lincoln signed the Emancipation Proclamation several months later, it freed slaves in Confederate-controlled territories. It took the 13th Amendment to the US Constitution, ratified in December 1865, to abolish all slavery in the United States.

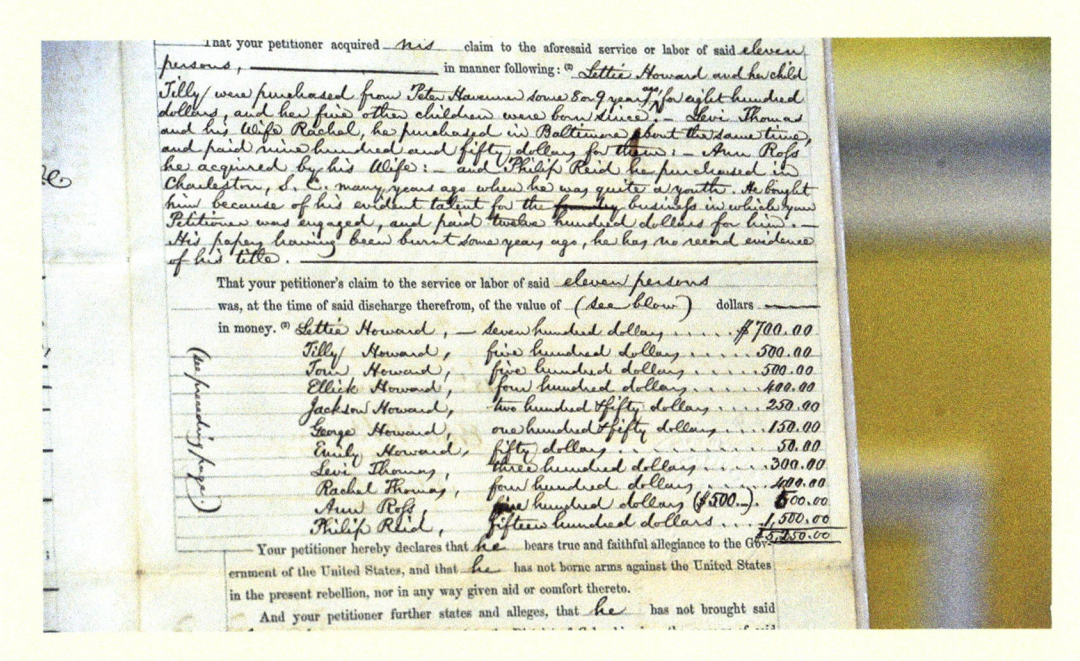

Petition used to free slaves, 1862. © MARVIN JOSEPH/THE WASHINGTON POST VIA GETTY IMAGES.

The most important result of the Virginia slavery debate was the legislature's failure to take a stand against slavery. By refusing to free its slaves, Virginia showed that the South had almost no chance of ever changing its views from pro-slavery to anti-slavery. As a result, the conflict between the

North and South increased, and the whole nation moved closer to a civil war. The debates also deepened the divisions between the eastern and western parts of Virginia. The opposing views within the state eventually caused Virginia to split in two, forming the states of Virginia and West Virginia.

Christmas Rebellion/Baptist War

LOCATION: Jamaica
DATE: 1831–1832

The British government took control of the Caribbean island of Jamaica in the mid-1600s. They used the island to grow crops that could be sold back in Great Britain. For many years, the British used slaves to work in the fields and harvest the crops. By the early 1800s, there were hundreds of thousands of slaves working in Jamaica.

In 1831 a slave named Samuel Sharpe (c. 1801–1832) developed a plan to gain freedom for the Jamaican slaves. Sharpe wanted to lead the slaves in a large strike after Christmas. When people strike, they refuse to work until their demands are met. The strike was supposed to be peaceful, but anger among the slaves pushed them to begin an uprising. They burned farms and crops and took control of several areas on the island.

The rebellion lasted for days until Jamaica's governor called in armed troops to stop the slaves. Hundreds of people were killed, and many farms were destroyed. The British punished many of the slaves involved in the rebellion. Some were beaten, while others were put on trial and executed. The size of the uprising shocked many people in Jamaica and in Great Britain. The rebellion was one of the main reasons the British government decided to end slavery in 1833.

Brief history of Jamaica

Jamaica is an island in the Caribbean Sea. It is about 160 miles (257 kilometers) south of the island of Cuba and about 530 miles (852 kilometers) south of Florida in the United States. Explorer Christopher Columbus (1451–1506) landed on Jamaica in 1494 and claimed the island for the nation of Spain. The Spanish used the island as a supply base for their troops who were trying to conquer land in South America.

In 1655 British forces defeated the Spanish and captured Jamaica. The British colonists who settled there began planting crops. The island's warm weather was perfect for growing sugarcane, which is a plant used to make sugar. Sugar was very popular in Great Britain, where it was used to sweeten tea and other drinks and foods. Because of the sweetener's popularity, the number of Jamaican sugar-producing farms, called plantations, grew from 57 in 1673 to about 430 by 1739.

Plantation owners needed workers for their farms, so they imported thousands of slaves from Africa. In 1673 there were fewer than 10,000 slaves in Jamaica; by 1800 there were about 300,000. Living conditions for slaves in Jamaica were very difficult. They were often mistreated, and many died from diseases common in tropical regions. During the 1700s and early 1800s, Jamaican slaves staged at least 16 rebellions.

Samuel Sharpe's plan

Samuel Sharpe was born in Jamaica about 1801. It was not common for slaves to read or to get an education, but Sharpe was different. He learned to read and write, and he taught himself by reading newspapers and books. Sharpe was very religious and became a preacher in the Baptist church. Sharpe often traveled from church to church speaking out against slavery. His speeches were very powerful and inspired many people.

Christmas Rebellion/Baptist War leader Samuel Sharpe. © GEORGIOS KOLLIDAS/SHUTTERSTOCK.COM.

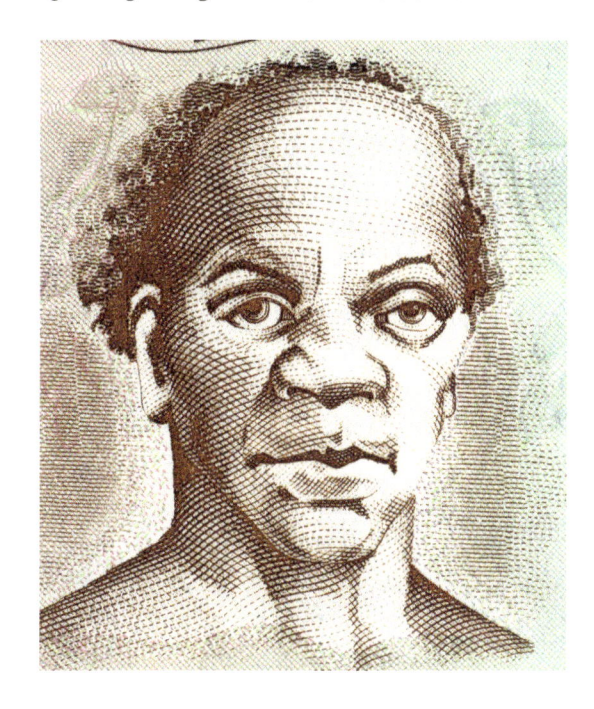

Sharpe kept up on world events by reading newspapers. He knew that feelings toward slavery had begun to change back in Great Britain. In 1807 the British government stopped transporting slaves from Africa to its colonies. By 1831 there was a movement growing in Great Britain to abolish, or end, slavery altogether. Sharpe believed it was just a matter of time before the British government freed the slaves in Jamaica and all the colonies.

Because of his position as a Baptist preacher, Sharpe was able to travel to churches around Jamaica. He spoke to other slaves and began to organize a plan he thought would win the slaves their freedom. He called for the slaves to go on strike and refuse to work after their three-day

Christmas break in 1831. They would return to work only if the plantation owners agreed to pay them wages.

The time after Christmas was very important to plantation owners. The sugarcane was ripe, and if it was not cut down quickly, it would spoil. Sharpe hoped the plantation owners would agree with the slaves' demands to keep their valuable crops from being ruined. He told the slaves that he wanted the strike to be peaceful. However, Sharpe and other strike leaders did plan for an armed revolt if the owners did not listen to their demands.

Beginnings of an uprising

Word spread across the island about the planned strike that was scheduled to begin on December 27. Plantation owners also became aware of Sharpe's plan and would not accept the slaves' demands. Some slaves thought that plantation owners were going to send in troops to force them back to work. Other slaves believed a false story that slavery had already ended in Great Britain. They thought the governor of Jamaica was ignoring the law and refusing to free them.

The stories and rumors angered many of the slaves. Instead of striking on December 27, a group of slaves in the Saint James section of Jamaica set fire to a large estate. The fire was seen as a signal that a rebellion had begun. The revolt soon spread to other areas of the island. The slaves burned houses, fields of crops, and storage buildings full of sugarcane. More than 60,000 slaves joined in the rebellion. They took control of large areas of land and burned or attacked more than 200 plantations.

Local military forces were unable to handle the uprising. The governor of Jamaica called in highly trained British soldiers and ordered them to stop the violence. A group of freed slaves called Maroons (pronounced muh-ROONS) helped the British troops. The name Maroon comes from the Spanish word *cimarrón* (pronounced sim-uh-rohn), meaning "wild." The Maroons were former Spanish slaves who escaped into the mountains when the British took control of Jamaica. In return for their freedom, the Maroons helped the British capture other escaped slaves on the island.

British troops were able to stop the main rebellion in about eight days. Scattered fighting continued around Jamaica into late January 1832. More than 300 slaves were killed in the uprising. Some were killed in the fighting, while others were shot by troops instead of being

The stories and rumors angered many of the slaves. Instead of striking on December 27, a group of slaves in the Saint James section of Jamaica set fire to a large estate. The fire was seen as a signal that a rebellion had begun.

arrested. Fourteen white farmers or plantation owners were also killed. The rebellion caused more than $1.2 million in property damage.

Aftermath in Jamaica

In the months after the rebellion, many slaves were arrested and put on trial. More than 500 were found guilty of committing a crime and more than 300 were executed. Other slaves were whipped or beaten as a punishment. In some cases, the beatings were so bad the slaves later died from their injuries. A smaller number of slaves were deported, or removed from Jamaica, and sent to Canada or Great Britain.

Because the rebellion was planned in Baptist churches, some white Jamaicans responded by burning down several places of worship. For this reason, the rebellion is sometimes called the Baptist War. Others call it the Christmas Rebellion because it occurred after the holiday.

Sharpe was among the hundreds of slaves arrested. Although his original plan was for a peaceful strike, the court accused him of leading the rebellion. He was found guilty and executed on May 23, 1832. His owners were paid about $20 for their "loss of property." In the 20th century, Jamaica named Sharpe a national hero. The country also renamed the site of his execution in the town of Montego Bay as Sam Sharpe Square.

Effect on British slavery

The rebellion was the largest slave uprising in the British Caribbean colonies. It raised fears among Jamaica's white plantation owners that the slaves could plan another revolt. Many plantation owners who were against abolishing slavery were now willing to consider it to prevent more violence. In Great Britain, the rebellion inspired anti-slavery groups to push harder to end slavery. More than 1 million people signed several formal requests asking lawmakers to end slavery in all British territories.

British lawmakers were already considering ending slavery. The Christmas Rebellion and the public's response to it prompted them to find a quicker solution. In September 1833, Great Britain passed the Slavery Abolition Act. The law officially ended slavery in all British colonies. The government paid plantation owners in the Caribbean colonies about $26 million to make up for financial losses.

Under the law, former slaves were required to work on their plantations for a period of six years. During that time, they were paid wages.

The plantation owner also provided them with housing, food, and clothing. Children under six were considered free and could work only with their parents' approval. The system did not work very well. Plantation owners sometimes abused their workers and treated them as if they were still slaves. The government of Jamaica decided to end the system. In June 1838, Jamaica passed a law granting all former slaves full freedom.

Harpers Ferry Raid

LOCATION: Harpers Ferry, Virginia

DATE: October 16–18, 1859

Slavery was a major part of American life for many years. However, it was abolished in many of the northern states after the American Revolution (1775–1783). The states that allowed slavery were mainly in the southern United States. In 1807 Congress passed a law to prohibit new slaves from being brought into the country. However, the law did not free the slaves already in the nation. By the mid-19th century, a growing number of people thought that slavery should end in all states.

The effort to end slavery was called the abolition movement and it first began to gain steam in the 1830s. It was led by individuals such as anti-slavery speaker Frederick Douglass (1817–1895) and *Uncle Tom's Cabin* author Harriet Beecher Stowe (1811–1896). People objected to slavery for different reasons. Some thought it was morally wrong. Others simply thought it was a bad way to do business. Whatever their reasons, many people thought it was time for slavery to end.

The battle over slavery quickly became heated. Many in the South wanted slavery to continue because it was important to their way of life. Many in the North wanted slavery to end because it was cruel and unfair. People became even more upset over slavery as the United States began to expand westward. The question of whether or not slavery should be allowed in new states left the country more divided than ever. By the late 1850s, the argument over slavery had reached a crisis point.

A major event in the slavery crisis was John Brown's (1800–1859) raid on the town of Harpers Ferry, Virginia (now part of West Virginia), in 1859. Brown was an abolition supporter and wanted the raid to be the first step in a large slave uprising. The raid was not successful, but it had a major effect on people on both sides of the slavery debate. The raid made Southerners more fearful of slave rebellions and also encouraged more Northerners to support abolition. In the end the Harpers Ferry raid was one of the important events that set the stage for the American Civil War (1861–1865).

The slavery debate

Slavery was the most hotly debated issue in mid-19th-century America. At this time, many people wanted the practice to end once and for all. They joined together to put pressure on the government to take action on the matter. This became known as the abolition movement. The abolition movement was mostly supported by people in the northern part of the country. Most people in the South, on the other hand, did not support the movement. Southern plantation owners depended on slaves to grow and harvest their crops. This meant that slaves were a very important part of the South's ability to support itself. Because of this most Southerners were strongly opposed to the Northern abolition movement.

Harriet Tubman was a conductor on the Underground Railroad. She escorted escaped slaves north to freedom. COURTESY OF THE LIBRARY OF CONGRESS.

The abolition movement became powerful in the 1830s because of the Underground Railroad. The Underground Railroad was a network of safe houses through which escaped slaves moved on their journey to freedom. As many as 100,000 slaves may have found their way to freedom through the Underground Railroad. Although this pathway to freedom may have been used as early as the 1780s, it did not become widely known until the 1830s. The success of the Underground Railroad helped further the abolition movement in the North. In the South it made people even more determined to keep slavery alive at any cost.

The nation's rapid growth intensified the fight over slavery. The United States started to expand into the West during the 19th century, eventually creating a number of new states and territories. This led to a major debate over whether or not slavery should be allowed in these new states and territories. The government's attempts to address this problem upset people on both sides and further divided the North and the South. By the late 1850s, the nation was so divided over the practice of slavery that a civil war seemed like a real possibility.

John Brown John Brown grew up in Connecticut and Ohio as part of a religious family that was strongly against slavery. Brown had spent most of his life struggling to find success in business before committing himself to the abolition movement. He attended his first abolition meeting in Cleveland in 1837. This meeting turned out to be an inspiring event that convinced him to make ending slavery his life's goal. From that moment forward Brown did everything he could to support the abolition movement.

Brown's fight against slavery took a violent turn in the 1850s when the debate over whether slavery should be allowed in new states was raging. Kansas was one of the new states in the middle of this debate. Brown and his five sons traveled to Kansas to help fight against pro-slavery forces there. On May 21, 1856 pro-slavery fighters attacked Lawrence, Kansas, an anti-slavery town, burning and looting many of the buildings. Several days later, Brown and a few other men attacked a pro-slavery settlement at Pottawatomie Creek and killed five men. The pro- and anti-slavery forces continued to fight back and forth. One of Brown's sons was killed by pro-slavery fighters. Brown swore his revenge.

Brown left Kansas in early 1858 and began making plans for a massive slave uprising that would scare the South into giving up on slavery. Brown first looked to find help from some of the abolition movement's most powerful leaders. He eventually convinced six such leaders to join him. They became known as the "Secret Six." With their help, Brown put together a small army of 20 men who agreed to take part in a raid. The target of Brown's raid was the US Armory at Harpers Ferry, Virginia. The army made and stored many of its weapons at the armory. Brown planned an attack on the US government that would send a clear message about the future of slavery in the country.

John Brown became so devoted to the anti-slavery cause that he led the raid on Harpers Ferry, Virginia (now West Virginia). He was later executed for his role in the insurrection.
COURTESY OF THE LIBRARY OF CONGRESS.

Slavery

The Sword of Rebellion

This primary source excerpt by Frederick Douglass, an African American social reformer, is from a speech he gave about John Brown on May 30, 1881, at Storer College. Douglass praised Brown for giving his life to help end slavery in the United States. In the audience was Andrew Hunter, the district attorney who had tried Brown. Douglass ended his speech as follows.

But the question is, Did John Brown fail? He certainly did fail to get out of Harpers Ferry before being beaten down by United States soldiers; he did fail to save his own life, and to lead a liberating army into the mountains of Virginia. But he did not go to Harpers Ferry to save his life.

The true question is, Did John Brown draw his sword against slavery and thereby lose his life in vain? And to this I answer ten thousand times, No! No man fails, or can fail, who so grandly gives himself and all he has to a righteous cause. No man, who in his hour of extremest need, when on his way to meet an ignominious [disgraceful] death, could so forget himself as to stop and kiss a little child, one of the hated race for whom he was about to die, could by any possibility fail.

Did John Brown fail? Ask Henry A. Wise in whose house less than two years after, a school for the emancipated slaves was taught.

Did John Brown fail? Ask James M. Mason, the author of the inhuman fugitive slave bill, who was cooped up in Fort Warren, as a traitor less than two years from the time that he stood over the prostrate body of John Brown....

If John Brown did not end the war that ended slavery, he did at least begin the war that ended slavery. If we look over the dates, places and men for which this honor is claimed, we shall find that not Carolina, but Virginia, not Fort Sumter, but Harpers Ferry, and the arsenal, not Col. Anderson, but John Brown, began the war that ended American slavery and made this a free Republic. Until this blow was struck, the prospect for freedom was dim, shadowy and uncertain. The irrepressible conflict was one of words, votes and compromises.

When John Brown stretched forth his arm the sky was cleared. The time for compromises was gone—the armed hosts of freedom stood face to face over the chasm of a broken Union—and the clash of arms was at hand. The South staked all upon getting possession of the Federal Government, and failing to do that, drew the sword of rebellion and thus made her own, and not Brown's, the lost cause of the century.

SOURCE: Douglass, Frederick. "Frederick Douglass at Harpers Ferry." US National Park Service. Available online at https://www.nps.gov/hafe/learn/historyculture/frederick-douglass-at-harpers-ferry.htm (accessed October 15, 2017). Courtesy of US National Park Service.

Harpers Ferry raid

Brown prepared for his raid by renting a farm in Maryland that was just across the Potomac River from Harpers Ferry. He gathered his men there and readied them for the attack. They left for Harpers Ferry on the night of October 16, 1859. After crossing the river, Brown and his men quietly

Slavery

captured a few watchmen. They also cut the armory's telegraph wires so no one could send out a call for help. Brown's forces took control of the armory over the next few hours. They also took 60 of the town's most important slave-owning citizens as prisoners. Brown had hoped their capture would convince their slaves to join the raid, but none actually did.

Few people learned about the raid until armory workers arrived in the morning. Then several groups of armed soldiers rushed to the armory, surrounded it, and prepared for a fight. It soon became clear that Brown and his men were outnumbered and in trouble. Brown took several of the prisoners and hid in the armory's firehouse. Some of Brown's men gave up on the raid and tried to escape. While several made it to safety, a few others were killed as they fled.

News of the raid soon reached the nation's capital in Washington, DC. President James Buchanan (1791–1868) sent army lieutenant colonel Robert E. Lee (1807–1870) to deal with the problem at Harpers Ferry. When Lee arrived, he prepared the town's soldiers and came up with a plan to end the standoff. Early the next morning Lee ordered Brown and his men to surrender. When they refused to cooperate, Lee ordered a group of marines to enter the firehouse. Brown's men fired on the marines and killed one of them. Fighting then broke out for a short time. Ten of Brown's men were killed. Two of those killed were Brown's sons. The fighting finally came to an end when Brown himself was wounded and captured two days after the Harpers Ferry raid began.

John Brown and others inside the engine house of the Harpers Ferry Armory just before the US military rams through the door. © EVERETT HISTORICAL/SHUTTERSTOCK.COM.

Results

After the raid, Brown was tried for treason and murder. He was eventually found guilty and hanged on December 2, 1859. News of his death shook the nation. While nearly everyone agreed that his raid was a reckless act, people in the North and the South felt differently about the meaning of his death. Abolition supporters in the North considered Brown a hero who died fighting to end slavery. People in the South thought he was a madman who threatened their way of life and got what he deserved.

Even though it failed, the Harpers Ferry raid was an important turning point in the slavery debate. It further divided the nation and angered people on both sides. After the raid it was clear that the North and South could not settle their differences peacefully. In the end the raid set the United States on the path to a civil war and was the beginning of the end of slavery in the country.

Fight to Stop Human Trafficking

LOCATION: Worldwide

DATE: Ongoing

Most of the world's nations officially ended the practice of slavery in the 1800s. The United Kingdom made it illegal in 1833. The United States ended slavery in 1865. In 1948 the United Nations (UN) declared that slavery should be made illegal in all countries. The UN is an organization of 193 world nations that tries to promote cooperation and peace between countries. In 1981 the West African nation of Mauritania (pronounced mohr-ah-TAH-nee-ah) was the last country to officially end slavery.

Despite the efforts to end the practice, slavery is still a serious problem in many places around the world. Millions of people in the 21st century are bought, sold, and forced into labor or are sexually exploited, or used to make money. Some are kidnapped, while others are threatened or tricked into a life of slavery. In many cases, the victims are children. Modern slavery is often referred to as human trafficking. Trafficking is the buying or selling of an illegal product or service.

Most nations have passed laws to fight human trafficking, but ending the practice has been difficult. People who commit the crime of human

Slavery

Members of Soroptimist International hold a protest against human trafficking on October 26, 2012, in Belfast, Northern Ireland. © STEPHEN BARNES/SOCIETY/ ALAMY.

trafficking often operate in secret. Many of the victims are afraid to escape or speak out, and some may not even be aware that help is available. In some countries, governments may not do enough to fight human trafficking. The United States publishes a yearly report that grades nations on the job they are doing to stop the practice.

There are many private organizations that are also trying to stop human trafficking. The Polaris Project, International Justice Mission, and Soroptimist International are just a few of the anti-trafficking groups worldwide. Their efforts include organizing rallies, demonstrations, and other events to raise awareness of the problem. Many also offer support for victims of human trafficking.

A look at the problem

According to a 2017 report by the International Labour Organization (ILO), about 40.3 million people worldwide were victims of modern slavery in 2016, either through forced labor (24.9 million) or forced marriage (15.4 million). The ILO is a part of the United Nations that deals with labor issues and improving working conditions. Other sources place the number of victims as high as 45.8 million.

The ILO reported that about 16 million people were forced into slavery as a source of labor in the private sector. They were made to work in industries such as construction, mining, manufacturing, or farming.

Some were forced to become domestic workers such as housekeepers. About 4.8 million people were forced to become sex workers. About 4 million were forced into labor by their governments.

About 71 percent of the victims of modern slavery were women or girls. About 25 percent were under the age of 18. Of those forced into slave labor, about 25 million, or 62 percent, lived in the Asia-Pacific region. This area includes countries such as China, India, and Thailand. About 9.2 million victims came from Africa, 2 million from the Americas, 3.6 million from Russia and Eastern Europe, and fewer than 1 million from Arab states.

One of the problems authorities have with fighting modern slavery is that it is a very profitable business. The ILO estimated in 2014 that human traffickers earned about $150 billion a year. Two-thirds of that money came from the sex industry. Forced labor in other industries is responsible for producing many common products that people buy. In 2016 the US government made a list of 139 goods from 75 countries made by forced or child labor. The list included clothes from India and Christmas decorations from China.

The victims

Many children and young people who are forced into slavery are runaways. According to the National Center for Missing and Exploited Children in 2016, one in six runaways under age 17 in the United States was likely to become a victim of sex trafficking. Some are abused and live in fear of their captors. Many are told that they are also guilty of a crime and warned to keep silent.

In some poor countries, people often struggle to find work to support their families. Human traffickers know this and use it to trick people into slavery. They may promise victims money for a few hours work or offer them a job in another country. When the individuals accept, they may find themselves forced to work long hours in jobs with little or no pay. In some cases, people who owe money may be told they can pay off the debt by working. However, no matter how long they work, they are told they still owe money.

If a person accepts a job in another country, the trafficker may take the victim's passport. A passport is an official document that allows people to travel from one country to another. Without a passport, people would not be able to return home. They may also be told they must work to pay for the cost of their travel. Trafficking victims may also be held captive by armed guards or kept in prisonlike buildings.

International efforts

In 1948 the UN passed the Universal Declaration of Human Rights, a list of 30 basic rights the UN believed every human being deserved. The fourth right on the list said that "no one shall be held in slavery" and that the slave trade should be made illegal worldwide. In 2000 the UN created laws that made human trafficking a criminal offense. It targeted people who try to force, trick, or convince others into becoming slaves. It also made it a crime to transport people to a place where they would be forced into slavery.

Also in 2000, the United States passed the Trafficking Victims Protection Act (TVPA). The TVPA made human trafficking a federal crime and created tougher punishments for those who break the law. It also set up a four-part system to monitor how other nations fight human trafficking.

The system is divided into tiers, or levels. Tier 1 means a country has met all its responsibilities under the law and is doing everything it can to stop human trafficking. As of 2017, the United States, the United Kingdom, and Canada are on the Tier 1 list. Tier 2 means a country has not met all its responsibilities but is making an effort to do so. Countries on the 2017 list include Mexico and India. If a nation is on the Tier 2 list but human trafficking is a serious problem or is increasing, that nation is placed on the Tier 2 watch list.

In 2017, 23 countries were placed on the Tier 3 list. The list is for nations that have not met their responsibilities under the law and are not doing enough to stop human trafficking. Russia and China, two of the largest nations in the world, were on the Tier 3 list.

Raising awareness

In addition to the efforts of world governments, there are many private organizations that help fight human trafficking. The Polaris Project is an organization based in Washington, DC. The Polaris Project operates a free telephone line for people to report suspected cases of human trafficking. Victims can call the line to find out how to get help. The organization also pushes federal and state governments to pass tougher anti-trafficking laws.

In the United Kingdom, the women's group Soroptimist International has been running an anti-trafficking effort called the Purple

In 1948 the United Nations passed the Universal Declaration of Human Rights, a list of 30 basic rights the UN believed every human being deserved. The fourth right on the list said that "no one shall be held in slavery" and that the slave trade should be made illegal worldwide.

Teardrop Campaign since 2008. The group tries to raise awareness of the issue by holding demonstrations and asking people to donate money and time to support its efforts. The campaign tries to inform the public of businesses that may use trafficking victims. It also promotes a free police phone number for people to call if they think someone is a victim of human trafficking.

In 2013 the UN designated July 30 as World Day against Trafficking in Persons. Groups across the world use the day to hold programs and rallies. Their goal is to bring the problem of human trafficking to the attention of government leaders and the public. In 2010 the British government named October 18 as Anti-Slavery Day. Demonstrations and events are held on that day across the United Kingdom and several other nations.

Other efforts

Many people around the world observe World Day against Trafficking in Persons and Anti-Slavery Day with rallies and other events to raise awareness of the problem. In 2014 hundreds of people marked Anti-Slavery Day by taking part in the Walk for Freedom. The A21 Campaign, an anti-slavery group, organized the walk. In 2015 marches were held at 200 locations in 26 nations. The Walk for Freedom was also held in 2016 and on October 14, 2017.

In 2012 the International Justice Mission (IJM), a US-based human rights group, started a campaign called Stand for Freedom. The first event took place on six college campuses in the United States. By 2015 it had grown to include thousands of people from 42 US states and 10 countries worldwide. The campaign asked people to stand for 24 hours in support of human trafficking victims. Many people took turns standing on college campuses or in public areas. They held anti-slavery signs or posters to get their message to the public. The event continued until 2016.

In 2017 the IJM asked Christians across the world to mark September 24 as Freedom Sunday. The campaign asked religious leaders to discuss the issue during services and bring the issue of human trafficking to a large audience.

For More Information

BOOKS

Horwitz, Tony. *Midnight Rising: John Brown and the Raid That Sparked the Civil War.* New York: Henry Holt, 2012.

Pernoud, Régine. *Those Terrible Middle Ages: Debunking the Myths.* Translated by Anne Englund Nash. San Francisco, CA: Ignatius Press, 2000, 85–88.

Rasmussen, Daniel. *American Uprising: The Untold Story of America's Largest Slave Revolt.* New York: HarperCollins, 2011.

Reynolds, David S. *John Brown, Abolitionist: The Man Who Killed Slavery, Sparked the Civil War, and Seeded Civil Rights.* New York: Vintage Books, 2006.

Shepherd, Verene. "Baptist War (1831–1832)." In *Encyclopedia of Antislavery and Abolition.* Volume 1. Edited by Peter Hinks and John McKivigan, 81–82. Westport, CT: Greenwood Press, 2007.

PERIODICALS

Blair, David. "The World Has Over 45 Million Slaves—Including 1.2 Million in Europe—Finds New Study." *Telegraph* (May 31, 2016). Available online at http://www.telegraph.co.uk/news/2016/05/31/the-world-has-over-45-million-slaves---including-12-million-in-e/ (accessed August 28, 2017).

WEBSITES

Alkhateeb, Firas. "The Bahia Muslim Slave Revolt." Lost Islamic History. http://lostislamichistory.com/the-bahia-muslim-slave-revolt (accessed August 25, 2017).

Fessenden, Marissa. "How a Nearly Successful Slave Revolt Was Intentionally Lost to History." *Smithsonian.* http://www.smithsonianmag.com/smart-news/its-anniversary-1811-louisiana-slave-revolt-180957760 (accessed August 25, 2017).

"45.8 Million People Are Enslaved across the World." Global Slavery Index, May 30, 2016. https://www.globalslaveryindex.org/media/45-8-million-people-enslaved-across-world/ (accessed August 28, 2017).

"Global Estimates of Modern Slavery: Forced Labour and Forced Marriage." International Labour Organization, September 19, 2017. http://www.ilo.org/global/publications/books/WCMS_575479/lang–en/index.htm (accessed October 11, 2017).

"Human Trafficking by the Numbers." Human Rights First, January 7, 2017. http://www.humanrightsfirst.org/resource/human-trafficking-numbers (accessed August 23, 2017).

"Jamaican History." Jamaica Information Service. http://jis.gov.jm/information/jamaican-history/ (accessed August 24, 2017).

"Profits and Poverty: The Economics of Forced Labour." International Labour Organization, May 20, 2014. http://www.ilo.org/global/publications/ilo-bookstore/order-online/books/WCMS_243391/lang–en/index.htm (accessed October 11, 2017).

"The Raid on Harpers Ferry." Public Broadcasting Service. http://www.pbs.org/wgbh/aia/part4/4p2940.html (accessed August 21, 2017).

"Slavery in Louisiana." Whitney Plantation. http://whitneyplantation.com/slavery-in-louisiana.html (accessed August 25, 2017).

"Slaves & Freemen." Public Broadcasting Service. http://www.pbs.org/empires/romans/empire/slaves_freemen.html (accessed August 28, 2017).

"Thousands to #Stand4Freedom and Shine Light on Modern-Day Slavery." International Justice Mission. http://news.ijm.org/thousands-to-stand4freedom-and-shine-light-on-modern-day-slavery (accessed August 23, 2017).

"Timeline of Atlantic Slave Trade." ABC News. http://abcnews.go.com/US/story?id=96659&page=1 (accessed August 28, 2017).

"Trafficking in Persons Report." US Department of State, June 2017. https://www.state.gov/documents/organization/271339.pdf (accessed August 23, 2017).

"Uncle Tom's Cabin." Harriet Beecher Stowe Center, 2015. https://www.harrietbeecherstowecenter.org/utc (accessed August 23, 2017).

20

War

International Congress of Women **657**

Student Armband Protest of Vietnam War **663**

Student Protest at Kent State **669**

Candlelight Vigils against Invasion of Iraq **676**

Chelsea Manning and WikiLeaks **684**

Protests against war have become a major feature of modern conflicts. Wars bring great destruction, and many people question their reasons and value when they finally end. Demonstrations against wars have taken place in many countries. Such protests took a strong hold in the United States and reached a peak there in the 1960s and 1970s. These demonstrations may take a wide variety of forms. Some protests are against a particular war, while others are more about promoting peace in general. Protests may be personal, in the case of people refusing to serve in the armed forces or writing essays against war. Protests may also be massive displays, marches, or even riots.

Organized mass protests against war have become common only in recent generations, even though wars have been a major part of the human experience for thousands of years. By the time of the ancient civilizations of Egypt, Greece, and Rome, war was a common fact of life for many people. History records few organized efforts in ancient times to prevent war. At the time, most common people had little, if any, political representation and could be seriously punished for speaking out against the will of their leaders. Only much later, when leaders and nations embraced concepts such as human rights and freedom of expression, were people able to more freely speak and act out against war.

Early anti-war ideas

A rare suggestion of organized anti-war sentiment in ancient times appears in *Lysistrata*, a comedic play by Greek writer Aristophanes (c. 450 BCE–c. 388 BCE). *Lysistrata* tells the story of a group of Greek women who force their husbands to stop fighting by refusing them any sexual attention until they sign a truce, which is an agreement not to fight. This play proved very popular among ancient audiences. It suggested disapproval about the wars

WORDS TO KNOW

Candlelight vigil: An assembly of people who hold candles to show support or opposition for a cause or event.

Communism: A political system in which private ownership of property is eliminated and government directs all economic production. The goods produced and accumulated wealth are, in theory, shared relatively equally by all.

Delegate: A person at a meeting who represents others.

Democracy: Government in which all people vote for officials to make laws for them.

Draft: A process by which young men (and sometimes women) are required to serve in the armed forces.

National Guard: A branch of the armed forces that usually deals with problems within the United States.

Pacifist: Someone who is strongly opposed to war and fighting.

Suffrage: The right to vote.

Transgender: A term used to describe a person whose gender identity differs from the sex he or she was assigned at birth.

Weapons of mass destruction (WMD): Powerful weapons that can destroy entire cities or regions.

Whistle-blower: A person who publicly reports the illegal activities of an organization or a government.

---

raging in and around Greece at the time. However, the play was just a work of fiction, and the Greek wars continued for many years.

Religion is a force that causes increasing numbers of people to seek to end conflicts. Although some religious groups directly or indirectly encourage fighting, others seek to end it. Most notably, the Christian groups known as the Quakers and Unitarians are pacifists who hold many anti-war ideas and practices. Pacifists are strongly opposed to war and fighting. People from these religions have often spoken out against war and suggested it is not only a social danger but also a violation of God's will.

Some pacifists, including many Christians, helped to introduce the idea of conscientious objection. The term *conscientious objector* refers to a person who refuses to serve in the military due to religious or moral beliefs. The first recorded conscientious objector was a Roman soldier named Maximilianus, a Christian of the late 3rd century CE who refused to participate in war. Although he was promptly beheaded, he set an example for other pacifists and was later honored as Saint Maximilian. Many other early conscientious objectors met similar ends, but in the

CRITICAL THINKING QUESTIONS

1. Do you think people can strongly disagree with their country's policies and still be considered patriotic citizens? Why or why not?

2. Do you agree with the US government's decision to enter the war with Iraq? Why or why not?

3. Why do you think public support was low for a war with Iraq?

4. The founders of the International Congress of Women believed that, in general, women are naturally more peace loving than men. Do you believe that is a fair judgment? Why or why not?

5. Do you think the students in *Tinker v. Des Moines* should have been allowed to wear their armbands in school? Explain your reasoning.

6. Do you think President Obama made the right decision to reduce Chelsea Manning's prison sentence? Why or why not?

coming centuries some leaders began showing some respect and understanding toward anti-war sentiment.

First demonstrations in the United States

The formation of the United States in 1776 led to a new era of thought about human rights and the roles of leaders and societies. The new country was based on democratic principles of government and greatly increased personal freedoms and protections. The idea that citizens could make their own decisions and freely disagree with national policies helped to create a growing force of anti-war behavior.

Many people spoke out against the fighting that helped to establish the United States. However, it was not until the first decades of the 1800s that anti-war thinking really gained a strong foothold in America. During this period, some people wrote about the importance of maintaining peace for the moral improvement of society. In other words, if there was no war, people could devote time to solving social issues such as providing better public education, taking on health-care reform, or improving living conditions for the poor. Pacifist religious groups spoke out more freely and loudly than ever in favor of peace. Social organizations such as the American Peace Society also called for international cooperation in settling conflicts without war.

Despite the calls for peace, tensions between the North and South led to the US Civil War (1861–1865). Many Americans on both sides

War

Abraham Lincoln. COURTESY OF THE LIBRARY OF CONGRESS.

disagreed with this war, which became horribly bloody over its four-year span. A strong anti-war movement began and made a great impression in the North. There, many voters attempted to oust President Abraham Lincoln (1809–1865) due to his determination to continue the war. Many people felt that the continued war between the North and South was proving costlier than could ever be justified.

Many of the anti-war protesters were young men who saw that an ongoing war might bring them personally onto the battlefield. When Lincoln announced a draft, which required young men to serve in the armed forces, disapproval grew in many northern cities. A feature of Lincoln's plan allowed people to avoid the draft by paying a large fee to hire someone to take their place in war. Although on the surface this might have seemed like a major benefit to conscientious objectors, it also came as a stinging insult, as most Americans could not afford to pay the fee. In that sense, Lincoln's plan allowed only the wealthiest citizens to avoid their responsibility to serve.

Outraged, many working-class people began to protest in the streets. In July 1863, these protests led to the New York draft riots, which remain among the most destructive events in US history. Thousands of men, mostly poor immigrants, began demonstrating violently against the draft. Many also lashed out at local African Americans, who were seen by some as the cause of the war since one of Lincoln's main goals was to end slavery in the South.

The 20th century begins

The horrors of the Civil War supported the belief of many Americans that war was to be avoided at all costs. In the early 20th century, however, violent tensions rose in Europe. Many Americans pushed to remain neutral in any conflict that might erupt there. A neutral country does not pick sides or become involved in the fighting. Many leaders and others in Europe also promoted peace, although their governments, still monarchies ruled by one person, had little patience for disagreement from citizens.

When World War I (1914–1918) began, some people made attempts to bring it to an early end. The International Congress of Women, for instance, was a peace convention made entirely of women from different nations. This group met in late April and early May 1915 in the Netherlands, a neutral nation, to discuss the possibilities for restoring peace. They recommended that warring nations discuss their conflicts with the help of neutral nations instead of continuing the war. Although the women spread their message widely, it was ultimately ignored.

World War I proved to be a disaster of an unimaginable scale. Many nations around the globe sent soldiers to fight, and millions died in lengthy battles. Millions of noncombatants, or people not directly involved in the fighting, died from bombings, starvation, disease, and other wartime dangers.

The overwhelming tragedy of World War I led to a strong rebirth of anti-war sentiment. Artists and writers condemned the horrors of modern warfare. Peace groups and international organizations attempted to settle conflicts that could lead to future wars. These actions proved powerless, however, to stop the coming of World War II (1939–1945). In this war, much of the world returned to the same battlefields to commit horrors even worse than the previous conflict. Anti-war feelings were not as strong in World War II, as the goals of this war were clearer.

The Cold War and beyond

With two world wars within 50 years, many people hoped that reasons for fighting had finally been exhausted. Potentially disastrous conflicts remained, however. Following the end of World War II, the world almost immediately entered a period known as the Cold War (1945–1991). During this time, two major groups of nations (the Eastern Bloc with the Soviet Union and the Western Bloc with the United States) competed for political power and influence, with war seemingly always a strong possibility. This possible war would be worse than all others, too, since both sides had adopted nuclear weapons, capable of extreme destructive force. For the first time, people faced the prospect of a war that could destroy humanity. However, much of the Cold War was a war of ideas rather than actual fighting.

During this period, most of the active fighting was contained to the relatively small Asian countries of Vietnam and Korea. A long-lasting war in Vietnam over the spread of Communism in that country drew international attention. The United States became economically and then militarily involved in the Vietnam War (1954–1975) not long after World War II. Although many Americans did not fully understand or support the war, US involvement increased slowly in the coming years.

By the mid-1960s, thousands of American soldiers were fighting in the Vietnam conflict, and leaders were planning a sharp increase in American involvement. By this point, the war had become unpopular in the United States. Anti-war protests sprang up in various cities. In 1968 thousands of anti-war protesters descended on Chicago, Illinois, during the Democratic National Convention in August. Chicago's law enforcement officers were well prepared. Violent clashes occurred between the demonstrators and the police. Due to the violence by police, who beat protesters with clubs and sprayed them with tear gas, a commission later described the response as a police riot.

In 1970, when word spread that President Richard M. Nixon (1913–1994) intended to expand the war and the draft, anti-war protests occurred in many cities. These protests were particularly common on educational campuses, where young people were taking a stand for their rights. Marches, protest songs, and various demonstrations, including the burning of draft documents, became common in America in the 1970s.

One of the most remembered war protests occurred at the Democratic National Convention in 1968. As shown here, a police officer escorts a protester to a squad car surrounded by dozens of anti–Vietnam War demonstrators in Chicago, Illinois. © HULTON ARCHIVE/ GETTY IMAGES.

Some of these protests were peaceful, and others became violent. Some, such as the *Tinker v. Des Moines Independent Community School District* case, ended in new rulings and insights into freedom of speech. Others, such as the Kent State University protest, ended in bloodshed.

The demonstrations of the Vietnam era were so widespread that they rooted the idea of the anti-war protest into American culture. From that point, Americans became more likely than ever to publicly demonstrate against wars with which they disagreed. The conflicts following the terrorist attacks of September 11, 2001, led to a great range of reactions. The US war in Afghanistan that began in 2001 was first widely supported, as it seemed like an inevitable reaction to the terror attacks. Later, however, the war became significantly less popular as it continued for many years and brought up troubling questions about what information about wars should be made public.

The Iraq War (2003–2011) was met with a great deal of public disapproval. Many people felt that the war was based on mistaken information, or even outright lies, from US leaders. Anti-war protests, notably candlelight demonstrations in support of peace, became a common sight. Americans continue to observe world events, and those who want peace and not war will doubtless make their opinions known in future conflicts.

International Congress of Women

LOCATION: The Hague, Netherlands

DATE: April 28 to May 1, 1915

The International Congress of Women was a peace convention that took place in The Hague, Netherlands, from April 28 to May 1, 1915. Organized by Dutch suffragist Aletta Jacobs (1854–1929), this conference was planned and conducted solely by women in the hopes of bringing peace during World War I (1914–1918).

Over the course of their discussions, the congress produced a list of recommendations. Some recommendations described ways of easing international tensions nonviolently. Others pushed for women's rights to become a new standard in the world.

Members of the congress spread their messages to many world leaders, but ultimately no direct changes resulted. The war lasted for three more years, and women had to continue to struggle for their rights. However, the congress introduced the beginning of women's participation in political discussions and international affairs that would build greatly in the coming generations. Some of their recommendations are part of international law today.

World War I and women's rights

In the early 20th century, the most powerful countries of Europe were divided into two military groups—the Allies (France, Russia, and the United Kingdom) and the Central powers (Austria-Hungary and Germany). In 1914 the assassination, or murder, of Archduke Franz Ferdinand (1863–1914), the heir to Austria-Hungarian throne, led to a major crisis. Conflicts between countries grew at an alarming rate. Soon, both large military groups had been drawn into a global war known as the Great War or the World War (it did not become known as World War I until after World War II started). Fighting between the countries quickly became an ongoing nightmare of death and suffering. Millions of soldiers died for a cause many of them did not even understand.

Prior to the war, groups of women in many countries had been developing plans and rallying support for women's rights. At that time, most countries denied women suffrage, which is the right to vote, and many other rights given to male citizens. Since the 1800s, a growing movement of women began trying to gain these rights. One group in this movement was the International Woman Suffrage Alliance, an association of women from many countries that met each year. Their 1915 meeting, set for Berlin, Germany, had to be canceled because of the war. This change of plans ultimately led to a unique demonstration by the activists.

Plans for the congress

Many of the women suffragists were already greatly concerned by the war. Across Europe, suffragists witnessed their husbands and sons marching off to join the war, many of whom would die on the battlefield. The cancellation of the 1915 meeting made some realize that there was a more urgently pressing cause than winning the right to vote—it was peace.

Dutch suffragist Jacobs wanted the women's organization to focus its efforts on returning peace to the world. She felt that women had a unique ability to see beyond political and military conflict and create inventive ways to solve problems. They could create a plan to convince the world's leaders to give up their anger and stop the fighting.

Jacobs began organizing a meeting of top women activists from around the world. She invited these activists to the Netherlands, which was a neutral country, or one that was not involved in the fighting. There, she led the International Congress of Women (sometimes called the Women's Peace Congress) in a creative and courageous bid to stop World War I.

Assembling the Congress

Jacobs's invitations to the congress went around the globe, to countries on both sides of the fighting. Jacobs felt it was necessary to have women from many lands participate to show their unity despite the international conflicts fueling the war. She invited the women to meet in The Hague, a city in the Netherlands.

Women hoping to attend the Congress faced several major difficulties. The dangers of warfare meant that many international borders were blocked or contested by soldiers. Attack ships and submarines patrolled the oceans. Many people were not able to leave their homes, or were too busy coping with immediate stresses of the conflict to participate in the women's meeting. In an age when it was rare for women to travel alone, unaccompanied by male family members, traveling during wartime was particularly challenging and dangerous.

Making the situation worse, several nations discouraged the conference by refusing to allow women to leave their country. France blocked all its delegates to the congress from exiting the country. Russia, Japan, and Serbia also did not send any representatives. British authorities closed a ferry connecting Great Britain with the Netherlands. This halted the progress of 177 of 180 British women who planned to attend the conference.

Even those women who were able to travel faced widespread criticism by people who felt their mission was vain and hopeless. Critics felt that these women were overstepping their boundaries. Some said the women were upsetting traditional male and female roles that gave men the responsibility of managing war and peace. These criticisms did little to discourage Jacobs and the other delegates from their goals.

Even those women who were able to travel faced widespread criticism by people who felt their mission was vain and hopeless. Critics felt that these women were overstepping their boundaries. Some said the women were upsetting traditional male and female roles that gave men the responsibility of managing war and peace.

War

The conference begins

Despite the challenges they faced, between 1,200 to 1,500 women arrived in the Netherlands in time for the conference. These women represented 12 countries: the United States, Sweden, Norway, the Netherlands, Italy, Hungary, Germany, Denmark, Canada, Belgium, Austria, and the United Kingdom.

Many of the women were, or would become, notable leaders, teachers, and reformers. Among them were American reformer Jane Addams (1860–1935), who had established housing for needy people in Chicago, and American university professors Emily G. Balch (1867–1961) and Alice Hamilton (1869–1970). Reformers such as German Lida Gustava Heymann (1868–1943), Hungarian Rosika Schwimmer (1877–1948), and

British and American delegates to the International Congress of Women are shown. The delegates include feminist and peace activist Emmeline Pethick-Lawrence (1867–1954), social activist and writer Jane Addams (1860–1935), and Annie E. Malloy, president of the Boston Telephone Operators' Union. COURTESY OF THE LIBRARY OF CONGRESS.

British Emmeline Pethick-Lawrence (1867–1954) brought their own views on women's rights, international politics, and the need for peace.

On April 28, 1915, Jacobs began the conference. She opened with a stirring speech to the assembled delegates in which she expressed her hopes that women from many lands could bring peace to the warring nations. She said that leaders of the 20th century had to find more peaceful means of settling disputes than using brute force alone.

Progress of the meeting

Over the next three days, the congress met each evening to give speeches and hold debates. One evening, the public was invited to watch, and interested onlookers filled every available seat. The delegates at the conference all held some essential goals in common. Among these were the need to bring peace using only nonviolent means, and to avoid debates about which countries were to blame for the war. In addition, all delegates linked their peacemaking mission to the establishment of women's rights in the warring nations and around the world.

Beyond those common goals, however, the delegates had many different ideas about the best ways to bring peace. They approached the problem from various angles. Many women were pacifists who were strongly opposed to war. These women wanted to work hard to stop the existing war. Other women took a more moderate stance to the issue and felt their main concern was to create means by which to prevent future wars.

Despite their differences, the women reached an agreement after four days. They created a plan for conflict resolution based on help from neutral outside groups. In this plan, neutral countries would help warring nations reach peace. They would discuss international problems and potential solutions with the nations at war until they could reach common ground and settle their conflicts through peaceful means.

The congress included in its platform demands for equal rights for women and increased education for children. The delegates established a new group, the Women's International League for Peace and Freedom, to help carry out their resolutions. They also made plans for a follow-up conference to take place upon the actual ending of the war. That meeting eventually took place in Zurich, Switzerland, in 1919.

Conclusion and effects

Delegates formalized their plans on May 1, 1917, and published them for distribution. The delegates also agreed to try a challenging, potentially

War

Resolutions from the International Congress of Women

This primary source is an excerpt from the Report of the International Congress of Women, *which was printed by the Woman's Peace Party. This excerpt features a few of the resolutions that were adopted during the business sessions.*

We women, in International Congress assembled, protest against the madness and horror of war, involving as it does a reckless sacrifice of human life and the destruction of so much that humanity has labeled through centuries to build up....

This International Congress of Women opposes the assumption that women can be protected under the conditions of modern warfare. It protests vehemently against the odious wrongs of which women are the victims in times of war, and especially against the horrible violation of women which attends all war....

This International Congress of Women of different nations, classes, creeds and parties is united in expressing sympathy with the suffering of all, whatever their nationality, who are fighting for their country or labouring under the burden of war.

Since the mass of the people in each of the countries now at war believe themselves to be fighting, not as aggressors but in self-defence and for their national existence, there can be no irreconcilable differences between them, and their common ideas afford a basis upon which a magnanimous and honourable peace might be established. The Congress therefore urges the Governments of the world to put an end to this bloodshed, and to begin peace negotiations. It demands that the peace which follows shall be permanent and therefore based on principles of justice....

That no territory should be transferred without the consent of the men and women in it, and that the right on conquest should not be recognized....

That women should be granted equal political rights with men.

SOURCE: *Report of the International Congress of Women: The Hague—The Netherlands, April 28th to May 1st, 1915.* Chicago: Women's Peace Party, 1915.

---

dangerous means of spreading their message. They enlisted a group of women to travel to the capitals of the main warring and neutral nations. These women would carry the congress's resolutions and ask to meet with top leaders.

Over the next four months, 13 women representing the congress visited the capitals of 14 nations. Although many people doubted these missions would be successful, most of the women were able to gain the attention of the kings and ministers they sought.

However, despite the official shows of interest, the reaction to the women's demands was almost nonexistent. Leaders did not offer the women the same considerations as male counterparts, nor did they offer any promises or valuable information. Some leaders later complained that the women were confused about important political matters. The media, already critical of the women and their mission, continued to belittle the congress and its breaking with traditional roles.

Legacy

Ultimately, the attempt by the International Congress of Women to bring peace was in vain. The group's resolutions were dismissed by most leaders. The war continued, and expanded, until November 1918. Millions of soldiers and citizens of war-torn areas lost their lives.

The International Congress of Women created some important practices. Although their ideas were not adopted at the time, they did help introduce the idea of negotiation by neutral countries as a means of avoiding war. This and several of their ideas for creating and preserving peace were influential in the Fourteen Points, which was a list of recommendations by US President Woodrow Wilson (1856–1924) for bringing order to postwar Europe.

In addition, the congress became an important example for peace protests and women's rights demonstrations. Women showed that they could successfully create resolutions for international affairs and make an impact in world politics. Several of the women involved in the congress went on to great accomplishments and honors in the name of reform.

Student Armband Protest of Vietnam War

LOCATION: Des Moines, Iowa
DATE: 1965–1969

In December 1965 a group of students at schools in Des Moines, Iowa, wore black armbands to school to protest the US involvement in the Vietnam War (1954–1975). The war had begun when Vietnamese Communists tried to take control of the country. Communism is a political system in which property is owned collectively, government directs all economic production, and people are paid according to what they need. The United States opposed Communism and wanted to stop Communist forces from spreading in Vietnam. The United States sent troops to Vietnam in the late 1950s. By 1965 US forces were fully entrenched in fighting against the Communists in Vietnam.

Small groups of Americans had begun to oppose the Vietnam War by late 1964. Most of these opponents were college students and other young people. They disapproved of US soldiers dying in a war that did not directly affect the United States. Children of the Tinker family in Des Moines, Iowa, were among those Americans who strongly opposed US involvement in the Vietnam War. In December 1965, teenagers Mary Beth Tinker (1952–), her brother John Tinker (c. 1950–), and fellow student Christopher Eckhardt (c. 1950–2012) all protested the Vietnam War at their schools by wearing black armbands. School authorities believed this to be disrespectful so they suspended the students.

However, the parents of the students felt their children had the right to express themselves freely. They argued this in various courts, saying the schools had taken away the students' right to free speech by suspending them. The question of whether the armbands were a protected form of free speech in school was eventually heard by the US Supreme Court, the most powerful court in the country.

Vietnam

The American people's protests against the Vietnam War were an important part of late-1960s American culture. However, the decade did not begin this way. By 1960 the United States had officially declared its support for South Vietnam. This was the southern half of Vietnam that had a government similar to that of the United States. The Communist North Vietnam wanted to take over South Vietnam and make the entire country Communist. The United States sent aid to South Vietnam in the early 1960s.

In 1964 North Vietnam attacked US forces. The United States responded in 1965 by striking back. At this time, many Americans supported the United States fighting North Vietnam. They believed Communists would take over the world if allowed to do so. Engaging in war showed Communists everywhere that the United States would always defend its allies from attack.

At the same time, a smaller portion of the American people strongly opposed the United States entering the war. They did not like that the war resulted in the loss of American lives and cost billions of dollars. War

Small groups of Americans had begun to oppose the Vietnam War by late 1964. Most of these opponents were college students and other young people. They disapproved of US soldiers dying in a war that did not directly affect the United States.

opponents also disliked how some US actions killed innocent Vietnamese people. The anti-war movement grew throughout the rest of the 1960s and into the 1970s.

Black armbands

Many American opponents of the Vietnam War were students. Some wore bracelets with the names of US soldiers missing in action or prisoners of war written on them. In 1965, 13-year-old Mary Beth Tinker, her 15-year-old brother John, and 16-year-old Christopher Eckhardt decided to wear black armbands. John and Christopher were high school students. Mary Beth was in junior high school.

The students met with their parents at the Eckhardts' house in December 1965 to discuss ways to protest. In the end they decided to wear black armbands in public around the Christmas and New Year's Day holidays. The armbands would show that the students and adults opposed US actions in Vietnam and that they wanted the violence there to end. Many other opponents of the war had already worn black armbands in this way.

Authorities at the students' Des Moines schools learned about the armband protest before it began. The principals of the schools met and created a single rule for students wearing armbands. Principals would ask students wearing black armbands to remove the bands from their arms. Any students who did not remove the armbands would be suspended. The students could return to school only if they were no longer wearing the bands.

Mary Beth and Christopher first wore their armbands to their schools on December 16, 1965. John wore his armband the next day. The students did not actively protest the Vietnam War or express their opinions with words. They simply wore the armbands to their classes.

Once school authorities saw the armbands, they asked the three students to remove them. When the students refused, the principals suspended the students, keeping with the new policy. Sticking to their plan, the Tinkers and Eckhardt returned to school after January 1, 1966, without their black armbands.

Legal actions

The students' suspensions became news in Des Moines. The president of the school board that had suspended the Tinkers and Eckhardt claimed

War

Burning Draft Cards, 1967

Beginning in the mid-1960s, Americans started strongly opposing US involvement in the Vietnam War. People protested the war in numerous ways. Some people marched in the streets. Some wore black armbands. Some sang protest songs. Others burned their draft cards. A military draft is a legal order that forces citizens to serve in their country's military.

Burning draft cards had become a popular form of anti-war protest by the late 1960s. The US draft forced many young Americans to go to war in Vietnam. Some of these young people opposed the war based on morality. They thought it was wrong to fight in the war and kill people. To protest the draft and the war, some people publicly burned the draft notices they had received in the mail. The US government made the act illegal in 1965.

David Miller became famous for burning his draft card in New York City later in 1965. Miller was a 22-year-old pacifist, or someone who does not believe in fighting in wars. He told the crowd around him that he was burning his card to show that he believed that US actions in Vietnam were wrong. Miller was later arrested and sentenced to several years in prison under the 1965 law. Miller tried to take his case to the US Supreme Court, but the court would not hear it. The court did not believe the 1965 law took away Americans' right to free speech.

Miller went to prison in April 1967. Soon after this, protesters in New York City staged their own demonstration against the war. Several hundred people burned their draft cards in Central Park before joining an anti-war march. That October protesters in 30 cities throughout the United States burned about 1,400 draft cards at the same time. Protesters staged similar card burnings in numerous American cities in April 1968. About 1,000 people burned their draft cards at these events.

Many Americans continued to burn their draft cards throughout US involvement in the Vietnam

the armbands would have negatively influenced the other students at the schools. The American Civil Liberties Union (ACLU) of Iowa opposed this view. The ACLU is an organization that defends and protects the civil rights of American citizens. The ACLU believed the students had a right to express themselves freely, even on school property.

The suspended students' parents worked with the ACLU to file a complaint against the school district in the US District Court for the Southern District of Iowa. District courts are part of the federal court system. Later in 1966, a judge of the court ruled in favor of the school district. He claimed the principals had a right to suspend the students to prevent the armbands from disturbing the school environment. Yet, the judge admitted that wearing the armbands was indeed a form of free speech.

War. As the war continued into the late 1960s and early 1970s, these burnings became less public and were done more by individuals than by large groups. The United States ended the draft in 1973, the same year US forces withdrew from Vietnam.

Goddard C. Graves, a former student of the University of Wisconsin, burns his draft card in front of 100 women on December 4, 1967. © BETTMANN/GETTY IMAGES.

The parents then took their case to the US Court of Appeals for the Eighth Circuit. US appeals courts are federal courts that hold more power than district courts. In 1967 the appeals court agreed with the district court that the principals had the right to suspend the students. So another appeal was made, this time to the US Supreme Court. The court started hearing arguments in *Tinker v. Des Moines Independent Community School District* in November 1968. The court had to decide whether students had to give up their rights to free speech when they entered school property.

Lawyers for the students argued that other students in the Iowa school district had worn political symbols on their clothing without disturbing school activities. Lawyers for the school district responded

War

Mary Beth Tinker and her brother, John, display two black armbands, the objects they wore to school that got them suspended. How much should schools be able to limit what political symbols students wear to class? That question went before the US Supreme Court in Tinker vs. Des Moines Independent Community School District.
© BETTMANN/GETTY IMAGES.

that the school board had the right to stop the students from wearing the black armbands. The schools had done this to prevent any possible disorder from occurring.

The Supreme Court decided *Tinker v. Des Moines* on February 24, 1969. The court ruled that the black armbands were an expression of free speech that the US Constitution protected. The court said the school district could not ban students from wearing the armbands unless school officials could prove the armbands had disturbed school activities. The court argued that the Iowa school district had banned the armbands only out of fear that disturbances would occur, not because any disturbances had actually taken place.

Tinker v. Des Moines protected free speech for students in all American public schools. In the end the *Tinker v. Des Moines* case guaranteed free political speech in schools as long as it did not interfere with the work of the school itself.

Mary Beth Tinker later became a registered nurse and an activist for student rights. Activists are people who publicly support or oppose certain issues. As an adult, her brother John worked as a distributor and an editor. In 2013 the Tinkers returned to the schools from which they had been suspended to encourage students to know their rights and to become more involved in civic affairs.

Student Protest at Kent State

LOCATION: Kent, Ohio

DATE: May 1–4, 1970

A protest at Kent State University in Kent, Ohio, that began on May 1, 1970, was a demonstration against the Vietnam War (1954–1975). Students and others gathered to show their disapproval for the president's plan to increase the US military presence in Vietnam and expand the fighting in the region.

In the coming days, protesters became destructive and violent. Soldiers from the National Guard arrived to try to restore order. On May 4, tensions rose between the soldiers and protesters, leading some soldiers to fire their rifles into the crowd. Four students were killed and nine were injured. The actions of the soldiers outraged many Americans and increased the spirit of protest against the war.

Background on the Vietnam War

The Vietnam War became one of the most debated conflicts in US history. This war began in Vietnam, a small country in Southeast Asia. The seriousness of the war and the ideas behind it soon drew many countries around the world into battle.

In the 1940s, different groups struggled for control in Vietnam. The country eventually split into two parts. North Vietnam wanted to follow the ideas of Communism. Meanwhile, South Vietnam wanted to have a more democratic government. Communism and democracy are two styles of government. Under Communism, citizens cannot own private property and powerful leaders make all of the decisions. In a democracy, citizens have more freedom to own property, make decisions, and choose their own leaders.

In the 1950s this political disagreement became a war. The United States and other countries quickly became involved. Many leaders believed that the United States had to fight in the war to protect democracy against Communism. The war continued for decades and became bloodier and more politically complicated.

War

Protest Songs of the Vietnam Era

People reacted to news of the Kent State shootings in many ways. For Canadian musician Neil Young (1945–), the news inspired an important song of protest. In his song "Ohio," Young expresses shock, anger, and despair over the killings. He also blames President Nixon and asks how many more people would have to die before the nations at war find peace. The song was recorded by Crosby, Stills, Nash, and Young.

Young was not alone. During the Vietnam War era, music became an important means of protest. Artists of many areas of music, from folk to rock to gospel, sang about their feelings on important world events, particularly the war. Many of the songs remain famous in the 21st century.

Some songs expressed the terror and tragedy of war. "Eve of Destruction," a 1965 song by Barry McGuire (1935–), describes a horrifying image of the world being burned and shot to pieces by conflict. In 1970's "War," Edwin Starr (1942–2003) asks and answers a question many people were pondering: "War—what is it good for? Absolutely nothing!"

"Fortunate Son," a 1969 hit by the band Creedence Clearwater Revival, accuses wealthy politicians of keeping their own children safe while forcing less powerful people to fight the country's battles. "What's Going On," a 1971 hit by American Marvin Gaye (1939–1984), asks why the world is so embroiled in war and violence.

Many other songs protested the war in a different way—by praising peace. British musician John Lennon (1940–1980) wrote many songs about the need to end the war and bring the world to harmony. Among his most famous was "Give Peace a Chance" from 1969. In it, he sings that many people with different interests and ideas must unite for the ultimate goal of restoring peace. Folk singers such as Pete Seeger (1919–2014), Joan Baez (1941–), Bob Dylan (1941–), Phil Ochs (1943–1976), and Peter, Paul, and Mary also lent their talents to the anti-war movement.

Protest songs of the Vietnam era have become some of the most famous tunes in history. At the same time, however, some

The expansion of the war

By 1970 tens of thousands of American soldiers had been sent to fight in Vietnam. Many were killed or wounded. Many others experienced terrible battles, cruelty, and suffering in the brutal war. Many Americans began to question the meaning of the war and the reasons why the United States was involved. Some felt that defending democracy was not worth continuing the horrible conflict.

Increasing numbers of citizens wanted the United States to stop fighting and let the soldiers return home. However, many other Americans

musicians wrote music in support of Nixon and the American effort in the war. One of the most notable of these songs was "Ballad of the Green Berets," a song recorded in 1966 by Staff Sergeant Barry Sadler (1940–1989). This song praises the bravery and sacrifices of the American armed forces, particularly the elite troops known as the Green Berets.

John Lennon protested for peace through his music. © EMKA74/SHUTTERSTOCK.COM.

felt that the United States could not afford to lose this lengthy conflict. They believed that even greater numbers of American troops had to be sent overseas to win the fight.

President Richard M. Nixon felt that more American troops were necessary. On April 30, 1970, Nixon made a speech on television. He said that he had decided to invade Cambodia, a country near Vietnam, in the hopes of hurting the North Vietnamese army. To do this, Nixon said 150,000 more American soldiers would be drafted. A draft meant that more young men would be required to serve in the armed forces.

War

"Four Dead in Ohio"

This primary source excerpt is from an article that John Kifner wrote for the New York Times *immediately following the shootings at Kent State. It provides details of the tense moments between the National Guard and student protesters.*

The students in the parking lot area, numbering about 500, began to move toward the rear of the troops, cheering. Again, a few in front picked up stones from the edge of the parking lot and threw them at the guardsmen. Another group of several hundred students had gathered around the sides of Taylor Hall watching.

As the guardsmen, moving up the hill in single file, reached the crest, they suddenly turned, forming a skirmish line and opening fire.

The crackle of the rifle volley cut the suddenly still air. It appeared to go on, as a solid volley, for perhaps a full minute or a little longer.

Some of the students dived to the ground, crawling on the grass in terror. Others stood shocked or half crouched, apparently believing the troops were firing into the air. Some of the rifle barrels were pointed upward.

Near the top of the hill at the corner of Taylor Hall, a student crumpled over, spun sideways and fell to the ground, shot in the head.

When the firing stopped, a slim girl, wearing a cowboy shirt and faded jeans, was lying face down on the road at the edge of the parking lot, blood pouring out onto the macadam, about 10 feet from this reporter.

Too Shocked to React

The youth stood stunned, many of them clustered in small groups staring at the bodies. A young man cradled one of the bleeding forms in his arms. Several girls began to cry. But many of the students who rushed from the scene seemed

The spirit of protest

Many Americans were shocked by Nixon's plan. They believed the attack on Cambodia would not help anyone and would lead to only more death and suffering. Some said that the United States had participated in the war for many years for the wrong reasons. Others were upset that college students and other young men would be drafted and forced to risk their lives against their will.

More Americans began to protest the Vietnam War. Most protests were peaceful. Some young men left the country to avoid the draft. Others burned their draft cards, which are papers that identified them as being registered to serve in the military. Some protesters took to the streets to hold demonstrations, rallies, and marches where they could spread their anti-war messages.

Meanwhile, many other Americans supported the war. They felt the United States had to remain strong and defend democracy at all costs.

almost too shocked to react. Several gathered around an abstract steel sculpture in front of the building and looked at the .30-caliber bullet hole drilled through one of the plates.

The hospital said that six young people were being treated for gunshot wounds, some in the intensive care unit. Three of the students who were killed were dead on arrival at the hospital.

One guardsman was treated and released at the hospital and another was admitted with heat prostration.

In early afternoon, students attempted to gather at various areas of the Commons but were ordered away by guardsmen and the Ohio Highway Patrol, which moved in as reinforcements.

There were no further clashes, as faculty members, graduate assistants and student leaders urged the crowd to go back to dormitories.

But a bizarre atmosphere hung over the campus as a Guard helicopter hovered overhead, grim-faced officers maneuvered their men to safeguard the normally pastoral campus and students, dazed, fearful and angry, struggled to comprehend what had happened and to find something to do about it.

Students carrying suitcases and duffel bags began leaving the campus this afternoon. Early tonight the entire campus was sealed off and a court injunction was issued ordering all students to leave.

A 5 P.M. curfew was declared in Kent, and road blocks were set up around the town to prevent anyone from entering. . . .

SOURCE: Kifner, John. "4 Kent State Students Killed by Troops." *New York Times* (May 4, 1970). Available online at http://www.nytimes.com/learning/general/onthisday/big/0504.html (accessed October 16, 2017). Courtesy of New York Times Company.

They did not want to see soldiers coming home in defeat. Some also felt that the anti-war protesters were unpatriotic, cowardly, or even criminal. The Vietnam War was turning many Americans against one another.

Crisis at Kent State

One of the largest anti-war protests began at Kent State University in Kent, Ohio. On May 1, 1970, some university students staged a rally against the Vietnam War and the draft. Although intended to be a peaceful gathering, the rally quickly turned violent. By the end of the day, protesters had lit bonfires. Others threw bottles or stones at the police officers who arrived to restore order on campus.

Local leaders tried to regain control of the situation. They sent in more police. They also closed nearby bars so the protesters could not drink

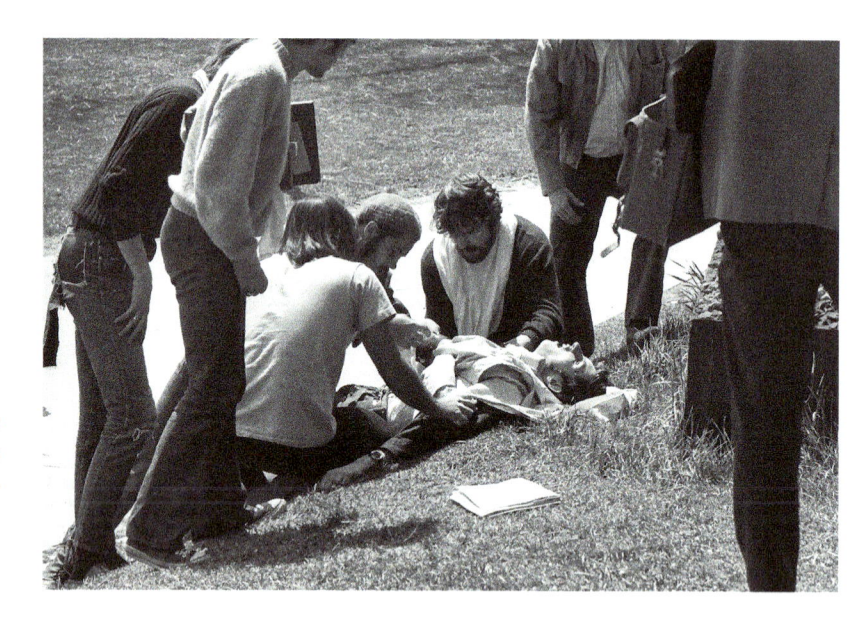

Wounded Kent State student John Cleary is attended to by other students, who helped save his life, May 4, 1970.
© HOWARD RUFFNER/GETTY IMAGES.

alcohol. Soon, protesters began smashing windows on campus and in the nearby areas. Some even looted, or broke into homes and businesses to steal. At the same time, many students tried to calm the protesters or clean up damage, but their efforts were largely ineffective.

By May 2, the situation at Kent State had only become worse. Someone set fire to the school's Reserve Officers' Training Corps (ROTC) building. The ROTC is a program that prepares school students to become military officers. The building was most likely burned by protesters. However, the building might have been set on fire by people who opposed the protest and wanted the demonstrators to take the blame. When firefighters arrived, some protesters treated them poorly and even damaged their hoses to make it harder to put out the flames.

State of emergency

The mayor of Kent, LeRoy Satrom (1919–2004), declared that the city was in a state of emergency. A state of emergency means that a place is in serious trouble and needs help. Ohio Governor James A. Rhodes (1909–2001) agreed with Satrom. Rhodes was known to dislike protesters, believing they were dangerous people whose beliefs were unpatriotic.

Governor Rhodes quickly ordered soldiers from the National Guard to Kent State. The National Guard is a branch of the armed forces that often helps with emergencies within the country. About 1,000 National Guardsmen arrived by May 3 with orders to calm the protesters and restore order to Kent State. The guardsmen began to break up demonstrations using tear gas, a gas that hurts people's eyes but does not cause permanent injury or death. The soldiers also carried rifles with bayonets, which are knives attached to guns.

School leaders hoped that the presence of the soldiers would end the demonstrations. Teachers planned to hold their classes as usual on May 4, a Monday. However, another protest rally disrupted these plans. The National Guardsmen tried to use tear gas to stop the protesters, but the wind blew the gas away. Protesters, yelling insults at the soldiers, threw the tear-gas cans back at the soldiers and threw rocks at them.

The Kent State shootings

Tensions continued to rise at the May 4 rally. The demonstrators were ordered to leave but refused to go. Seventy-seven guardsmen, who had loaded their rifles with the bayonets attached, began moving toward the protesters. The unarmed students ran over Blanket Hill toward a fenced campus athletic field, some veering off toward a parking lot. The guard followed and found themselves between the student mob and the fenced field. Rather than retreating farther, the protesters continued throwing objects and yelling at the soldiers. The guardsmen headed back up the hill. Then suddenly, 29 of the guardsmen began firing—some at the crowd, others in the air. The shooting lasted for about 13 seconds, during which time the soldiers fired nearly 70 bullets. Others thought it went on longer.

Researchers are unsure what caused the firing to begin. Some believe that the soldiers feared for their lives and fired in self-defense. Others believe confusion caused the soldiers to open fire. A few people have even suggested that armed protesters began the shooting. Regardless of the exact cause, the results of the shooting were deadly.

After the gunfire stopped, witnesses could see that many of the protesters were lying on the ground or running away. Four students in the group had been killed. These students were Jeffrey Miller (1950–1970), Allison Krause (1951–1970), William Schroeder (1950–1970), and Sandra Scheuer (1949–1970). Two of these students had not even been involved in the protests and were simply bystanders. In addition, nine other students and protesters had been seriously hurt by the gunfire.

About 1,000 National Guardsmen arrived by May 3 with orders to calm the protesters and restore order to Kent State. The guardsmen began to break up demonstrations using tear gas. The soldiers also carried rifles with bayonets.

War

Aftermath

The gunfire at Kent State became a source of shock and outrage around the country. Millions of Americans read about the shootings in newspapers or saw coverage on television. Many felt sympathy for the protesters and their families. Americans realized that the protesters were not criminals or traitors to their country. Rather, they were well-educated students from good families who just felt passionately about the troubles of the world.

Many people thought the National Guardsmen had committed murder. Others defended their actions and said the soldiers were responding to acts of violence from the protesters. Eight of the soldiers were tried in court, but their case was eventually ended due to lack of evidence that they had committed a crime. Researchers still study and debate the soldiers' actions.

Protests against the Vietnam War actually increased following the shootings at Kent State. Many colleges and universities were overwhelmed by protests, and school officials feared further riots and violence. Some schools canceled their classes for days or weeks. Kent State shut down for six weeks following the shootings.

Within two years, however, protests were quickly ending. President Nixon had decided to ease American involvement in Vietnam, and in 1973 agreed to the Paris Peace Accords. This treaty ended most US activity in the war. Many Americans viewed the Vietnam War era as a dark time in American history. The war cost thousands of American lives, failed to achieve its goals, and made many Americans turn against one another. However, it also showed the power of protest to bring changes to public opinion and official policy.

Candlelight Vigils against Invasion of Iraq

LOCATION: Worldwide

DATE: March 16, 2003

Many people worldwide opposed the United States and other countries entering into war with Iraq in 2003. The United States was already involved in a war in Afghanistan that started in response to the September 11, 2001, terrorist attacks. As time passed and little progress was made in the Afghanistan war, support for war in general faded.

People around the world began organizing protests against the war in Iraq. While many of these demonstrations were loud marches and rallies, a group of people came up with an idea for a peaceful event: a candlelight vigil. At a candlelight vigil, individuals gather with candles to show support or opposition for a cause or event. A worldwide candlelight vigil to oppose a war in Iraq was set for the night of March 16, 2003.

People in more than 100 countries gathered at thousands of vigils held around the world that evening. Some of these vigils were formal gatherings with speakers, music, and more, while others were informally held outside people's homes. The vigil began in the country of New Zealand and then spread to other countries as night fell. The United States, the United Kingdom, and a coalition of other countries officially invaded Iraq a few days later.

Terrorists attacks of September 11, 2001

On September 11, 2001, which is commonly known as 9/11, militant Islamists from the group al-Qaeda (pronounced al-KY-duh) carried out terrorist attacks against the United States. A militant group uses violent or aggressive means in support of a cause. That day, nearly 3,000 people died in four separate airplane attacks in New York City; Washington, DC; and near Shanksville, Pennsylvania. The attacks directly led to the war in Afghanistan and the Iraq War in an attempt to destroy al-Qaeda forces and capture its leader, Osama bin Laden (1957–2011), who claimed responsibility for the attacks.

Events of 9/11 American Airlines Flight 11 took off from Boston, Massachusetts, near 8 a.m. on September 11, 2001. It had 92 people aboard to Los Angeles, California. About 15 minutes later, United Airlines Flight 175, which was carrying 65 people, also took off from Boston and was headed to Los Angeles. About 8:20 a.m., Flight 11 crew members notified officials that people had hijacked, or took control by force, of the plane. Then, American Airlines Flight 77 left Washington, DC, heading to Los Angeles with 64 people on board. After a flight delay of about 40 minutes—unrelated to the other incidents—United Airlines Flight 93 with 40 people on board took off at 8:41 a.m. from Newark, New Jersey, and headed to San Francisco, California.

War

One Thousand Coffins

Hundreds of groups planned a protest for New York City on the days leading up to the 2004 Republican National Convention, which was held on August 30. Participants protested President George W. Bush's Republican nomination for the presidency. Protesters were angry and upset with the president for keeping the nation involved in the wars in Afghanistan and Iraq, and destroying the country's economy with the cost of the two conflicts.

United for Peace and Justice was the major planner of the protest, but hundreds of other groups took part in the event. Rallies, performances, demonstrations, and a march took place that weekend. One of the groups involved was One Thousand Coffins. It planned a demonstration for the march on August 29, which was the day before the start of the convention. During the march, the group carried nearly 1,000 fake coffins made out of cardboard and draped with American flags. The coffins represented the US soldiers killed in the Iraq War.

The march drew hundreds of thousands of participants, who filled a 2-mile (3.2-kilometer) route. The protesters included the Reverend Jesse Jackson (1941–), actor Danny Glover (1947–), and filmmaker Michael Moore (1954–), among numerous other celebrities. The group marched for six hours from the Chelsea section of Manhattan to Midtown and back to Union Square.

The march was mostly nonviolent, and a peaceful post-march gathering was held in Central Park. Other participants traveled to Times Square and became unruly, where they harassed people attending convention events. Some engaged in fights with police, who arrested more than 200 of these protesters that day. All in all, it is considered one of the largest protests ever held in US history.

As the Federal Bureau of Investigation (FBI) rushed to send fighter planes into the air to stop the hijacked Flight 11, the terrorists on board the airplane crashed it into the North Tower of the World Trade Center (WTC) in New York City at 8:46 a.m. Everyone on the plane and many people in the building were killed. The crash set the building on fire. The New York City Police Department, the fire department, and other officials responded to the scene to help the injured and get people out of the burning building.

As people were rushing to leave the scene, hijackers crashed a second airplane, Flight 175, into the South Tower of the WTC at 9:03 a.m. Everyone on board the plane died, and many people in the building were killed. In the minutes that followed, the Federal Aviation Administration (FAA) banned all flights to New York City and all aircraft from being in the air above the city. The Port Authority of New York and New Jersey then closed all bridges and tunnels to the city.

One thousand flag-draped mock coffins, one for each soldier who has died in Iraq, are carried by volunteers. Thousands of protesters took to the streets to rally against the George W. Bush administration and the Republican National Convention during an event organized by the United for Peace and Justice group. © RAMIN TALAIE/CORBIS VIA GETTY IMAGES.

After 9 a.m., authorities learned that Flight 77 was also hijacked. President George W. Bush (1946–) announced that the United States was under a terrorist attack at 9:31 a.m. Six minutes later, Flight 77 crashed into the western side of the Pentagon building in Washington, DC. All 59 people on the plane and 125 people in the building were killed.

A few minutes later, the FAA made history when it banned all flights over or on their way to the United States. Flights were rerouted to other countries in the hours that followed. The government then emptied the White House, Capitol building, and other important buildings, landmarks, and locations as a safety measure. Right before 10 a.m., the South Tower of the WTC collapsed.

Flight 93 from Newark was also hijacked that morning. Passengers and crew members on this flight learned about the other attacks while they were in the air and came up with a plan to take back control of the

War

President Bush on Going to War in Iraq

This primary source excerpt is from President George W. Bush's "Address to the Nation on Military Operations in Iraq," given on March 19, 2003. In the speech, Bush explains why the nation is going to war.

My fellow citizens, at this hour, American and coalition forces are in the early stages of military operations to disarm Iraq, to free its people and to defend the world from grave danger.

On my orders, coalition forces have begun striking selected targets of military importance to undermine Saddam Hussein's ability to wage war. These are opening stages of what will be a broad and concerted campaign. More than 35 countries are giving crucial support—from the use of naval and air bases, to help with intelligence and logistics, to the deployment of combat units. Every nation in this coalition has chosen to bear the duty and share the honor of serving in our common defense.

To all the men and women of the United States Armed Forces now in the Middle East, the peace of a troubled world and the hopes of an oppressed people now depend on you. That trust is well placed.

The enemies you confront will come to know your skill and bravery. The people you liberate will witness the honorable and decent spirit of the American military. In this conflict, America faces an enemy who has no regard for conventions of war or rules of morality....

I want Americans and all the world to know that coalition forces will make every effort to spare innocent civilians from harm. A campaign on the harsh terrain of a nation as large as California could be longer and more difficult than some predict.

---

plane from the hijackers. The attempt caused the hijackers to crash the plane into a field at 10:07 a.m. in western Pennsylvania. All 40 people on board the plane died. The North Tower of the WTC fell to the ground around 10:30 a.m. When the WTC towers collapsed, not only were the employees and visitors inside the building killed but so were the first responders (police, firefighters, emergency medical technicians, and other rescue workers).

A short time later, New York Mayor Rudolph Giuliani (1944–) called for people in other parts of the city, including Lower Manhattan south of Canal Street, to leave the area. This affected more than 1 million people. At the site of the WTC, people continued to flee the scene, as others searched for survivors.

The president put the US military on high alert that afternoon. He later addressed the nation about the terrorist attacks. In his speech, he said the country and its allies would "stand together to win the war against terrorism."

And helping Iraqis achieve a united, stable and free country will require our sustained commitment.

We come to Iraq with respect for its citizens, for their great civilization and for the religious faiths they practice. We have no ambition in Iraq, except to remove a threat and restore control of that country to its own people.

I know that the families of our military are praying that all those who serve will return safely and soon. Millions of Americans are praying with you for the safety of your loved ones and for the protection of the innocent. For your sacrifice, you have the gratitude and respect of the American people. And you can know that our forces will be coming home as soon as their work is done.

Our nation enters this conflict reluctantly—yet, our purpose is sure. The people of the United States and our friends and allies will not live at the mercy of an outlaw regime that threatens the peace with weapons of mass murder. We will meet that threat now, with our Army, Air Force, Navy, Coast Guard and Marines, so that we do not have to meet it later with armies of fire fighters and police and doctors on the streets of our cities. . . .

My fellow citizens, the dangers to our country and the world will be overcome. We will pass through this time of peril and carry on the work of peace. We will defend our freedom. We will bring freedom to others and we will prevail.

May God bless our country and all who defend her.

SOURCE: Bush, George W. "Address to the Nation on Military Operations in Iraq." *Selected Speeches of President George W. Bush: 2001–2008*. White House Archives. Available online at https://georgewbush-whitehouse.archives.gov/infocus/bushrecord/documents/Selected_ Speeches_George_W_Bush.pdf (accessed October 15, 2017). Courtesy of George W. Bush.

War in Afghanistan begins

The US government announced that it had evidence to believe that al-Qaeda leader Osama bin Laden (1957–2011) was responsible for the attacks. It accused the Taliban in the South Asia country of Afghanistan of hiding bin Laden. The Taliban is a militant Islamist group that operated much like al-Qaeda. It ruled Afghanistan at the time. The United States tried to work out a deal with the Taliban in exchange for bin Laden. The Taliban wanted to give bin Laden to a third country, where he would stand trial for the attacks. The US government refused the offer and instead decided that it would have to go to war to catch bin Laden. This was the beginning of the War on Terror.

On October 7, 2001, the United States officially began the war in Afghanistan. At this time, many US citizens supported the decision to go to war. Many were angry, scared, and upset over the 9/11 attacks and believed the nation needed to stop the terrorist groups. The country

War

along with a coalition that included Great Britain and Australia launched air and ground strikes. Over the next few months, the fighting continued. In December 2001, bin Laden released a tape admitting responsibility for the 9/11 attacks. By the end of 2001, forces pushed al-Qaeda, including bin Laden, and the Taliban from Afghanistan to bordering countries.

Opposition to another war

In January 2002, Bush identified Iraq, Iran, and North Korea as terror threats. That September, in an address to the United Nations (UN), Bush warned that the United States would be forced to take military action if Iraq did not agree to calls to disarm. The UN is an organization of more than 100 countries that works to protect international order. US officials claimed that Iraq had weapons of mass destruction (WMD), which are powerful weapons that can destroy entire regions. The UN gave Iraqi President Saddam Hussein (pronounced hoo-SAYN; 1937–2006) several opportunities to get rid of the weapons, and it began to inspect Iraq for WMD over the next few months. (None was found.)

By February, talk of a war in Iraq loomed, angering many people worldwide. Individuals began to organize public events to show their opposition to invading Iraq. A worldwide protest was held on February

Callie Gates (left) of Boston, Massachusetts, and Amelia Rutter (right) of Minneapolis, Minnesota, sing during an anti-war candlelight vigil on March 16, 2003, at the Lincoln Memorial in Washington, DC. On the day US President George W. Bush met with British Prime Minister Tony Blair and Spanish Prime Minister José María Aznar for a summit on Iraq, anti-war activists held candlelight vigils to protest a possible US-led invasion of Iraq. © ALEX WONG/GETTY IMAGES.

16, 2003. Anti-war demonstrators organized marches throughout numerous cities on that day in the United States and Europe. These events drew millions of protesters from around the globe. Despite the opposition to the war, UN talks about what to do about Iraq continued.

Candlelight vigils

On the evening of March 16, 2003, thousands of candlelight vigils were held around the world. This event was held as part of a worldwide protest to prevent a war in Iraq. Nearly 6,700 vigils were held in 139 nations. Many were held in front of government buildings, courthouses, and statues and in town squares and parks. Some were even held in backyards and on house porches.

People used the Internet and local channels to organize the gatherings throughout the world. The event began on the night of March 16 in New Zealand and then spread to other places as evening set in those countries. In New York City, people gathered at more than 50 locations at 7 p.m. for the vigils. Other locations that held vigils included London, United Kingdom; Bangalore, India; Manama, Bahrain; Antwerp, Belgium; Lucerne, Switzerland; Boston, Massachusetts; and Amman, Jordan.

The idea of a peaceful vigil was in contrast to the anti-war demonstrations that were held previously. Some vigils had speakers and singers. At others, people chanted, sang, and carried signs to protest the war. Many, however, were silent gatherings. Attendees at the vigils all had the same message. They did not support a war in Iraq.

The Iraq War

While many people opposed another war, some world leaders believed the threat Iraq posed was too great. Eventually, other UN member countries supported a war against Iraq. The United States gave Hussein a final chance to disarm and leave the country on March 17, 2003. The next day, the United Kingdom agreed to send forces to Iraq. On March 20, 2003, the United States, the United Kingdom, and forces from several other countries began the war with Iraq. Other nations joined the war effort against Iraq in the years that followed. The Iraq War lasted until 2011, which was the same year bin Laden was captured and killed. The war in Afghanistan, however, continued as terrorism threatened the safety of many countries worldwide.

Chelsea Manning and WikiLeaks

LOCATION: Global
DATE: 2010

The Chelsea Manning/WikiLeaks case involved US Army soldier Chelsea Manning (1987–), who was known as Bradley Manning at the time. Manning stole secret information from the US military in 2010. The information revealed US military activities that had killed innocent civilians in Iraq and Afghanistan. Civilians are people who are not in the military or a police force. The United States was fighting wars in Iraq and Afghanistan at the time.

Manning disliked that the United States was killing civilians and treating other people harshly in the wars. Manning stole evidence of US military actions and leaked it to WikiLeaks, an international organization that publishes stolen secrets about governments around the world. Manning was eventually arrested and sentenced to prison for stealing the information. Meanwhile, WikiLeaks published the information.

For releasing the secret documents about the US military, Manning became known as a whistle-blower. Whistle-blowers are people who publicly report organizations' secret, improper, or harmful actions taken by companies, agencies, or other organizations. Anyone can be a whistleblower—it may be an employee or a customer of the organization. The US government protects whistle-blowers by banning organizations from seeking revenge on the whistle-blower who reported the activity.

However, it is illegal to steal and use US government property. This is why Manning's case was different from other whistle-blower cases. Manning stole sensitive government property and had it published. Supporters of Manning called her a hero and a whistle-blower who told the world the truth about US actions in the war. In 2010 people in several countries protested for Manning's release. They believed she had been right to expose violent actions taken by the United States during wartime.

Others called Manning a traitor, or someone who betrays his or her country. Critics said Manning had put members of the US military in danger by exposing secret information about them. In 2013 Manning was sentenced to 35 years in prison for releasing the stolen secrets. In early

2017, however, President Barack Obama (1961–) reduced Manning's sentence. Manning was released from prison in May 2017 after having served a total of seven years in prison since her arrest in 2010.

Manning's early life

Chelsea Manning was born Bradley Manning on December 17, 1987, in Oklahoma. Her father was American, and her mother was Welsh (British). As a child, Manning was often lonely and had strong opinions about various subjects. She was also intensely interested in computers. Manning's parents divorced when she was a teenager. In 2001 Manning traveled to Wales to live with her mother. Around this time, Manning began to realize she was transgender. Transgender individuals have a gender identity that differs from the sex they were assigned at birth. Gender identity is a person's internal experience of gender. Although labeled male at birth, Manning had a female gender identity.

Manning returned to the United States in 2005. She had trouble keeping a job. In 2007 Manning joined the US Army. In 2009 the army assigned Manning to work in Iraq as a junior intelligence analyst. Intelligence analysts examine information from numerous sources to learn about possible attacks from a nation's enemies.

Communications with WikiLeaks

Soon after arriving in Iraq, Manning became troubled after seeing some of the actions carried out by the US military. These included bombings that killed civilians in Iraq and Afghanistan. This violence greatly disturbed Manning. After working in Iraq for only a few weeks, Manning decided she would somehow steal evidence of these killings and release it to the public.

Manning learned about the website WikiLeaks in 2009. Australian computer programmer Julian Assange (pronounced ah-SAHNJ; 1971–) had founded the site in 2006. WikiLeaks is an organization that publishes international government secrets and other leaked information. Its purpose is to present the public with information governments want to hide. While still in Iraq, Manning downloaded hundreds of thousands of files exposing violent actions in Iraq, Afghanistan, and elsewhere by the United States.

Manning brought the files back to the United States with her while on leave, or vacation, in early 2010. At first she was unsure of what to

Soon after arriving in Iraq, Manning became troubled after seeing some of the actions carried out by the US military. These included bombings that killed civilians in Iraq and Afghanistan. This violence greatly disturbed Manning.

do with the information. She offered the stolen files to newspapers such as the *Washington Post* and the *New York Times*. The papers did not respond enthusiastically. Manning then sent her files to the WikiLeaks site. She got no immediate response. Manning then returned to duty in Iraq.

WikiLeaks published some of Manning's files in February 2010. However, the first major release of the information came in April. That month WikiLeaks released a video showing a US military helicopter shooting Iraqi civilians and news reporters. The event had been a case of friendly fire, in which soldiers mistake non-enemies for enemies. In this case, the helicopter crew had mistaken the cameras of two Reuters news photographers for weapons and opened fire, killing a dozen people including the journalists. WikiLeaks continued releasing hundreds of thousands of Manning's files into late 2011. Other files proved that many US attacks in the wars killed civilians. They also showed that the United States sometimes tortured and killed prisoners captured during the war. Torture is the act of causing someone severe pain and suffering as punishment.

Manning's arrest and trial

In an online chat in May 2010, Manning told an American computer hacker about her theft. Hacking involves breaking into computers to access information. The hacker told the Federal Bureau of Investigation (FBI)

US Army Private First Class Bradley Manning (center; now Chelsea Manning) and military officials depart a US military court facility as the sentencing phase continues in Manning's trial at Fort Meade, Maryland on August 20, 2013. Manning was convicted of espionage for giving classified government documents to WikiLeaks. © SAUL LOEB/AFP/GETTY IMAGES.

about what Manning had done. The FBI investigates threats to national security. The FBI then told the US Army about Manning. Authorities arrested Manning in Iraq at the end of May 2010. She was brought to Virginia, where she was kept in solitary confinement for about nine months. Solitary confinement involves keeping prisoners in cells by themselves for extended periods.

News about Manning divided the international public. Some called Manning a traitor. Critics claimed Manning had put the US military in danger by revealing classified information about its activities in its wars. Some US leaders claimed Manning's release of the information to WikiLeaks directly benefited the United States' enemies in the Middle East. They said Manning knew terrorists would read the information. For these reasons, many Americans believed Manning was no hero.

Others said Manning was a hero. American film director Michael Moore encouraged people around the world to protest for Manning's release from prison. Moore praised Manning for telling the truth about US military actions in the wars. He claimed Manning was being unfairly punished simply for exposing the illegal activities of the United States. People in the United States, Canada, and Australia demonstrated to call for Manning's release in September 2010. American protesters held rallies in 18 US cities. The organization Courage to Refuse staged the main protest in California. The group called for Americans to oppose the wars in Iraq and Afghanistan.

The US government charged Manning with numerous crimes in 2010 and 2011. These included obtaining secret information, leaking that information, and helping the enemies of the United States. This last charge had come in response to reports that enemies in the Middle East had read the files Manning released. In the end, Manning faced a total of 22 criminal charges. She admitted to being guilty of 10 of the charges. These 10 charges alone would have landed Manning a 20-year prison sentence.

Manning's trial began in Maryland in June 2013. Lawyers arguing against Manning presented several forms of evidence proving she had leaked the information. The evidence included Manning's online chat records, admissions of guilt, and awareness of Assange, the WikiLeaks founder. At the end of July 2013, the court found Manning not guilty of aiding enemies of the United States. However, Manning was found guilty of 20 other charges.

War

Walter Reed Medical Center Neglect Scandal

As negative stories were being released about what was going on during the wars in Iraq and Afghanistan, another issue was unfolding. Whistle-blowers said that US veterans' hospitals were neglecting their patients and subjecting them to poor conditions. One of these hospitals was the Walter Reed National Military Medical Center in Bethesda, Maryland, just outside of Washington, DC.

A series of articles in the *Washington Post* in 2007 detailed the conditions at Walter Reed. Newspaper reporters talked with several soldiers, their family members, and staff from the medical center. The reporters also visited Walter Reed. Some of the whistle-blowers agreed to have their names used. Others feared what the US military might do to them if they gave their real names. They asked to remain anonymous, or secret.

According to the reports, some of the soldiers were treated in smelly rooms with torn walls and holes in the ceiling. The carpets and mattresses were old, dirty, and stained. Evidence of mice and bugs existed. Army veterans at the medical center suffered from various injuries, including brain issues, amputations, and mental conditions. Some had been there for months or even years.

The whistle-blowers hoped that exposing the conditions at the hospital would change things. However, some whistle-blowers found themselves at odds with the army for revealing what was going on. Some felt that the army turned its back on them because they spoke out for veterans who needed continued medical care.

When the public found out about the conditions at Walter Reed, many were angry. They were concerned that the soldiers who risked their lives for the country were not treated better. More people came forward with stories about other veterans' hospitals across the country. This led to more investigations over the next several years. Army officials vowed to

Throughout the trial, Manning claimed she had never meant to put any Americans in danger by releasing the stolen files. She wanted only to allow the world to see the unfortunate results of war. In August the trial judge sentenced Manning to 35 years in prison. This was one of the longest sentences ever given to a whistle-blower who leaked US secrets.

Imprisonment and release

Manning was to serve her sentence at the US military prison in Fort Leavenworth, Kansas. Her imprisonment there over the next few years was difficult. Manning had recently revealed she was transgender and wished to transition to living publicly as a woman. She asked that people refer to her as Chelsea. She said workers at the prison bullied her and

clean up the hospitals and require stricter cleaning procedures. Also, they replaced the administrators who ran the hospitals. Nevertheless, problems continued.

A wounded army specialist reveals problems with the wallpaper. He is assigned a room at Building 18, which is a facility used by Walter Reed National Military Medical Center to house wounded soldiers recovering from their injuries. Over the years, the facilities had fallen into disrepair. © MICHEL DU CILLE/THE WASHINGTON POST/GETTY IMAGES.

treated her unfairly due to her being transgender. While in prison, Manning tried to kill herself several times.

In late 2016 Manning protested her prison treatment by starting a hunger strike. This involved her refusing to eat until her conditions improved. She specifically wanted to undergo sex-reassignment surgery. This is surgery to remove or change sexual organs to help individuals transition to their inner gender identity. The US Army eventually agreed to allow Manning to have the surgery. However, she did not have surgery before leaving prison.

Throughout Manning's imprisonment, protesters across the United States publicly called for her release. They claimed she had suffered greatly in prison and deserved freedom. Protesters requested that

President Obama reduce Manning's 35-year sentence. Obama did this in January 2017, days before leaving office as president. He said Manning had already served a difficult sentence. Obama also felt that the US government had served justice in this case. He hoped Manning's sentence would stop possible future whistle-blowers from stealing and leaking secret government information. Obama did not officially pardon, or forgive, Manning for her crimes though. While some people were happy Manning was to be released, others were angry, believing the sentence was not long enough.

Manning was released from prison on May 17, 2017. She had served about seven years of her 35-year sentence. Manning said she would obtain her own health care to complete her gender transition. She was considering writing a book about her experiences. Manning said she was not a traitor to the United States. She claimed she had made what she thought was the best decision regarding releasing the stolen military information.

Despite having many supporters, Manning remained a subject of controversy. In September 2017 after inviting Manning to be a visiting fellow at Harvard Kennedy School, the school withdrew its offer. Harvard had received complaints from Central Intelligence Agency director Mike Pompeo (1963–) and others. They did not believe Manning deserved the honor of being a visiting fellow after revealing classified US military secrets.

For More Information

BOOKS

Addams, Jane, et al. *Women at the Hague: The International Congress of Women and Its Results.* New York: Macmillan, 1915.

Çinar, Özgür Heval. *Conscientious Objection to Military Service in International Human Rights Law.* New York: Palgrave Macmillan, 2013.

Elmer, Jerry. *Felon for Peace: The Memoir of a Vietnam-Era Draft Resister.* Nashville, TN: Vanderbilt University Press, 2005, 60–62.

Gold, Susan Dudley. *Tinker v. Des Moines: Free Speech for Students.* Tarrytown, NY: Marshall Cavendish Benchmark, 2007.

Means, Howard. *67 Shots: Kent State and the End of American Innocence.* Boston: Da Capo Press, 2016.

Stienstra, Deborah. *Women's Movements and International Organizations.* New York: St. Martin's Press, 1994.

PERIODICALS

Bakkila, Blake. "'Please, Give Me Help': Chelsea Manning Goes on Hunger Strike to Protest Her Treatment in All-Male Prison." *People* (September 10, 2016).

Available online at http://people.com/crime/chelsea-manning-goes-on-hunger-strike-to-protest-her-treatment-in-prison/ (accessed September 20, 2017).

Lueck, Thomas J. "Threats and Responses: Protests; Candlelight Vigils Are Held around the World to Oppose Military Action against Iraq." *New York Times* (March 17, 2003). Available online at http://www.nytimes.com/2003/03/17/world/threats-responses-protests-candlelight-vigils-are-held-around-world-oppose.html?mcubz=1 (accessed September 22, 2017).

McFadden, Robert D. "The Republicans: The Convention in New York—The March; Vast Anti-Bush Rally Greets Republicans in New York." *New York Times* (August 30, 2004). Available online at http://www.nytimes.com/2004/08/30/us/republicans-convention-new-york-march-vast-anti-bush-rally-greets-republicans.html?mcubz=1 (accessed September 22, 2017).

Michaels, Samantha. "The Inside Story of Chelsea Manning's Unlikely Release from Prison." *Mother Jones* (May 11, 2017). Available online at http://www.motherjones.com/politics/2017/05/chelsea-manning-free-from-prison-commutation-transgender-wikileaks/ (accessed September 22, 2017).

Pilkington, Ed. "Bradley Manning a Traitor Who Set Out to Harm US, Prosecutors Conclude." *Guardian* (July 25, 2013). Available online at https://www.theguardian.com/world/2013/jul/25/bradley-manning-traitor-wikileaks-prosecution (accessed October 16, 2017).

Priest, Dana, and Anne Hull. "Soldiers Face Neglect, Frustration at Army's Top Medical Facility." *Washington Post* (February 18, 2007). Available online at http://www.washingtonpost.com/wp-dyn/content/article/2007/02/17/AR2007021701172.html (accessed September 22, 2017).

Rothman, Lily. "This Photo Shows the Vietnam Draft-Card Burning That Started a Movement." *Time* (October 15, 2015). Available online at http://time.com/4061835/david-miller-draft-card/ (accessed August 31, 2017).

Selk, Avi. "Chelsea Manning Denies Betraying the U.S., Feels as If She Lives in a 'Dystopian Novel.'" *Washington Post,* (September 18, 2017). Available online at https://www.washingtonpost.com/news/checkpoint/wp/2017/09/18/chelsea-manning-denies-betraying-the-u-s-feels-like-she-lives-in-a-dystopian-novel/?utm_term=.b8229403101a (accessed October 16, 2017).

Stegmeir, Mary. "Iowa Activists Return to Schools That Suspended Them." *USA Today* (November 20, 2013). Available online at https://www.usatoday.com/story/news/nation/2013/11/20/iowa-activists-suspended-protesting-vietnam-return/3651047/ (accessed August 31, 2017).

WEBSITES

Adams, Cydney. "May 4, 1970: Guardsmen Open Fire on Kent State Protesters." CBS News, May 4, 2016. https://www.cbsnews.com/news/on-this-day-may-4-1970-guardsmen-open-fire-on-kent-state-protesters/ (accessed September 7, 2017).

"Afghanistan Profile—Timeline." BBC News, September 4, 2017. http://www.bbc.com/news/world-south-asia-12024253 (accessed September 22, 2017).

Alihusain, C. "International Congress of Women of 1915." Peace Palace Library, February 6, 2015. https://www.peacepalacelibrary.nl/2015/02/international-congress-of-women-of-1915/ (accessed September 8, 2017).

Bowman, Tom. "Walter Reed Was the Army's Wake-Up Call in 2007." National Public Radio, August 31, 2011. http://www.npr.org/2011/08/31/139641856/in-2007-walter-reed-was-the-armys-wakeup-call (accessed September 22, 2017).

"Chelsea Manning: Wikileaks Source and Her Turbulent Life." BBC News, May 16, 2017. http://www.bbc.com/news/world-us-canada-11874276 (accessed September 20, 2017).

Iannacci, Nicandro. "Tinker v. Des Moines: Protecting Student Free Speech." National Constitution Center, February 24, 2017. https://constitutioncenter.org/blog/tinker-v-des-moines-protecting-student-free-speech (accessed August 31, 2017).

"International Anti-war," CBS News. https://www.cbsnews.com/pictures/international-anti-war (accessed September 22, 2017).

International Congress of Women. "Final Programme." Gothenburg University Library. http://www.ub.gu.se/kvinndata/portaler/fred/samarbete/pdf/program_1915.pdf (accessed September 8, 2017).

"Kent State Shootings." Ohio History Central. http://www.ohiohistorycentral.org/w/Kent_State_Shootings (accessed September 7, 2017).

Lewis, Jerry M., and Thomas R. Hensley. "The May 4 Shootings at Kent State University: The Search for Historical Accuracy." Kent State University. http://www.kent.edu/may-4-historical-accuracy (accessed September 7, 2017).

Lindsay, James M. "The Twenty Best Vietnam Protest Songs." Council on Foreign Relations, March 5, 2015. https://www.cfr.org/blog/twenty-best-vietnam-protest-songs (accessed September 7, 2017).

"September 11th Terror Attacks Fast Facts." CNN, August 24, 2017. http://www.cnn.com/2013/07/27/us/september-11-anniversary-fast-facts/index.html (accessed September 22, 2017).

"Timeline: Iraq War." BBC News, July 5, 2016. http://www.bbc.com/news/magazine-36702957 (accessed September 22, 2017).

"Tinker v. Des Moines Independent Community School Dist." Cornell Law School. https://www.law.cornell.edu/supremecourt/text/393/503 (accessed August 31, 2017).

Weeks, Linton. "Whatever Happened to the Anti-war Movement?" National Public Radio, April 15, 2011. http://www.npr.org/2011/04/15/135391188/whatever-happened-to-the-anti-war-movement (accessed September 22, 2017).

"WikiLeaks Fast Facts." CNN. http://www.cnn.com/2013/06/03/world/wikileaks-fast-facts/index.html (accessed September 20, 2017).

21

Women's Rights

Hunger Strikes by Suffragettes in Prison **701**

Women's Suffrage Protest at the White House **707**

Baladi Campaign **714**

Malala Yousafzai All-Girls School **718**

Women's March on Washington **724**

Throughout history, women have struggled to have the same rights as men. Whether it be to own land, have access to education, have the right to vote, or to even have a job, women have raised their voices in protest against unfair treatment. Many women organized to stand up and fight for their rights. Several movements throughout history, such as the suffrage movements, have successfully secured rights for women. The suffrage movements helped women gain voting rights in several countries.

In many countries, such as the United States and the United Kingdom, men and women have equal rights. In many other countries, however, women experience unfair treatment. They do not have the same rights as men do. For example, in some areas of the world, women cannot be in public without a related male present. In addition, many women who have equal rights must continue to fight to keep these rights from being taken away.

Women's rights in the British colonies

In the early 17th century, women in the British colonies of North America had the same rights as they did in Britain. According to the law, single women, who were either unmarried or widowed, could own and sell property. They could keep the money they earned. Once a woman married, however, she signed over these rights to her husband. Married women were the property of their husbands. They could not own land. Their houses and children belonged to their husbands. Any money they earned was considered their husband's profits.

A woman's role was that of a domestic or homemaker. She would oversee the household and care for the children. She also tended to gardens and grew food to eat. During the early 17th century, not many women traveled to the colonies. Many people thought that the New

Women's Rights

> ### WORDS TO KNOW
>
> **Abolitionist movement:** A campaign held during the 19th century to end slavery in the United States.
>
> **Electoral votes:** Votes cast by a select group of people from each state to elect the president of the United States.
>
> **Etiquette:** A social custom or skill that guides the way people behave in the presence of others.
>
> **Force-feed:** To make a person eat by forcefully putting food down his or her throat.
>
> **Hunger strike:** The act of refusing to eat to bring about a desired change.
>
> **Indentured servant:** A person who works for another person in exchange for travel, food, and housing for a specified amount of time.
>
> **Militant:** Using violent or aggressive means in support of a cause.
>
> **Picket:** To stand or march in a public place to protest something.
>
> **Sharia:** Islamic law based on the teachings of the Koran.
>
> **Suffrage:** The right to vote.
>
> **Suffragist:** A person who works to gain voting rights for people who are not allowed to vote.
>
> **Tactic:** Something used to effect change.

World was a harsh place—too harsh for a woman. In the early days, men outnumbered women there. Since women were scarce, many men were responsible for performing household duties. The men pleaded with British officials to get more women to come to the colonies, and eventually, more women traveled from Great Britain to North America.

Many women who first traveled to the colonies worked as indentured servants, who performed work in exchange for travel and housing costs. These servants usually worked in the fields, planting and harvesting crops, until their debts were paid. Some women came to the colonies to look for husbands. It was easy for a woman at this time to find a man to marry since the men outnumbered the women in America. In exchange for being provided for by their husbands, these married women became their husband's property, according to the law.

During the late 17th and early 18th centuries, Great Britain passed many laws to limit the rights of women. For example, women who spoke poorly about their husbands or other men could be held underwater as punishment. Women struggled with their newfound duties in the colonies, and sometimes their roles were unclear. They were supposed to obey their husbands, take care of the children, clean the home, and grow food as needed. Yet, many women found themselves leading a household.

CRITICAL THINKING QUESTIONS

1. Do you think it is important for women to have the same rights as men? Why or why not?

2. What is the importance of having the right to vote?

3. What do you think was the real reason Saudi Arabia shut down the Baladi campaign?

4. Do you believe women will ever achieve full equal rights in Islamic countries? Why or why not?

5. Why do you think education is important to young women?

6. What are some other strategies women could have used during the suffrage movements in the United Kingdom and United States?

7. What are some of the rights that women worldwide still lack in the 21st century?

8. What are some of the ways that men and women are unequal in the United States in the 21st century?

9. Do you think the Women's March on Washington was successful? Why or why not?

10. Do you believe that women are in danger of having some of their rights taken away from them in the United States? In other countries? Why or why not?

These women were not used to managing house staff, including slaves. Because the women were in charge of staff and slaves, they sometimes clashed with their husbands over who was really in control. Many women felt that since they were in charge of the household they did not have to obey their husband's commands. The men did not like this since wives were supposed to be obedient.

By the mid-18th century, the responsibility of women changed again. At this time, mothers were in charge of educating their children. They instructed them in reading, writing, math, and religion. They also taught etiquette, or proper social skills, to prepare the children to enter society. Mothers taught their daughters how to perform domestic duties to prepare the girls for marriage.

While these were the accepted norms of the times, not all women followed these rules. Some single women, who had either never married or had been widowed because their husbands died, preferred to keep their independence by not marrying or remarrying. A single woman at the time could keep many of the rights that were taken away once she married. Some married women held jobs outside the home. They worked at taverns, shops, or mills, and others became midwives or seamstresses. Since many of the jobs performed by women outside the home were domestic duties, these did not challenge gender roles set forth by the colonies.

Women's Rights

The role of women in the early United States

In the late 18th century, the colonies began to break away from British control. Many colonists were unhappy with the taxes put on them by Great Britain, so they decided to protest by not importing British items. Women had to learn how to produce these items, such as soap, clothing, and candles. Women learned how to spin and weave cloth and make clothing. This helped women feel important and part of the fight against British rule.

The fighting with Great Britain led to the American Revolution (1775–1783), also known as the American War of Independence. The colonies gained their freedom and established the United States of America. During the fight for independence, Abigail Adams (1744–1818) urged her husband, Congress member and future president John Adams (1735–1826), to "remember the ladies." Adams and the other men, however, ignored this request. After the colonies gained freedom from British control, not everyone in the colonies had equal rights. White men controlled the country and denied white women many political and legal rights. African American slaves had no rights and were considered the property of their owners.

Origins of the women's rights movement in the United States

By the 19th century, women began to speak out for equal rights. They wanted to own property and vote. In the 1830s and 1840s, women began to organize and work for these reforms. This was the start of the women's rights movement.

Women also spoke out against slavery. As a way to get their voices heard, many women joined the abolitionist movement, which was a campaign to end slavery in the United States. Many women believed that fighting for the rights of enslaved African Americans would lead to equal human rights for all people.

Some women decided to focus solely on gaining rights for women. One of these women, Elizabeth Cady Stanton (1815–1902), along with a few others organized the Woman's Rights Convention, also known as the Seneca Falls Convention, in 1848. The women who attended spoke out in favor of changes to laws related to childcare, divorce, education, equal wages, and the right to vote. While all of these rights were important, suffrage, or the right to vote, became the central fighting point. This began the suffrage movement in the United States. Women thought that

Women's Rights

This graphic shows the portraits of seven prominent figures of the early women's suffrage and women's rights movements in the United States, with Anna E. Dickinson in the middle, the others are (clockwise from the top) Lucretia Mott, Elizabeth Cady Stanton, Mary Livermore, Lydia Maria Child, Susan B. Anthony, and Grace Greenwood. COURTESY OF THE LIBRARY OF CONGRESS.

if they gained the right to vote, they could influence many laws and gain greater rights. They could hold political office and fight for the rights most important to not only women but also to all citizens.

The suffrage movements Women in the United States were not the only ones fighting for the right to vote. Groups of women began to organize suffrage campaigns in the United Kingdom in the 1860s. They held protests and used both nonviolent and violent means to make their voices heard. Many women in the United Kingdom were jailed for their actions. Some of these women began to use tactics, or ways to cause change, while they were in prison. They found refusing to eat a very effective way to get the government's attention.

Women's Rights

American women who visited the United Kingdom during this time brought back some of these ideas to the United States to use in their fight for suffrage. However, the United States had become deeply divided over the issue of slavery, which became more urgent to some people than the women's suffrage movement at the time. Tensions were mounting between the southern states, which wanted slavery to continue because their economy depended on it, and the northern states, which wanted slavery to end. This disagreement eventually led to the US Civil War (1861–1865). The war halted the women's progress, and many women joined the war effort instead.

The end of the war brought freedom to slaves in the United States. In the years that followed, Congress passed amendments that gave all people born in the United States citizenship and all men the right to vote; however, women still lacked voting privileges. This helped to spur women to continue to fight for equal rights. The fight led to the formation of several women's organizations that used many different actions, such as protests and demonstrations, to make their voices heard. Eventually, women in the United States gained the right to vote nationally on August 26, 1920. All women in the United Kingdom received voting rights in 1928.

Alice Paul, national chair of the National Woman's Party, unfurled a banner after Tennessee became the 36th state to ratify the 19th Amendment, which gave women the right to vote nationally in 1920. COURTESY OF THE LIBRARY OF CONGRESS.

Women's rights in the 21st century

Although women can hold political office in the United States, there are far fewer than men in local, state, and federal government positions. Fewer women than men hold seats in nearly every political field. No woman has ever been elected president of the United States. However, former Senator, First Lady, and Secretary of State Hillary Rodham Clinton (1947–) ran for the presidency two times, in 2008 and 2016. She made history in 2016 when she received the Democratic Party's presidential nomination. She eventually lost the election to Republican candidate Donald Trump (1946–). Despite this loss, and in a number of cases, because of it, women continue to make bids for political office in an effort to fight for the rights of all people.

Women also continue to rally against people who try to take their rights away. Areas that women tend to concentrate their efforts on include access to affordable health care, childcare, equal wages, and reproductive rights protections. US lawmakers continue to challenge some of these rights.

While women in the United States and the United Kingdom have gained the right to vote and have equal rights to men, women in some other countries are still denied these rights in the 21st century. In some parts of the world, religion prevents women from being considered equal to men. In Saudi Arabia, for example, women stood up to fight for the right to vote with the formation of the Baladi (pronounced buh-LAH-dee) campaign in 2011. The group, which met opposition from the government, challenged the country's laws. Saudi Arabian women eventually gained voting and political participation rights in 2015 elections.

While Saudi Arabian women received the right to take part in elections and hold office, they still do not have many of the same rights as men do in their own country. They also lack rights that women have in other countries. For example, Saudi women must dress a certain way in public. Also, they were banned from driving. In September 2017, however, the Saudi government agreed to lift its ban on women driving. Many women around the world have even fewer legal protections. They cannot own property. Some women do not have access to education, health care, employment, or equal wages. They do not have protection from violence or sexual harassment.

Women's Rights

Michelle Obama: The Importance of Educating Girls

This primary source excerpt is from a weekly address given by First Lady Michelle Obama on May 10, 2014. In the address, she speaks about the Nigerian schoolgirls who were kidnapped by militant Islamists.

Like millions of people across the globe, my husband and I are outraged and heartbroken over the kidnapping of more than 200 Nigerian girls from their school dormitory in the middle of the night.

This unconscionable act was committed by a terrorist group determined to keep these girls from getting an education—grown men attempting to snuff out the aspirations of young girls. . . .

In these girls, Barack and I see our own daughters. We see their hopes, their dreams—and we can only imagine the anguish their parents are feeling right now.

Many of them may have been hesitant to send their daughters off to school, fearing that harm might come their way.

But they took that risk because they believed in their daughters' promise and wanted to give them every opportunity to succeed.

The girls themselves also knew full well the dangers they might encounter.

Their school had recently been closed due to terrorist threats . . . but these girls still insisted on returning to take their exams.

They were so determined to move to the next level of their education . . . so determined to one day build careers of their own and make their families and communities proud.

And what happened in Nigeria was not an isolated incident . . . it's a story we see every day as girls around the world risk their lives to pursue their ambitions.

It's the story of girls like Malala Yousafzai from Pakistan.

Some, like the 276 Nigerian schoolgirls who were kidnapped by militant Islamists in 2014, were denied an education and subjected to abuse. The girls, ranging in age from 15 to 18, were studying to become doctors, lawyers, and other professionals when they were violently taken at gunpoint by men who would rather enslave them than see them go to school. Since that time, some of the girls have escaped and others have been released. Others remained missing. Girls and women in other parts of the world are also denied an education. Some in poverty cannot afford an education so they end up marrying and becoming young mothers in order to have a future. Many movements and organizations have formed worldwide to help women fight for equal and basic human rights. However, gender inequality remains an important issue in many countries worldwide.

Malala spoke out for girls' education in her community ... and as a result, she was shot in the head by a Taliban gunman while on a school bus with her classmates.

But fortunately Malala survived ... and when I met her last year, I could feel her passion and determination as she told me that girls' education is still her life's mission.

As Malala said in her address to the United Nations, she said "The terrorists thought that they would change our aims and stop our ambitions but nothing changed in my life except this: Weakness, fear and hopelessness died. Strength, power and courage was born."

The courage and hope embodied by Malala and girls like her around the world should serve as a call to action.

Because right now, more than 65 million girls worldwide are not in school.

Yet, we know that girls who are educated make higher wages, lead healthier lives, and have healthier families.

And when more girls attend secondary school, that boosts their country's entire economy.

So education is truly a girl's best chance for a bright future, not just for herself, but for her family and her nation.

And that's true right here in the U.S. as well ... so I hope the story of these Nigerian girls will serve as an inspiration for every girl—and boy—in this country....

So today, let us all pray for their safe return ... let us hold their families in our hearts during this very difficult time ... and let us show just a fraction of their courage in fighting to give every girl on this planet the education that is her birthright. Thank you.

SOURCE: Obama, Michelle. "Weekly Address: The First Lady Marks Mother's Day and Speaks Out on the Tragic Kidnapping in Nigeria." White House, Office of the Press Secretary (May 10, 2014). Available online at https://www.whitehouse.gov/the-press-office/2014/05/10/weekly-address-first-lady-marks-mother-s-day-and-speaks-out-tragic-kidna (accessed October 16, 2017). Courtesy of the White House.

Hunger Strikes by Suffragettes in Prison

LOCATION: United Kingdom

DATE: Early 20th century

Hunger strikes are a form of protest to bring about a desired change. Activists and prisoners have long used hunger strikes in which people refuse to eat to draw attention to their causes in the hope of producing change. In the early 20th century, some imprisoned women used this measure while fighting for suffrage, or the right to vote, throughout the United Kingdom. The countries of England, Northern Ireland, Scotland, and Wales make up the United Kingdom.

The suffrage movement, which began in the United Kingdom in the late 19th century, gained strength and received much notice by the beginning of the early 20th century. Women did not think it was fair that their country did not allow them to vote. They formed groups to fight for voting rights. These groups used both violent and nonviolent means to make their voices heard. Some women were jailed for their actions.

One of these jailed women came up with a plan so she could receive better treatment in prison. The woman wanted to be seen as a political prisoner. Political prisoners received special privileges in prison, such as being allowed to wear their own clothes or read books. She decided to refuse to eat as an act of protest. Prison officials did not know what to do with her, so they released the woman.

Other imprisoned women followed her lead and stopped eating, so they could be let out of jail also. Eventually, the prison began to force-feed these women and took other actions to keep them locked up. The women did not give up and continued to fight. The start of World War I (1914–1918) delayed some of the women's efforts. Some women halted their voting rights' work to support the war. Others continued to fight. Gradually, British women received partial voting rights in 1918. In 1928 women over the age of 21 received full voting rights in the United Kingdom.

Women's suffrage movement in the United Kingdom

Women and men did not always have the same rights. During the 18th century, women could not participate in political affairs. They could not vote or hold office. Many people felt that women did not need the right to vote because men in the family took care of political matters. The role of women was in the home, taking care of the household and raising children.

This role eventually began to change for women during the Industrial Revolution of the late 18th and early 19th centuries. More women entered the workforce. Women met other women at these jobs. They found that they had more to talk about than just their families. They began to debate political and social issues. Eventually, they realized they wanted the right to political participation.

Women's Rights

Groups of women began to organize suffrage campaigns in the United Kingdom in the 1860s. In 1867 the British government considered making changes to Parliament, its lawmaking body. Parliament member John Stuart Mill (1806–1873) suggested an amendment, or change, to the law that would give women the right to vote. Parliament rejected the amendment.

The suffrage movement began to gain support and followers known as suffragists after this time. Suffragist Millicent Fawcett (1847–1929) formed the National Union of Women's Suffrage Societies (NUWSS) to oversee the suffrage groups. NUWSS wanted to gain the right to vote for middle-class women who owned property. Members of the organization used peaceful measures such as demonstrations and written requests to spread their message. Women such as Fawcett believed that the government would listen to polite and responsible women.

By the beginning of the 20th century, members of Parliament introduced several bills granting women the right to vote, but none of the laws passed. In 1903 a second group of suffragists formed. This group, known as the suffragettes, broke from NUWSS. Emmeline Pankhurst (1858–1928), a former member of NUWSS, organized the new group because she did not believe that peaceful measures were working. This organization, which included working-class women, became known as the Women's Social and Political Union (WSPU).

By 1907 WSPU split into two groups after Pankhurst had conflicting views with other members. Pankhurst remained with WSPU. The women who left over the disagreements formed another group called the Women's Freedom League (WFL). The groups did not agree with each other over the campaign's tactics. However, they worked together at times since they were fighting for the same cause.

In the years that followed, WSPU spread its reach throughout the country and even published its own newspaper, *Votes for Women*. NUWSS also gained a nationwide following. However, the suffragettes from both WSPU and WFL were unhappy with how long the government was taking to make any changes. About this time, they adopted more aggressive ways to carry out their message.

They broke laws, made violent threats, and held protests as ways to effect change. Police arrested many suffragettes, and some went to jail for their actions. Not everyone agreed that women should have the right to political participation. Groups of both women and men formed anti-suffrage movements. These groups campaigned against allowing women to vote.

A trio of WFL members participated in a protest in 1908. Muriel Matters (1877–1969), Violet Tillard (1874–1922), and Helen Fox protested

They broke laws, made violent threats, and held protests as ways to effect change. Police arrested many suffragettes, and some went to jail for their actions. Not everyone agreed that women should have the right to political participation. Groups of both women and men formed anti-suffrage movements. These groups campaigned against allowing women to vote.

Women's Rights

Women's suffrage leader Sylvia Pankhurst, daughter of suffragette Emmeline Pankhurst, is shown leaving the East End of London in a bath chair in June 1914. Weakened by hunger, thirst, and sleep strikes, Pankhurt is surrounded by suffragettes and male supporters who are trying to prevent the police from rearresting her during a temporary release from prison. Pankhurst had been released due to ill health caused by her hunger and other strikes. Once prisoners like Pankhurst recovered at home after their strikes, the police would rearrest them and return them to prison to complete their sentences. © MUSEUM OF LONDON/HERITAGE IMAGES/GETTY IMAGES.

the grille, or iron gate, used to keep women separate from the men during parliamentary meetings. Matters and Fox chained themselves to the grille and refused to leave. Police had to remove the grille with the women attached to it and cut them from its iron rails. The three women along with several others were arrested and sent to prison for their involvement in the protest.

Hunger strikes

While in prison, the suffragettes found a nonviolent tactic to use to draw attention to their cause: hunger strikes. On July 5, 1909, Marion Wallace Dunlop (1864–1942), a suffragette who belonged to the WSPU, was

Emily Wilding Davison's Derby Day Protest

Emily Wilding Davison (1872–1913) was a British woman who died during the suffrage movement in the United Kingdom. A horse trampled her in what many historians believe was an attempt to attach a suffrage banner to the animal. Davison was the first woman in the United Kingdom to die in the fight for voting rights.

Davison was born in London in 1872. She attended Royal Holloway College and Oxford University. She then worked as a teacher. Davison became involved with the suffrage movement in 1906 when she joined the Women's Social and Political Union (WSPU). Within three years, she decided to quit her teaching job to devote herself fully to the suffrage movement.

The suffragette quickly became known for using militant tactics to make her voice heard. She was daring and got into trouble for several incidents. She held public demonstrations and burned down mailboxes. Police arrested her nine different times. She spent time in jail on several occasions.

In 1909 she threw rocks at the carriage carrying UK Chancellor David Lloyd George (1863–1945). She was arrested by the police and was sentenced to jail for one month. While in prison, she held a hunger strike, refusing to eat. Prison officials tried to force-feed her, but she resisted. She sat in front of her jail cell's door and blocked prison guards from getting to her. Eventually, the guards forced her out by flooding her cell with water.

After her release from prison, Davison continued to fight for the right to vote for women. In 1913 at the Epsom Derby, a horse race near London, her fight ended. During the race, she ran out onto the track in front of the horse of King George V. According to accounts written at the time, some believed that she was trying to attach a women's suffrage banner to the bridle of the horse. Instead, the horse trampled her. Davison died a few days later on June 8, 1913.

This edition of the Suffragette *commemorated the death of Emily Wilding Davison. She died as a result of her injuries after being knocked down by the king's horse during a protest in support of women's voting rights at the Epsom Derby.* © POPPERFOTO/GETTY IMAGES.

Estimates of more than 5,000 women marched in Davison's funeral procession through London. Thousands more stood in silence along the route, paying respect to the woman who died trying to get women the right to vote.

arrested and imprisoned. She was jailed at HM Prison Holloway for posting part of the Bill of Rights on a wall in the House of Commons. Dunlop wanted the prison to treat her like other political prisoners, so she refused to eat to bring support to her cause. A political prisoner is someone who has been imprisoned because of his or her political views, which may disagree with the government and its laws. Often times, political prisoners receive special treatment, such as being able to read books or wear their own clothing. Instead of granting her "political prisoner" status, she was released after she went three days without eating.

The suffragettes realized how useful hunger strikes could be to their cause. Other jailed suffragettes began to use this tactic. The prison tried to tempt the prisoners with delicious foods, but the suffragettes stayed strong and refused to eat. After the release of several prisoners who staged hunger strikes, government and prison officials decided to force-feed the prisoners. The process of feeding a person by putting food down his or her throat by force was seen as dangerous and cruel to the prisoners. Some women received physical injuries from being force-fed. The prisons fed numerous suffragettes this way.

When people found out what was happening at the prisons, they demanded that the prison officials stop feeding the inmates against their will. In response, Parliament passed the Prisoners (Temporary Discharge for Ill-Health) Act, also known as the Cat and Mouse Act, in 1913. The law allowed the prisoners to starve themselves until they were ill. They were then released from prison. Once the released prisoners regained health, they were once again arrested so they could serve the rest of their sentences.

The suffragettes continued with the hunger strikes and released accounts to the media of women who were force-fed. The stories of force-feedings angered the public and encouraged more people to join the suffrage movement. By this time, World War I had begun. The government, which had more pressing issues at the time, decided to release the suffragettes from prison. Some suffragettes temporarily halted their actions. They chose to support the war effort instead.

The process of feeding a person by putting food down his or her throat by force was seen as dangerous and cruel to the prisoners. Some women received physical injuries from being force-fed. The prisons fed numerous suffragettes this way.

Aftermath

After the war ended in 1918, Parliament passed the Representation of the People Act. This gave some women over the age of 30 the right to vote. The act required that the women own property and belong to the Local Government Register. The act also allowed women to be elected to Parliament. The Representation of the People Act gave all men over the

Women's Rights

age of 21 full voting rights. It did not require them to be landowners or live in the country for a certain amount of time. It also allowed male soldiers over the age of 19 to vote. While many activists saw this law as a triumph, it did not give all women equal voting rights.

Women continued to speak out and hold protests. Eventually, the government expanded voting rights with the Representation of the People (Equal Franchise) Act, also known as the Equal Suffrage Act, in 1928. This law granted all women in the United Kingdom over the age of 21 the right to vote. The act had no landowner requirements. In 1969 the UK government amended the law to lower the voting age from 21 to 18. In Scotland officials passed another revision to the act in 2015. This allowed residents of the country over the age of 16 to vote in certain elections.

Women's Suffrage Protest at the White House

LOCATION: Washington, DC

DATE: 1917

Women in the United States began seeking equal rights during the 19th century. Much of the fight centered on suffrage, or the right to vote. During this era, major human and civil rights movements were taking place in the country, competing with the suffrage movement. Despite this, women continued to work to gain support for their cause.

One of the struggles for human rights was taking place at the same time as the early women's suffrage movement. The rights of enslaved African Americans and the issue of slavery divided much of the country. This led to the US Civil War (1861–1865). Many women abandoned their work with the suffrage movement to focus on the war effort. These women hoped that maybe they would gain equal rights when the war ended. After the Civil War, Congress passed an amendment to the US Constitution that granted African American men voting rights.

Women did not receive voting rights. Many people felt this was unfair. After all, if men could have the right to vote, why not women? This helped rally support for the suffrage movement. Over the next

U•X•L Protests, Riots, and Rebellions: Civil Unrest in the Modern World

707

Women's Rights

Seneca Falls Convention, 1848

The Seneca Falls Convention, also known as the Woman's Rights Convention, took place on July 19 and 20, 1848, in Seneca Falls, New York. It started with two women who were working toward the abolition, or end, of slavery. While attending the 1840 World Anti-Slavery convention in London, Lucretia Mott (1793–1880) and Elizabeth Cady Stanton (1815–1902) were upset that because they were women, they could only listen at the event. They could not participate. This gave them an idea for a women's convention, an event in which women could participate.

The pair worked with Martha Wright (1806–1875), Mary Ann M'Clintock, and Jane Hunt (1812–1889) to organize the event. The group decided to hold it near Stanton's home near Seneca Falls. Many people in the area were abolitionists who fought for an end to slavery. The women thought they could convince these activists to join their movement too. They ran an advertisement in a local newspaper a few days before the event. They invited women for the first day, and both men and women on the second day.

About 300 people came to the conference. On the first day, Stanton spoke and read the Declaration of Sentiments, which she and the other four women had worked on for the meeting. It listed the ways in which women were not treated the same as men in the United States. It was similar to the Declaration of Independence, but its main goal was to gain voting and other equal rights for women.

Elizabeth Cady Stanton is shown speaking during the first Woman's Rights Convention, held in the Wesleyan Methodist Chapel in Seneca Falls, New York, in July 1848. © BETTMANN/GETTY IMAGES.

A few dozen men, including African American social reformer Frederick Douglass (1817–1895), joined the women on the second day. After some debate, the people at the meeting signed and adopted the Declaration of Sentiments. This marked the start of the women's suffrage movement in the United States.

several years, women tried various methods to appeal for their cause. They used nonviolent campaigns, parades, and protests to make their voices heard. It took many years and much fighting, but women were finally granted the right to vote nationally in the United States in 1920 with the passage of the 19th Amendment.

The Civil War halts women's progress

Just as the women's suffrage movement was gaining support, the fight against slavery became more prominent. For several centuries, Africans were brought to North America as slaves. They did not have the same rights as whites and were treated unfairly. Slavery was legal in the United States but mostly practiced in the southern states, where plantation owners needed cheap or free labor to work in the fields. The economy in the North was more industry-focused and did not depend on the work of slaves. The issue of slavery eventually divided the United States and led to the Civil War.

After four long years of fighting, the Civil War came to an end, and with it, an end to slavery throughout the United States. In 1865 the US Congress passed the 13th Amendment to the US Constitution. This amendment officially ended slavery in the country. In 1868 Congress passed the 14th Amendment, which granted citizenship to "all persons born or naturalized in the United States, and subject to the jurisdiction thereof." This included African Americans who had been slaves.

A short time later, Congress proposed the 15th Amendment. This amendment would give citizens the right to vote regardless of race, color, or previous condition of servitude (meaning slave). The passage of the 14th Amendment and the proposed 15th Amendment were of particular interest to women suffragists.

However, women soon learned that the passage of the 15th Amendment would not help them gain voting rights. This angered many women and inspired them to fight for equality. Suffragists called on women to protest the passage of the 15th Amendment. Some women sided with the southern states, which tried to ban African Americans from obtaining voting rights. Officials from these states argued that women should be given the right to vote, too. However, they wanted to grant women voting rights only so votes from white women could be used to cancel out votes cast by African American men.

In the late 1860s several groups of women formed suffrage associations. Some opposed the passage of the 15th Amendment unless it included women in its wording. Others felt that it was unfair of women not to support the right to vote for African American men. They wanted to keep the two issues separate. In the end, Congress

Elizabeth Cady Stanton read the "Declaration of Sentiments" at the first Woman's Rights Convention in Seneca Falls, New York, in 1848. It is modeled after the Declaration of Independence, but it specifically includes "women" in the language. © 2018 CENGAGE®.

Declaration of Sentiments

... We hold these truths to be self-evident; that all men **and women** are created equal; that they are endowed by their Creator with certain inalienable rights; that among these are life, liberty, and the pursuit of happiness; that to secure these rights governments are instituted, deriving their just powers from the consent of the governed. Whenever any form of government becomes destructive of these ends, it is the right of those who suffer from it to refuse allegiance to it, and to insist upon the institution of a new government....

SOURCE: Stanton, Elizabeth Cady. "Declaration of Sentiments." Seneca Falls, New York, 1848.

Women's Rights

passed the 15th Amendment in 1870 and granted African American men the right to vote. The amendment did not include voting rights for women.

A united front for women's suffrage

Women's suffrage groups continued to campaign for political participation rights for women. Some women in these groups voted illegally and faced arrests and jail time. By 1890 many of the groups united and formed the National American Woman Suffrage Association (NAWSA). Elizabeth Cady Stanton (1815–1902) served as the first president of the new organization. Later Carrie Chapman Catt (1859–1947) became the group's leader. Members of the NAWSA argued that they deserved the right to vote because women were different from men and had distinct responsibilities.

This helped the group gain many followers. NAWSA continued its efforts to get women the right to vote state by state rather than at the national level. Several states began granting women the right to vote, but these women could vote only in their own state's elections. They were not allowed to participate in federal elections. For example, they could vote for governor, but they could not vote for president.

The movement finally began to receive notice. In 1912 former US President Theodore Roosevelt's (1858–1919) Progressive Party, also known as the Bull Moose Party, recognized women's suffrage. The following year, Alice Paul (1885–1977) and Lucy Burns (1879–1966) formed the Congressional Union for Woman Suffrage, later called the National Woman's Party (NWP). This group used protests and rallies to gain support.

Paul and other women suffragists organized a parade in Washington, DC, on March 3, 1913. This was the day before the inauguration of President Woodrow Wilson (1856–1924). About 8,000 women took part in the march, which was held to bring attention to women's efforts to gain the right to vote. Many people in town for the inauguration lined up to watch the women protesters. Some of these people mistreated the women marching. They tripped them, pushed them, spit at them, and injured them. More than 100 of the marchers needed medical attention after the event. Nevertheless, the protesters brought awareness to their cause and continued the fight for women's suffrage.

More states began allowing women to vote, and women's groups continued to hold protests and parades around the nation. The start of World War I (1914–1918) slowed the support for the suffrage movement, as many women joined the war effort instead. Some women

Do You Know?

This primary source excerpt comes from a booklet created by women's rights activist Carrie Chapman Catt in 1918, in an era before women got the right to vote nationally in the United States. What follows is a sampling of the statistics that Chapman used in making a case for women's suffrage.

DO YOU KNOW that the question of votes for women is one which is commanding the attention of the whole civilized world; that woman suffrage organizations of representative men and women exist in twenty-seven different countries; that in this country alone there are more than 1,000 woman suffrage organizations; that there is an International and a National Men's League for Woman Suffrage and numbers of local men's leagues....

DO YOU KNOW that in our own country women have been voting on the same terms as men in Wyoming since 1869, in Colorado since 1893, in Utah and Idaho since 1896; that in 1910, the state of Washington voted to one to extend the full suffrage to women; that in 1911, California doubled the number of voting women in this country by giving the full suffrage to more than half a million women citizens; that in 1912, the men of Kansas, Oregon, and Arizona voted to give votes to their women; that in 1913, the legislature of the State of Illinois passed measure giving to women all the voting rights within the power of the legislature to bestow, including presidential electors, all municipal officers and some country and some state officers; and that the territorial legislature of Alaska granted full suffrage to women?...

DO YOU KNOW that ... large numbers of men are utterly indifferent to their rights as voters; that in the presidential election of 1912, the total vote cast was only 14,720,038, while the number of men eligible to vote was 24,335,000....

DO YOU KNOW that extending the franchise to women actually increases the proportion of intelligent voters, that there is now and has been for years, according to the report of the Commissioner of Education, one-third more girls in the high schools of the country than boys and that, according to the last census, the illiterate men of the country greatly outnumbered the illiterate women?...

DO YOU KNOW that there are in the United States about 8,000,000 women in gainful occupations outside the home who need the protection of the ballot to regulate the conditions under which they must labor; and that the efforts of working women to regulate these conditions without the ballot have been practically unavailing?...

DO YOU KNOW one single sound, logical reason why the intelligence and individuality of women should not entitle them to the rights and privileges of self-government?

SOURCE: Catt, Carrie Chapman. *Do You Know?* (1918). National American Woman Suffrage Association Collection, Library of Congress. Available online at https://memory.loc.gov/ (accessed August 29, 2017). Courtesy of Library of Congress.

---

continued to work toward suffrage. In 1916 Jeannette Rankin (1880–1973) made history when she became the first woman to hold a seat in Congress. She was elected to the US House of Representatives in Montana. At that time, women still did not have the right to vote in national elections.

Women's Rights

Picketing for suffrage at the White House

During his reelection campaign in 1916, President Wilson stated that the Democratic Party would support suffrage. After he was reelected president, he did not immediately hold up to his promise to give women voting rights. A group of NWP members organized a picket, which is a protest that involves a group of people marching at a site with signs on posts or sticks. The NWP demonstration began in January 1917 in front of the White House in Washington, DC.

Women known as "silent sentinels" traveled from around the nation to the White House. At first they stood quietly outside, but then they burned copies of the president's speeches. They hung banners and carried signs that read, "How Long Must Women Wait for Liberty" and "Mr. President: What Will You Do for Woman Suffrage."

The president ignored his promise for supporting suffrage. The women continued to picket at the White House each day. Wilson mostly ignored the protesters, as he was dealing also with the war. He sometimes tipped his hat to them as he passed by or asked them in for tea, but they refused his invitations.

The National Woman's Party demonstrates in front of the White House in 1917. The activists are taking part in a college day protest. They are protesting President Woodrow Wilson's failure to support women's suffrage. Their banners ask the president for help in obtaining voting rights. COURTESY OF THE LIBRARY OF CONGRESS.

In the months that followed, more than 1,000 women participated in the daily pickets. In June 1917, violence and fighting erupted between the protesters and ordinary citizens. Until this time, the protesters were mostly peaceful and did not cause much trouble. Police became involved and arrested many demonstrators. Some were jailed. The White House protests continued, however.

On August 28, women outside the White House protested in support of the proposed Anthony amendment, named after suffragist Susan B. Anthony (1820–1906), which would finally give women the right to vote. During the protest, police arrested 10 suffragists, including NWP leader Alice Paul. They were sentenced to six months in prison. Paul, who formerly spent time in England, learned some of the tactics, including hunger strikes, that the British suffragists used. While in prison in October, Paul and others decided to hold hunger strikes, in which they refused to eat. In response, prison officials force-fed the women.

In November, more than 30 suffragists were arrested including Burns. Many were taken to the Occoquan Workhouse in Virginia where they were beaten and kicked. Burns was hand-cuffed to her cell, arms above her head, and forced to stand all night long. Another protester suffered a heart attack but was denied medical treatment for several hours. To the suffragists, November 14, 1917, became known as the "Night of Terror." People became angry when they learned of these events against the silent sentinels. They called on the president to put an end to the force-feedings, beatings, and harsh treatment. They also called on the president to end the protests and arrests by granting women the right to vote.

"Votes for Women"

In late November 1917, the government shut down the protests outside the White House. During the 10 months that the pickets took place, officials had arrested more than 200 protesters. Of these, nearly 100 protesters received jail time. At this point, more and more people pressured Wilson to allow women to vote. In January 1918, the president finally supported women's suffrage. The 19th Amendment, giving women the right to vote nationally, was passed by Congress on June 4, 1919. It finally became law on August 26, 1920. This day was later dedicated as Women's Equality Day in the United States.

Women's Rights

Baladi Campaign

LOCATION: Saudi Arabia

DATE: 2011–2015

Activists in Saudi Arabia began the Baladi campaign to fight for women's right to vote. Historically, women in the country did not have the right to political participation. Saudi Arabia did not permit women to vote or hold any political position. Many people felt this was unfair, and they worked to change the laws.

In September 2011, Saudi Arabia held its second municipal, or local, elections in its history. The first elections of this kind were held in 2005. Women were not allowed to vote in either of these elections. Officials said that women were not ready to vote. They stated that women did not know how the process worked, and the government could not teach them in time for the elections. They also said they were not sure how to allow women to vote since women needed males to accompany them in public. These males are typically family members since women in Saudi Arabia are not allowed to interact publicly with men who are not related to them.

This ban on political participation angered many Saudi women. Some tried to register to vote anyway but were denied. In response, a group of women formed the Baladi campaign to enact change. *Baladi* means "my country." The goal of the campaign was to fight for the right for women to vote. Since women were the main caretakers of families, they knew best what women and families needed. Members of the Baladi campaign believed women could stand up and fight for these needs. The campaign helped to educate citizens about the importance of women running for political positions to improve social services and other conditions. The Baladi campaign also shed light on the broader issue of equal women's rights in Saudi Arabia.

Background of women's rights in Saudi Arabia

In the Middle Eastern country of Saudi Arabia, women's rights are limited. Women cannot do many of the things that men can do. One family, the al Sauds (pronounced al sah-OOD), controls the country with the help of an elected cabinet. The government has no lawmaking bodies, such as parliament, or leaders, such as a president or prime minister. It does have a municipal council, which oversees local decisions, but the body holds no real power.

Sharia (pronounced shah-REE-ah), also called Islamic law, governs Saudi Arabia. *Sharia* means "the path." The laws state how Muslims, who are followers of Islam, should lead their lives. Sharia is based on the Koran (pronounced KAH-ran), or Quran, which is the holy book of the religion of Islam. The Koran contains words from the prophet Muhammad (c. 570–632), the founder of Islam, who gave his followers direction on how to live in their private and public lives according to his teachings.

The Koran includes the basic principles of the religion of Islam. It also has rules concerning women and men, marriage, divorce, and crime. It has detailed punishments for those who do not follow the laws. Muslims interpret the Koran in various ways, and not all Muslims follow the teachings in the same way. Some Muslims try to follow the Koran exactly and have strict laws. Other Muslims have broader interpretations of Islamic law.

Saudi Arabia and Iraq are two countries that rule by Sharia. However, the ways in which they apply its teachings and rules vary. Saudi Arabia is the birthplace of Muhammad. It is where Islam was founded, where the Koran was written, and where Sharia was established.

In modern times, the majority of Saudi Arabia's citizens follow the teachings of Islam, and the country practices a strict version of Sharia. The country does not allow people to practice other religions there. It also has a police force known as *mutawa* (pronounced MOO-tah-wah), which enforces Islamic law. Those who do not follow the laws are arrested, sent to prison, or subjected to violent punishments such as beatings.

Sharia is especially strict for women. In Saudi Arabia, women cannot travel without the permission of a male relative. According to Saudi Arabian law, women need a male with them to participate in public activities. Another area in which women's rights are limited is politics. Throughout the years, many people have protested against denying women the right to vote and hold political positions.

In September 2011, days before the municipal elections in Saudi Arabia, King Abdullah bin Abdulaziz al Saud (1924–2015) made history when he granted women the right to vote and run for political positions.

A king's decision

In September 2011, days before the municipal elections in Saudi Arabia, King Abdullah bin Abdulaziz al Saud (1924–2015) made history when he granted women the right to vote and run for political positions. Women in the country saw this move as a victory

Women's Rights

toward equal rights in the country. Pressure from Saudi and international women's groups and criticism from other nations prompted the change.

While women were granted the right to cast their ballots and campaign for office, they were not allowed to do so until the country's next election cycle in 2015. Women who were eager to enter politics had other concerns. They wanted to know how they would get to polling places or run political campaigns since they could not drive themselves and had to be in the presence of a male relative in public. In Saudi Arabia, women were not allowed to drive. The law was changed in September 2017 but was not scheduled to go into effect until 2018. Many women wondered if they would ever be able to vote or hold office. They questioned whether the change in law was just a move to quiet them.

King Abdullah also allowed women to serve on the country's advisory board, known as the Shura (pronounced SHUR-ah) Council. He appointed 30 women to the Shura at the beginning of 2013. The board does not have power to make laws, but its members can make suggestions to the king.

Goals of the Baladi campaign

A group of women established the Baladi campaign in 2011. Baladi's main goal was to give women the right to vote. Some of these women were

Cofounders of the Baladi Initiative, Laila al-Kadhem (center) and Iman Fallata (left), accepted the Chaillot Prize from Adam Kulach, the head of the European Union delegation in Riyadh, Saudi Arabia. The Chaillot Prize honors those who promote human rights. © FAYEZ NURELDINE/AFP/GETTY IMAGE.

educated and held leadership roles within their fields. They knew the importance of political participation. The Baladi organization sought to teach women the electoral process so they would be ready to vote in the 2015 elections.

The Baladi campaign did not want the government to be able to use the same excuse it did in 2005 and 2011 to bar women from voting. It set up free educational workshops to teach women how elections and the voting process worked. The Baladi campaign wanted to make sure women were ready for the 2015 elections. It also wanted to ensure women were voting for the person, man or woman, best suited for the job. It did not want women to vote based on the candidates their husbands or fathers were voting for in the elections. The organization wanted women to find their own voices and not just echo the views of the males in their lives.

From 2011 to 2015, the Baladi campaign held numerous classes to educate women throughout the country. Members of the organization showed women how to work around driving bans and having a male present to organize political campaigns. They showed women how to use social media sites and other electronic forms of communication to their advantage. King Abdullah died in January 2015 before seeing his order of women's political participation officially carried out in the country. King Salman bin Abdulaziz al Saud (1935–) replaced him. Many feared the new king would halt the progress that women had made up to this point.

In August 2015, a woman made history when she became the first female registered to vote in Saudi Arabia. Prior to the elections in 2015, however, the Saudi government shut down the Baladi campaign. It said the organization was profiting from the classes it offered. The organization denied these claims since it offered services free of charge. Many people felt it was just another way to try to keep women from voting in the country and keep denying women other rights.

Aftermath

The Baladi campaign remained shut down, but its goal to educate women and get them to participate in the country's political system was achieved. Voting arrangements were set up to keep men and women voters separate, according to law. In addition, female candidates had special rules to follow. They were able to present their campaigns from behind areas away from men. They also used social media sites and other media platforms to address male supporters without breaking Islamic law. Some women had a male present their campaigns for them.

More than 130,000 women registered to vote in the country by the time of the elections in December 2015. More than 1.3 million men registered to vote. These numbers were very low compared to the 5 million people who were eligible to vote in the country. In December 2015, Saudi women made history when they cast their ballots. More than 900 women ran for the 2,100 open municipal seats. Of these, 21 women were elected.

Malala Yousafzai All-Girls School

LOCATION: Lebanon
DATE: 2015

The Malala Yousafzai All-Girls School is located in the Middle Eastern country of Lebanon. It is in the Bekaa (pronounced bee-KAH) valley, which is close to the country's border with Syria. Malala Yousafzai (pronounced YU-suf-zi; 1997–), a Pakistani education activist and the youngest winner of the Nobel Peace Prize, opened the school. The Nobel Peace Prize is an award given to people who work to spread peace throughout the world.

As part of her mission to give all girls an opportunity to receive an education, she opened the Malala Yousafzai All-Girls School in 2015. The school admitted Syrian refugee girls, who left their country because of the unrest in their nation due to civil war. The four-year school teaches students life skills and traditional subjects to prepare the young women for careers.

Yousafzai fights for education rights

Yousafzai was born in the Swat valley of Pakistan in 1997. Pakistan is an Islamic country, meaning that most people practice the Islamic faith. It is one of the countries in the world where women do not have the same rights as men. Pakistan has its own legal system, which includes elements of Sharia, or Islamic law. Sharia states how Muslims, who are followers of Islam, should lead their private and public lives. The rules are based on the teachings of Islam's holy book, known as the Koran or Quran. Under Sharia, women's rights are limited and they must follow certain rules that do not apply to men.

Yousafzai and her family are Muslims and follow the teachings of the Koran. Yousafzai's parents raised her in a household where women and men were treated equally. They also stressed the importance of education to their daughter, even though they knew education for women was limited in their country. Growing up, Yousafzai loved school. She enjoyed reading and learning new things.

Everything changed in the Swat valley around 2007. At this time, the Taliban, which is a militant Islamist group, began to take control of the area. A militant group uses violent or aggressive means in support of a cause. The Taliban followed Sharia. It made the residents follow many rules. It even banned people from playing music and owning a television. The group punished people who did not follow orders. These punishments included beatings, executions, and beheadings. At the end of 2008, the Taliban banned all girls in the Swat valley from attending school. The group ordered the schools to close.

Yousafzai was angry and upset that the Taliban had taken away her education. She decided to use a fake name to write about how she felt on a blog, a type of online diary, for BBC News. In a series of posts, she wrote about fighting for education for girls. Throughout 2009, the Pakistani army fought the Taliban in an effort to force the group from the Swat valley. Many residents, including Yousafzai and her family, left their homes in the war zone.

In late 2009, the *New York Times* featured her in a documentary film, which is a true story about a person's life. After the documentary was released, Yousafzai became known worldwide for her efforts. She spent the next two years continuing to promote education for all girls, despite knowing she might become a target of the Taliban. Her father joined her efforts. By late 2011, the Pakistani army defeated the Taliban in the Swat valley, and many people returned home. Yousafzai's school reopened. For her work, she won Pakistan's first National Youth Peace Prize.

Despite her young age, Malala Yousafzai has fought for educational rights for girls throughout the world. Her efforts earned her the Nobel Peace Prize in 2014. © JSTONE/SHUTTERSTOCK.COM.

Women's Rights

"It Is the Story of Many Girls"

This primary source excerpt is from Malala Yousafzai's lecture when she won the Nobel Peace Prize in 2014. After surviving a brutal attack by Taliban militant extremists in her home country of Afghanistan, Malala went on to be an advocate for girls' education. She discusses how she is just one of many girls in the world who either lost access or had no access to education.

Dear sisters and brothers, today is a day of great happiness for me. I am humbled that the Nobel Committee has selected me for this precious award....

This award is not just for me. It is for those forgotten children who want education. It is for those frightened children who want peace. It is for those voiceless children who want change....

I tell my story, not because it is unique, but because it is not.

It is the story of many girls....

One of my very good school friends, the same age as me, who had always been a bold and confident girl, dreamed of becoming a doctor. But her dream remained a dream. At the age of 12, she was forced to get married. And then soon she had a son, she had a child when she herself was still a child—only 14. I know that she could have been a very good doctor.

But she couldn't ... because she was a girl....

The world can no longer accept that basic education is enough. Why do leaders accept that for children in developing countries, only basic literacy is sufficient, when their own children do homework in Algebra, Mathematics, Science and Physics?

Leaders must seize this opportunity to guarantee a free, quality, primary and secondary education for every child.

Yousafzai continued to speak out in support of education for girls. Because of this, the Taliban became angry and wanted to stop Yousafzai's efforts, which the group saw as going against Islamic law. On October 12, 2012, the Taliban shot Yousafzai in the head while she was on her school bus. She survived the attack. As she recovered over the next year, she became an internationally known supporter of education rights. She vowed to keep fighting for girls' education.

Forgotten students in Syria

Pakistan was not the only country in the region experiencing unrest. A civil war began in Syria around 2011. The fighting led to the destruction of many communities in the country. People had nowhere to live, work, or learn. Since the civil war began, millions of people fled Syria. Numerous students were among the people forced from the country. The refugees settled in other nations, including Lebanon, Jordan, Iraq, Egypt, and Turkey. Some

> Some will say this is impractical, or too expensive, or too hard. Or maybe even impossible. But it is time the world thinks bigger.
>
> Dear sisters and brothers, the so-called world of adults may understand it, but we children don't. Why is it that countries which we call "strong" are so powerful in creating wars but are so weak in bringing peace? Why is it that giving guns is so easy but giving books is so hard? Why is it, why is it that making tanks is so easy, but building schools is so hard? . . .
>
> Dear sisters and brothers, dear fellow children, we must work . . . not wait. Not just the politicians and the world leaders, we all need to contribute. Me. You. We. It is our duty.
>
> Let us become the first generation to decide to be the last, let us become the first generation that decides to be the last that sees empty classrooms, lost childhoods, and wasted potentials.
>
> Let this be the last time that a girl or a boy spends their childhood in a factory.
>
> Let this be the last time that a girl is forced into early child marriage.
>
> Let this be the last time that a child loses life in war.
>
> Let this be the last time that we see a child out of school.
>
> Let this end with us.
>
> Let's begin this ending . . . together . . . today . . . right here, right now. Let's begin this ending now.
>
> Thank you so much.
>
> **SOURCE:** Yousafzai, Malala. "Malala Yousafzai—Nobel Lecture." Nobel Prize (December 2014). Available online at http://www.nobelprize.org/nobel_prizes/peace/laureates/2014/yousafzai-lecture_en.html (accessed October 16, 2017). Courtesy of Nobelprize.org.

also went to Europe. Many of these countries could not handle the arrival of so many people. The refugees put a strain on services such as education and health care in these countries.

Before the war, Syria had numerous schools and colleges, where both men and women gained the skills needed to enter the workforce. When the fighting began, it became difficult for students to travel to these schools. The military blocked roadways. Many streets were not passable due to the destruction. Some students chose to leave school to join the fighting. Others fled the country. As the fighting continued, many schools in Syria were destroyed.

Difficulties for refugees Students who fled the country found it difficult to continue their education. Education became less important to many people, as they feared for their lives and looked for new places to live. Basic survival needs such as food, water, and shelter became the focus.

Women's Rights

Bring Back Our Girls

Bring Back Our Girls is a social media campaign started in response to the kidnapping of 276 girls in Chibok (pronounced CHEE-bahk), Nigeria. In April 2014, militants from a group known as Boko Haram (pronounced BOH-koh hah-RAHM) kidnapped the girls from their school. Boko Haram is a militant Islamist group that uses terrorism to spread fear. It overtook parts of the West African country of Nigeria around 2009. The group wanted to rid the country of people who did not follow Islamic law. Boko Haram took the girls because it did not believe women should receive an education.

A few of the kidnapped girls escaped from Boko Haram, but 219 remained missing. In May 2014, the Boko Haram leader, Abubakar Shekau (c. 1965–), announced that God told him to sell the girls as brides and released a video showing some of the girls. After the Nigerian government failed to find the girls, numerous people worldwide got involved. They took part in a Twitter campaign called #BringBackOurGirls to raise awareness of the situation.

Boko Haram released another video showing some of the girls in April 2016. The girls asked the Nigerian government to give into the demands of Boko Haram. One of the girls, Amina Ali Nkeki, was found in May 2016. She escaped from the group.

In August 2016, Boko Haram released another video. In it, one of the girls asked the government for help. In October, 21 of the girls were released as part of a deal made by the International Committee of the Red Cross (ICRC). Another girl who escaped from the kidnappers was found in November.

A military raid in January 2017 led to another lost Chibok girl being found. The ICRC convinced the group to free 82 girls in May. By this time, 113 girls were still missing. The government continued to plead with Boko Haram for the girls' release. The government

Some people felt it was not necessary to enroll in school in the country where they sought refuge since they planned to return to Syria as soon as the war ended.

Language barriers also existed. For example, in Lebanon many schools taught in French or English, and in Turkey, the schools used Turkish. This created issues for many Syrians who only spoke and wrote in Arabic.

Many refugees did not have the money to send their children to private schools and had to rely on public education. Countries such as Jordan experienced overcrowding at public schools, leaving many refugees with nowhere to attend. Some countries did not have developed educational systems like Syria did. Many refugees who were in college could not get documents required for them to transfer to new schools. These documents were destroyed by the war in their home country.

believed Boko Haram still had the girls as of late 2017. The Bring Back Our Girls movement was set to protest in the streets again beginning in October 2017.

Protesters march in Abuja, Nigeria, during a "Bring Back Our Girls" campaign in August 2014. The Nigerian schoolgirls were kidnapped by Boko Haram militants and, at that time, only about 54 of the girls had returned, while authorities said about 219 remained missing. © MAC JOHN AKENDE/ANADOLU AGENCY/GETTY IMAGES.

Some organizations established programs to assist Syrian refugee students. Language classes were available to teach English, Turkish, and other languages. Some schools did not charge fees for refugees who could not afford the instruction. Other colleges no longer required documents, such as birth certificates or copies of previous grades, to enroll in classes.

The United Kingdom also provided help to refugee students who wanted to attend school there. It offered aid with payment, language classes, and other programs designed to keep Syrian refugees in school. In addition, many organizations began to build schools for the growing Syrian refugee population. Despite all of this aid available, many refugees, in particular young girls, still had trouble acquiring education in new countries.

School opened

Yousafzai continued her mission to give all girls worldwide an opportunity to get an education. In 2013 she set up the Malala Fund, an organization to help raise money and promote education for girls around the globe. In response to the widespread destruction in Syria, Yousafzai wanted to do something for the girls forced from their homes in that country.

She knew how hard it was for refugees, especially girls, to obtain an education. She feared generations of girls would suffer due to a lack of education. She also knew that many Syrian parents were forcing their daughters to marry at a young age to protect the girls' futures. Yousafzai wanted to give these girls another option.

With the help of the Malala Fund and the Kayany Foundation, Yousafzai established an all-girls school for refugees near the Syrian border in Lebanon. She chose Lebanon because of the high numbers of Syrian refugees in that country. She knew she had to do something to help the uneducated children affected by the war. The Kayany Foundation works to provide education to students in Syria. It has established several schools, including the Malala Yousafzai All-Girls School, which officially opened on July 12, 2015, Yousafzai's 18th birthday.

The secondary school can host up to 200 girls from ages 14 to 18. The school is similar to US high school programs where students learn both traditional subjects and job skills. The aim of the school is to provide girls with an education so they can find job opportunities. The school also offers skills in fields such as computer literacy, embroidery and sewing, hairdressing and cosmetics, and nursing. Graduates of the school receive a certificate from the Lebanese Ministry of Education and Higher Education. Yousafzai hoped that girls at the school could gain an education and become independent.

Women's March on Washington

LOCATION: Washington, DC

DATE: January 21, 2017

The Women's March on Washington took place on January 21, 2017. People marched in support of women's rights, among other issues. Nearly 500,000 people participated in the demonstration, which was held at the nation's capital. More than an estimated 3 million people took part in similar marches worldwide. Protests were even held on all seven continents.

The idea for the event came from a Hawaiian woman who was upset by the results of the 2016 US presidential election. She used social media to propose a women's march. The small event quickly grew into the massive Women's March on Washington.

On the day of the march, supporters traveled to the nation's capital from across the United States and from countries around the world. Participants peacefully marched and listened to speakers and entertainers. Groups in other countries held marches to show their support. Organizers of the event hoped to inspire all people, not just women, to continue to stand up and fight for their rights.

The 2016 US presidential election

The 2016 US presidential race was not like previous elections. After months of campaigning and primary elections to narrow down the field of nominees, the two major candidates emerged. Donald Trump, a wealthy businessman who had no experience in politics, became the Republican candidate. Former First Lady, New York Senator, and Secretary of State Hillary Rodham Clinton was the Democratic Party candidate.

Clinton spent decades serving in political office. She would have been the first female president of the United States if elected. She focused her campaign on issues such as protecting the nation's health-care policy, changing immigration and gun control laws, and creating new jobs. Trump would have been the oldest and wealthiest person ever to attain the presidency. Also, he would have been the first president without any experience in politics or the military. He focused on reforming immigration laws and promised to build a wall along the US-Mexican border. He also vowed to change the country's health-care policy.

The election included many months of political campaigning. The candidates had several troubles and conflicts. The Federal Bureau of Investigation (FBI) examined claims that Clinton used a private e-mail server for government work when she was secretary of state. The FBI did not find her guilty of any crime, but the investigation hurt her image in the public. Other issues that harmed her reputation included questions about foreign donations to her family foundation and leaked e-mails between her and members of her campaign team that were stolen by computer hackers.

Throughout his campaign, Trump was very outspoken and made negative remarks about women, Mexicans, Muslims, other foreign

Throughout his campaign, Trump was very outspoken and made negative remarks about women, Mexicans, Muslims, other foreign people, and other groups. He used his personal Twitter account to voice his opinions on a range of issues.

Women's Rights

people, and other groups. He used his personal Twitter account to voice his opinions on a range of issues. Media outlets reported that Trump did not pay federal income tax for nearly two decades. People asked to see his tax returns. He refused to make his tax returns viewable to the public like other candidates before him. A leaked video from 2005 surfaced showing Trump bragging about how he could touch women inappropriately because he was famous. After the video was made public, Trump apologized for the crude talk. Much of this damaged his reputation among voters, especially women and immigrants.

Many people considered Trump the long shot to win. They predicted that Clinton would succeed in the election. Several opinion polls showed her ahead of Trump. On November 8, 2016, voters elected Trump to the presidency. He received more electoral votes, which are votes cast by a select group of people (called electors) for each state for president. Clinton won the popular vote, which are votes cast directly by individuals. Clinton had nearly 2.9 million more votes than Trump, but that was not enough for her to win the election. This upset many Clinton voters.

Election sparks a movement

After the election, Teresa Shook (c. 1957–), a woman from Hawaii, was upset with the election results. She did not understand how a man who made negative comments about many groups of people, including women, could be elected president. She did not have many people she could talk to about her feelings in her small Hawaiian community, so she took to the Internet. Shook proposed the idea of a women's march on the Facebook page of a private group called Pantsuit Nation. The group supported Clinton. Only one woman responded to Shook's proposal.

Shook then created an event page for the march and invited 40 people. Women began to share the idea with others, and the small group grew to more than 10,000 names overnight. Then some women began to share their feelings. Some were angry that Trump threatened to take away funding for women's health care. Others were mad about the comments he made concerning women and his opponent, Clinton.

Within a matter of a few weeks, the number of women interested in the march grew to more than a few hundred thousand people. Shook was

Clinton won the popular vote, which are votes cast directly by individuals. Clinton had nearly 2.9 million more votes than Trump, but that was not enough for her to win the election. This upset many Clinton voters.

shocked that her idea had gained so much interest. Others joined the planning of the march and set the date for January 21, 2017, the day after Trump took office.

Support for the event was not all positive. Some people criticized the demonstration for not including enough minority women in the planning. They also did not agree with the name of the event, which at the time was Million Women March. Organizers added minority groups to the planning committee and changed the name of the event to the Women's March on Washington. They altered the focus of the march to highlight other important issues such as the discrimination of groups because of their race, the language they speak, the country they come from, or the religion they practice. Discrimination occurs when people treat others unfairly because they are different.

The event continued to grow. Organizers expected supporters to travel from all over the United States by bus, car, and airplane to Washington, DC. Many hotels and motels in the area were fully booked for the day of the march. Organizers raised money for the march through donations and by selling items related to the march such as T-shirts and hats. The money was used to pay for the costs related to hosting such a large event, including security, parking, and portable toilets.

Women's March on Washington

On January 21, 2017, about 500,000 men, women, and children arrived at the National Mall in Washington, DC. The event was one of the largest protests in US history. The marchers kept the event peaceful, as they chanted, sang, and listened to speakers. Many women wore pink hats with cat ears in support of women's rights. Many people were there in support of other issues such as health care, ending violence against women, immigration, LGBTQ rights, racial justice, gun control, and climate change.

The marchers brought signs that read, "Love Trumps Hate!" and "Less Fear More Love." Some described themselves as "nasty women" in response to a comment Trump made about Clinton during the election. They chanted, "When they go low, we go high!," a line from a speech by First Lady Michelle Obama (1964–) during the 2016 campaign. Many participants were concerned about the policies that Trump would pursue; some were afraid he would follow up on his campaign promises and begin mass deportations of immigrants in the country illegally or ban Muslims from coming to the United States.

Many of the people who participated in the march took part in similar events in past years. Some fought for African American civil

Women's Rights

Women's Strike for Equality

The Women's Strike for Equality took place on August 26, 1970. This date marked the 50th anniversary of when women gained the right to vote in the United States. The National Organization for Women (NOW) planned a protest to bring awareness to the fact that women were paid less than men to perform the same jobs.

At a NOW meeting in March 1970, members discussed an idea for a strike, which is a refusal to work. While women had gained the right to vote in 1920, they still did not have all of the same rights as men did, especially equal wages. At that time, studies showed that on average, a woman earned 59 cents for every dollar a man earned for doing the same job. NOW President Betty Friedan (1921–2006) asked women to refuse to work for one day. She asked them not to cook, clean, or work outside the home that day. While a work stoppage was the original intent of the day, it turned into organized marches and protests in more than 90 cities across the United States.

On August 26, 1970, women went on strike for equality. In New York City, about 50,000 women, including Friedan, blocked Fifth Avenue. Another group held a demonstration at the Statue of Liberty. The protesters held signs that read, "Don't Iron While the Strike Is Hot!" and "Equal Jobs and Educational Opportunities!"

Similar events occurred across the United States. Women in Washington, DC, carried a banner that read, "We Demand Equality." Women working at the *Detroit Free Press* newspaper did not allow the men who worked there to use the second men's restroom since women had only one. Around the country, women entered all-male businesses and held rallies, marches, and protests.

The women marched for more than equal pay. They also demanded other rights such as education equality, access to quality health care, and affordable childcare. While the strike only lasted one day, women continued to fight for

rights and protested the Vietnam War (1954–1975). Many said they attended the Women's March on Washington because they did not want to see their past achievements taken away from them by the new administration.

Speakers and famous participants For a few hours, the marchers listened to speeches from a variety of women and men, including event organizers Linda Sarsour (1980–), Tamika Mallory (c. 1981–), and Carmen Perez (1980–); US senator from Massachusetts Elizabeth Warren (1949–); activist Gloria Steinem (1934–); and Planned Parenthood president Cecile Richards (1957–). Planned Parenthood is an organization that provides affordable health care to women, especially those with low incomes. Trump and some members of Congress had been threatening to cut Planned Parenthood's federal funding.

Women's Rights

these changes in the years that followed. As a result of the strike, US President Richard M. Nixon (1913–1994) dedicated August 26 as Women's Equality Day in the United States.

Feminist leader Betty Friedan (right) at the Women's Strike for Equality on August 26, 1970. The strike was held on the 50th anniversary of women getting the right to vote nationally in the United States. © ZUMA PRESS/ ALAMY.

Sophie Cruz (c. 2010–), a child activist who made headlines for speaking out for the rights of undocumented immigrants, gave a speech. Actors America Ferrera (1984–) and Ashley Judd (1968–) and filmmaker Michael Moore (1954–) spoke to the crowds. Performers such as Madonna (1958–), Alicia Keys (1981–), Janelle Monáe (1985–), the Indigo Girls, and Mary Chapin Carpenter (c. 1958–) showed their support for the cause and provided entertainment. Those who could not participate in the march used social media sites to extend their support. Clinton posted a message to Twitter thanking the demonstrators.

Sister marches held In addition to the march in Washington, DC, women in cities across the United States held similar marches. Some of these cities included Concord, New Hampshire; Chicago, Illinois; New York, New York; Portland, Oregon; and Los Angeles, California. In

Women's Rights

Women of all ages, races, and social backgrounds descended on Washington, DC, for the Women's March on Washington on January 21, 2017. Marches were held in cities through the United States and around the world.
© CATLAUREN/SHUTTERSTOCK.COM.

Chicago, the event turnout was so large that organizers had to change the route of the march. People worldwide also held marches and demonstrations. Marchers in Paris, France, gathered at the Eiffel Tower, where they chanted and sang. People in other cities around the world hosted events, including in Berlin, Germany; Toyko, Japan; London, United Kingdom; Sydney, Australia; New Delhi, India; Nairobi, Kenya; Halifax, Canada; Bogotá, Colombia; and Copenhagen, Denmark. Protesters even included people on an expedition ship in Antarctica. That meant the demonstrations occurred on all seven continents.

Aftermath

Organizers of the march hoped that people would continue to speak out in support of their rights. They urged people to contact members of Congress to ask for their support on human rights issues or to object when those rights are taken away. They asked people to participate in special elections and to vote candidates into office who support the views important to them.

The Women's March on Washington inspired other events in the months that followed. Those unhappy with Trump's remarks on climate change and global warming and proposed budget cuts to science agencies helped spur the March for Science. Demonstrators at this event gathered on Earth Day on April 22, 2017, at the National Mall in Washington,

DC. Speakers addressed the crowd on the importance of science in creating policies concerning the environment.

The march also led to A Day without a Woman, which was held on March 8, 2017. The day was organized to show the importance of women in the US economy. Women participated by wearing red in support, taking the day off from work, and avoiding shopping at businesses, except for stores owned by women or minorities.

The Women's March on Washington inspired people to get involved and to take a stand on important issues. Many were inspired to run for political office. Others chose to volunteer to help those less fortunate. Even others took on the task of making sure that their elected officials were representing the views of the people who elected them. The Women's March was repeated in various cities during the third weekend in January 2018, bringing more than 1 million women and men out to protest Trump and his policies while encouraging people to vote and run for office.

For More Information

BOOKS

Jalalzai, Farida. *Shattered, Cracked, or Firmly Intact?: Women and the Executive Glass Ceiling Worldwide.* Oxford, UK: Oxford University Press, 2013.

Kristof, Nicholas D., and Sheryl WuDunn. *Half the Sky: Turning Oppression into Opportunity for Women Worldwide.* New York: Vintage, 2009.

McMillen, Sally. *Seneca Falls and the Origins of the Women's Rights Movement.* Oxford: Oxford University Press, 2008.

PERIODICALS

Cohen, Sascha. "The Day Women Went on Strike." *Time* (August 26, 2015). Available online at http://time.com/4008060/women-strike-equality-1970 (accessed August 21, 2017).

Gaffey, Conor. "Bring Back Our Girls: A Brief History of What We Know about the Missing Chibok Women." *Newsweek* (April 14, 2017). Available online at http://www.newsweek.com/chibok-girls-boko-haram-583584 (accessed August 21, 2017).

Myers, Rebecca. "General History of Women's Suffrage in Britain." *Independent* (May 27, 2013). Available online at http://www.independent.co.uk/news/uk/home-news/general-history-of-women-s-suffrage-in-britain-8631733.html (accessed August 21, 2017).

Purvis, June. "Suffragette Hunger Strikes, 100 Years On." *Guardian* (July 6, 2009). Available online at https://www.theguardian.com/commentisfree/libertycentral/2009/jul/06/suffragette-hunger-strike-protest (accessed August 21, 2017).

Stuart, Tessa. "Inside the Historic Women's March on Washington." *Rolling Stone* (January 21, 2017). Available online at http://www.rollingstone.com/politics/features/inside-the-historic-womens-march-on-washington-w462325 (accessed August 21, 2017).

Taylor, Alan. "The 1913 Women's Suffrage Parade." *Atlantic* (March 1, 2013). Available online at https://www.theatlantic.com/photo/2013/03/100-years-ago-the-1913-womens-suffrage-parade/100465 (accessed October 16, 2017).

WEBSITES

Kearney, Laila. "Hawaii Grandma's Plea Launches Women's March in Washington." Reuters, December 5, 2016. http://www.reuters.com/article/us-usa-trump-women-idUSKBN13U0GW (accessed August 21, 2017).

Kurtzleben, Danielle. "100 Days In, Women's March Still Inspires. But Can the Enthusiasm Hold?" National Public Radio, April 28, 2017. http://www.npr.org/2017/04/28/525764938/100-days-in-womens-march-still-inspires-but-can-the-enthusiasm-hold (accessed August 21, 2017).

"Malala's Story," Malala Fund. https://www.malala.org/malalas-story (accessed August 21, 2017).

National Women's History Project. http://www.nwhp.org/ (accessed October 17, 2017).

"Saudi Women React to Election Results." National Public Radio, December 20, 2015. https://www.npr.org/templates/transcript/transcript.php?storyId=460464070 (accessed November 18, 2017).

Tuysuz, Gul. "What Is Sharia Law?" CNN, August 16, 2016. http://www.cnn.com/2016/08/16/world/sharia-law-definition/index.html (accessed August 21, 2017).

"US Election 2016: All You Need to Know." BBC News, November 8, 2016. http://www.bbc.com/news/world-us-canada-35356941 (accessed August 21, 2017).

Westall, Sylvia. "Nobel Winner Malala Opens School for Syrian Refugees." Reuters, July 13, 2015. http://www.reuters.com/article/us-lebanon-malala-idUSKCN0PM0L520150713 (accessed August 21, 2017).

"What Democracy Looks Like: Women's March on Washington." CBS News, January 22, 2017. http://www.cbsnews.com/news/what-democracy-looks-like-womens-march-on-washington (accessed August 21, 2017).

"Woman Suffrage Timeline (1840–1920)." National Women's History Museum. https://www.nwhm.org/education-resources/history/woman-suffrage-timeline (accessed August 21, 2017).

"Women's Suffrage Movement." BBC. http://www.bbc.co.uk/bitesize/higher/history/britsuff/suffrage/revision/1/ (accessed August 21, 2017).

Research and Activity Ideas

Animal Rights

Some of the animals discussed in this chapter include whales, elephants, and monkeys. Choose one animal mentioned in the chapter, or select an animal you would like to learn more about. Research that animal on the Internet or in the school library. Create a poster that includes a picture of the animal and facts about it. Be sure to include information about where the animal lives, what makes it unique, and how it interacts with humans. Present your poster to the rest of the class, and explain why you chose the animal you did.

Civil Rights, African American

The Freedom Riders protested segregation in the southern United States. The Freedom Riders' protests helped bring about the desegregation of public transportation. Many Freedom Riders were threatened and some were beaten for their protests. Write an editorial to a newspaper about why you think the Freedom Riders' protests were important and should be remembered today. Include specific details about the Freedom Riders and explain specific outcomes of their protests.

Civil Rights, Hispanic and Latino

Dolores Huerta was the cofounder of the National Farm Workers Association, which later became United Farm Workers (UFW). Huerta advocated for workers' rights throughout her life. Use the Internet or school library resources to research Huerta's life. Write a paragraph describing one event in which Huerta participated or one part of her life story that most interests you. Share your writing with the group.

Economic Discontent

The citizens of the United Kingdom launched campaigns for and against Britain's break from the European Union, which became known as "Brexit." Demonstrate the opposing sides by organizing into two groups: one to research economic arguments in support of leaving the European Union and the other to research economic arguments in support of staying in the European Union. With your group, prepare a speech explaining why the UK should leave or stay in the European Union. Then choose one representative from each group to present the speech to the whole class.

Environment

The Pacific Climate Warriors tried to prevent coal ships from leaving an Australian port in 2014. Use the Internet or school library resources to search for images of the Pacific Climate Warriors' protest. Have the class vote on one image to print. Post the image at the front of the class. Then, break into small groups to discuss what the image shows and how the people in the picture most likely felt. With your group, write a journal entry from the point of view of one of the protesters in the picture. Explain how that person felt during the protest and why that person wanted to protest. Also describe what the person hoped to change by protesting.

Free Speech

In 2001 a church group burned Harry Potter books. People have burned and banned books for many reasons throughout history. Use the Internet or your school library to learn about one of these banned books: *The Absolutely True Diary of a Part-Time Indian*, *The Adventures of Huckleberry Finn*, *The Call of the Wild*, *The Catcher in the Rye*, *Go Ask Alice*, *The Handmaid's Tale*, *I Know Why the Caged Bird Sings*, *The Outsiders*, or *Twilight*. Read about the history of the book and why it is considered controversial. Pretend leaders in your community are planning to ban the book you chose from the community library. Write and present a speech about why they should or should not ban the book from the library's shelves.

RESEARCH AND ACTIVITY IDEAS

Globalization

Banksy is an artist whose works have shared messages about many topics, including globalization. Do you agree or disagree with Banksy's opinions about consumerism and globalization? Use the Internet or the school library to find images of anti-globalization artwork. Imagine that you are an artist. Create a piece of art in response to Bansky's art shown in this chapter. You may create a drawing, a painting, or a collage with pictures from magazines or the Internet. Present your artwork to the class.

Gun Control/Gun Rights

The Black Panther protest of 1967 and the "I Will Not Comply" rally in 2014 both supported gun rights. However, these protests had different goals and different methods pertaining to gun rights. Create a compare-contrast chart on a poster. Fill in details about each protest to show how they were similar and how they were different. Present your poster to the class.

Human Rights

In 1971 prisoners at the Attica prison rioted in response to overcrowding, lack of food, and a lack of medical care. The riot ended in a great deal of violence. In 2016 prisoners from at least a dozen prisons in the United States commemorated the Attica Prison Riot by refusing to work. Use the Internet or your school library to research this protest from 2016. Which conditions were the prisoners protesting in 2016? How did those conditions compare to the conditions at Attica in 1971? How did the 2016 protest differ from the 1971 protest? How was it similar? Write a two-paragraph essay comparing and contrasting the conditions both groups were protesting.

Immigrant Rights

The 1844 riots in Philadelphia focused on Irish immigrants, most of whom were Catholic. The 2017 travel ban protests focused mostly on Middle Eastern and African immigrants, most of whom were Muslim. Use the Internet or the school library to research immigration in the United States from the early 1800s to the present. How have immigration rates from various parts of the world changed over time? How did this change most likely affect protests for immigrants' rights? What role has religion or race played in who was allowed into the country? Write a short essay

RESEARCH AND ACTIVITY IDEAS

(a couple of paragraphs) about how changes in immigration over time have affected protests for immigrants' rights in the United States.

Independence Movements

Imagine that you are a citizen of India in 1930. You want India to have independence from the United Kingdom. One day you see Mohandas Gandhi and a few hundred followers marching toward the sea. Some of them tell you about their plans to collect salt. You decide to join the march. Write a letter to a friend about your experience on the Salt March with Gandhi. Tell your friend why you joined the march and how you felt after collecting salt. Describe to your friend your hope for the future of India.

Indigenous Peoples' Rights

Imagine that you have a friend from another part of the world who learned about the Dakota Access Pipeline and the protests by the Standing Rock Sioux in the news. Your friend wants to learn more about the protests. He or she wants to know about the protesters' goals. Gather information about the protest from the chapter. Use the Internet or your school library to do research if you need more information. Then, write a two-paragraph email to your friend explaining the reasons for the protests, the protesters' goals, and the outcome of the protests.

Labor Rights

In 1936 and 1937 workers at a General Motors plant went on strike. Imagine that you are a newspaper journalist living in Flint, Michigan, in the 1930s. You just learned that the workers at General Motors have gone on strike. Write a newspaper article about the strike. Include at least one made-up quotation from a striking worker in your article. If you need more information about the strike, use the Internet or school library resources to research the topic.

LGBTQ Rights

The Stonewall Riots are one of the earliest protests for LGBTQ rights. Since then, many important events have helped shape the LGBTQ rights movement. Use the Internet or school library resources to research important events that happened around the world and shaped this movement. Then create a timeline poster starting in the 1960s and ending in the present. Mark at least 10 important events that happened in the LGBTQ rights movement during that time.

Political/Government Uprisings

The Arab Spring started in December 2010 in Tunisia. Many protests followed the one in Tunisia. The effects of the Arab Spring are still being felt in the Middle East today. Use the Internet or the school library to research the events of the Arab Spring. Make a poster with a timeline listing the most important events from the Arab Spring. Start the timeline in 2010 and end it in the present. Present your timeline to the class and compare it to the timelines your classmates made. Discuss with classmates how the timelines are similar or different.

Racial Conflict

In 1976 thousands of black students in Soweto, South Africa, protested unfair government laws. Imagine that you are a news reporter covering the Soweto uprising. You have an opportunity to interview a number of protesters after the uprising ends. Write a list of questions you would ask them about their protest. Then make up answers that you think the protesters might give based on what you have read. Share your questions and answers with a small group.

Reproductive Rights

Reproductive rights differ from one country to another. Track the reproductive rights of different countries around the world. Organize into five groups and have each group choose a different continent (Africa, Asia, Europe, North America, and South America). Try to determine which country on your chosen continent offers the most reproductive rights and which country offers the fewest reproductive rights. Use the Internet or your school library to research the reproductive rights in different countries. With your group, prepare a two-minute presentation about the reproductive rights in the countries you studied. Share your presentation with the class.

Resistance to Nazis

The White Rose movement published informational pamphlets as a way to resist Nazis. Consider the information the White Rose movement most likely included in its pamphlets. Organize into small groups. Imagine you are members of the White Rose movement, and you are

RESEARCH AND ACTIVITY IDEAS

designing another pamphlet to hand out in Germany. Use the Internet or school library resources to research the White Rose movement's pamphlets. Make a similar pamphlet with your group. Include information in the pamphlet that you want other Germans to know about the Nazis. Present your finished pamphlets to the class.

Slavery

Enslaved Africans were unable to protest to gain their freedom. People who escaped enslavement, however, often wanted to share their stories. They wanted people to understand the horrors of slavery and the terrible conditions enslaved people faced. Many enslaved people who were freed or who escaped wrote stories about their lives. Using the Internet or the school library, find one of these stories written by Frederick Douglass, Olaudah Equiano, Harriet Ann Jacobs, Solomon Northup, William Wells Brown, Briton Hammon, or Mary Prince. Read part of the story. Write a paragraph explaining how anti-slavery protesters could have benefited from reading the story.

War

In 1965 a group of students in Des Moines, Iowa, decided to wear black arm bands to protest the Vietnam War. Their school tried to stop them. In response, the students' families sued the school. The court case, *Tinker v. Des Moines*, eventually reached the US Supreme Court. Imagine that you are a lawyer defending one of the students in *Tinker v. Des Moines*. Write a one- or two-paragraph statement that you want to present in the courtroom to support your client's protest. Be sure to include information about why the students protested and why you think they should be allowed to take part in such a protest.

Women's Rights

Both the women from Saudi Arabia who were involved in the Baladi campaign in 2015 and the American women who were involved in the women's suffrage protest in 1918 were protesting to gain the right to vote. Talk about the two protests with a partner. Discuss what one of the Saudi protesters and one of the American protesters might say to each other about their protests if they could meet each other. Write down notes about this imaginary conversation. Then, perform a short skit in front of the class to show what the two protesters might say when talking about their protests.

Where to Learn More

Books

Amison Lüsted. *Tiananmen Square Protests*. Edina, MN: ABDO, 2011.

Arsenault, Raymond. *Freedom Riders: 1961 and the Struggle for Racial Justice*. New York: Oxford University Press, 2006.

Bledsoe, Karen E. *Consumption and Waste*. New York: Bloomsbury, 2014.

Çinar, Özgür Heval. *Conscientious Objection to Military Service in International Human Rights Law*. New York: Palgrave Macmillan, 2013.

Cunningham, Anne. *Critical Perspectives on Gun Control*. Berkeley Heights, NJ: Enslow, 2017.

David, Laurie, and Cambria Gordon. *The Down-to-Earth Guide to Global Warming*. New York: Scholastic, 2007.

Fredrickson, George M. *Racism: A Short History*. Princeton, NJ: Princeton University Press, 2002.

Gitlin, Todd. *Occupy Nation: The Roots, the Spirit, and the Promise of Occupy Wall Street*. New York: HarperCollins Publishers, 2012.

Henderson, Timothy J. *The Mexican Wars for Independence*. New York: Hill and Wang, 2009.

Jenkins, Henry. *Convergence Culture: Where Old and New Media Collide*. New York: New York University Press, 2006.

Kelly, Nigel. *The Fall of the Berlin Wall: The Cold War Ends*. Rev. ed. Chicago: Heinemann, 2006.

Kinsbruner, Jay. *Independence in Spanish America: Civil Wars, Revolutions, and Underdevelopment*. Albuquerque: University of New Mexico Press, 2000.

Laine, Carolee. *Book Banning and Other Forms of Censorship*. Minneapolis, MN: ABDO, 2017.

Lennox, Corinne, and Damien Short, eds. *Handbook of Indigenous Peoples' Rights*. New York: Routledge, 2016.

WHERE TO LEARN MORE

Mize, Ronald L., and Grace Peña Delgado. *Latino Immigrants in the United States.* Cambridge, UK: Polity Press, 2012.

Oberg, Michael Leroy. *Native America: A History.* 2nd ed. Hoboken, New Jersey: Wiley-Blackwell, 2017.

Parks, Rosa. *Rosa Parks: My Story.* New York: Penguin, 1992.

Poehlmann, Tristan. *The Stonewall Riots: The Fight for LGBT Rights.* Minneapolis, MN: ABDO, 2017.

Reagan, Leslie J. *When Abortion Was a Crime: Women, Medicine, and Law in the United States, 1867–1973.* Berkeley: University of California Press, 1998.

Regan, Tom. *The Case for Animal Rights.* 2nd ed. Berkeley: University of California Press, 2004.

Robinson, J. Dennis. *Striking Back: The Fight to End Child Labor Exploitation.* Mankato, MN: Compass Point Books, 2010.

Rosinsky, Natalie M. *The Kent State Shootings.* Minneapolis: Compass Point Books, 2009.

Singer, Peter. *Animal Liberation: The Definitive Classic of the Animal Movement.* 40th anniversary ed. New York: Open Road Media, 2015.

Shuter, Jane. *Resistance to the Nazis.* Chicago: Heinemann, 2003.

Skocpol, Theda, and Vanessa Williamson. *The Tea Party and the Remaking of Republican Conservatism.* Oxford, UK: Oxford University Press, 2012.

Skurzynski, Gloria. *Sweat and Blood: A History of U.S. Labor Unions.* Minneapolis, MN: Twenty-First Century Books, 2009.

Stienstra, Deborah. *Women's Movements and International Organizations.* New York: St. Martin's Press, 1994.

Townsend, Riley M. *The European Migrant Crisis.* Morrisville, NC: Lulu, 2015.

Periodicals

Abend, Lisa. "In Spain, Human Rights for Apes." *Time* (July 18, 2008). Available online at http://content.time.com/time/world/article/0,8599,1824206,00.html (accessed July 10, 2017).

Abouzeid, Rania. "Bouazizi: The Man Who Set Himself and Tunisia on Fire." *Time* (January 21, 2011). Available online at http://content.time.com/time/magazine/article/0,9171,2044723,00.html (accessed August 18, 2017).

Aisch, Gregor, and K. K. Rebecca Lai. "The Conflicts along 1,172 Miles of the Dakota Access Pipeline." *New York Times* (March 23, 2017). Available online at https://www.nytimes.com/interactive/2016/11/23/us/dakota-access-pipeline-protest-map.html (accessed August 21, 2017).

Alexander, Harriet. "Who Is Chelsea Manning and Why Is She Being Released from Prison?" *Telegraph* (May 17, 2017). Available online at http://www.telegraph.co.uk/news/2017/05/17/chelsea-manning-released-prison/ (accessed September 20, 2017).

Anderson, John Ward. "Cartoons of Prophet Met with Outrage." *Washington Post* (January 31, 2006). Available online at http://www.washingtonpost.com/wp-dyn/content/article/2006/01/30/AR2006013001316.html (accessed July 25, 2017).

Archibold, Randal C. "Immigrants Take to U.S. Streets in Show of Strength." *New York Times* (May 2, 2006). Available online at http://www.nytimes.com/2006/05/02/us/02immig.html (accessed July 17, 2017).

"A Background Guide to 'Brexit' from the European Union." *Economist* (February 24, 2016). Available online at https://www.economist.com/blogs/graphicdetail/2016/02/graphics-britain-s-referendum-eu-membership (accessed July 24, 2017).

Bacon, John, and Alan Gomez. "Protests against Trump's Immigration Plan Rolling in More than 30 Cities." *USA Today* (January 29, 2017). Available online at https://www.usatoday.com/story/news/nation/2017/01/29/homeland-security-judges-stay-has-little-impact-travel-ban/97211720/ (accessed August 3, 2017).

Blair, David. "The World Has Over 45 Million Slaves—Including 1.2 Million in Europe—Finds New Study." *Telegraph* (May 31, 2016). Available online at http://www.telegraph.co.uk/news/2016/05/31/the-world-has-over-45-million-slaves---including-12-million-in-e/ (accessed August 28, 2017).

Blythe, Anne. "NC Law Replacing HB2 Is Still a Bathroom Bill That Discriminates, Challengers Claim." *News & Observer* (July 21, 2017). Available online at http://www.newsobserver.com/news/politics-government/state-politics/article162850673.html (accessed August 22, 2017).

Burton, Lynsi. "WTO Riots in Seattle: 15 Years Ago." *Seattle Post Intelligencer* (November 29, 2014). Available online at http://www.seattlepi.com/local/article/WTO-riots-in-Seattle-15-years-ago-5915088.php (accessed July 25, 2017).

"Casting Ballots, Saudi Women Proudly 'Make History.'" *Times of Israel* (December 13, 2015). Available online at http://www.timesofisrael.com/casting-ballots-saudi-women-proudly-make-history (accessed August 21, 2017).

Chertoff, Emily. "Occupy Wounded Knee: A 71-Day Siege and a Forgotten Civil Rights Movement." *Atlantic* (October 23, 2012). Available online at https://www.theatlantic.com/national/archive/2012/10/occupy-wounded-knee-a-71-day-siege-and-a-forgotten-civil-rights-movement/263998/ (accessed August 21, 2017).

Cobb, James C. "The Voting Rights Act at 50: How It Changed the World." *Time* (August 6, 2015). Available online at http://time.com/3985479/voting-rights-act-1965-results/ (accessed July 18, 2017).

Cohen, Sascha. "The Day Women Went on Strike." *Time* (August 26, 2015). Available online at http://time.com/4008060/women-strike-equality-1970 (accessed August 21, 2017).

Collins, Mike. "The Pros and Cons of Globalization." *Forbes* (May 6, 2015). Available online at https://www.forbes.com/sites/mikecollins/2015/05/06/the-pros-and-cons-of-globalization/#60ffb291ccce (accessed July 27, 2017).

"Dalit Anger Singes West India." *Times of India* (December 1, 2006). Available online at https://www.pressreader.com/india/the-times-of-india-new-delhi-edition/20061201/281552286366605 (accessed September 21, 2017).

Davis, Julie Hirschfeld, and Helene Cooper. "Trump Says Transgender People Will Not Be Allowed in the Military." *New York Times* (July 26, 2017). Available online at https://www.nytimes.com/2017/07/26/us/politics/trump-transgender-military.html (accessed August 23, 2017).

Davis, Kenneth C. "America's True History of Religious Tolerance." *Smithsonian* (October 2010). Available online at http://www.smithsonianmag.com/history/americas-true-history-of-religious-tolerance-61312684/ (accessed August 1, 2017).

Day, Elizabeth. "#BlackLivesMatter: The Birth of a New Civil Rights Movement." *Guardian* (July 19, 2015). Available online at https://www.theguardian.com/world/2015/jul/19/blacklivesmatter-birth-civil-rights-movement (accessed September 15, 2017).

Drezner, Daniel W. "A Clash between Administrators and Students at Yale Went Viral. Why That Is Unfortunate for All Concerned." *Washington Post* (November 9, 2015). Available online at https://www.washingtonpost.com/posteverything/wp/2015/11/09/a-clash-between-administrators-and-students-at-yale-went-viral-why-that-is-unfortunate-for-all-concerned/?utm_term=.bdfae3d5f34b (accessed July 25, 2017).

Eddy, Melissa. "Big Anti-Immigration Rally in Germany Prompts Counterdemonstrations." *New York Times* (January 12, 2015). Available online at https://www.nytimes.com/2015/01/13/world/europe/big-anti-immigration-rally-in-germany-prompts-counterdemonstrations.html (accessed July 27, 2017).

"800 Arrested at Berkeley; Students Paralyze Campus." *Harvard Crimson* (December 4, 1964). Available online at http://www.thecrimson.com/article/1964/12/4/800-arrested-at-berkeley-students-paralyze/ (accessed July 25, 2017).

Eilperin, Juliet. "The Keystone XL Pipeline and Its Politics, Explained." *Washington Post* (February 4, 2014). Available online at https://www.washingtonpost.com/news/the-fix/wp/2013/04/03/the-keystone-xl-pipeline-and-its-politics-explained/?utm_term=.2b02fc9a65c7 (accessed July 22, 2017).

Ellingwood, Ken. "In Mexico City, Crowds Protest Drug Violence." *Los Angeles Times* (May 8, 2011). Available online at http://articles.latimes.com/2011/may/08/world/la-fg-mexican-violence-protest-20110509 (accessed July 18, 2017).

Engler, Mark, and Paul Engler. "How Did Gandhi Win? Lessons from the Salt March." *Dissent* (October 10, 2014). Available online at https://www.dissentmagazine.org/blog/gandhi-win-lessons-salt-march-social-movements (accessed August 2, 2017).

Erb, Kelly Phillips. "Considering the Death Penalty: Your Tax Dollars at Work." *Forbes* (May 1, 2014). Available online at https://www.forbes.com/

sites/kellyphillipserb/2014/05/01/considering-the-death-penalty-your- tax-dollars-at-work/#3dbe69c7664b (accessed September 7, 2017).

Federoff, Nina. "Can We Trust Monsanto with Our Food?" *Scientific American* (July 25, 2013). Available online at https://www.scientificamerican.com/article/can-we-trust-monsanto-with-our-food/ (accessed July 25, 2017).

Fitz, Nicholas. "Economic Inequality: It's Far Worse than You Think." *Scientific American* (March 31, 2015). Available online at https://www.scientificamerican.com/article/economic-inequality-it-s-far-worse-than-you-think/ (accessed July 28, 2017).

Ford, Matt. "Can Europe End the Death Penalty in America?" *Atlantic* (February 18, 2014). Available online at https://www.theatlantic.com/international/archive/2014/02/can-europe-end-the-death-penalty-in-america/283790/ (accessed September 7, 2017).

Gaffey, Conor. "South Africa: What You Need to Know about the Soweto Uprising 40 Years Later." *Newsweek* (June 16, 2016). Available online at http://www.newsweek.com/soweto-uprising-hector-pieterson-memorial-471090 (accessed September 15, 2017).

Gopalakrishnan, Amulya, and Vaibhav Ganjapure. "10 Years Later, Khairlanji Shows How Caste Crimes Fester." *Times of India* (September 28, 2016). Available online at http://timesofindia.indiatimes.com/city/nagpur/10-years-later-Khairlanji-shows-how-caste-crimes-fester/articleshow/54568908.cms (accessed September 19, 2017).

Gordon, Noah. "The Little Rock Nine: How Far Has the Country Come?" *Atlantic* (September 25, 2014). Available online at https://www.theatlantic.com/politics/archive/2014/09/the-little-rock-nine/380676/ (accessed July 18, 2017).

Greenhouse, Steven. "With Day of Protests, Fast-Food Workers Seek More Pay." *New York Times* (November 30, 2012). Available online at http://www.nytimes.com/2012/11/30/nyregion/fast-food-workers-in-new-york-city-rally-for-higher-wages.html?mcubz=3 (accessed August 25, 2017).

Gregory, Alice. "A Brief History of the Zoot Suit: Unraveling the Jazzy Life of a Snazzy Style." *Smithsonian* (April 2016). Available online at http://www.smithsonianmag.com/arts-culture/brief-history-zoot-suit-180958507 (accessed September 15, 2017).

Grossman, David. "The Dakota Pipeline Controversy Explained." *Popular Mechanics* (January 24, 2017). Available online at http://www.popularmechanics.com/technology/infrastructure/a23658/dakota-pipeline-protests (accessed August 21, 2017).

Grossman, Ron. "Flashback: 'Swastika War': When the Neo-Nazis Fought in Court to March in Skokie." *Chicago Tribune* (January 1, 2002). Available online at http://www.chicagotribune.com/news/opinion/commentary/ct-neo-nazi-skokie-march-flashback-perspec-0312-20170310-story.html (accessed July 25, 2017).

WHERE TO LEARN MORE

Hall, Sarah. "Harry Potter and the Sermon of Fire." *Guardian* (January 1, 2002). Available online at https://www.theguardian.com/world/2002/jan/01/books.harrypotter (accessed July 25, 2017).

Havard, Kate, and Lori Aratani. "Nearly 1,000 March in D.C. for Gun Control." *Washington Post* (January 26, 2013). Available online at https://www.washingtonpost.com/local/trafficandcommuting/newtown-residents-among-those-at-dc-march-for-gun-control/2013/01/26/1813a3f6-67cb-11e2-85f5-a8a9228e55e7_story.html?utm_term=.c1c727450d42 (accessed August 8, 2017).

Hendel, John. "The Freedom Riders for Civil Rights, Half a Century Later." *Atlantic* (May 4, 2011). Available online at https://www.theatlantic.com/national/archive/2011/05/the-freedom-riders-for-civil-rights-half-a-century-later-life-photos/238342/ (accessed July 18, 2017).

Herszenhorn, David M. "Armenia, on Day of Rain and Sorrow, Observes 100th Anniversary of Genocide." *New York Times* (April 24, 2015). Available online at https://www.nytimes.com/2015/04/25/world/europe/armenian-genocide-100th-anniversary.html?mcubz=1&module=ArrowsNav&contentCollection=Europe&action=keypress&region=FixedLeft&pgtype=article (accessed September 8, 2017).

Herszenhorn, David M., and Emmarie Huetteman. "House Democrats' Gun-Control Sit-In Turns into Chaotic Showdown with Republicans." *New York Times* (June 23, 2016). Available online at https://www.nytimes.com/2016/06/23/us/politics/house-democrats-stage-sit-in-to-push-for-action-on-gun-control.html (accessed August 8, 2017).

Hingston, Sandy. "Bullets and Bigots: Remembering Philadelphia's 1844 Anti-Catholic Riots." *Philadelphia Magazine* (December 17, 2015). Available online at http://www.phillymag.com/news/2015/12/17/philadelphia-anti-catholic-riots-1844/ (accessed August 1, 2017).

Holmes, Steven A. "Disabled Protest and Are Arrested." *New York Times* (March 14, 1990). Available online at http://www.nytimes.com/1990/03/14/us/disabled-protest-and-are-arrested.html (accessed September 21, 2017).

Iracheta, Michelle. "Houston Group Protests Texas' Death Penalty." *Houston Chronicle* (October 26, 2014). Available online at http://www.chron.com/news/houston-texas/houston/article/Houston-group-protests-Texas-death-penalty-5848226.php (accessed September 7, 2017).

Iyengar, Rishi. "6 Questions You Might Have about Hong Kong's Umbrella Revolution." *Time* (October 5, 2014). Available online at http://time.com/3471366/hong-kong-umbrella-revolution-occupy-central-democracy-explainer-6-questions/ (accessed August 21, 2017).

Jacobs, Andrew. "Gay Festival in China Pushes Official Boundaries." *New York Times* (June 15, 2009). Available online at http://www.nytimes.com/2009/06/15/world/asia/15shanghai.html (accessed August 16, 2017).

Jaschik, Scott. "Racial Tensions Escalate." *Inside Higher Ed* (November 9, 2015). Available online at https://www.insidehighered.com/news/2015/

11/09/racial-tensions-escalate-u-missouri-and-yale (accessed July 25, 2017).

Kafanov, Lucy. "Turkey, Armenians Battle over Genocide 100 Years Later." *USA Today* (April 23, 2015). Available online at https://www.usatoday.com/story/news/world/2015/04/23/turkey-armenia-genocide-massacre-anniversary/26261059/ (accessed September 8, 2017).

Kaleem, Jaweed. "The Death Penalty Has Long Divided Americans. Here's Why Those Who Oppose It Are Winning." *Los Angeles Times* (April 27, 2017). Available online at http://www.latimes.com/nation/la-na-death-penalty-arkansas-20170427-htmlstory.html (accessed September 7, 2017).

Kifner, John. "Armenian Genocide of 1915: An Overview." *New York Times*, n.d. Available online at http://www.nytimes.com/ref/timestopics/topics_armeniangenocide.html?mcubz=0 (accessed September 8, 2017).

Koch, Wendy. "Tens of Thousands Demand Action on Climate Change." *USA Today* (February 17, 2013). Available online at https://www.usatoday.com/story/news/nation/2013/02/17/climate-change-rally-human-pipeline/1925719/ (accessed July 22, 2017).

Kopel, David. "The Warsaw Ghetto Uprising: Armed Jews vs. Nazis." *Washington Post* (October 10, 2015). Available online at https://www.washingtonpost.com/news/volokh-conspiracy/wp/2015/10/10/the-warsaw-ghetto-uprising-armed-jews-vs-nazis/?utm_term=.914e605236fd (accessed August 8, 2017).

Levitin, Michael. "The Triumph of Occupy Wall Street." *Atlantic* (June 10, 2015). Available online at https://www.theatlantic.com/politics/archive/2015/06/the-triumph-of-occupy-wall-street/395408/ (accessed July 27, 2017).

Liu, Melinda. "China Gay-Pride Event Meets Obstacles." *Newsweek* (June 12, 2009). Available online at http://www.newsweek.com/china-gay-pride-event-meets-obstacles-80291 (accessed August 16, 2017).

Lueck, Thomas J. "Threats and Responses: Protests; Candlelight Vigils Are Held around the World to Oppose Military Action against Iraq." *New York Times* (March 17, 2003). Available online at http://www.nytimes.com/2003/03/17/world/threats-responses-protests-candlelight-vigils-are-held-around-world-oppose.html?mcubz=1 (accessed September 22, 2017).

"Marchers in over 400 Cities Protest Monsanto." *Washington Post* (May 25, 2013). Available online at https://www.washingtonpost.com/politics/marchers-in-over-400-cities-protest-monsanto/2013/05/25/938dd988-c59b-11e2-914f-a7aba60512a7_story.html?utm_term=.cd0efcd95a22 (accessed July 25, 2017).

McCarthy, Tom. "Under the Umbrellas: What Do Hong Kong's Protesters Want from China?" *Guardian* (September 29, 2014). Available online at https://www.theguardian.com/world/2014/sep/29/hong-kong-democracy-protests-china-umbrellas-police (accessed August 21, 2017).

McFadden, Robert D. "The Republicans: The Convention in New York—The March; Vast Anti-Bush Rally Greets Republicans in New York." *New York Times* (August 30, 2004). Available online at http://www.nytimes.com/

2004/08/30/us/republicans-convention-new-york-march-vast-anti-bush-rally-greets-republicans.html?mcubz=1 (accessed September 22, 2017).

Mejia, Brittny, et al. "Armenian Genocide: Massive March Ends at Turkish Consulate in L.A." *Los Angeles Times* (April 24, 2015). Available online at http://www.latimes.com/local/lanow/la-me-ln-armenian-genocide-march-los-angeles-20150424-story.html (accessed September 8, 2017).

Meyer, Robinson. "The Standing Rock Sioux Claim 'Victory and Vindication' in Court." *Atlantic* (June 14, 2017). Available online at https://www.theatlantic.com/science/archive/2017/06/dakota-access-standing-rock-sioux-victory-court/530427/ (accessed August 21, 2017).

"Millions March against GM Crops." *Guardian* (May 25, 2013). Available online at https://www.theguardian.com/environment/2013/may/26/millions-march-against-monsanto (accessed July 25, 2017).

Minder, Raphael. "Animal Welfare Activists to Protest Bullfighting in Spain." *New York Times* (August 20, 2010). Available online at http://www.nytimes.com/2010/08/21/world/europe/21iht-spain.html (accessed July 12, 2017).

Patterson, Romaine. "Let Westboro Baptist Have Their Hate Speech. We'll Smother It with Peace." *Washington Post* (March 6, 2011). Available online at http://www.washingtonpost.com/wp-dyn/content/article/2011/03/04/AR2011030406330.html (accessed August 14, 2017).

Peters, Jeremy W., et al. "Pence Tells Anti-Abortion Marchers That 'Life Is Winning.'" *New York Times* (January 27, 2017). Available online at https://www.nytimes.com/2017/01/27/us/politics/march-for-life.html (accessed August 30, 2017).

"Prophet Mohammed Cartoon Controversy: Timeline." *Telegraph* (May 4, 2015). Available online at http://www.telegraph.co.uk/news/worldnews/europe/france/11341599/Prophet-Muhammad-cartoons-controversy-timeline.html (accessed July 25, 2017).

Rayman, Noah. "6 Things You Should Know about the Tiananmen Square Massacre." *Time* (June 4, 2014). Available online at http://time.com/2822290/tiananmen-square-massacre-facts-time/ (accessed August 23, 2017).

Remnick, Noah. "Yale Grapples with Ties to Slavery in Debate over a College's Name." *New York Times* (September 12, 2015). Available online at https://www.nytimes.com/2015/09/12/nyregion/yale-in-debate-over-calhoun-college-grapples-with-ties-to-slavery.html (accessed July 25, 2017).

Richmond, Emily. "Civics Lessons from the House Democrats' Sit-in." *Atlantic* (June 28, 2016). Available online at https://www.theatlantic.com/education/archive/2016/06/civics-lessons-from-the-house-democrats-sit-in/489167/ (accessed August 8, 2017).

Ross, Winston. "Protests Hit Netherlands in Wake of Paris Attack." *Newsweek* (January 7, 2015). Available online at http://www.newsweek.com/protests-hit-netherlands-wake-paris-attack-297459 (accessed July 25, 2017).

Rothman, Lily. "What We Still Get Wrong about What Happened in Detroit in 1967." *Time* (August 3, 2017). Available online at http://time.com/4879062/detroit-1967-real-history/ (accessed September 15, 2017).

Sanchez, Raf. "WikiLeaks Q & A: Who Is Bradley Manning and What Did He Do?" *Telegraph* (July 30, 2013). Available online at http://www.telegraph.co.uk/news/worldnews/wikileaks/10210160/WikiLeaks-Q-and-A-who-is-Bradley-Manning-and-what-did-he-do.html (accessed September 20, 2017).

Santora, Marc. "Yale Report Clears Police Officer in Encounter with Student." *New York Times* (March 5, 2015). Available online at https://www.nytimes.com/2015/03/05/nyregion/yale-report-clears-police-officer-in-encounter-with-student.html (accessed July 25, 2017).

Smith, Mitch. "Standing Rock Protest Camp, Once Home to Thousands, Is Razed." *New York Times* (February 23, 2017). Available online at https://www.nytimes.com/2017/02/23/us/standing-rock-protest-dakota-access-pipeline.html (accessed July 22, 2017).

Smith, Noah. "The Dark Side of Globalization: Why Seattle's 1999 Protesters Were Right." *Atlantic* (January 6, 2014). Available online at https://www.theatlantic.com/business/archive/2014/01/the-dark-side-of-globalization-why-seattles-1999-protesters-were-right/282831/ (accessed July 27, 2017).

Stack, Liam. "A Brief History of Deadly Attacks on Abortion Providers." *New York Times* (November 29, 2015). Available online at https://www.nytimes.com/interactive/2015/11/29/us/30abortion-clinic-violence.html (accessed August 31, 2017).

Steinfels, Peter. "Paris, May 1968: The Revolution That Never Was." *New York Times* (May 11, 2008). Available online at http://www.nytimes.com/2008/05/11/world/europe/11iht-paris.4.12777919.html (accessed July 24, 2017).

Steyn, Paul. "African Elephant Numbers Plummet 30 Percent, Landmark Survey Finds." *National Geographic* (August 31, 2016). Available online at http://news.nationalgeographic.com/2016/08/wildlife-african-elephants-population-decrease-great-elephant-census/ (accessed July 11, 2017).

Swarns, Rachel L. "Yale College Dean Torn by Racial Protests." *New York Times* (November 15, 2015). Available online at https://www.nytimes.com/2015/11/16/nyregion/yale-college-dean-torn-by-racial-protests.html (accessed July 25, 2017).

"Tiananmen Square 25 Years On: 'Every Person in the Crowd Was a Victim of the Massacre.'" *Guardian* (June 1, 2014). Available online at https://www.theguardian.com/world/2014/jun/01/tiananmen-square-25-years-every-person-victim-massacre (accessed August 23, 2017).

"A Timeline of the Dakota Access Oil Pipeline." *U.S. News & World Report* (February 22, 2017). Available online at https://www.usnews.com/news/north-dakota/articles/2017-02-22/a-timeline-of-the-dakota-access-oil-pipeline (accessed August 21, 2017).

Tremlett, Giles. "Spain Protesters Vote to Dismantle Puerta del Sol Tent City." *Guardian* (June 8, 2011). Available online at https://www.theguardian.com/

world/2011/jun/08/spain-protesters-dismantle-puerta-sol (accessed August 1, 2017).

"Why Islam Prohibits Images of Muhammad." *Economist* (January 19, 2015). Available online at https://www.economist.com/blogs/economist-explains/2015/01/economist-explains-12 (accessed July 25, 2017).

Wilkinson, Tracy. "New Report Raises Chilling Possibility That Mystery of 43 Mexican Students' Disappearance Will Never Be Solved." *Los Angeles Times* (April 25, 2016). Available online at http://www.latimes.com/world/mexico-americas/la-fg-mexico-students-20160425-story.html (accessed July 18, 2017).

Winkler, Adam. "The Secret History of Guns." *Atlantic* (September 2011). Available online at https://www.theatlantic.com/magazine/archive/2011/09/the-secret-history-of-guns/308608/ (accessed August 8, 2017).

Woo, Elaine. "'60s 'Blowouts': Leaders of Latino School Protest See Little Change." *Los Angeles Times* (March 7, 1988). Available online at http://articles.latimes.com/1988-03-07/local/me-488_1_lincoln-high-school-graduate (accessed July 13, 2017).

Worthington, Danika. "Meet the Disabled Activists from Denver Who Changed a Nation." *Denver Post* (July 5, 2017). Available online at http://www.denverpost.com/2017/07/05/adapt-disabled-activists-denver/ (accessed September 21, 2017).

Yee, Vivian, Kenan Davis, and Jugal K. Patel. "Here's the Reality about Illegal Immigrants in the United States." *New York Times* (March 2, 2017). Available online at https://www.nytimes.com/interactive/2017/03/06/us/politics/undocumented-illegal-immigrants.html (accessed July 19, 2017).

Yong, Ed. "How the March for Science Finally Found Its Voice." *Atlantic* (April 23, 2017). Available online at https://www.theatlantic.com/science/archive/2017/04/how-the-march-for-science-finally-found-its-voice/524022/ (accessed July 22, 2017).

Websites

"About." 18th Annual March to Abolish the Death Penalty – Oct 28, 2017. http://marchforabolition.org/about-2/ (accessed September 7, 2017).

Badcock, James. "Will Spain Ever Ban Bullfighting?" BBC News, December 3, 2016. http://www.bbc.com/news/world-europe-38063778 (accessed July 12, 2017).

Batha, Emma. "Europe's Refugee and Migrant Crisis in 2016. In Numbers." World Economic Forum, December 5, 2016. https://www.weforum.org/agenda/2016/12/europes-refugee-and-migrant-crisis-in-2016-in-numbers (accessed July 27, 2017).

Black, Richard. "Copenhagen Climate Accord: Key Issues" BBC News, December 19, 2009. http://news.bbc.co.uk/2/hi/science/nature/8422186.stm (accessed July 22, 2017).

WHERE TO LEARN MORE

Botelho, Greg. "Arab Spring Aftermath: Revolutions Give Way to Violence, More Unrest." CNN, March 2015. http://www.cnn.com/2015/03/27/middleeast/arab-spring-aftermath/index.html (accessed August 18, 2017).

"Chicano Movement." Brown University. http://www.brown.edu/Research/Coachella/chicano.html (accessed July 13, 2017).

"Civil Rights at Stonewall National Monument." National Park Service, October 17, 2016. https://www.nps.gov/places/stonewall.htm (accessed August 17, 2017).

Connolly, Katie. "What Exactly Is the Tea Party?" BBC News, September 16, 2010. http://www.bbc.com/news/world-us-canada-11317202 (accessed July 14, 2017).

Convention on International Trade in Endangered Species of Wild Fauna and Flora (CITES). https://www.cites.org/ (accessed July 10, 2017).

"Czech Republic Slovakia: Velvet Revolution at 25." BBC News, November 17, 2014. http://www.bbc.com/news/world-europe-30059011 (accessed August 4, 2017).

"The Death Penalty in United States of America." Cornell Center on the Death Penalty Worldwide, March 10, 2014. http://www.deathpenaltyworldwide.org/country-search-post.cfm?country=united+states+of+america (accessed September 7, 2017).

Dwyer, Colin. "Protests against Planned Parenthood Rouse Dueling Rallies Nationwide." National Public Radio, February 11, 2017. http://www.npr.org/sections/thetwo-way/2017/02/11/514717975/protests-against-planned-parenthood-rouse-dueling-rallies-nationwide (accessed August 31, 2017).

"Episode 337: The Secret Document That Transformed China." *Planet Money*, National Public Radio, May 14, 2014. http://www.npr.org/sections/money/2014/05/14/312488659/episode-337-the-secret-document-that-transformed-china (accessed July 19, 2017).

Fessenden, Marissa. "How a Nearly Successful Slave Revolt Was Intentionally Lost to History." *Smithsonian*. http://www.smithsonianmag.com/smart-news/its-anniversary-1811-louisiana-slave-revolt-180957760 (accessed August 25, 2017).

"45.8 Million People Are Enslaved across the World." Global Slavery Index, May 30, 2016. https://www.globalslaveryindex.org/media/45-8-million-people-enslaved-across-world/ (accessed August 28, 2017).

"The Freedom Rides: CORE Volunteers Put Their Lives on the Road." Congress of Racial Equality (CORE). http://www.core-online.org/History/freedom%20rides.htm (accessed July 18, 2017).

Friedman, Gail. "March of the Mill Children." Encyclopedia of Greater Philadelphia. http://philadelphiaencyclopedia.org/archive/march-of-the-mill-children/ (accessed August 25, 2017).

Gamboa, Suzanne. "For Latinos, 1965 Voting Rights Act Impact Came a Decade Later." NBC News, August 6, 2015. http://www.nbcnews.com/

WHERE TO LEARN MORE

news/latino/latinos-1965-voting-rights-act-impact-came-decade-later-n404936 (accessed July 20, 2017).

"The Global Divide on Homosexuality." Pew Research Center, June 4, 2013. http://www.pewglobal.org/2013/06/04/the-global-divide-on-homosexuality/ (accessed August 16, 2017).

"Globalization." *National Geographic*, March 28, 2011. https://www.nationalgeographic.org/encyclopedia/globalization/ (accessed July 27, 2017).

Goodman, Al. "Thousands of Spaniards Call for Economic Reform in New Protest." CNN, June 19, 2011. http://www.cnn.com/2011/WORLD/europe/06/19/spain.protests/ (accessed August 1, 2017).

"The Grito de Lares: The Rebellion of 1868." Library of Congress. https://www.loc.gov/collections/puerto-rico-books-and-pamphlets/articles-and-essays/nineteenth-century-puerto-rico/rebellion-of-1868 (accessed July 31, 2017).

"Gun Violence." Brady Campaign to Prevent Gun Violence. http://www.bradycampaign.org/gun-violence (accessed August 8, 2017).

"Hate Crimes Law." Human Rights Campaign. http://www.hrc.org/resources/hate-crimes-law (accessed August 15, 2017).

Hersher, Rebecca. "Key Moments in the Dakota Access Pipeline Fight." National Public Radio, February 22, 2017. http://www.npr.org/sections/thetwo-way/2017/02/22/514988040/key-moments-in-the-dakota-access-pipeline-fight (accessed August 21, 2017).

"Hispanics in the US Fast Facts." CNN, March 31, 2017. http://www.cnn.com/2013/09/20/us/hispanics-in-the-u-s-/index.html (accessed July 27, 2017).

"History—Incident at Wounded Knee." US Marshals Service. https://www.usmarshals.gov/history/wounded-knee/ (accessed August 21, 2017).

"Hong Kong Protests: Timeline of the Occupation." BBC News, December 11, 2014. http://www.bbc.com/news/world-asia-china-30390820 (accessed August 21, 2017).

"How the United States Immigration System Works." American Immigration Council, August 12, 2016. https://www.americanimmigrationcouncil.org/research/how-united-states-immigration-system-works (accessed July 19, 2017).

"India's Dalits: Between Atrocity and Protest." Human Rights Watch, January 12, 2007. https://www.hrw.org/news/2007/01/12/indias-dalits-between-atrocity-and-protest (accessed September 21, 2017).

"Indigenous Peoples." The World Bank. http://www.worldbank.org/en/topic/indigenouspeoples (accessed August 21, 2017).

International Congress of Women. "Final Programme." Gothenburg University Library. http://www.ub.gu.se/kvinndata/portaler/fred/samarbete/pdf/program_1915.pdf (accessed September 8, 2017).

Johnson, Troy. "We Hold the Rock." National Park Service, February 27, 2015. https://www.nps.gov/alca/learn/historyculture/we-hold-the-rock.htm (accessed August 21, 2017).

Jones, Owen. "The People Are Revolting—the History of Protest." BBC. http://www.bbc.co.uk/timelines/ztvxtfr (accessed August 15, 2017).

Kauffman, Stephen. "They Abandoned Their Wheelchairs and Crawled Up the Capitol Steps." ShareAmerica, March 12, 2015. https://share.america.gov/crawling-up-steps-demand-their-rights/ (accessed September 21, 2017).

Kennedy, Merrit. "A Look at Egypt's Uprising, 5 Years Later." National Public Radio, January 25, 2016. http://www.npr.org/sections/thetwo-way/2016/01/25/464290769/a-look-at-egypts-uprising-5-years-later (accessed August 15, 2017).

Kim, Inga. "The 1965–1970 Delano Grape Strike and Boycott." United Farm Workers, March 7, 2017. http://ufw.org/1965-1970-delano-grape-strike-boycott (accessed August 25, 2017).

Kurtzleben, Danielle. "100 Days In, Women's March Still Inspires. But Can the Enthusiasm Hold?" National Public Radio, April 28, 2017. http://www.npr.org/2017/04/28/525764938/100-days-in-womens-march-still-inspires-but-can-the-enthusiasm-hold (accessed August 21, 2017).

Lee, Brianna, and Danielle Renwick. "Mexico's Drug War." Council on Foreign Relations, May 25, 2017. https://www.cfr.org/backgrounder/mexicos-drug-war (accessed July 18, 2017).

Lee, Trymaine. "Justice for All: Thousands March against Police Violence." MSNBC, July 21, 2015. http://www.msnbc.com/msnbc/justice-all-thousands-expected-march-washington-against-police-violence (accessed September 15, 2017).

Lewis, Jerry M., and Thomas R. Hensley. "The May 4 Shootings at Kent State University: The Search for Historical Accuracy." Kent State University. http://www.kent.edu/may-4-historical-accuracy (accessed September 7, 2017).

"LGBT Rights Milestones Fast Facts." CNN, July 4, 2017. http://www.cnn.com/2015/06/19/us/lgbt-rights-milestones-fast-facts/index.html (accessed August 23, 2017).

"Little Rock Central High School: Crisis Timeline." National Park Service. https://www.nps.gov/chsc/learn/historyculture/timeline.htm (accessed July 18, 2017).

López, Gustavo, and Kristen Bialik. "Key Findings about U.S. Immigrants." Pew Research Center, May 3, 2017. http://www.pewresearch.org/fact-tank/2017/05/03/key-findings-about-u-s-immigrants/ (accessed July 17, 2017).

"Malala's Story." Malala Fund. https://www.malala.org/malalas-story (accessed August 21, 2017).

Malik, Asad. "Charles Deslondes and the American Uprising of 1811." Pan-African Alliance. https://www.panafricanalliance.com/charles-deslondes (accessed August 25, 2017).

WHERE TO LEARN MORE

"Māori Land Rights." Museum of New Zealand. http://sites.tepapa.govt.nz/sliceofheaven/web/html/landrights.html (accessed August 21, 2017).

"March for Science." EarthDay.org, April 22, 2017. http://www.earthday.org/marchforscience/ (accessed July 22, 2017).

"March on Washington for Jobs and Freedom." National Park Service. https://www.nps.gov/articles/march-on-washington.htm (accessed July 18, 2017).

"The Matthew Shepard and James Byrd, Jr., Hate Crimes Prevention Act of 2009." US Department of Justice. https://www.justice.gov/crt/matthew-shepard-and-james-byrd-jr-hate-crimes-prevention-act-2009-0 (accessed August 15, 2017).

Meincke, Paul. "Protests Mark 100th Anniversary of Armenian Massacres." ABC News 7, April 24, 2015. http://abc7chicago.com/news/protests-mark-100th-anniversary-of-armenian-massacres-/679914/ (accessed September 8, 2017).

Michals, Debra. "Ruby Bridges (1954–)." National Women's History Museum, 2015. https://www.nwhm.org/education-resources/biography/biographies/ruby-bridges (accessed July 18, 2017).

"The Modern Environmental Movement." Public Broadcasting Service. http://www.pbs.org/wgbh/americanexperience/features/earth-days-modern-environmental-movement/ (accessed July 22, 2017).

"Murder in Mississippi." Public Broadcasting Service. http://www.pbs.org/wgbh/americanexperience/features/freedomsummer-murder/ (accessed July 18, 2017).

"Muslims Protest Danish Muhammad Cartoons." NBC News, February 15, 2008. http://www.nbcnews.com/id/23186467/ns/world_news-europe/t/muslims-protest-danish-muhammad-cartoons/#.WW9wZITyuUl (accessed July 25, 2017).

National Rifle Association (NRA). https://home.nra.org/ (accessed August 8, 2017).

"1943: Zoot Suit Riots." *National Geographic*. https://www.nationalgeographic.org/thisday/jun3/zoot-suit-riots (accessed September 15, 2017).

"Obergefell v. Hodges." Oyez. https://www.oyez.org/cases/2014/14-556 (accessed August 18, 2017).

"The Official Harvey Milk Biography." Milk Foundation. http://milkfoundation.org/about/harvey-milk-biography (accessed August 22, 2017).

"Our History." Royal Society for the Prevention of Cruelty to Animals (RSPCA). https://www.rspca.org.uk/whatwedo/whoweare/history (accessed July 11, 2017).

Pao, Maureen. "Cesar Chavez: The Life behind a Legacy of Farm Labor Rights." National Public Radio, August 12, 2016. http://www.npr.org/2016/08/02/488428577/cesar-chavez-the-life-behind-a-legacy-of-farm-labor-rights (accessed July 14, 2017).

Pilgrim, David. "What Was Jim Crow." Ferris State University, September 2000. https://ferris.edu/HTMLS/news/jimcrow/what/ (accessed August 23, 2017).

"Polish Resistance and Conclusions." United States Holocaust Memorial Museum. https://www.ushmm.org/learn/students/learning-materials-and-resources/poles-victims-of-the-nazi-era/polish-resistance-and-conclusions (accessed August 2, 2017).

"The Raid on Harpers Ferry." Public Broadcasting Service. http://www.pbs.org/wgbh/aia/part4/4p2940.html (accessed August 21, 2017).

Ravitz, Jessica. "The Surprising History of Abortion in the United States." CNN, June 27, 2016. http://www.cnn.com/2016/06/23/health/abortion-history-in-united-states/index.html (accessed August 31, 2017).

"Rescue in Denmark." United States Holocaust Memorial Museum. https://www.ushmm.org/outreach/en/article.php?ModuleId=10007740 (accessed August 2, 2017).

"Rock Hill, South Carolina, Students Sit-In for US Civil Rights, 1960." Global Nonviolent Action Database at Swarthmore College. http://nvdatabase.swarthmore.edu/content/rock-hill-south-carolina-students-sit-us-civil-rights-1960 (accessed July 18, 2017).

"'Satanic' Harry Potter Books Burnt." BBC News, December 31, 2001. http://news.bbc.co.uk/2/hi/entertainment/1735623.stm (accessed July 25, 2017).

Schwartz, Daniel. "What Happened after the Arab Spring?" CBC News, August 4, 2014. http://www.cbc.ca/news/world/what-happened-after-the-arab-spring-1.2723934 (accessed August 18, 2017).

"September 11th Terror Attacks Fast Facts." CNN, August 24, 2017. http://www.cnn.com/2013/07/27/us/september-11-anniversary-fast-facts/index.html (accessed September 22, 2017).

"Shanghai to Show Pride with Gay Festival." BBC News, June 6, 2009. http://news.bbc.co.uk/1/hi/world/asia-pacific/8083672.stm (accessed August 16, 2017).

Smith, Natalie. "What Is Occupy Wall Street?" Scholastic. http://www.scholastic.com/browse/article.jsp?id=3756681 (accessed July 27, 2017).

"Spain's Indignados Protest Here to Stay." BBC News, May 15, 2012. http://www.bbc.com/news/world-europe-18070246 (accessed July 18, 2017).

"Syrian War Monitor Says 465,000 Killed in Six Years of Fighting." Reuters, March 13, 2017. http://www.reuters.com/article/us-mideast-crisis-syria-casualties-idUSKBN16K1Q1 (accessed August 18, 2017).

"Timeline: Iraq War." BBC News, July 5, 2016. http://www.bbc.com/news/magazine-36702957 (accessed September 22, 2017).

"Timeline: Tiananmen Protests." BBC News, June 2, 2014. http://www.bbc.com/news/world-asia-china-27404764 (accessed August 23, 2017).

WHERE TO LEARN MORE

"Tinker v. Des Moines Independent Community School Dist." Cornell Law School. https://www.law.cornell.edu/supremecourt/text/393/503 (accessed August 31, 2017).

"Topics in Chronicling America—The Haymarket Affair." Library of Congress. https://www.loc.gov/rr/news/topics/haymarket.html (accessed August 25, 2017).

"Trafficking in Persons Report." US Department of State, June 2017. https://www.state.gov/documents/organization/271339.pdf (accessed August 23, 2017).

"Treblinka Death Camp Revolt." United States Holocaust Memorial Museum. https://www.ushmm.org/research/the-center-for-advanced-holocaust-studies/miles-lerman-center-for-the-study-of-jewish-resistance/medals-of-resistance-award/treblinka-death-camp-revolt (accessed July 31, 2017).

"The Triangular Slave Trade: Overview." BBC. http://www.bbc.co.uk/bitesize/ks3/history/industrial_era/the_slave_trade/revision/2/ (accessed August 28, 2017).

Tuysuz, Gul. "What Is Sharia Law?" CNN, August 16, 2016. http://www.cnn.com/2016/08/16/world/sharia-law-definition/index.html (accessed August 21, 2017).

"2015 Charlie Hebdo Attacks Fast Facts." CNN, December 22, 2016. http://www.cnn.com/2015/01/21/europe/2015-paris-terror-attacks-fast-facts/index.html (accessed July 25, 2017).

"The 2016 ITUC Global Rights Index: The World's Worst Countries for Workers." International Trade Union Confederation (ITUC). https://www.ituc-csi.org/IMG/pdf/ituc-violationmap-2016-en_final.pdf (accessed August 25, 2017).

"The Velvet Revolution, November 1989." Association for Diplomatic Studies and Training. http://adst.org/2015/10/the-velvet-revolution-november-1989 (accessed August 4, 2017).

"Warsaw." United States Holocaust Memorial Museum. https://www.ushmm.org/wlc/en/article.php?ModuleId=10005069 (accessed August 8, 2017).

Weeks, Linton. "Whatever Happened to the Anti-War Movement?" National Public Radio, April 15 2011. www.npr.org/2011/04/15/135391188/whatever-happened-to-the-anti-war-movement (accessed September 22, 2017).

"What Are Human Rights?" United Nations Human Rights Office of the High Commissioner. http://www.ohchr.org/EN/Issues/Pages/WhatareHumanRights.aspx (accessed September 19, 2017).

"What Does Free Speech Mean?" US Courts. http://www.uscourts.gov/about-federal-courts/educational-resources/about-educational-outreach/activity-resources/what-does (accessed July 25, 2017).

"What Is Fracking and Why Is It Controversial?" BBC News, December 16, 2015. http://www.bbc.com/news/uk-14432401 (accessed July 22, 2017).

"What Is the Americans with Disabilities Act (ADA)?" ADA National Network. https://adata.org/learn-about-ada (accessed September 21, 2017).

"White Rose." United States Holocaust Memorial Museum. https://www.ushmm.org/wlc/en/article.php?ModuleId=10007188 (accessed August 4, 2017).

"WikiLeaks Fast Facts." CNN. http://www.cnn.com/2013/06/03/world/wikileaks-fast-facts/index.html (accessed September 20, 2017).

"Woman Suffrage Timeline (1840–1920)." National Women's History Museum. https://www.nwhm.org/education-resources/history/woman-suffrage-timeline (accessed August 21, 2017).

"World Trade Organization Protests in Seattle." Seattle.gov. https://www.seattle.gov/cityarchives/exhibits-and-education/digital-document-libraries/world-trade-organization-protests-in-seattle (accessed July 25, 2017).

"Yale Students March over Concerns of Racism." CBS News, November 9, 2015. http://www.cbsnews.com/news/yale-students-march-over-concerns-of-racism/ (accessed July 25, 2017).

Zhou, David. "Operation Rescue Activists Resist Abortion Clinic in Wichita, Kansas (Summer of Mercy), 1991." Global Nonviolent Action Database, April 30, 2012. http://nvdatabase.swarthmore.edu/content/operation-rescue-activists-resist-abortion-clinic-wichita-kansas-summer-mercy-1991 (accessed August 28, 2017).

Other

Blackfish. Documentary. Directed by Gabriela Cowperthwaite. New York: Magnolia Pictures, 2013.

Britches. Documentary. Directed by Lori Gruen, Norfolk, VA: PETA, 1986.

A Day without a Mexican. DVD. Directed by Sergio Arau. Los Angeles: Altavista Films, 2004.

Gasland. Documentary. Directed by Josh Fox. Brooklyn, NY: International WOW Company, 2010.

An Inconvenient Truth. Documentary. Directed by Davis Guggenheim. Los Angeles: Paramount Pictures, 2006.

The Ivory Game. Documentary. Directed by Richard Ladkani and Kief Davidson. Vienna, Austria: Terra Mater Factual Studios, 2016.

General Index

Italic type indicates volume numbers; **boldface** indicates main entries. Illustrations are marked by (ill.).

A

A21 Campaign, *3:* 647
Abdullah bin Abdulaziz al Saud, King of Saudi Arabia, *3:* 715–716
Abernathy, Ralph, *1:* 36 (ill.)
Ableism, *2:* 276
Abolition of slavery, *2:* 267–268; *3:* 511–512. *See also* **Slavery**
    Harpers Ferry Raid (1859), *3:* 638–643, 642 (ill.)
    Mauritania, *3:* 643
    United Kingdom, *3:* 637
    United States, *3:* 633
    Washington, D.C., *3:* 633
Abolitionist movement, *3:* 622, 638, 639
Aboriginal Land Rights Protest (1988), *2:* 375–379, 378 (ill.). *See also* **Indigenous peoples' rights**
Aboriginals, *2:* 365–366, 375–379
Abortion, *3:* 549. *See also* **Reproductive rights**
    anti-abortion laws, *3:* 552–553
    blocking access to clinics, *3:* 557–558, 562–568, 566–567
    history, *3:* 551–553
    late-term, *3:* 566
    legalization of, *3:* 575–576
Abzug, Bella, *3:* 560
ACCD (American Coalition of Citizens with Disabilities), *2:* 279
ACLU (American Civil Liberties Union), *2:* 460, 461–462, 464
ACT UP, HIV/AIDS demonstration, *2:* 433 (ill.)
Activists
    animal rights, *1:* 4, 7–11, 10 (ill.), 12–13, 25–26
    labor, *1:* 75–76
    scientists, *1:* 168
ADA (United States. Americans with Disabilities Act), *2:* 277, 280–283
ADAPT (American Disabled for Accessible Public Transit), *2:* 279–280, 283
Addams, Jane, *3:* 660, 660 (ill.)
ADL (Anti-Defamation League), *2:* 446
Afghanistan War, *3:* 681–682
    civilian casualties, *3:* 684
    refugees, *2:* 319
AFL (American Federation of Labor), *2:* 409
Africa
    child labor, *2:* 399
    slavery, *3:* 620–621
African American civil rights, *1:* **35–70**, 36 (ill.), 39 (ill.), 45 (ill.), 52 (ill.), 53 (ill.), 56 (ill.), 58 (ill.), 61 (ill.), 65 (ill.). *See also* Civil rights; **Racial conflict**
    Bridges, Ruby, *1:* 53, 53 (ill.)
    desegregation in Birmingham, Alabama, *1:* 62
    Freedom Rides (1961), *1:* 54–59, 56 (ill.)
    Little Rock Nine Crisis (1957), *1:* 47–52, 52 (ill.)
    Lunch Counter Protest, McCrory's (1961), *1:* 59–63, 61 (ill.)
    March on Washington for Jobs and Freedom (1963), *1:* 39 (ill.), 63–69, 65 (ill.)

GENERAL INDEX

Mississippi Summer Project/Freedom Summer Voter Registration, *1:* 58, 58 (ill.)
Montgomery Bus Boycott (1955–1956), *1:* 36 (ill.), 42–47
African Americans
  racial discrimination, *1:* 36–37; *3:* 512, 513–515
  violence against, *1:* 38, 40, 56–57, 56 (ill.), 58, 62; *3:* 526–527
  voting rights, *1:* 40
African slave trade, *3:* 620–621, 621 (ill.)
  end of, *3:* 622
  triangular trade, *3:* 621
Afrikaans, *3:* 534–535
Afrikaners, *3:* 533
Agent Orange, *1:* 223
Agha-Soltan, Neda, *3:* 490–491, 491 (ill.)
Agricultural Workers Organizing Committee (AWOC), *2:* 418
Ahmadinejad, Mahmoud, *3:* 490
AIM (American Indian Movement), *2:* 364–365, 371–372
AIM (American Indian Movement) Occupation of Wounded Knee (1973), *2:* 364–365, 367–375, 374 (ill.). *See also* **Indigenous peoples' rights**
Airports, anti-Trump travel ban protests, *2:* 330–331, 330 (ill.)
Alabama
  desegregation, *1:* 62
  Freedom Rides, *1:* 56, 56 (ill.), 57
  Montgomery Bus Boycott (1955–1956), *1:* 36 (ill.), 42–47
Alamagordo, NM, book burning, *1:* 181 (ill.)
Alamagordo Public Library, *1:* 182
Alcatraz, occupation by Native Americans, *2:* 370–371, 371 (ill.)
Alexander the Great, *2:* 430
Alexis, Aaron, *2:* 253
ALF (Animal Liberation Front), *1:* 7–11
  activists, *1:* 10 (ill.)
  debate over methods, *1:* 11
  founding, *1:* 8
  use of arson, *1:* 10–11
Allende, Salvador, *1:* 106–107, 107 (ill.)
Alliance of Small Island States (AOSIS), *1:* 146, 147
Allred, Gloria, *3:* 577 (ill.)

Alt Right, *3:* 542, 543
Amazon rain forest, *2:* 366, 379–384
Amazonian indigenous peoples, *2:* 366, 379–384. *See also* Indigenous peoples
Ambedkar, Bhimrao Ramji, *2:* 291–293, 295
American Airlines Flight 11, *3:* 677, 678
American Airlines Flight 77, *3:* 677
American Civil Liberties Union (ACLU), *2:* 460, 461–462, 464
American Coalition of Citizens with Disabilities (ACCD), *2:* 279
American Federation of Labor (AFL), *2:* 409
American Horse, *2:* 373
American Indian Movement (AIM), *2:* 364–365, 371–372
American Indian Movement (AIM) Occupation of Wounded Knee (1973), *2:* 364–365, 367–375, 374 (ill.)
American Library Association, *1:* 180
American Protestant Association, *2:* 315, 316
American Psychiatric Association (APA), *2:* 432
American Recovery and Reinvestment Act (ARRA), *1:* 113
American Republican Association, *2:* 315
American Revolutionary War (1775–1783), *2:* 233, 335–337; *3:* 471. *See also* United States
American Society for the Prevention of Cruelty to Animals (ASPCA), *1:* 3
  circus animals, *1:* 29
  position on ALF methods, *1:* 11
American War of Independence (1775–1783), *2:* 233, 335–337; *3:* 471. *See also* United States
American westward expansion, *3:* 638, 639–640. *See also* United States
Americans for Responsible Solutions, *2:* 248
Americans with Disabilities Act (ADA), *2:* 277, 280–283
Amherst, NY, Operation Rescue protests, *3:* 562–568
Amnesty International, *3:* 474
Anarchists, *1:* 213–214
Ancient Greece
  free speech, *1:* 172
  slavery, *3:* 617–619
Anderson, John Ward, *1:* 185

Andry, Manuel, *3:* 625–627
Angel Action, *2:* 449–451, 449 (ill.), 451
Anielewicz, Mordechai, *3:* 605
Animal cruelty, *1:* 4
Animal experimentation, *1:* 7–11. See also **Animal rights**
Animal Liberation: A New Ethics for Our Treatment of Animals (1975), *1:* 3–4
Animal Liberation Front (ALF), *1:* 7–11
    activists, *1:* 10 (ill.)
    debate over methods, *1:* 11
    founding, *1:* 8
    use of arson, *1:* 10–11
Animal rights, *1:* **1–33**, 6 (ill.), 10 (ill.), 13 (ill.), 17 (ill.), 23 (ill.), 24 (ill.)
    Bilbao Anti-bullfighting Protest (2010), *1:* 12–18, 17 (ill.)
    Blackfish Documentary and SeaWorld Protests (2013-2014), *1:* 25–31
    Circus animals, *1:* 5, 29, 29 (ill.)
    Global March for Elephants and Rhinos, *1:* 18–25, 24 (ill.)
    Greenpeace and whaling, *1:* 22–23, 23 (ill.)
    ongoing fight for, *1:* 4–5
    PETA antifur campaign, *1:* 12–13, 13 (ill.)
    protests, *1:* 5–7
    UCR Lab Raid (1985), *1:* 7–11
Animal rights activists, *1:* 4
    ALF, *1:* 10 (ill.)
    anti-fur campaign, *1:* 12–13
    SeaWorld protests, *1:* 25–26
    UCR lab raid, *1:* 7–11
Animal rights movement
    history, *1:* 1–7
    modern, *1:* 3–4
Animal rights organizations, *1:* 2–3
Animal Welfare Act of 1966, *1:* 3
Anima-Naturalis, *1:* 17, 17 (ill.)
Anniston, Alabama, *1:* 56
Anthony, Susan B., *3:* 697 (ill.), 713
Anti-abortion laws, *3:* 552–553, 561, 580
Anti-abortion protesters, *3:* 558, 564 (ill.), 567 (ill.)
Anti-Catholicism, *2:* 313
Anti-Defamation League (ADL), *2:* 446
Antifa, *3:* 542

Anti-fur campaign, *1:* 12–13, 13 (ill.)
Anti-gay laws. See also **LGBTQ rights**
    protests against in Russia, *2:* 455 (ill.)
    Russia, *2:* 454–455
    United States, *2:* 432
Anti-gay protests
    counterprotests, *2:* 448, 449–451
    Westboro Baptist Church, *2:* 448, 449–451, 451
Anti-immigrant riots, *2:* 328–329, 329 (ill.)
Anti-Islam movement, *2:* 322–323
Anti-migrant protests
    Dresden, Germany, *2:* 321, 323 (ill.)
    Warsaw, Poland, *2:* 323
Anti-slavery Day, *3:* 647
Anti-slavery petitions, *3:* 628–634
Anti-war protests, *3:* **651–692**, 656 (ill.), 660 (ill.), 667 (ill.), 668 (ill.), 679 (ill.), 674 (ill.), 679 (ill.), 682 (ill.), 686 (ill.). See also Pacifists
    burning draft cards, *3:* 666–667, 667 (ill.)
    Candlelight Vigils against Invasion of Iraq (2003), *3:* 676–683, 682 (ill.)
    Democratic National Convention (DNC) (1968), *3:* 656 (ill.)
    International Congress of Women, *3:* 657–663, 660 (ill.)
    Iraq War (2003–2011), *3:* 657, 682 (ill.)
    Manning, Chelsea, and WikiLeaks, *3:* 684–690, 686 (ill.)
    One Thousand Coffins Protest (2004), *3:* 678–679, 679 (ill.)
    Student Armband Protest of Vietnam War (1965–1969), *3:* 663–668, 668 (ill.)
    United States, *3:* 653–657
    Vietnam War (1954–1975), *3:* 655–656, 663–668, 669–676
AOSIS (Alliance of Small Island States), *1:* 146, 147
APA (American Psychiatric Association), *2:* 432
Apartheid, *3:* 531, 534, 539. See also Desegregation/Segregation; Racial discrimination
Apprentices, *2:* 395
Arab Spring, *1:* 90, 120, 219; *3:* 486–493. See also **Political/Government uprisings**
    Bahrain, *3:* 489
    Egypt, *3:* 495
    Libya, *3:* 489–490

GENERAL INDEX

origins, *3:* 487–488
spread of, *3:* 489–490
Syria, *3:* 491–493, 492 (ill.)
Tunisia, *2:* 318–319
Yemen, *3:* 488–489
Argentina, March against Monsanto, *1:* 228
Aristophanes, *3:* 651–652
Arizona, mass shooting, *2:* 248
Arkansas, school integration, *1:* 47–52
Armenia
   genocide survivors, *2:* 298–300, 299
   history, *2:* 297–298
Armenian Genocide Protests (2015), *2:* 297–302, 301 (ill.). *See also* Genocide; **Human rights**
Army of God, *3:* 558
ARRA (United States. American Recovery and Reinvestment Act), *1:* 113
Arson, *1:* 10–11
Aryan race, *3:* 598–599
Asia. *See also* Specific Asian countries
   independence movements, *2:* 339–340
   use of rhino horn, *1:* 19
Asia for Educators, *3:* 569
Asner, Ed, *3:* 560
ASPCA (American Society for the Prevention of Cruelty to Animals), *1:* 3
   circus animals, *1:* 29
   position on ALF methods, *1:* 11
Assad, Bashar al-, *2:* 319; *3:* 487, 491–492
Assange, Julian, *3:* 685, 687
Assassination attempts, Hitler, Adolf, *3:* 590–591
Assault weapons, *2:* 234–235
Athens (city state), *1:* 172
Athletes, protests by, *3:* 516–517
Atkins v. Virginia, *2:* 285
Atlantic, *1:* 198
ATSIC (Aboriginal and Torres Strait Islander Commission), *2:* 379
Attica Prison Riot (1971), *2:* 270–276, 274 (ill.). *See also* **Human rights**
   investigation and outcome, *2:* 275–276
   manifesto of demands, *2:* 273
   prisoner conditions, *2:* 271–272
Austerity measures, Spain, *1:* 116–122, 117–118, 121

Austin, TX, March to Abolish the Death Penalty, *2:* 287
Australia
   aboriginals, *2:* 365–366, 375–379
   land rights protests, *2:* 375–379
   pro-migrant rallies, *2:* 318–325
Australia Day, *2:* 365–366, 375, 376–377
Australian aboriginals, *2:* 365–366, 375–379
Automobile industry, working conditions, *2:* 408–409
AWOC (Agricultural Workers Organizing Committee), *2:* 418
Axis Powers, *3:* 585

B

Background checks, *2:* 236, 252. *See also* **Gun control/Gun rights**
   federal law, *2:* 253
   gun shows, *2:* 257
   private sales, *2:* 256
   Washington (state), *2:* 253–254
Baez, Joan, *1:* 68, 198, 199 (ill.); *3:* 670
Bahrain, Arab Spring, *3:* 489
Baladi campaign, *3:* 699, 714–718, 716 (ill.). *See also* **Women's rights**
   goals of, *3:* 716–717
   leaders, *3:* 716 (ill.)
Balch, Emily G., *3:* 660
Bald and Golden Eagle Protection Act, *1:* 135
Baldwin, James, *1:* 68
Baldwin-Felts, *2:* 410
Banks, Dennis, *2:* 372, 374, 390–391
Banksy, *1:* 212, 212 (ill.)
Banned books, *1:* 180. *See also* Censorship
Baptist War (1831–1832), *3:* 634–638. *See also* **Slavery**
Barbagelata, John, *2:* 443
Bassey, Nnimmo, *1:* 148
Bates, Berke, M.M., *3:* 543
Bates, Daisy, *1:* 50–51
Battle in Seattle, World Trade Organization Protests (1999), *1:* 209–216, 214 (ill.). *See also* **Globalization**

Battle of Blair Mountain (1921), *2:* 410–411
Battle of Matewan, *2:* 410
Battle of Stalingrad (1943), *3:* 594–595, 609. *See also* World War II (1939–1945)
Bavaud, Maurice, *3:* 590–591
Bear Runner, Oscar, *2:* 374 (ill.)
Bearbaiting, *1:* 2
Beijing, China, Tiananmen Square protests, *3:* 473–478, 476 (ill.)
Belarus, human rights protests, *2:* 270
Belo Monte Dam, *2:* 381, 384
Belvis, Segundo Ruiz, *2:* 344–345
Ben Ali, Zine El-Abidine, *3:* 488, 495
Bergh, Henry, *1:* 3
Berlin, Germany
    division of, *3:* 480
    fall of the Berlin Wall (1989), *3:* 478–486
Berlin Wall, *3:* 483 (ill.)
    building of, *3:* 482–483
    fall of, *3:* 485–486
    history, *3:* 478–479
    Reagan, Ronald speech, *3:* 484–485
Bernard, Sheila C., *3:* 530–531
Betances, Ramón Emeterio, *2:* 344–345, 345 (ill.)
Bhopal, India
    torch rally, *1:* 136 (ill.)
    toxic chemical spills, *1:* 136
Bhotmange family, *2:* 293–294, 296
Bialystok Ghetto, Poland, *3:* 607
Bias, danger of, *1:* 167
Bible, *2:* 314–316
Biden, Joe, *2:* 250
Big Pharma, *1:* 226–227, 227 (ill.)
Biko, Steve, *3:* 532–533
Bilbao (Spain) Anti-bullfighting Protest (2010), *1:* 12–18, 17 (ill.). *See also* **Animal rights**
bin Laden, Osama, *3:* 681
Binghamton, NY, Operation Rescue protests, *3:* 563
Birmingham, AL
    desegregation, *1:* 62
    Freedom Rides, *1:* 56, 57
Birth control, *3:* 550. *See also* One child policy; **Reproductive rights**
    access to information, *3:* 553, 575
    China, *3:* 568–574

    health insurance plans and, *3:* 556
    laws limiting, *3:* 555
    oral contraceptives, *3:* 558–559
Birth rate, China, *3:* 569, 573
Bisexuals. *See* LGBTQ people
Black armbands, *3:* 664, 665
Black consciousness movement, *3:* 532–533
Black Lives Matter, *2:* 244; *3:* 515, 539
    demonstrators, *3:* 540 (ill.)
    origins, *3:* 540–544
Black Panthers, *2:* 239–245, 240–241, 243 (ill.)
Blackfish (2013), *1:* 4–5, 25–31, 28, 30
Blair Mountain, Battle of (1921), *2:* 410–411
Blake, James F., *1:* 44–45
Blankenship, Geraldine Green, *2:* 413
Blasphemy, *1:* 183
Blow, Charles M., *1:* 196
Blow, Tahj, *1:* 196
Blowouts, Mexican American students, *1:* 77–82
Blue Star Boy, Suzanne, *2:* 247–249
Bly, Nellie, *2:* 278, 278 (ill.)
Boehner, John, *1:* 115
Boko Haram, *3:* 700, 722–723
Bolívar, Simón, *2:* 338, 338 (ill.)
Book burning. *See also* Censorship; **Free speech**
    Alamagordo, New Mexico, *1:* 181 (ill.)
    Harry Potter (book series), *1:* 175, 177–183, 181 (ill.)
    history, *1:* 178–179
    Mayan texts, *1:* 178
    Nazi Germany, *1:* 179
    protests against in Alamagordo, *1:* 182
Boston Harbor, *2:* 337 (ill.)
Boston Tea Party (1773), *1:* 99, 111–112; *2:* 336–337, 337 (ill.); *3:* 471
Bouazizi, Mohamed, *3:* 487–488
Boutilier v. Immigration and Naturalization Service, *2:* 432
Boycotts. *See also* Protests
    defined, *1:* 35
    Delano Grape Strike and Boycott, *2:* 414–422, 421 (ill.)
    farm produce, *1:* 78–79
    Great American, *1:* 88
    Japan, *1:* 126–127

GENERAL INDEX

Montgomery Bus Boycott (1955–1956), *1:* 35, 36 (ill.)
NCAA, of North Carolina, *2:* 460–461
North Carolina, *2:* 461–462
South African products, *3:* 538
Boynton v. Virginia, 1: 55
Brady, James, *2:* 236
Brady Campaign to Prevent Gun Violence, *2:* 236–237, 250
Brady Handgun Violence Prevention Act, *2:* 236–237, 253
Brancheau, Dawn, *1:* 26, 27 (ill.)
Brando, Marlon, *1:* 68; *2:* 375
Brazil
    Malê Revolt of 1835, *3:* 626–627
    Preservation of Amazon Rain Forest Awareness Campaign, *2:* 379–384
Bressler, Isak, *1:* 215
Brexit, *1:* 103–104, 103 (ill.), 122–129, 124 (ill.). *See also* **Economic discontent**
    demonstrations, *1:* 103 (ill.), 124 (ill.), 125–128
    EU anniversary demonstration, *1:* 127–128
    May, Theresa, speech, *1:* 128–129
    referendum, *1:* 124–125
Bridges, Ruby, *1:* 53, 53 (ill.)
Bring Back Our Girls, *3:* 722–723
    demonstrators, *3:* 723 (ill.)
    Obama, Michelle, speech, *3:* 700–701
Britches, *1:* 8, 9
Britches (1986), *1:* 9
British colonies, *2:* 336–337. *See also* Colonization; United Kingdom
    Australia, *2:* 376
    Hong Kong, *3:* 499
    India, *2:* 347–349
    women's rights, *3:* 693–695
British East India Company (EIC), *2:* 347–348
British Raj, *2:* 348–349
Brock, Jack, *1:* 178, 181–182
Brotherhood of Sleeping Car Porters, *1:* 64
Brown, John, *3:* 640–643, 640 (ill.), 642 (ill.)
    anti-slavery activity in Kansas, *3:* 640
    Douglass, Frederick speech, *3:* 641
    Harpers Ferry Raid, *3:* 641–643, 642 (ill.)
Brown, Minnijean, *1:* 50, 51

Brown v. Board of Education, 1: 38–39, 49
BUC (Buffalo United for Choice), *3:* 565
Buchanan, James, *3:* 642
Buenos Aires, Argentina, March against Monsanto, *1:* 228
Buffalo, NY, Operation Rescue protests, *3:* 562–568
Buffalo United for Choice (BUC), *3:* 565
Bull Moose Party, *3:* 710
Bullbaiting, *1:* 1–2
Bullfighting, *1:* 6, 12–13, 14–15 (ill.)
    arguments against, *1:* 15
    Bilbao, Spain, protest, *1:* 16–18, 17 (ill.)
    interview with former bullfighter, *1:* 16
Burgdorf, Robert L., Jr., *2:* 282
Burma. *See* Myanmar
Burns, Lucy, *3:* 710
Burwell v. Hobby Lobby, 3: 555
Bush, George H.W., *2:* 281; *3:* 478
Bush, George W., *1:* 112
    position on reproductive rights, *3:* 561
    protests at RNC, *3:* 678–679
    speech on Iraq invasion, *3:* 680–681

C

Cacerolaza protests, *1:* 106–107. *See also* **Economic discontent**
Caesar, Julius, *3:* 469, 469 (ill.)
Cairo, Egypt, Tahrir Square Protests (2011), *3:* 495–498, 496 (ill.)
Calderón, Felipe, *1:* 91, 94–95
Calhoun, John C., *1:* 195
California. *See also* East Los Angeles, CA; Los Angeles, CA
    Black Panthers protest Mulford Act, *2:* 239–245, 243 (ill.)
    Delano Grape Strike and Boycott (1965–1970), *2:* 414–422, 421 (ill.)
    occupation of Alcatraz (1969–1970), *2:* 370–371, 371 (ill.)
    protest against Trump travel bans, *2:* 327, 330 (ill.)
    San Bernardino terrorist attack, *2:* 328
    San Diego SeaWorld protest, *1:* 30

California. Mulford Act, *2:* 242–243, 244
California. Senate. Resolution No. 16 (2017), *2:* 327
California redwoods, *1:* 152
California State Capitol, Sacramento, CA, *2:* 239–245, 243 (ill.)
Cameron, David, *1:* 124–125; *2:* 321
Camus, Albert, *1:* 93
Canada
    indigenous peoples, *2:* 365 (ill.), 382
    land rights protests, *2:* 365 (ill.), 382
Candlelight Vigils against Invasion of Iraq (2003), *3:* 676–683, 682 (ill.). *See also* **War protests**
Capital punishment, *2:* 284–285. *See also* **Human rights**
    declining use, 289
    history, *2:* 285
    legal challenges to, *2:* 285–286
    support and opposition, *2:* 286–287
Capitalism, *1:* 212
Capitol Crawl (1990), *2:* 276–284, 282 (ill.). *See also* **Human rights**
Carlos, John, *3:* 516, 517 (ill.)
Carpenter, Mary Chapin, *3:* 729
Carson, Rachel, *1:* 135
Carter, Jimmy, *1:* 143; *2:* 280–281
Cartoons, of Muhammad, *1:* 184–187
The Cartoons That Shook the World (2009), *1:* 184, 187
CAS International, *1:* 17, 17 (ill.)
The Case for Animal Rights (1983), *1:* 4
Casper, WY, anti-gay protests by WBC, *2:* 448
Caste systems, *2:* 290–291
    discrimination, *2:* 296
    India, *2:* 290–297
Castro, Fidel, *1:* 106
Castro, Sal, *1:* 80, 82
Castro Village Association, *2:* 442
Catalonia, Spain, *1:* 17–18
Catholic Church, *1:* 173
Cats, animal testing, *1:* 10 (ill.)
Catt, Carrie Chapman, *3:* 710, 711
La Causa, *1:* 78
Cavanagh, Jerome, *3:* 528
CCP (Chinese Communist Party), *1:* 105, 107

Censorship, *1:* 171. *See also* Banned books; Book burning
    Catholic Church, *1:* 173
    Nazi Germany, *1:* 179
CERCLA (United States. Comprehensive Environmental Response, Compensation, and Liability Act), *1:* 143
Chaillot Prize, *3:* 716 (ill.)
Chaney, James Earl, *1:* 58, 58 (ill.)
Charlie Hebdo, *1:* 176, 187, 190–191
    publication of Muhammad cartoons, *1:* 191
    terrorist attack on offices, *1:* 191
Charlotte Magazine, *2:* 462, 463
Charlottesville Protests (2017), *3:* 542–543, 543 (ill.). *See also* **Racial conflict**
Chávez, César
    Delano Grape Strike and Boycott (1965–1970), *2:* 414–415, 419–421, 421 (ill.)
    Hispanic and Latino civil rights, *1:* 75–76, 78–79, 79 (ill.), 86
    state holiday, *1:* 79
Chechnya, *2:* 454–455
Chemical weapons, use in Syria, *3:* 492
Chen Guangcheng, *3:* 571
Chernobyl nuclear accident, *1:* 136–137
Cherokees, *2:* 386–387
Chicago, IL
    DNC anti-war protests, *3:* 656 (ill.)
    Haymarket Square Riot, *2:* 418–419
Chicano movement, *1:* 76, 79
Child, Lydia Maria, *3:* 697 (ill.)
Child labor, *2:* 393–394, 400–401, 400 (ill.), 402–403, 403 (ill.). *See also* **Labor rights**
    Africa, *2:* 399
    labor laws, *2:* 407
    Mother Jones's "Children's Crusade," *2:* 399–407, 406 (ill.)
    NYC protest of 1909, *2:* 402–403, 403 (ill.)
    textile mills, *2:* 400 (ill.)
Children
    cruelty to animals, *1:* 4
    disabled, *2:* 277–278
    Love Canal protests, *1:* 143 (ill.)
    runaway, *3:* 645

GENERAL INDEX

Children's Crusade of 1903, *2:* 399–407, 406 (ill.).
See also **Labor rights**
Chile, *Cacerolaza* protests, *1:* 106–107
China, *1:* 103
   birth rate, *3:* 569, 573
   book burning, *1:* 178
   collective farms and communes, *1:* 108–110
   Cultural Revolution (1966), *1:* 108
   economic reforms, *1:* 110–111
   farmers' secret agreement, *1:* 105–111, 109 (ill.)
   fur production, *1:* 12, 13
   history, *1:* 105–108
   ivory trade, *1:* 25
   labor rights, *2:* 398
   LGBTQ rights, *2:* 452–453, 458
   one child policy, *3:* 568–574
   relationship with Hong Kong, *3:* 499–500
   rhino horn, *1:* 19
   sanctions by United States, *3:* 478
   Shanghai Pride Festival (2009), *2:* 452–458, 456 (ill.)
   Tiananmen Square protests, *3:* 473–478, 476 (ill.)
   transgender rights, *2:* 452–453
China Daily, 2: 455, 457
Chinese Classification of Mental Disorders, 2: 452
Chinese Communist Party (CCP), *1:* 105, 107
Chinese farmers
   one child policy, *3:* 570
   secret agreement, *1:* 105–111, 109 (ill.)
Chinese immigrants. See also Immigrants and immigration
   riots against, Denver, Colorado, *2:* 328–329, 329 (ill.)
   United States, *2:* 307, 415–416
Chinese traditional medicine, *1:* 19
Chinese workers, working conditions, *2:* 398
Christ Community Church, Alamagordo, New Mexico, *1:* 175, 177–183
Christakis, Erika, *1:* 195, 197–198, 200
Christakis, Nicholas, *1:* 197–198, 200
Christian X, King of Denmark, *3:* 600
Christmas Rebellion (1831–1832), *3:* 634–638.
   See also **Slavery**

Cigar workers, *1:* 85 (ill.)
   strikes, *1:* 84
   violence against, *1:* 84
Circus animals, *1:* 5, 29, 29 (ill.)
CITES (Convention on International Trade in Endangered Species of Wild Fauna and Flora), *1:* 21
Citizen journalism, *3:* 490–491
Citizens for a Sound Economy, *1:* 111
Citrin, Jack, *1:* 177
City of Hope National Medical Center, *1:* 9
Civic Forum, *2:* 355
Civil disobedience, *1:* 139. See also Nonviolent resistance
   "I Will Not Comply" Rally, *2:* 254
   Indian independence movement, *2:* 346–347, 349, 350
Civil rights. See also **African American civil rights; Free speech; Hispanic and Latino civil rights; Human rights; Indigenous peoples' rights; LGBTQ rights**
   defined, *1:* 71
   DOJ lawsuit against North Carolina, *2:* 463
   farm workers, *1:* 78–79
   summary of laws, *1:* 41
Civil rights, African American. See **African American civil rights**
Civil rights, Hispanic and Latino. See **Hispanic and Latino civil rights**
Civil Rights Act of 1957, *1:* 41
Civil Rights Act of 1960, *1:* 41
Civil Rights Act of 1964, *1:* 40, 41, 69
Civil Rights Act of 1968, *1:* 40, 41
Civil rights movement, *1:* 35–36, 38–42, 42
   Freedom Rides, *1:* 54–59, 56 (ill.)
   Hispanic and Latino, *1:* 75–76
   legislation, *1:* 40–41
   origins, *1:* 38–39
   resulting legislation, *1:* 40–41
   United States, *3:* 472
Civilian casualties, *3:* 684, 686
Cleary, John, *3:* 674 (ill.)
Cleveland, Ohio, *1:* 135–136
Climate change. See also **Environment**; Global warming
   COP 15, *1:* 144–145
   greenhouse gases, *1:* 137, 145, 157
   island nations, *1:* 157–158
   US attitudes about, *1:* 164, 164 (ill.)

Climate deniers, *1:* 165–166
Climate Justice Action (CJA), *1:* 145, 146
Climate Justice Now (CJN), *1:* 146
Climate refugees, *1:* 159
Clinton, Bill, *1:* 52
    Gay and Lesbian Pride Month, *2:* 441
    gays in military policy, *2:* 434
    gun control laws, *2:* 253
    position on reproductive rights, *3:* 561
    support of gun control sit-in, *2:* 259
    WTO meeting, *1:* 211
Clinton, Hillary Rodham, *2:* 426; *3:* 578, 699, 725–726
Clovis, Sam, *1:* 168
Coal miners and coal mining
    environmental impact, *1:* 159
    global warming, *1:* 159
    strikes, *2:* 410–411
    working conditions, *2:* 312
Cockfighting, *1:* 2
Code Noir, *3:* 624
Coffee, Linda, *3:* 576
Cold War (1945–1991), *1:* 178; *3:* 479, 483, 484, 486, 655
Collective farms, *1:* 108–110
Collin, Frank, *1:* 189 (ill.)
Collins, Susan, *2:* 260
Colonization, *1:* 204; *2:* 335. *See also* British colonies; French colonies; Portuguese colonies; Spanish colonies
    impact on indigenous peoples, *2:* 361, 375–376
    impact on Native Americans, *2:* 362–363, 386–387
    North America, *1:* 72
    prison colonies, *2:* 376
    South America, *1:* 72; *3:* 533
Colorado, A Day without Immigrants protests, *1:* 88
Columbus, Christopher, *2:* 343
Comfort Women (Korean), protests, *2:* 269 (ill.)
Communes, *1:* 108–110
Communism and communists, *2:* 352; *3:* 587, 663–664, 669
    Chile, *1:* 106
    China, *1:* 107–108
    resistance to Nazis, *3:* 587–588

Compensated Emancipation Act, *3:* 633, 633 (ill.)
Comprehensive Environmental Response, Compensation, and Liability Act (CERCLA), *1:* 143
Compton, Jim, *1:* 215
Comstock Act, *3:* 553, 575
Conception, *3:* 562
Confederate symbols, *3:* 515–517
Congress of Racial Equality (CORE), *1:* 54–57
    Berkeley free speech movement, *1:* 198
    sit-ins, *1:* 60–61, 62
Congressional Union for Woman Suffrage, *3:* 710
Connecticut, Sandy Hook mass shooting, *2:* 246–247
Conscientious objectors, *3:* 652–653
Constitution of India, *2:* 292
Consumerism, *1:* 212
Contraceptives, *3:* 549
Convention on International Trade in Endangered Species of Wild Fauna and Flora (CITES), *1:* 21
Cooper, Roy, *2:* 462, 463
COP 15 (Conference of the Parties 15), *1:* 144–145, 145–146, 146–148. *See also* **Environment**
Copenhagen, Denmark, protests (2009), *1:* 144–151, 150 (ill.). *See also* **Environment**
    clashes with police, *1:* 148–150
    protest groups plan, *1:* 146–148
    response of Danish government, *1:* 147–150
Copernicus, Nicolaus, *1:* 173
CORE (Congress of Racial Equality), *1:* 54–57
    Berkeley free speech movement, *1:* 198
    sit-ins, *1:* 60–61, 62
Cornell Center on the Death Penalty Worldwide, *2:* 284
Coulter, Ann, *1:* 176
Cowperthwaite, Gabriela, *1:* 26–27
Cree First Nations, *2:* 382. *See also* Indigenous peoples
Creedence Clearwater Revival, *3:* 670
Criminal justice system, human rights abuses, *2:* 270–271
Cruz, Sophie, *3:* 729
C-SPAN, *2:* 259
Cuba, independence movements, *2:* 338–339
Cuernavaca, Mexico, *1:* 91 (ill.), 93–94
Cullen, H. Jay, *3:* 542–543

U•X•L Protests, Riots, and Rebellions: Civil Unrest in the Modern World

Cullors, Patrice, *3:* 541
Cultural exchange, *1:* 206
Cultural Revolution (1966), *1:* 108; *3:* 473. *See also* China
Cultural studies, Los Angeles Unified School District, *1:* 82
Cuomo, Mario, *2:* 382
Cuyahoga River, *1:* 135–136
Cyrus the Great, King of Persia, *2:* 265
Czech Republic, *2:* 357–358
Czech resistance (World War II), *3:* 589
Czechoslovakia
    independence movements, *2:* 341–342, 352–358
    invasion of 1968, *2:* 354 (ill.)
    under Soviet Union, *2:* 353–354

D

Dakota Access Pipeline (DAPL), *1:* 140; *2:* 384, 385
    Native American opposition, *1:* 144; 366–367, 367 (ill.), 384–391, 388 (ill.)
    Trump, Donald, *2:* 367
Dakota Access Pipeline (DAPL) Protest (2016–2017), *2:* 366–367, 367 (ill.), 384–391, 388 (ill.). *See also* **Indigenous peoples' rights**
    Dennis Banks, *2:* 390–391
    Native Americans, *2:* 367 (ill.), 388 (ill.)
Dalit Protests in India (2006), *2:* 290–297, 295 (ill.). *See also* **Human rights**
Dalits, *2:* 290, 291–293, 295 (ill.)
    continuing discrimination, *2:* 296–297
    murder of family in Khairlanji, India, *2:* 293–294
    violence against, *2:* 293–294, 297
Dallas, TX, Huey P. Newton Gun Club demonstrations, *2:* 244
Dams
    land rights protests by Cree First Nations, *2:* 382
    land rights protests by Kayapo, *2:* 379–384
Dandi March, *2:* 346–352, 351 (ill.)
Danish Jews, *3:* 597, 601–602
Danish resistance (World War II), *3:* 589, 597–602
DAPL (Dakota Access Pipeline), *1:* 140; *2:* 384, 385
    Native American opposition, *1:* 144
    Trump, Donald, *2:* 367

DAPL (Dakota Access Pipeline) Protest (2016–2017), *2:* 366–367, 367 (ill.), 384–391, 388 (ill.). *See also* **Indigenous peoples' rights**
    Dennis Banks, *2:* 390–391
    Native Americans, *2:* 367 (ill.)
Dart, Justin, Jr., *2:* 282
Davis, Sammy, Jr., *1:* 68
Davison, Emily Wilding, *3:* 705, 705 (ill.)
A Day without a Mexican (2004), *1:* 86
A Day without a Woman (2017), *3:* 731
A Day without Immigrants, *1:* 83–89, 88 (ill.)
DDT, *1:* 135
De Klerk, F.W., *3:* 539
Death camps, *3:* 585–586, 587, 604–605, 608–609
Death penalty, *2:* 284–285. *See also* **Human rights**
    declining use, *2:* 289
    history, *2:* 285
    legal challenges to, *2:* 285–286
    support and opposition, *2:* 286–287
Declaration of Independence, *2:* 337
Declaration of Sentiments, *3:* 708, 709 (ill.)
Declaration of the Rights of Animals, *1:* 3
Declaration of the Rights of Man and of the Citizen, *2:* 267
Defense of Marriage Act, *2:* 438
Deforestation, *1:* 138
DeGeneres, Ellen, *2:* 434
Delano (CA) Grape Strike and Boycott (1965–1970), *2:* 414–422, 421 (ill.). *See also* **Labor rights**
Democracia Real Ya (DRY), *1:* 116, 120
Democracy, *3:* 467, 493, 669
Democratic Congressional Representatives Sit-in for Gun control (2016), *2:* 256–260, 259 (ill.). *See also* **Gun control/Gun rights**
Democratic National Convention (DNC), *3:* 564, 656 (ill.)
Deng, Xiaoping, *1:* 108, 110
Denmark
    Holocaust Resistance in Denmark (1943), *3:* 597–602, 601 (ill.)
    Nazi occupation, *3:* 598–600
    Nazi occupation ends, *3:* 602
    protests against *Jyllands-Posten* cartoons, *1:* 183–188
    response to Copenhagen protests, *1:* 147–148

Denver, CO, A Day without Immigrants protests, *1:* 88
Deportations
    to death camps, *3:* 604–605
    to Mexico by the United States, *1:* 74
Derby Day Protest (1913), *3:* 705
Des Moines, IA, Vietnam War protest (1965–1969), *3:* 663–668
Desegregation/Segregation, *1:* 38–39, 42. *See also* Apartheid
    Birmingham, Alabama, *1:* 62
    Little Rock, Arkansas, *1:* 47–52
    national defense jobs, *1:* 64
Desertification, *1:* 138
Deslondes, Charles, *3:* 625–627
Detroit Riots (MI) (1967), *3:* 524–530, 528 (ill.). *See also* **Racial conflict**
    aftermath, *3:* 529–530
    origins in "blind pig," *3:* 525
    Romney, George, interview, *3:* 530–531
Developing countries, advantages of globalization, *1:* 206
Development, Relief, and Education for Alien Minors Act (United States. DREAM Act), *1:* 89
Diagnostic and Statistical Manual of Mental Disorders, *2:* 432
Dickinson, Anna E., *3:* 697 (ill.)
Dictators, *3:* 467–468
Disability rights, *2:* 276–284. *See also* **Human rights**
    ADA passage, *2:* 280–283
    legislation, *2:* 278–279
    ongoing efforts, *2:* 283–284
    organizations, *2:* 279–280
Disabled children, education, *2:* 277–278
Discrimination. *See also* Racial discrimination
    against LGBTQ people, *2:* 431, 432, 436, 454–455
    Mexican American students, *1:* 79–80
District of Columbia. *See* Washington, D.C.
DNC (Democratic National Convention), *3:* 564, 656 (ill.)
"Don't Ask, Don't Tell," *2:* 434, 435
Douglass, Frederick, *3:* 638, 641
Dowell, Denzil, *2:* 241
Draft cards, burning, *3:* 666–667, 667 (ill.)

Draft (military)
    United States Civil War, *3:* 526, 654
    Vietnam War, *3:* 666
Drag shows, *2:* 457
DREAM Act, *1:* 89
Dresden, Germany, anti-migrant protests, *2:* 321, 323 (ill.)
Drug trade
    Mexico, *1:* 75, 90, 91
    violence, *1:* 91–92
DRY (Democracia Real Ya), *1:* 116, 120
Dubček, Alexander, *2:* 353
Dublin, Ireland, Easter Rebellion (1916), *3:* 480–481, 481 (ill.)
Duckwitz, Georg Ferdinand, *3:* 600–601
Duncan, Arne, *2:* 249
Dunlop, Marion Wallace, *3:* 704, 706
Durant, William C., *2:* 408
Dutilleux, Jean-Pierre, *2:* 381–382
Dylan, Bob, *1:* 68; *3:* 670

E

Earth Day, *1:* 136, 164; *3:* 730–731
Earth Liberation Front (ELF), *1:* 11
Earthquakes, *1:* 154
East Los Angeles, CA. *See also* California; Los Angeles, CA
    blowouts, *1:* 77–82
    commemoration of East LA blowouts, *1:* 81 (ill.)
    Mexican American students, *1:* 77
Easter Rebellion (1916), *3:* 480–481, 481 (ill.). *See also* **Political/Government uprisings**
Eckford, Elizabeth, *1:* 50–51, 52 (ill.)
Eckhardt, Christopher, *3:* 664, 665
Economic discontent, *1:* **99–131**, 103 (ill.), 109 (ill.), 114 (ill.), 119 (ill.), 121 (ill.), 124 (ill.). *See also* **Globalization**
    Brexit, *1:* 103, 103 (ill.), 122–129, 124 (ill.)
    Cacerolazo Protests in Chile (1971), *1:* 106–107
    15-M Movement (2011), *1:* 116–122, 121 (ill.)
    Porkulus Protests, Tea Party (2009–2010), *1:* 111–116, 114 (ill.)
    Rice Riots of 1918 (Japan), *1:* 126–127

GENERAL INDEX

Secret Document of the Farmers of Xiaogang (1978), *1:* 105–111, 109 (ill.)
student protests in France (May 1968), *1:* 118–119, 119 (ill.)
Economic inequality, *1:* 208
    protest against, *1:* 216–217
    Wall Street, *1:* 218
Ecoterrorism, *1:* 11. *See also* Terrorism
Education
    for disabled children, *2:* 277–278
    discrimination against Mexican American students, *1:* 79–80
    for girls and women, *3:* 718–724
Education for All Handicapped Children Act, *2:* 278
Educational Issues Coordinating Committee (EICC), *1:* 82
EEC (European Economic Community), *1:* 123
Egypt
    labor rights, *2:* 398
    post-revolution, *3:* 497–498
    Tahrir Square Protests (2011), *3:* 493–498, 495–498, 496 (ill.)
Egyptian Revolution (2011), *3:* 488, 493–498, 496 (ill.). *See also* **Political/Government uprisings**
EIA (United States. Energy Information Administration), *1:* 155
EIC (British East India Company), *2:* 347–348
EICC (Educational Issues Coordinating Committee), *1:* 82
8888 Uprising, Myanmar (1988), *3:* 502–503, 503 (ill.)
Eilperin, Juliet, *1:* 141
Eisenhower, Dwight D., *1:* 48, 52
El Rhazoui, Zineb, *1:* 194
Elections
    disputed, Iran, *3:* 490
    source of unrest in Hong Kong, *3:* 499–500
    US presidential (2016), *3:* 725–726
Elephants
    poaching, *1:* 18–19, 25
    population decline, *1:* 20–22
    postage stamp, *1:* 29 (ill.)
    in Ringling Bros. circus, *1:* 29, 29 (ill.)
ELF (Earth Liberation Front), *1:* 11

Elizabeth I, Queen of England, *1:* 173; *2:* 347
Elser, Georg Johann, *3:* 591
Emancipation Proclamation, *3:* 633
Emergency Economic Stabilization Act of 2008, *1:* 112
Emerson, Ralph Waldo, *2:* 387, 387 (ill.)
Encyclopedia of Environmental Issues, 3: 573
Endangered Species Act, *1:* 136
Energy Transfer Partners, *2:* 384, 385, 386–387
England. Bill of Rights, *1:* 173; *2:* 266–267
ENGOs (Environmental nongovernmental organizations), *1:* 146
Enlightenment, *2:* 265–267
Environment, *1:* **133–170**, 135 (ill.), 136 (ill.), 142 (ill.), 143 (ill.), 150 (ill.), 153 (ill.), 155 (ill.), 161 (ill.), 162 (ill.), 165 (ill.). *See also* Climate change; Global warming
    Copenhagen Protests (2009), *1:* 144–151, 150 (ill.)
    Forward on Climate Rally (2013), *1:* 139–144, 142 (ill.)
    Fukushima nuclear power protests, *1:* 160–161, 161 (ill.)
    Global Frackdown (2014), *1:* 151–156, 155 (ill.)
    Gore, Al, *1:* 148–149
    Hill, Julia "Butterfly," *1:* 152, 153 (ill.)
    human impact, *1:* 137–138
    Love Canal, NY, *1:* 136, 143, 143 (ill.)
    March for Science (2017), *1:* 163–168, 165 (ill.)
    Pacific Climate Warriors Blockade (2014), *1:* 157–163, 162 (ill.)
    21st century challenges, *1:* 137–138
Environmental movement
    history, *1:* 133–137
    methods, *1:* 138–139
Environmental nongovernmental organizations (ENGOs), *1:* 146
Environmentalists, *1:* 133, 138–139
EPA (United States. Environmental Protection Agency), *1:* 136
Equal pay, *3:* 728–729
Equal Rights Amendment (ERA), *3:* 558–559
Equanimal, *1:* 17, 17 (ill.)
Espionage, *2:* 285
Estonia, independence movements, *2:* 348
Ethnicity, *3:* 509

EU (European Union)
    exit of United Kingdom, *1:* 103–104, 122–129
    immigrants and immigration, *2:* 309–310
    refugee crisis, *2:* 324–325
    refugees, *2:* 319–321
Europe, pro-migrant rallies, *2:* 318–325, 324 (ill.)
European Court of Human Rights, *2:* 454
European Economic Community (EEC), *1:* 123
European Union (EU)
    exit of United Kingdom, *1:* 103–104, 122–129
    immigrants and immigration, *2:* 309–310
    refugee crisis, *2:* 324–325
    refugees, *2:* 319–321
Euroscepticism, *1:* 125
Eviction protests, *1:* 120
Evidence-based policies, *1:* 163–164
Executions
    declining use, 2890
    lethal injection, 2890
    Texas, *2:* 284

F

FACE Act (United States. Freedom of Access to Clinic Entrances Act), *3:* 568
Fair Housing Act of 1968, *1:* 40, 41
Fair Labor Standards Act of 1938, *2:* 397–398, 407
Fairchild, Morgan, *3:* 560
Fall of the Berlin Wall (1989), *3:* 478–486, 483 (ill.). *See also* **Political/Government uprisings**
Fallata, Iman, *3:* 716 (ill.)
Famines, *3:* 569
Farage, Nigel, *1:* 125
Farm workers. *See also* Workers
    civil rights, *1:* 78–79
    labor unions, *1:* 75–76
    Mexican, *1:* 75 (ill.)
    working conditions, *2:* 416
Fast Food Forward, *2:* 424, 425
Fast-food Workers' Strike (2012), *2:* 422–426, 424 (ill.). *See also* **Labor rights**
    global recognition, *2:* 425
    sit-ins, *2:* 425
Faubus, Orbal, *1:* 48, 50–52

Fawcett, Millicent, *3:* 703
FBI (United States. Federal Bureau of Investigation), *3:* 686–687, 725
Federal Assault Weapons Ban, *2:* 234–235
Federal Society of Journeymen Cordwainers, *2:* 396
Federalists, *1:* 175
Feld Entertainment, *1:* 29
Feminists, *3:* 558. *See also* **Women's rights**
Ferdinand II, King of Spain, *2:* 343
Ferrera, America, *3:* 729
Feudal societies, *3:* 469–470, 619–620
Fields, James Alex, *3:* 542
15-M Movement, *1:* 90, 116–122, 121 (ill.). *See also* **Economic discontent**
Fight for $15, *2:* 422
Fight to Stop Human Trafficking, *3:* 643–647. *See also* **Slavery**
Filipino workers, *2:* 416, 418–419. *See also* Workers
Final Solution, *3:* 608
Finding Dory, *1:* 28
Firearms Owners' Protection Act, *2:* 234
First Landing Day (Australia), *2:* 365–366, 375, 376–377
Fisher Body Plant No. 1, Flint, MI, *2:* 410
Fisher Body Plant No. 2, Flint, MI, *2:* 410
Fitz, Nicholas, *1:* 100
Flag burning, Palestinian students, *1:* 186 (ill.)
Flint (MI) Sit-Down Strike against General Motors (1936–1937), *2:* 407–414, 412 (ill.). *See also* **Labor rights**
Florida
    mass shootings at Pulse nightclub, *2:* 257
    Tea Party movement, *1:* 114 (ill.)
    Ybor City Cigar Strike (1931), *1:* 84
Floyd, John, *3:* 632
Fonda, Jane, *3:* 560
Food & Water Watch, *1:* 155
Food labeling, *1:* 229–230
Forced abortions, *3:* 571
Forced labor, *3:* 644–646
Forced sterilization, *3:* 571
Force-feeding, *3:* 702, 706, 713
Ford v. Wainwright, *2:* 285
Fort Myers, FL, Tea Party movement, *1:* 114 (ill.)

Forward on Climate Rally (2013), *1:* 139–144, 142 (ill.). *See also* **Environment**
Fossey, Dian, *1:* 20
Foundation Day (Australia), *2:* 365–366, 375, 376–377
Fox, Helen, *3:* 703–704
Fox, Maggie, *3:* 556
Fracking, *1:* 151–154; *2:* 385. *See also* **Environment**
    bans on, *1:* 156
    environmental impact, *1:* 154–155
    origins, *1:* 153–154
    toxic wastes, *1:* 153–154
France
    attack on *Charlie Hebdo* offices, *1:* 191
    student protests of 1968, *1:* 118–119, 119 (ill.)
Frantz (William) Elementary School, *1:* 53
Free blacks, *3:* 630–632. *See also* African Americans
Free speech, *1:* **171–202,** 177 (ill.), 181 (ill.), 186 (ill.), 189 (ill.), 190 (ill.), 192 (ill.), 197 (ill.), 199 (ill.). *See also* Civil rights
    Banned book list, *1:* 180
    Harry Potter Book Burning (2001), *1:* 177–183, 181 (ill.)
    history of, *1:* 171–174
    "Je Suis Charlie" protests (2015), *1:* 189–194, 192 (ill.)
    limits of, *1:* 171, 175–177
    Muslim protests against *Charlie Hebdo*, *1:* 190 (ill.), 193
    Muslim protests of Danish cartoons (2005–2008), *1:* 183–188, 186 (ill.)
    Nazi Book Burning, *1:* 179
    proposed Skokie neo-Nazi march, *1:* 188–189, 189 (ill.)
    religion and, *1:* 176, 183
    Supreme Court decisions, *3:* 667–668
    United States, *1:* 173–174
    University of California, Berkeley, *1:* 176–177, 177 (ill.), 198–199, 199 (ill.)
    Yale Student Protests (2015), *1:* 194–201, 197 (ill.)
Free Syrian Army, *3:* 492
Free trade. *See also* **Globalization**
    defined, *1:* 203
    opponents of, *1:* 211

Free trade agreements, *1:* 205–206
Freedom of Access to Clinic Entrances Act (FACE Act), *3:* 568
Freedom of religion, *2:* 265
Freedom of speech. *See* **Free speech**
Freedom Riders, *1:* 39, 56 (ill.)
Freedom Rides (1961), *1:* 39, 54–59, 56 (ill.). *See also* **African American civil rights**
    first ride, *1:* 56–57
    origins, *1:* 54–55
Freedom Sunday, *3:* 647
French colonies. *See also* Colonization
    Haitian Revolution (1791–1804), *3:* 625
    independence movements, *2:* 338
    slavery in, *3:* 624–625
French resistance (World War II), *3:* 589
French Revolution (1789–1799), *2:* 267; *3:* 471
French Student Protests of 1968, *1:* 118–119, 119 (ill.)
Friedan, Betty, *3:* 558, 728, 729 (ill.)
Friendship Junior College, *1:* 59, 61
Friendship Nine, *1:* 59, 61, 63
Frost, Robert, *1:* 149
Fryberg, Jaylen, *2:* 253
Fugitive Slave Law, *3:* 631
Fukushima nuclear power protests, *1:* 160–161, 161 (ill.)
Fulton, Sybrina, *3:* 545–546
Fur farms, *1:* 11
Furman v. Georgia, *2:* 285
Furs, PETA protests against, *1:* 12–13, 13 (ill.)

G

G20 Summit, Hamburg, Germany (2017), *1:* 208–209, 208 (ill.)
Gandhi, Mahatma, *1:* 78; *2:* 340–341, 341, 351 (ill.)
    Indian independence movement, *2:* 348–352
    Salt March, *2:* 341–342, 346–352, 351 (ill.)
    speech before the Salt March, *2:* 349
Gandhi, Mohandas. *See* Gandhi, Mahatma
Gandhi's Salt March (1930), *2:* 340–341, 346–352, 351 (ill.). *See also* **Independence movements**
Garfield High School, East LA, *1:* 81

Garner, Eric, *3:* 541–542, 544–545
Garner, Esaw, *3:* 546
Garza, Alicia, *3:* 541
Gasland (2010), *1:* 154
Gaulle, Charles de, *1:* 118–119
Gay and Lesbian Alliance against Defamation (GLAAD), *2:* 458
Gay and Lesbian Pride Month, *2:* 441
Gay pride
    parades, *2:* 441
    Shanghai Pride Festival, *2:* 452–458, 456 (ill.)
Gaye, Marvin, *3:* 670
Gays. *See* LGBTQ people
Gdansk Shipyard Strike, Poland (1980), *2:* 356–357, 357 (ill.)
Gender identity, *2:* 429, 435
Genderqueer, *2:* 429–430
General Motors Co. (GM)
    Flint Sit-Down Strike, *2:* 407–414, 412 (ill.)
    working conditions, *2:* 408–409
Genetically modified organisms (GMOs), *1:* 224
    food, *1:* 223
    labeling, *1:* 229–230
    seeds, *1:* 223
Genocide, *2:* 297, 300. *See also* Holocaust
George III, King of Great Britain, *2:* 376
Gerber, Henry, *2:* 432
German immigrants, *2:* 307. *See also* Immigrants and immigration
Germany. *See also* Nazi Germany
    anti-migrant protests, *2:* 321, 323 (ill.)
    Fukushima nuclear energy protests, *1:* 161 (ill.)
    Nazi resistance, *3:* 592–597
    nuclear energy policy, *1:* 161
    post-World War II division, *3:* 479–481
    reunification, *3:* 486
Gestapo, *3:* 592, 593, 594. *See also* Nazi Germany
Ghettos, *3:* 602
    Bialystok, Poland, *3:* 607
    Warsaw, Poland, *3:* 602–605
Ghost dance, *2:* 369, 369 (ill.)
Giffords, Gabrielle, *2:* 248, 248 (ill.)
Giumarra, John, Sr., *2:* 421 (ill.)
GLAAD (Gay and Lesbian Alliance against Defamation), *2:* 458

Glacier Point, Yosemite Valley, *1:* 135 (ill.)
Global Frackdown (2014), *1:* 151–156, 155 (ill.). *See also* **Environment**
Global March for Elephants and Rhinos (GMFER), *1:* 18–25, 24 (ill.). *See also* **Animal rights**
Global Recession of 2008, *1:* 219
    Spain, *1:* 104–105, 116–117
    United States, *1:* 112–113
Global Slavery Index, *3:* 623
Global warming, *1:* 145, 159. *See also* Climate change; **Environment**
Globalization, *1:* **203–231,** 208 (ill.), 212 (ill.), 214 (ill.), 222 (ill.), 227 (ill.), 228 (ill.). *See also* **Economic discontent**
    Banksy street art protests, *1:* 212, 212 (ill.)
    Battle in Seattle, World Trade Organization protests (1999), *1:* 209–216, 214 (ill.)
    benefits and disadvantages, *1:* 206–207
    Big Pharma, *1:* 226–227, 227 (ill.)
    history, *1:* 204–205
    March against Monsanto (2013), *1:* 223–230, 228 (ill.)
    Occupy Wall Street (2011), *1:* 216–222, 222 (ill.)
    21st century, *1:* 205–206
Glover, Danny, *3:* 678
Glyphosate, *1:* 224
GM (General Motors Co.)
    Flint Sit-Down Strike, *2:* 407–414, 412 (ill.)
    working conditions, *2:* 408–409
GMFER (Global March for Elephants and Rhinos), *1:* 18–25, 24 (ill.). *See also* **Animal rights**
GMOs (Genetically modified organisms), *1:* 224
    foods, *1:* 223
    labeling, *1:* 229–230
    seeds, *1:* 223
Goddard, Colin, *2:* 249–250
Goebbels, Joseph, *1:* 179
Goldsmith, Judy, *3:* 559–560
Goodman, Andrew, *1:* 58, 58 (ill.)
Gorbachev, Mikhail, *3:* 476, 478, 484, 485
Gore, Al, *1:* 148–149
Gorillas, *1:* 20
Gorsuch, Neil, *3:* 579
Govea, Jessica, *2:* 417
Graffiti, *1:* 212

GENERAL INDEX

Graves, Goddard C., *3:* 667 (ill.)
Gray, Freddie, *3:* 544
Gray, Nellie, *3:* 559
Gray, Vincent, *2:* 250
Great American Boycott, *1:* 88. *See also* Boycotts
Great Britain. Tea Act, *2:* 336–337
Great Depression, *1:* 74, 218; *2:* 409, 419
Great Recession. *See* Global Recession of 2008
Green, Ernest, *1:* 50, 52
Green, Jay J., *2:* 413
Greenhouse gases. *See also* **Environment**
    from agriculture, *1:* 225–226
    climate change, *1:* 137, 145, 157
    Newcastle Harbor, New South Wales, *1:* 160–161
Greenpeace, *1:* 22–23, 23 (ill.)
Greensboro, NC, sit-ins, *1:* 59, 60
Greenwich Village, NY, *2:* 436–437, 441
Greenwood, Grace, *3:* 697 (ill.)
Grito de Lares (1868), *2:* 340, 342–346. *See also* **Independence movements**
Guangdong, China, *3:* 570–573
Guangxi, China, *3:* 570–573
Guardian, 1: 158, 181
Guggenheim Museum, Bilbao, Spain, *1:* 12, 16–18
Guiliani, Rudolph, *3:* 680
Gun Control Act, *2:* 234
Gun control laws
    background checks, *2:* 253
    California, *2:* 242–243
    history in the United States, *2:* 233–235
Gun control/Gun rights, *2:* **233–262**, 237 (ill.), 238 (ill.), 243 (ill.), 248 (ill.), 249 (ill.), 254 (ill.), 259 (ill.)
    Black Panthers Protest Mulford Act (1967), *2:* 239–245, 243 (ill.)
    Democratic Congressional Representatives Sit-in for Gun Control (2016), *2:* 256–260, 259 (ill.)
    demonstrators, *2:* 237 (ill.), 238 (ill.)
    gun control arguments, *2:* 235–237
    gun rights arguments, *2:* 237–238
    Huey P. Newton Gun Club demonstrations, *2:* 244
    "I Will Not Comply" Rally (2014), *2:* 252–256, 254 (ill.)
    March on Washington for Gun Control (2013), *2:* 246–252, 249 (ill.)
    Seale, Bobby, on Mulford Act, *2:* 240, 242
    Vocal Majority Tour (2016), *2:* 248, 248 (ill.)
Gun ownership
    history in United States, *2:* 233–235
    United States, *2:* 235, 235 (ill.)
Gun shows, *2:* 257
Gunn, David, *3:* 554
Gutenberg, Johannes, *1:* 172
Guttmacher Institute, *3:* 556

H

The Hague, Netherlands, International Congress of Women (1915), *3:* 657–663, 660 (ill.)
Haitian Revolution (1791–1804), *2:* 338; *3:* 625
Hamid bin Isa Al Khalifa, King of Bahrain, *3:* 489
Hamilton, Alice, *3:* 660
Handguns, *2:* 235
Harbor blockades, *1:* 157–163
Harding, Warren G., *2:* 411
Harpers Ferry Raid (1859), *3:* 638–643, 642 (ill.). *See also* **Slavery**
Harry Potter Book Burning (2001), *1:* 177–183, 181 (ill.). *See also* **Free speech**
Harry Potter (book series), *1:* 175
    book burning, *1:* 177–183, 181 (ill.)
    opposition to, *1:* 179–180
Hate crimes
    expanding definition, *2:* 447–448, 451
    laws, *2:* 434, 446, 450
    United States, *3:* 518 (ill.)
Hate groups, *3:* 518 (ill.), 542
Hatfield, Sid, *2:* 410
Hatshepsut, *2:* 430–431
Havel, Václav, *2:* 355, 356
Hawke, Bob, *2:* 378–379
Haymarket Square Riot (1886), *2:* 418–419, 419 (ill.)
HDI (Human Development Index), *1:* 102
Health insurance plans, birth control and, *3:* 555, 556
Heart (music group), *1:* 30
Heine, Heinrich, *1:* 179
Heller, Aron, *3:* 610

Henderson, Russell, *2:* 447, 451
Henry VII, King of England, *2:* 265
Henry VIII, King of England, *1:* 173; *2:* 285
Heston, Charlton, *1:* 68
Heydrich, Reinhard, *3:* 589
Heyer, Heather, *3:* 542
Heymann, Lida Gustava, *3:* 660
Hidalgo, Miguel, *2:* 338
Hill, Julia "Butterfly," *1:* 152, 153 (ill.)
Himmler, Heinrich, *3:* 604, 605
Hinckley, John, Jr., *2:* 236–237
Hinduism, *2:* 290–291
Hispanic and Latino civil rights, *1:* **71–98**, 76 (ill.), 81 (ill.), 88 (ill.), 91 (ill.), 95 (ill.). *See also* Civil rights
   Day without Immigrants protests (2006), *1:* 83–89, 88 (ill.)
   Day without Latinos (2006), *1:* 87
   early history, *1:* 73
   East LA blowouts (1968), *1:* 77–82, 81 (ill.)
   Mexican Indignados movement, *1:* 90–96, 91 (ill.), 95 (ill.)
   Sicilia, Javier, *1:* 90, 91 (ill.), 92–93, 94
   Tlatelolco Massacre (1968), *1:* 94, 95
   Ybor City Cigar Strike (1931), *1:* 84–85
Hispanics and Latinos. *See also* Mexican Americans
   definitions, *1:* 71
   United States population, *1:* 75–76
Hitler, Adolf, *1:* 179; *3:* 479–480, 585–586, 590–591, 592, 607
HIV/AIDS
   demonstrations, *2:* 433 (ill.)
   drugs protests, *1:* 226–227, 227 (ill.)
   epidemic, *2:* 433–434
Hobby Lobby, *3:* 555
Holloway, Jonathan, *1:* 200
Holocaust, *1:* 179; *2:* 297; *3:* 586, 613. *See also* Genocide
Holocaust Resistance in Denmark (1943), *3:* 597–602, 601 (ill.). *See also* **Resistance to Nazis**
Homosexuality. *See also* LGBTQ people
   as mental disorder, *2:* 432, 452
   opposition to by WBC, *2:* 448, 452
   as personality disorder, *2:* 432
Hong Kong
   relationship with China, *3:* 499–500
   Umbrella Revolution (2014), *3:* 498–505, 500 (ill.), 504 (ill.)
Hopper, Grace Murray, *1:* 200
Horn, Jerry, *3:* 560
Houston, TX
   anti-abortion demonstrators, *3:* 564 (ill.)
   March to Abolish the Death Penalty, *2:* 287
HPI (Human Poverty Index), *1:* 102
Hu Yaobang, *3:* 473–474
Huerta, Dolores, *1:* 75, 76 (ill.), 78, 86; *2:* 414–415, 419–420
Human development, *1:* 101–102
Human Development Index (HDI), *1:* 102
Human migrations, *2:* 305–306
Human Poverty Index (HPI), *1:* 102
Human rights, *2:* **263–304**, 269 (ill.), 274 (ill.), 278 (ill.), 282 (ill.), 287 (ill.), 295 (ill.), 301 (ill.). *See also* Civil rights; Disability rights; **Immigrant rights**
   Americans with Disabilities Act (ADA), *2:* 277, 280–283
   Armenian Genocide Protests, *2:* 297–302, 301 (ill.)
   Attica Prison Riot (1971), *2:* 270–276, 274 (ill.)
   Bly, Nellie, investigation of mental hospital, *2:* 278, 278 (ill.)
   Capitol Crawl (1990), *2:* 276–284, 282 (ill.)
   Dalit Protests in India (2006), *2:* 290–297, 295 (ill.)
   definition and nature of, *2:* 263
   history, *2:* 264–268
   March to Abolish the Death Penalty, *2:* 284–289, 287 (ill.)
   Strangeways Prison Riot (1990), *2:* 271
Human Rights Campaign, *2:* 458
Human trafficking, *3:* 623, 643–647. *See also* **Slavery**
Humane Society of the United States, *1:* 11
Hunger strikes, *3:* 476, 701–702
   Manning, Bradley/Chelsea, *3:* 689
   Pankhurst, Sylvia, *3:* 704 (ill.)
   by Suffragettes in Prison, *3:* 701–707
   Women's Suffrage Protest at the White House, *3:* 713
Hunt, Jane, *3:* 708
Hussein, Saddam, *3:* 682

Hutton, Bobby, *2:* 245
Hyde Amendment, *3:* 578
Hydro-Quebec, *2:* 382

I

"I Have a Dream" speech, *1:* 39, 63, 68
"I Will Not Comply" Rally (2014), *2:* 252–256
    See also **Gun control/Gun rights**
IAT (Indians of All Tribes), *2:* 370–371
Idle No More, *2:* 365 (ill.)
Iglesias, Pablo, *1:* 121–122
Iguala, Mexico, *1:* 95–96
IJM (International Justice Mission), *3:* 647
Illinois
    DNC anti-war protests, *3:* 656 (ill.)
    Haymarket Square Riot, *2:* 418–419
    proposed Skokie neo-Nazi march, *1:* 188–189
ILO (International Labour Organization), *3:* 644
Immigrant rights, *2:* **305–334**, 313 (ill.), 317 (ill.), 323 (ill.), 324 (ill.), 329 (ill.), 330 (ill.). *See also* **Human rights**
    anti-Chinese riots, Denver, CO (1980), *2:* 328–329, 329 (ill.)
    California. Senate. Resolution No. 16 (2017), *2:* 327
    Molly Maguires, *2:* 312–313, 313 (ill.)
    Nativist Riots (1844), *2:* 311–318, 317 (ill.)
    Patriotic Europeans against the Islamization of the West (PEGIDA), *2:* 322–323, 323 (ill.)
    Pro-migrant Rallies in Europe and Australia (2015-2016), *2:* 318–325, 324 (ill.)
    Protests against President Trump's Travel Ban (2017), *2:* 325–332, 330 (ill.)
Immigrants and immigration. *See also* **Refugees**
    Chinese, *2:* 307, 328–329, 329 (ill.), 415–416
    Day without Immigrants protests, *1:* 83–89
    EU (European Union), *2:* 309–310
    German, *2:* 307
    Irish, *2:* 307, 312, 314
    Latin American, *2:* 308–309
    Mexican, *2:* 308–309
    undocumented immigrants, *1:* 74, 83–84; *2:* 325
    United Kingdom, *1:* 123, 124
    United States, *1:* 74, 83–85; *2:* 306–309

INC (Indian National Congress), *2:* 348–349
Income inequality, *1:* 99–100
Indentured servants, *3:* 510–511, 694
Independence movements, *2:* **335–359**, 345 (ill.), 337 (ill.), 345 (ill.), 351 (ill.), 354 (ill.), 357 (ill.)
    Asia, *2:* 339–340
    Cuba, *2:* 338–339
    Czechoslovakia, *2:* 341–342, 352–358, 354 (ill.)
    Estonia, Singing Revolution, *2:* 348
    French colonies, *2:* 338; *3:* 625
    Gandhi leads Salt March (1930), *2:* 340–341, 346–352, 351 (ill.)
    Gdansk Shipyard Strike, Poland (1980), *2:* 356–357, 357 (ill.)
    Grito de Lares (1868), *2:* 342–346, 345 (ill.)
    history, *2:* 335–340
    India, *2:* 340–341, 346–352
    Jamaica, *2:* 339
    Mexico, *2:* 338
    Puerto Rico, *2:* 342–346
    Spanish colonies, *2:* 338–339
    Velvet Revolution (1989), *2:* 352–358
India
    caste systems, *2:* 290–297
    colonial history, *2:* 347–349
    Dalit protests, *2:* 290–297, 295 (ill.)
    8888 anniversary protest, *3:* 503 (ill.)
    independence movements, *2:* 340–341, 346–352
    reservation system, *2:* 292–293, 294–295
India. Constitution, *2:* 292
India. National Crime Record Bureau, *2:* 296–297
Indian Mutiny (1857–1858), *2:* 348
Indian National Congress (INC), *2:* 348–349
Indian reservations. *See also* Native Americans
    land rights, *2:* 362–363
    Pine Ridge Reservation, *2:* 370, 372, 374
    Standing Rock Reservation, *2:* 369, 370, 384
Indians of All Tribes (IAT), *2:* 370–371
Indigenous Australians. *See* Aboriginals
Indigenous peoples. *See also* Native Americans
    Amazonian, *2:* 366, 379–384
    Canada, *2:* 365 (ill.)
    Copenhagen protests, *1:* 146, 149
    Cree First Nations, *2:* 382
    impact of colonization, *2:* 361, 375–376

Kayapo, *2:* 366, 380–384
land rights, *2:* 361
New Zealand, *2:* 364
Pacific Climate Warriors Blockade, *1:* 162, 162 (ill.)
South Africa, *3:* 532–533, 534
Taino, *2:* 343
Indigenous peoples' rights, *2:* **361–392**, 365 (ill.), 367 (ill.), 369 (ill.), 371 (ill.), 374 (ill.), 378 (ill.), 383 (ill.), 388 (ill.). *See also* Civil rights
Aboriginal Land Rights Protest (1988), *2:* 365–366, 375–379, 378 (ill.)
AIM Occupation of Wounded Knee (1973), *2:* 364–365, 367–375, 374 (ill.)
Cree First Nations dam protest, *2:* 382
Dakota Access Pipeline Protest (2016–2017), *2:* 366–367; 367 (ill.), 384–391, 388 (ill.)
history, *2:* 362–364
occupation of Alcatraz, *2:* 370–371, 371 (ill.)
Preservation of Amazon Rain Forest Awareness Campaign (1989), *2:* 366, 379–384, 383 (ill.)
Trail of Tears protest, *2:* 386–387, 387 (ill.)
Indignados movement, *1:* 90–96
Indigo Girls, *3:* 729
Individuals with Disabilities Education Act (IDEA), *2:* 278
Industrial Revolution, *1:* 133–134; *2:* 393, 395, 395 (ill.)
Industrialization, *2:* 400
International Congress of Women (1915), *3:* 657–663, 660 (ill.). *See also* Anti-war protests
goals of, *3:* 661
impact of, *3:* 661–663
resolutions, *3:* 662
International Justice Mission (IJM), *3:* 647
International Labour Organization (ILO), *2:* 407; *3:* 644
International March for Elephants, *1:* 22–23. *See also* **Animal rights**
International Union, United Automobile, Aerospace and Agricultural Implement Workers of America, *2:* 414. *See also* UAW (United Auto Workers)
International Whaling Commission (IWC), *1:* 22
International Woman Suffrage Alliance, *3:* 658
International Workers Day, *1:* 86

Internet
citizen journalism, *3:* 490–491
role in organizing protests, *1:* 213
Interstate Commerce Commission, *1:* 54–55, 57, 59
Iowa, Student Armband Protest of Vietnam War (1965–1969), *3:* 663–668, 668 (ill.)
IPCC (United Nations. Intergovernmental Panel on Climate Change), *1:* 137, 148
Iranian demonstrators, violence against, *3:* 490–491, 491 (ill.)
Iranian Green Movement (2009), *3:* 490–491, 491 (ill.)
Iraq War (2003–2011), *3:* 682–683
anti-war protests, *3:* 657, 682 (ill.)
Bush, George W., speech, *3:* 680–681
Candlelight Vigils against Invasion of Iraq (2003), *3:* 676–683
civilian casualties, *3:* 684
Ireland
Brexit demonstrations, *1:* 126
Easter Rebellion (1916), *3:* 480–481, 481 (ill.)
Irish immigrants, *2:* 307, 312, 314. *See also* Immigrants and immigration
Irish Republican Brotherhood, *3:* 480
Irish War of Independence (1919–1921), *3:* 481
Irwin, Lord, *2:* 351
Islam, *1:* 184
Islamic extremists, *2:* 326–328
Islamic law, *3:* 715, 718, 719
Islamization, *2:* 322
Island nations, *1:* 146
climate change, *1:* 157–158
Pacific Climate Warriors Blockage, *1:* 162
Ivory trade, *1:* 18–19
IWC (International Whaling Commission), *1:* 22

J

Jackson, Jesse, *3:* 678
Jackson, Mahalia, *1:* 67, 68
Jackson, MS, Freedom Rides, *1:* 57
Jacobs, Aletta, *3:* 657, 658–659
"Jail, no bail," *1:* 61

Jamaica
    Christmas Rebellion/Baptist War (1831–1832), *3:* 634–638
    history, *3:* 634–635
    independence movements, *2:* 339
James II, King of England, *1:* 173; *2:* 266
Japan
    nuclear energy policy, *1:* 160
    rice riots of 1918, *1:* 126–127
    Tokyo Big March, *1:* 160
Jati, *2:* 291
"Je Suis Charlie" Protests (2015), *1:* 189–194, 192 (ill.). *See also* **Free speech**
    Muslim protests against *Charlie Hebdo*, *1:* 190 (ill.), 193
    pro free speech, *1:* 192–193
Jefferson County Courthouse, West Virginia, *2:* 411 (ill.)
Jewish Combat Organization (ZOB), *3:* 604–606, 605
Jewish Holocaust, *1:* 179; *2:* 297; *3:* 586, 613. *See also* Genocide
Jews
    assistance to, *3:* 588–589
    Danish, *3:* 597, 601–602
    under Nazis, *3:* 585–586, 607
Jim Crow laws, *1:* 37, 43–44. *See also* Racial discrimination
    changes to, *1:* 48
    school segregation, *1:* 48–49
    segregation, *1:* 55
John, King of England, *3:* 470
Johnson, Lyndon B., *1:* 69
    civil rights, *1:* 40
    Detroit Riots, *3:* 529
Jones, Mary Harris
    crusade against child labor, *2:* 399–407, 406 (ill.)
    excerpt from autobiography, *2:* 404–405
    Kensington textile mill strike, *2:* 401–403
Journey of Reconciliation (1947), *1:* 55
Judd, Ashley, *3:* 729
July 20 Plot (1944), *3:* 591
Juste, Carsten, *1:* 186
Justice for All March (2014), *3:* 515, 539–546, 545 (ill.). *See also* **Racial conflict**
Jyllands-Posten, *1:* 183–188, 191

K

Kadhem, Laila al-, *3:* 716 (ill.)
Kaepernick, Colin, *3:* 515, 516–517, 517 (ill.)
Kansas
    Brown, John, anti-slavery activity, *3:* 640
    debate over slavery, *3:* 640
    Summer of Mercy Protest, *3:* 566–567
Kayany Foundation, *3:* 724
Kayapo, *2:* 366, 380–384. *See also* Indigenous peoples
Keelan, Jennifer, *2:* 282 (ill.)
Keller, Helen, *1:* 179
Kelly, Mark, *2:* 248, 248 (ill.)
Kennedy, Anthony, *2:* 439
Kennedy, John F., *1:* 54
    assassination, *2:* 234
    Freedom Rides, *1:* 57, 59
    March on Washington, *1:* 66–67
Kennedy, Robert, *1:* 57, 69
Kennedy (John F.) International Airport, *2:* 330
Kenrick, Francis Patrick, *2:* 314–315, 316
Kensington Textile Mill Strike (1903), *2:* 401–403
Kent State University student protests, *3:* 669–676, 674 (ill.). *See also* Anti-war protests
Kenya, Global March for Elephants and Rhinos, *1:* 22–23, 24 (ill.)
Kerner Commission, *3:* 529–530
Kerr, Clark, *1:* 199
Kerr, Stanley, *2:* 299
Keys, Alicia, *3:* 729
Keystone XL project, *1:* 139, 140–141, 144
Khairlanji, India, Dalit family murder, *2:* 293–294
Kifner, John, *3:* 672–673
Killer whales, *1:* 4–5
    SeaWorld protests, *1:* 25–31
    treatment by SeaWorld, *1:* 26–27, 30–31
King, Martin Luther, Jr., *1:* 36, 78
    assassination, *1:* 41, 69
    Birmingham, AL, desegregation, *1:* 62
    civil rights movement, *1:* 75; *3:* 472
    "I Have a Dream" speech, *1:* 39
    March on Washington, *1:* 63, 67, 68
    Montgomery bus boycott, *1:* 36 (ill.), 45–46, 47

King, Rodney, *3:* 522
KKK (Ku Klux Klan), *1:* 47, 58; *3:* 542
Klausen, Jytte, *1:* 184, 185
KMT (Kuomintang), *1:* 107
Knights of Labor, *2:* 397
Koch, Charles, *1:* 111
Koch, David, *1:* 111
Kopp, James C., *3:* 563–564
Koran, *3:* 498, 715, 718
Kozachenko, Kathy, *2:* 433
Krause, Allison, *3:* 675
Ku Klux Klan (KKK), *1:* 47, 58; *3:* 542
Kulach, Adam, *3:* 716 (ill.)
Kuomintang (KMT), *1:* 107
Kyoto Protocol, *1:* 146

L

Labeling, genetically modified organisms, *1:* 229–230
Labor activists, *1:* 75–76
Labor Day, *2:* 402
Labor laws, *2:* 393
    child labor, *2:* 407
    United States, *2:* 397–398
Labor movement, *2:* 395–398, 401
Labor rights, *2:* **393–428**, 395 (ill.), 400 (ill.), 403 (ill.), 406 (ill.), 411 (ill.), 412 (ill.), 419 (ill.), 421 (ill.), 424 (ill.). *See also* Child labor; Workers
    Battle of Blair Mountain strike (1921), *2:* 410–411, 411 (ill.)
    Delano Grape Strike and Boycott (1965–1970), *2:* 414–422, 421 (ill.)
    Fast-Food Workers' Strike (2012), *2:* 422–426, 424 (ill.)
    Flint Sit-down Strike against General Motors (1936–1937), *2:* 407–414, 412 (ill.)
    Haymarket Square Riot (1886), *2:* 418–419, 419 (ill.)
    Mother Jones's "Children's Crusade" (1903), *2:* 399–407, 406 (ill.)
    Solidarity movement, *2:* 356–357, 357 (ill.)
    United States, *2:* 394
    worldwide, *2:* 398–399
Labor unions, *2:* 396–397
    employer resistance to, *2:* 397–398
    farmworkers, *1:* 75–76

Lafayette, LA, mass shooting, *2:* 251
Lake Oahe, *2:* 386
Lakota Sioux, *2:* 369, 369 (ill.), 370, 372. *See also* Native Americans
Lam, Carrie, *3:* 504–505
Lambda Legal, *2:* 433, 464
Land rights
    Indian reservations, *2:* 362–363
    indigenous peoples, *2:* 361
    Māori, *2:* 363–364
Land rights protests, *2:* 364–367. *See also* **Indigenous peoples' rights**
    Aboriginals, *2:* 365–366
    Amazonian indigenous peoples, *2:* 366, 379–384
    Australia, *2:* 375–379
    Canada, *2:* 365 (ill.)
    Cree First Nations, *2:* 382
    Native Americans, *2:* 364–365, 366–367, 384–391, 388 (ill.)
Lanza, Adam, *2:* 246–247, 253
Laramie, WY
    anti-gay protests by Westboro Baptist Church, *2:* 449–451
    murder of Matthew Shepard, *2:* 445–446
The Laramie Project, *2:* 456–457
Las Vegas, NV, mass shootings, *2:* 260
Lasn, Kalle, *1:* 219
Latin America, *1:* 71, 72
Latin American immigrants, *2:* 308–309. *See also* Immigrants and immigration; Mexican Americans
Latino civil rights. *See* **Hispanic and Latino civil rights**
Latinos. *See* Hispanics and Latinos
Law Center to Prevent Gun Violence, *2:* 256
Law Enforcement Officers Protection Act, *2:* 234
Lebanon, Yousafzai, Malala, All-Girls School, *3:* 718–724
Lectors, *1:* 84, 85 (ill.)
Lee, Robert E., *3:* 642
Lee, Ronnie, *1:* 8
Lemay, Tiffany, *2:* 454
Lennon, John, *3:* 670, 671 (ill.)
Lesbians, *2:* 430. *See also* LGBTQ people
Lethal injection, *2:* 289. *See also* Death penalty
Leung, Trini, *3:* 474–475
Leung Chun-ying, *3:* 500–501, 504–505

Levi-Strauss, Claude, *1:* 166
Lewis, John, *1:* 56, 66–67, 68; *2:* 258, 259 (ill.)
LGBTQ people. *See also* Homosexuality
    definition, *2:* 429–430
    discrimination against, *2:* 431, 432, 436, 454–455
    lesbians, *2:* 430
    transgender people, *2:* 429, 435
LGBTQ rights, *2:* **429–466,** 433 (ill.), 439 (ill), 440 (ill.), 444 (ill.), 449 (ill.), 455 (ill.), 456 (ill.), 461 (ill.), 463 (ill.). *See also* Civil rights
    China, *2:* 452–453, 458
    history, *2:* 430–431
    Marriage equality, *2:* 438–439, 439 (ill.)
    modern movement, *2:* 431–435
    NCAA boycott of North Carolina, *2:* 460–461, 461 (ill.)
    organizations, *2:* 432, 436
    protests against, *2:* 445–452
    Protests of North Carolina House Bill 2 (2016), *2:* 458–464, 461 (ill.), 463 (ill.)
    Russia, *2:* 454–455, 455 (ill.)
    Shanghai Pride Festival (2009), *2:* 452–458, 456 (ill.)
    Stonewall Riots (1969), *2:* 435–441, 440 (ill.)
    Westboro Baptist Church Protests of Matthew Shepard (1998–1999), *2:* 445–452, 449 (ill.)
    White Night Riots (1979), *2:* 441–445, 444 (ill.)
Li Peng, *3:* 475
Li Yinhe, *2:* 452
Liberal Democratic Party (Japan), *1:* 160
Libya
    Arab Spring, *3:* 489–490
    civil war, *3:* 490
Lincoln, Abraham, *3:* 654, 654 (ill.)
Little Rock, AR, school integration, *1:* 47–52
Little Rock Central High School, *1:* 47–52
Little Rock Nine Crisis (1957), *1:* 47–52, 52 (ill.).
    See also **African American civil rights**
Livermore, Mary, *3:* 697 (ill.)
Lloyd George, David, *3:* 705
Lobbyists, *1:* 139
Locke, John, *2:* 266
Loeak, Milañ, *1:* 158
London, UK, anti-fracking protesters, *1:* 155 (ill.)

Longley, Kristin, *2:* 413
Los Angeles, CA. *See also* California; East Los Angeles, CA
    Armenian genocide protests, *2:* 301 (ill.), 302
    A Day without Immigrants protests, *1:* 88
    King, Rodney, riots, *3:* 522–523, 523 (ill.)
    March for Women's Lives (1986), *3:* 556–561
    Occupy Wall Street demonstration, *1:* 222 (ill.)
    race riots (1992), *3:* 522–523, 523 (ill.)
    Watts Riots, *3:* 514 (ill.)
    Zoot Suit Riots, *3:* 518–524, 521 (ill.)
Los Angeles Race Riots (1992), *3:* 522–523, 523 (ill.)
Los Angeles Unified School District
    cultural studies introduced, *1:* 82
    discrimination in education, *1:* 79–80
Loughner, Jared Lee, *2:* 248
Louisiana
    mass shooting, *2:* 251
    school desegregation, *1:* 53
    slavery, *3:* 624–625
Louisiana Rebellion (German Coast) (1811), *3:* 623–628. *See also* **Slavery**
Love, William T., *1:* 143
Love Canal, NY, *1:* 136, 143, 143 (ill.)
Lowell, Arthur, *2:* 413
Luddites, *2:* 395 (ill.)
Lunch Counter Protest, McCrory's (1961), *1:* 59–63, 61 (ill.). *See also* **African American civil rights**
Luther, Martin, *2:* 312
Lyden, Jack, *2:* 450
Lysistrata, 3: 651–652

M

Macy's Thanksgiving Parade, *1:* 28, 30
Madonna, *3:* 729
Mafia, *2:* 436–437
Magazinet, 1: 185
Magna Carta (1215), *2:* 265; *3:* 470
Maharashtra, India, *2:* 296
Malala Fund, *3:* 724
Malala Yousafzai All-Girls School, *3:* 718–724
El Malcriado: The Voice of the Farm Worker, 2: 417

Malê Revolt of 1835, *3:* 626–627, 627 (ill.). *See also* **Slavery**
Mallory, Tamika, *3:* 728
Malloy, Annie E., *3:* 660 (ill.)
Manama, Bahrain, *3:* 489
Manchester, England, Strangeways Prison riot, *2:* 271
Mandela, Nelson, *3:* 539
Manning, Bradley/Chelsea, *3:* 684–690, 686 (ill.). *See also* **Transgender people**
   arrest and trial, *3:* 686–688
   communication with WikiLeaks, *3:* 685–686
Mao Zedong, *1:* 107, 108; *3:* 473, 569
Māori, land rights, *2:* 363–364
March against Monsanto (2013), *1:* 223–230, 228 (ill.). *See also* **Globalization**
March for Life (1986), *3:* 558, 559
March for Life Education and Defense Fund, *3:* 559
March for Marriage, *2:* 439 (ill.)
March for Science (2017), *1:* 163–168, 165 (ill.); *3:* 730–731. *See also* **Environment**
March for Women's Lives (1986), *3:* 556–561, 557 (ill.), 559. *See also* **Reproductive rights**
March of the Mill Children, *2:* 399–407, 406 (ill.). *See also* **Labor rights**
March on Washington for Gun Control (2013), *2:* 246–252, 249 (ill.). *See also* **Gun control/Gun rights**
March on Washington for Jobs and Freedom (1963), *1:* 39, 39 (ill.), 63–69, 65 (ill.); *3:* 472. *See also* **African American civil rights**
   King Jr., Martin Luther, *1:* 63, 67, 68
   leaders, *1:* 65–66, 65 (ill.)
   Lewis, John, *1:* 66–67
   origins, *1:* 64
March to Abolish the Death Penalty, *2:* 284–289, 287 (ill.). *See also* **Human rights**
Marine Mammal Protection Act, *1:* 136
Maroons, *3:* 636
Marriage equality, *2:* 434
   defined, *2:* 430
   legal battle, *2:* 438–439
   Washington, D.C., protest against, *2:* 439 (ill.)
Married women, rights of, *3:* 693–695
Marshall, Thurgood, *1:* 39

Marshall Islands, *1:* 158
Martin, Richard, *1:* 2
Martin, Trayvon, *3:* 540–541
Martin's Act, *1:* 2
Mary II, Queen of England, *1:* 173
Marysville Pilchuck High School shootings, *2:* 253
Mass shootings, *2:* 239, 253–254, 257
   Lafayette, Louisiana, *2:* 251
   Las Vegas, Nevada, *2:* 260
   Obama, Barack speech, *2:* 251
   Sandy Hook Elementary School, *2:* 246–247
   Tucson, Arizona, *2:* 248
   Umpqua Community College, *2:* 251
   Virginia Tech, *2:* 249
Mateen, Oscar, *2:* 257
Matewan Massacre (1921), *2:* 410
Mattachine Society, *2:* 432
Matters, Muriel, *3:* 703–704
Matthew Shepard and James Byrd, Jr., Hate Crimes Prevention Act, *2:* 450, 451
Mauritania, abolition of slavery, *3:* 643
Maximilian, Saint, *3:* 652
Maximilianus, *3:* 652
May, Theresa, *1:* 125, 128–129
May Day, *1:* 86
Mayan texts, book burning, *1:* 178
McAuliffe, Terry, *3:* 542
McCartney, Stella, *1:* 12–13
McCormick Reaper Works, *2:* 418
McCorvey, Norma, *3:* 576–577, 577 (ill.)
McCoy, Rose, *1:* 28, 30
McCrory, Pat, *2:* 459
McCrory's Lunch Counter Protest (1961), *1:* 59–63, 61 (ill.). *See also* **African American civil rights**
McDonald's, *2:* 422, 424, 425
McGuire, Barry, *3:* 670
McKinney, Aaron, *2:* 447, 451
M'Clintock, Mary Ann, *3:* 708
McSpadden, Lesley, *3:* 545–546
Means, Russell, *2:* 372, 374
Mechanics' Union of Trade Associations, *2:* 396–397
Medicaid, *2:* 283–284; *3:* 578
Medina, Francisco Ramírez, *2:* 345

Melchior, Bent, *3:* 598–599, 599 (ill.)
Meltdowns. *See* Nuclear accidents
Mental institutions, *2:* 278
Mercado, Mark, *2:* 255–256
Merkel, Angela, *1:* 161; *2:* 321, 322
Merkley, Jeff, *1:* 230
Methane gas, *1:* 159
Metropolitan Coalition against Nukes, *1:* 160
Mexican American students
    discrimination in education, *1:* 79–80
    East LA blowouts, *1:* 77–82
Mexican-American War (1846–1848), *1:* 73
Mexican Americans. *See also* Hispanics and Latinos
    racial conflict, *3:* 518–524
    racial discrimination, *3:* 519
    Zoot Suit Riots, *3:* 512 (ill.), 521 (ill.)
Mexican farm workers, *1:* 75 (ill.). *See also* Workers
Mexican immigrants, *2:* 308–309. *See also* Immigrants and immigration
Mexican Indignados movement, *1:* 90–96
Mexican students
    demonstrations, *1:* 95 (ill.)
    murder of in Iguala, *1:* 95–96
    Tlatelolco massacre, *1:* 94
    violence against, *1:* 90, 94
Mexican workers, *2:* 416, 418–419. *See also* Workers
Mexico
    drug trade, *1:* 75, 90, 91
    independence movements, *2:* 338
    Indignados movement, *1:* 90–96
    Tlatelolco Massacre (1968), *1:* 94, 95
    war on drugs, *1:* 91–95
Mexico City, Mexico, *1:* 93–94
MIA (Montgomery Improvement Association), *1:* 45–46
Michigan
    Detroit Riots (1967), *3:* 524–530
    strike against GM, *2:* 407–414, 412 (ill.)
Middle Ages
    political/government uprisings, *3:* 469–470
    slavery, *3:* 619–620
Middle East, Arab Spring, *1:* 90; *3:* 486–493
Middle Eastern refugees, *2:* 318–319
Migrant workers, *2:* 415, 416. *See also* Workers

Military draft
    United States Civil War, *3:* 526, 654
    Vietnam War, *3:* 666
Military servicemen, Zoot Suit Riots, *3:* 520–522
Milk (2008), *2:* 445
Milk, Harvey, *2:* 433, 441, 442, 445
Mill, John Stuart, *3:* 703
Miller, David, *3:* 666
Miller, Hannah, *2:* 454
Miller, Jeffrey, *3:* 675
Minimum wage, *2:* 422–423, 426. *See also* **Labor rights**
Minks, *1:* 11
Mississippi, Freedom Rides, *1:* 57
Mississippi Summer Project/Freedom Summer Voter Registration, *1:* 58, 58 (ill.). *See also* **African American civil rights**
Mitchell, George P., *1:* 154
Molly Maguires, *2:* 312–313, 313 (ill.)
Moms Demand Action, *2:* 238 (ill.)
Monáe, Janelle, *3:* 729
Monkeys, animal testing, *1:* 7–8, 10
Monopolies, *1:* 224–225, 228
Monsanto Co., *1:* 223–230
    concerns about products, *1:* 224–225
    product benefits, *1:* 225–226
Montgomery, AL
    bus boycott, *1:* 42–47
    Freedom Rides, *1:* 57
Montgomery Bus Boycott (1955–1956), *1:* 36 (ill.), 42–47. *See also* **African American civil rights**
Montgomery Improvement Association (MIA), *1:* 45–46
Moore, Gwen, *2:* 425
Moore, Michael, *3:* 678, 729
Moore, Tim, *2:* 462
Morgan, Ephraim, *2:* 410
Morgan, J.P., *1:* 217–218
Morgan v. Virginia, *1:* 55
Morsi, Mohamed, *3:* 498
Moscone, George Richard, *2:* 441, 442, 443, 445
Mother Jones
    crusade against child labor, *2:* 399–407, 406 (ill.)
    excerpt from autobiography, *2:* 404–405
    Kensington textile mill strike, *2:* 401–403

Mother Jones's "Children's Crusade" (1903), *2:* 399–407, 406 (ill.). *See also* **Labor rights**
Mothershed, Thelma, *1:* 50
Mott, Charles Stewart, *2:* 408
Mott, Lucretia, *3:* 697 (ill.), 708
Movement for Peace with Justice and Dignity, *1:* 93
Mubarak, Hosni, *3:* 488, 494, 496–497
Muhammad, images of, *1:* 176, 183, 184, 190
Muir, John, *1:* 135, 135 (ill.)
Mulford, Donald, *2:* 242–243
Mulford Act (California), *2:* 242–243, 244
Múnera, Álvaro, *1:* 16
Murder. *See also* Violence
    of Dalit family in Khairlanji, India, *2:* 293–294
    by pro-life advocates, *3:* 554–555, 563–564, 567
Murphy, Christopher, *2:* 258
Murphy, Frank, *2:* 412
Muslim Brotherhood, *3:* 498
Muslim protesters
    against *Charlie Hebdo* use of images of Muhammad, *1:* 190 (ill.), 193
    Muhammad cartoons, *1:* 186–187, 186 (ill.)
Muslim Protests of Danish Cartoons, *1:* 183–188, 186 (ill.). *See also* **Free speech**
Muslims, Trump travel bans, *2:* 325–326, 328–329, 330 (ill.)
Mutawa, 3: 715
Myanmar
    8888 Uprising (1988), *3:* 502–503
    violence against the Rohingya, *3:* 503

N

NAACP (National Association for the Advancement of Colored People)
    founding, *1:* 35
    legal actions, *1:* 38–39
    March on Washington, *1:* 65
    Montgomery bus boycott, *1:* 44
NAFTA (North American Free Trade Agreement), *1:* 205
Naidu, Sarojina, *2:* 351 (ill.)
NAN (National Action Network), *3:* 539, 544

Nat Turner's Rebellion (1831–1832), *3:* 628–634, 629 (ill.). *See also* **Slavery**
National Action Network (NAN), *3:* 539, 544
National Advisory Commission on Civil Disorders, *3:* 529–530
National American Woman Suffrage Association (NAWSA), *3:* 710
National Association for the Advancement of Colored People (NAACP)
    founding, *1:* 35
    legal actions, *1:* 38–39
    March on Washington, *1:* 65
    Montgomery bus boycott, *1:* 44
National Center for Missing and Exploited Children, *3:* 645
National Child Labor Committee, *2:* 407
National Collegiate Athletic Association (NCAA), *2:* 460–461, 461 (ill.)
National Conference of Dalit Organizations, *2:* 295 (ill.), 296
National Council on the Handicapped (NCH), *2:* 282
National defense jobs, desegregation, *1:* 64
National Democratic Party (Egypt), *3:* 495
National Family Planning Program, *3:* 577–578
National Farm Workers Association (NFWA), *1:* 75, 78; *2:* 419
National Firearms Act, *2:* 234
National Football League (NFL), *3:* 515
National Geographic, 1: 21–22
National Guard, *2:* 275, 389
    Arkansas, *1:* 48, 50–52, 52 (ill.)
    Michigan, *3:* 528, 528 (ill.), 531
    Ohio, *3:* 674–675
National Instant Criminal Background Check System, *2:* 253
National Labor Relations Act of 1935, *2:* 397
National Socialist German Workers' Party (Nazi Party), *3:* 585, 592, 607
National Socialist Party of America, *1:* 188
National Socialists German Students' Association, *1:* 179
National Urban League (NUL), *1:* 35
National Women's Party (United States), *3:* 698 (ill.), 710, 712 (ill.)

National Youth Peace Prize (Pakistan), *3:* 719
Nationwide Tea Party Coalition, *1:* 114
Native Americans. *See also* Indian reservations; Indigenous peoples
   Dakota Access Pipeline Protest, *2:* 366–367, 367 (ill.), 384–391, 388 (ill.)
   impact of colonization, *2:* 362–363, 386–387
   Lakota Sioux, *2:* 369, 369 (ill.), 370, 372
   land rights protests, *2:* 364–365, 366–367, 384–391, 388 (ill.)
   occupation of Alcatraz, *2:* 370–371, 371 (ill.)
   opposition to oil pipelines, *1:* 144
   slavery, *3:* 624
   Standing Rock Sioux, *2:* 384–385, 387–388, 388 (ill.)
   treaties with federal government, *2:* 368, 386
   treatment in the United States, *2:* 368–369
Nativism, *2:* 314
Nativist Riots (1844), *2:* 311–318, 317 (ill.). *See also* **Immigrant rights**
   eyewitness account, *2:* 314–315
   Protestant-Catholic conflict, *2:* 312–313
NATO (North Atlantic Treaty Organization), *3:* 490
NAWSA (National American Woman Suffrage Association), *3:* 710
Nazi Germany, *3:* 585–586, 592. *See also* Germany; Gestapo; **Resistance to Nazis**
   book burnings, *1:* 179
   deportations to death camps, *3:* 604–605
Nazi Party (National Socialist German Workers' Party), *3:* 585, 592, 607
Nazis, *1:* 188. *See also* Neo-Nazis
NCAA (National Collegiate Athletic Association), *2:* 460–461, 461 (ill.)
NCH (National Council on the Handicapped), *2:* 282
Ne Win, *3:* 502–503
Nelson, Willie, *1:* 30
Neo-Nazis, *1:* 188–189; *3:* 542, 543 (ill.). *See also* Nazis
Neumann-Ortiz, Christine, *1:* 87
Nevada, mass shootings, *2:* 260
New Delhi, India, 8888 anniversary protest, *3:* 503 (ill.)

New Mexico, Alamagordo book burning, *1:* 181 (ill.)
New Orleans, LA, school desegregation, *1:* 53
New York, NY
   child labor protest of 1909, *2:* 402–403, 403 (ill.)
   draft riots of 1863, *3:* 526–527, 527 (ill.)
   Occupy Wall Street, *1:* 216–222
   One Thousand Coffins Protest (2004), *3:* 678–679, 679 (ill.)
   racial conflict, *3:* 526–527
New York. State Police, *2:* 275
New York Act (1866), *1:* 3
New York City Draft Riots (1863), *3:* 526–527, 527 (ill.), 654. *See also* **Racial conflict**
New York Communities for Change (NYCC), *2:* 422, 423, 424
New York (state)
   Love Canal, *1:* 136, 143, 143 (ill.)
   Operation Rescue protests, *3:* 562–568, 563
New York State Liquor Authority, *2:* 436
New York Times, 3: 555–556
New Zealand, indigenous peoples, *2:* 364
Newcastle Harbor, New South Wales, *1:* 160–161
Newman, Paul, *1:* 68
Newsweek, 2: 452
Newton, Huey P., *2:* 240, 242
Newton (Huey P.) Gun Club, *2:* 244
Newtown, Connecticut, mass shooting, *2:* 246–247
NFL (National Football League), *3:* 515
NFWA (National Farm Workers Association), *1:* 75, 78; *2:* 419
Nigeria, Boko Haram kidnappings, *3:* 700, 722–723
Nixon, Richard M., *2:* 371
   decision to invade Cambodia, *3:* 671
   expansion of Vietnam War, *3:* 656
   moves to end Vietnam War, *3:* 676
   Women's Equality Day, *3:* 729
No Taxpayer Funding for Abortion and Abortion Insurance Full Disclosure Act, *3:* 580
NOAA (United States. National Oceanic and Atmospheric Administration), *1:* 136
Nobel Peace Prize
   Gore, Al, speech, *1:* 148–149
   Suu Kyi, Aung San, *3:* 503
   Yousafzai, Malala, *3:* 718, 720–721

Nonviolent resistance, *2:* 341, 420–421. *See also* Civil disobedience
Norman, Peter, *3:* 516, 517 (ill.)
North America
    British colonies, *2:* 336–337
    colonization, *1:* 72
North American Free Trade Agreement (NAFTA), *1:* 205
North Atlantic Treaty Organization (NATO), *3:* 490
North Carolina
    boycott, *2:* 461–462
    NCAA boycott, *2:* 460–461
    sit-ins, *1:* 59, 60
    transgender rights, *2:* 458–464
North Carolina. General Assembly. HB2, *2:* 458–459
    protests, *2:* 458–464, 461 (ill.), 463 (ill.)
    repeal, *2:* 463–464
North Carolina. General Assembly. HB142, *2:* 460, 464
North Dakota
    Dakota Access Pipeline protest, *2:* 366–367, 367 (ill.), 388 (ill.)
    land rights protests, *2:* 384–391, 388 (ill.)
North Vietnam, *2:* 340 (ill.). *See also* Vietnam
Northern Ireland, Brexit demonstrations, *1:* 126
Norway
    publication of cartoons of Muhammad, *1:* 185
    whaling, *1:* 22–23
No-till farming, *1:* 225–226
NOW (National Organization for Women), *3:* 554, 558–561, 560–561, 728
NPS (United States. National Park Service), *1:* 135
NRA (National Rifle Association), *2:* 238–239, 245, 250, 252, 257
Nuclear accidents
    Chernobyl, Ukraine, *1:* 136–137
    Fukushima, Japan, *1:* 160–161
Nuclear power plants, post-Fukushima protests, *1:* 160–161, 161 (ill.)
NUL (National Urban League), *1:* 35
Nunez, David, *2:* 255–256
NUWSS (National Union of Women's Suffrage Societies), *3:* 703

NYCC (New York Communities for Change), *2:* 422, 423, 424
Nye, Bill, *1:* 165 (ill.)

O

Oakes, Richard, *2:* 370
Oakland, CA, Global Frackdown, *1:* 156
Obama, Barack, *1:* 76 (ill.), 113
    Dakota Access Pipeline, *2:* 385
    declares Stonewall Inn a national landmark, *2:* 441
    hate crimes laws, *2:* 451
    Keystone XL project, *1:* 139, 141, 144
    Manning, Chelsea, sentence reduction, *3:* 685, 690
    on mass shootings, *2:* 251
    minimum wage, *2:* 422–423, 426
    repeal of "Don't Ask, Don't Tell," *2:* 435
    support of gun control sit-in, *2:* 259
Obama, Michelle, *3:* 700–701, 727
Obergefell, Jim, *2:* 438–439
Obergefell v. Hodges, *2:* 434, 438–439
Occupation of Alcatraz (1969–1970), *2:* 370–371, 371 (ill.)
Occupy Central with Love and Peace, *3:* 500–501
Occupy Wall Street (2011), *1:* 216–222, 222 (ill.). *See also* **Globalization**
    declaration of principles, *1:* 220–221
    expansion beyond NYC, *1:* 220–221, 222 (ill.)
    origins, *1:* 219
Ochs, Phil, *3:* 670
Ogallala Aquifer, *1:* 141
Ohio, Kent State University student protests, *3:* 669–676, 674 (ill.)
Oil leaks, *1:* 140
Oil pipelines, *1:* 140–141, 142. *See also* Dakota Access Pipeline (DAPL); Keystone XL project
Olympic Games, Mexico City (1968), *3:* 516, 517 (ill.)
One child policy, *3:* 568. *See also* Birth control; **Reproductive rights**
    enforcement of, *3:* 570–572
    introduction of, *3:* 569–570
    results of, *3:* 573
    revision of, *3:* 573–574

GENERAL INDEX

One Child Policy Riots (2007), *3:* 568–574, 572 (ill.)
One Million Moms for Gun Control, *2:* 248
One Thousand Coffins Protest (2004), *3:* 678–679, 679 (ill.). *See also* Anti-war protests
Open carry, *2:* 235. *See also* **Gun control/Gun rights**
    Black Panthers protest, *2:* 239–245, 243 (ill.)
    Huey P. Newton Gun Club demonstrations, *2:* 244
Operation Rescue (1992), *3:* 562–568. *See also* **Reproductive rights**
    demonstrators, *3:* 564 (ill.), 567 (ill.)
    history, *3:* 562–563
    methods, *3:* 563–564
Operation Save America, *3:* 563
Opletal, Jan, *2:* 355
Orcas, *1:* 4–5
    SeaWorld protests, *1:* 25–31
    treatment by SeaWorld, *1:* 26–27, 30–31
Orestiada, Greece, pro-migrant rally, *2:* 324 (ill.)
Origliasso, Jessica, *1:* 13 (ill.)
Origliasso, Lisa, *1:* 13 (ill.)
Orlando, FL, mass shootings at Pulse nightclub, *2:* 257
O'Sullivan, Michael, *1:* 28
Oswald, Lee Harvey, *2:* 234
Oswald, Russell, *2:* 273
Ottoman Empire, *2:* 297–300
Outsourcing, *1:* 207
Oxfam, *1:* 100
Oxford, Mississippi, *1:* 58

P

Pacific Climate Warriors Blockade (2014), *1:* 157–163, 162 (ill.). *See also* **Environment**
Pacific Lumber Company, *1:* 152
Pacifists, *3:* 652, 661. *See also* Anti-war protests
Paddock, Stephen, *2:* 260
PAH (Platform for People Affected by Mortgages), *1:* 120
Palestinian students, flag burning, *1:* 186 (ill.)
Paltrow, Gweneth, *1:* 229
Pankhurst, Emmeline, *3:* 703
Pankhurst, Sylvia, *3:* 704 (ill.)

Pantaleo, Daniel, *3:* 541–542, 544–545
Pantsuit Nation, *3:* 726
Parent, Elena, *2:* 238 (ill.)
Paris, France
    attack on *Charlie Hebdo* offices, *1:* 191
    student protests of 1968, *1:* 118–119, 119 (ill.)
Paris Agreement, *1:* 168
Paris Peace Accords, *3:* 676
Parks, Rosa, *1:* 36 (ill.), 42–43, 45 (ill.), 47
Partial-Birth Abortion Act, *3:* 561
Partisans, *3:* 589
Patents, genetically modified seeds, *1:* 224
Patriot Guard Riders, *2:* 452
Patriotic Europeans against the Islamization of the West (PEGIDA), *2:* 322–323, 323 (ill.)
Patterson, Romaine, *2:* 449
Pattillo, Melba, *1:* 50
Paul, Alice, *3:* 698 (ill.), 710, 713
Paul, Rand, *1:* 115–116
PayPal, *2:* 462
Pearse, Patrick, *3:* 480
Peasants' Revolt of 1381, *3:* 470
PEGIDA (Patriotic Europeans against the Islamization of the West), *2:* 322–323, 323 (ill.)
Pence, Mike, *3:* 559, 578–579
Penn, Sean, *2:* 445
Pennsylvania
    Kensington textile mill strike, *2:* 401–403
    Nativist Riots (1844), *2:* 311–318, 317 (ill.)
Peño Nieto, Enrique, *1:* 95, 96
Pentagon terror attack (2001), *2:* 326; *3:* 677–680. *See also* Terrorism
People for the Ethical Treatment of Animals (PETA)
    antifur campaign, *1:* 12–13, 13 (ill.)
    circus animals, *1:* 29
    founding, *1:* 4
    SeaWorld protests, *1:* 30
    support for ALF, *1:* 11
People's Climate March, *1:* 156
Perez, Carmen, *3:* 728
Periscope, *2:* 259
Perry, John B., *2:* 314–315
Perry, Rick, *2:* 288
Pesticides, *1:* 135, 224

PETA (People for the Ethical Treatment of Animals)
    antifur campaign, *1:* 12–13, 13 (ill.)
    circus animals, *1:* 29
    founding, *1:* 4
    SeaWorld protests, *1:* 30
    support for ALF, *1:* 11
Peter, Paul, and Mary, *3:* 670
Pethick-Lawrence, Emmeline, *3:* 660 (ill.), 661
Pew Research Center, *2:* 308, 453; *3:* 541 (ill.)
Pharmaceutical industry, *1:* 226–227, 227 (ill.)
Phelps, Fred, *2:* 446, 448
Philadelphia, PA, Nativist Riots (1844), *2:* 311–318, 317 (ill.)
Phipps, Benjamin, *3:* 629 (ill.)
Picketing, *3:* 563
Pieterson, Hector, *3:* 537
Pine Ridge Reservation, *2:* 370, 372, 374
Pixar Animation Studios, *1:* 28
Planned Parenthood, *3:* 558, 574, 575–576, 728.
    See also **Reproductive rights**
    anti-abortion demonstrators, *3:* 564 (ill.)
    debate over government funding for, *3:* 577–579
    pro-choice supporters, *3:* 579 (ill.)
    protests (2017), *3:* 574–580, 579 (ill.)
Planned Parenthood of Southeastern Pennsylvania v. Casey, 3: 561
Platform for People Affected by Mortgages (PAH), *1:* 120
Plessy v. Ferguson, 1: 48–49
Poaching
    elephants, *1:* 18–19, 25
    gorillas, *1:* 20
    rhinos, *1:* 18–19, 25
Podemos, *1:* 121–122
Poitier, Sidney, *1:* 68
Poland, Bialystok Ghetto, *3:* 607
Poland. Home Army, *3:* 589–590, 604
Polaris Project, *3:* 644, 646
Police
    impact of police shootings, *3:* 541 (ill.)
    racial discrimination, *3:* 513–514
    Watts Riots, *3:* 514 (ill.)
Police brutality, *3:* 525
Polish Home Army, *3:* 589–590, 604

Polish resistance (World War II), *3:* 589–590, 590 (ill.)
Political prisoners, *3:* 706
Political/Government uprisings, *3:* 467–507, 476 (ill.), 481 (ill.), 483 (ill.), 491 (ill.), 492 (ill.), 496 (ill.), 500 (ill.), 503 (ill.), 504 (ill.)
    Arab Spring and the Syrian Civil Uprising (2011), *3:* 486–493, 492 (ill.)
    causes of, *3:* 467–468
    Easter Rebellion (1916), *3:* 480–481, 481 (ill.)
    8888 Uprising, Myanmar (1988), *3:* 502–503, 503 (ill.)
    Fall of the Berlin Wall (1989), *3:* 478–486, 483 (ill.)
    history, *3:* 469–472
    Iranian Green Movement (2009), *3:* 490–491, 491 (ill.)
    Middle Ages, *3:* 469–470
    Tahrir Square Protests (Egyptian Revolution, 2011), *3:* 493–498, 496 (ill.)
    Tiananmen Square Protests (1989), *3:* 473–478, 476 (ill.)
    Umbrella Revolution (2014), *3:* 498–505, 500 (ill.), 504 (ill.)
PoliticsNation, 3: 544
Pollution, *1:* 134–135
Pompeo, Mike, *3:* 690
Popular Party (Spain), *1:* 121, 122
Populist movement, *1:* 218
Porkulus protests, Tea Party, *1:* 111–116, 114 (ill.).
    See also **Economic discontent**
Portuguese colonies. *See also* Colonization
    slave rebellions, *3:* 626–627
    slave trade, *3:* 621
    slavery, *3:* 511
Potter (Harry) Book Burning (2001), *1:* 177–183
Potter (Harry) (book series), *1:* 175
    book burning, *1:* 177–183
    opposition to, *1:* 179–180
Poverty, *1:* 101
Prague Spring, *2:* 353, 354 (ill.)
Preservation of Amazon Rain Forest Awareness Campaign (1989), *2:* 379–384
Presidential elections, *3:* 725–726
Presidential Medal of Freedom, *1:* 76 (ill.), 79

GENERAL INDEX

El Primer Congreso Mexicanista, *1:* 73
Prison colonies, *2:* 376. *See also* **Colonization**
Prisoners' rights, *2:* 270–276. *See also* **Human rights**
Prisons, human rights abuses, *2:* 270–271
Probst, Christoph, *3:* 593, 596
Pro-choice groups, *3:* 550–551, 554, 556, 574, 579 (ill.). *See also* **Reproductive rights**
Pro-democracy protests. *See* **Political/Government uprisings**
Progressive Party (United States), *3:* 710
Prohibition (1920–1933), *2:* 233–234
Project Confrontation, *1:* 62
Pro-life groups, *3:* 550, 554, 557, 574. *See also* **Reproductive rights**
   March for Life, *3:* 559
   murder by, *3:* 554–555
Pro-migrant rallies. *See also* **Immigrant rights**
   Europe and Australia, *2:* 318–325, 324 (ill.)
   Orestiada, Greece, *2:* 324 (ill.)
Protest literature, *3:* 631
Protest songs, *3:* 670–671
Protestant Reformation, *2:* 312–313
Protestants, *2:* 312
#ProtestPP, *3:* 574, 579–580
Protests. *See also* Boycotts; Riots; Sit-ins; Student protests
   African American civil rights, *1:* 35–70
   animal rights, *1:* 1–33
   athletes, *3:* 516–517
   economic discontent, *1:* 99–131
   environment, *1:* 133–170
   free speech, *1:* 171–202
   globalization, *1:* 203–231
   gun control/gun rights, *2:* 233–262, 237 (ill.), 238–239, 238 (ill.)
   Hispanic and Latino civil rights, *1:* 71–98
   HIV/AIDS drugs, *1:* 226–227
   human rights, *2:* 263–304
   immigrant rights, *2:* 305–334
   independence movements, *2:* 335–359
   indigenous peoples' rights, *2:* 361–392
   labor rights, *2:* 393–428
   LGBTQ rights, *2:* 429–466
   Mexican American students, *1:* 77–82
   political/government uprisings, *3:* 467–507

   racial conflict, *3:* 509–548
   reproductive rights, *3:* 549–583
   resistance to Nazis, *3:* 585–615
   slavery, *3:* 617–649
   in sports, *3:* 516–517
   tax, *1:* 111–116
   war, *3:* 651–692
   whaling, *1:* 22–23
   women's rights, *3:* 693–732
Protests against President Trump's travel ban (2017), *2:* 325–332, 330 (ill.). *See also* **Immigrant rights**
Protests of North Carolina House Bill 2 (2016), *2:* 458–464, 463 (ill.). *See also* **LGBTQ rights**
PSOE (Spanish Socialist Workers' Party), *1:* 120–121
Puerta del Sol, Madrid, Spain, *1:* 119, 121 (ill.)
Puerto Rico
   independence movements, *2:* 342–346
   as Spanish colony, *2:* 343–344
Pulse nightclub shootings, *2:* 257
Purple Teardrop Campaign, *3:* 646–647
Putin, Vladimir, *2:* 454

Q

Qaddafi, Mu'ammar al-, *3:* 488–489
al-Qaeda, *1:* 191
Qatar, labor rights, *2:* 398–399
Qin Shi Huang, *1:* 178
Qing Dynasty, *1:* 105–106
QR codes, *1:* 229
Quakers, *3:* 630, 652
Queer, *2:* 429. *See also* **LGBTQ people**
Quinn, William, *2:* 274

R

Race and racism, *3:* 509–510. *See also* White supremacists
   motivation for Zoot Suit riots, *3:* 523
   myth of racial superiority, *3:* 512–513

Racial conflict, *3:* **509–548**, 512 (ill.), 514 (ill.), 517 (ill.), 521 (ill.), 523 (ill.), 527 (ill.), 528 (ill.), 535 (ill.), 540 (ill.), 543 (ill.), 545 (ill.). *See also* **African American civil rights**; Black Lives Matter
   Black Consciousness Movement, *3:* 532–533
   Charlottesville Protests (2017), *3:* 542–543, 543 (ill.)
   Detroit Riots (1967), *3:* 524–530, 528 (ill.)
   Justice for All March (2014), *3:* 539–546, 545 (ill.)
   Los Angeles Race Riots (1992), *3:* 522–524, 523 (ill.)
   Mexican Americans, *3:* 518–524
   New York City Draft Riots (1863), *3:* 526–527, 527 (ill.)
   Soweto Uprising (1976), *3:* 530–539, 535 (ill.)
   Sports, protests in, *3:* 516–517, 517 (ill.)
   United States, *3:* 515–518
   Zoot Suit Riots (1943), *3:* 512, 512 (ill.), 518–524, 521 (ill.)
Racial discrimination, *1:* 35. *See also* Apartheid; Discrimination; Jim Crow laws
   African Americans, *1:* 36–37; *3:* 512, 513–515
   bus service, *1:* 54–59
   Mexican Americans, *3:* 519
   police, *3:* 513–514
   segregation and, *1:* 42
   South Africa, *3:* 513
Racial profiling, *3:* 539
Racial sensitivity, *1:* 194, 200
Racial superiority, *3:* 509–510, 512–513
Rain forests, *2:* 366, 379–380
Randolph, A. Philip, *1:* 64, 65–66, 68
Rankin, Jeannette, *3:* 711
Raoni (1977), *2:* 382
Raoni Metuktire, *2:* 366, 380–381, 383 (ill.)
Ray, Gloria, *1:* 50, 51
Reagan, Leslie J., *3:* 552
Reagan, Ronald, *2:* 245, 281
   Berlin Wall speech, *3:* 484–485
   position on reproductive rights, *3:* 559
   reproductive rights, *3:* 558
Redwoods, *1:* 152
Reed (Walter) Medical Center, *3:* 688–689, 689 (ill.)
Refugees. *See also* Immigrants and immigration
   Afghanistan, *2:* 319

   camps, *2:* 319–320, 320
   climate, *1:* 159
   crisis in Europe, *2:* 309–310, 324–325
   dangerous journeys, *2:* 323–324
   defined, *2:* 320
   EU (European Union), *2:* 319–321
   Middle Eastern, *2:* 318–319
   Syrian, *2:* 319, 321; *3:* 493, 720–724
Regan, Tom, *1:* 4
Reich, Robert, *2:* 425
Reid, Eric, *3:* 517 (ill.)
Religion, free speech and, *1:* 176, 183
Religious freedom, *2:* 311
Reproductive health services, *3:* 575
Reproductive rights, *3:* **549–583**, 557 (ill.), 564 (ill.), 567 (ill.), 572 (ill.), 577 (ill.), 579 (ill.). *See also* Abortion; Pro-choice groups; Pro-life groups; **Women's rights**
   debate over, *3:* 549–550
   history, *3:* 551–555
   laws limiting, *3:* 555
   March for Life (1986), *3:* 558, 559
   March for Women's Lives (1986), *3:* 556–561, 557 (ill.)
   McCorvey, Norma, *3:* 576–577, 577 (ill.)
   One Child Policy Riots (2007), *3:* 568–574, 572 (ill.)
   ongoing fight over, *3:* 555–556
   Operation Rescue (1992), *3:* 562–568, 564 (ill.)
   Planned Parenthood Protests (2017), *3:* 574–580, 579 (ill.)
   Summer of Mercy Protest (1991), *3:* 566–567
Republican National Convention (RNC), *3:* 564, 678
Reservation system
   India, *2:* 292–293
   private businesses, *2:* 294–295
Resistance to Nazis, *3:* **585–615**, 590 (ill.), 593 (ill.), 596 (ill.), 601 (ill.), 606 (ill.), 611 (ill.). *See also* Nazi Germany
   beginnings, *3:* 587–588
   Holocaust Resistance in Denmark (1943), *3:* 597–602, 601 (ill.)
   peaceful resistance, *3:* 588–589
   Treblinka Death Camp Revolt (1943), *3:* 607–614, 611 (ill.)

violent resistance, *3:* 590–591
  Warsaw Ghetto Uprising (1943), *3:* 602–607, 606 (ill.)
  White Rose Movement (1942–1943), *3:* 592–597, 593 (ill.), 596 (ill.)
Revolutionary Committee of Puerto Rico, *2:* 344–345
Rhino horn, *1:* 19
Rhinos
  poaching, *1:* 18–19, 25
  population decline, *1:* 21–22
Rhodes, James A., *3:* 674–675
Rice Riots of 1918 (Japan), *1:* 126–127
Richards, Cecile, *3:* 579, 728
Rig Veda, *2:* 290–291
Ringling Bros. and Barnum & Bailey Circus, *1:* 5, 29, 29 (ill.)
Riots. *See also* Protests; Violence
  anti-immigrant, *2:* 328–329
  Detroit Riots (MI) (1967), *3:* 524–530, 528 (ill.)
  Los Angeles Race Riots (1992), *3:* 522–523, 523 (ill.)
  Nativist riots, Philadelphia, Pennsylvania, *2:* 311–318, 317 (ill.)
  New York City Draft Riots (1863), *3:* 526–527, 527 (ill.), 654
  One Child Policy Riots (2007), *3:* 568–574, 572 (ill.)
  Rice Riots of 1918, *1:* 126–127
  Stonewall Riots (1969), *2:* 432–433, 435–441, 440 (ill.)
  White Night Riots (1979), *2:* 441–445, 444 (ill.)
  Zoot Suit Riots (1943), *3:* 512, 512 (ill.), 518–524, 521 (ill.)
RNC (Republican National Convention), *3:* 564, 678
Roberts, John, *1:* 87
Roberts, Terrence, *1:* 50
Robinson, Jackie, *1:* 68
Rock Hill, SC, Freedom Rides, *1:* 56
Rockefeller, Nelson, *2:* 273, 275
Roe v. Wade, 3: 554, 556, 575–576. *See also* McCorvey, Norma.
Roeder, Scott, *3:* 567
Rohingya, violence against, *3:* 503

Rolling Stone, 1: 177
Roman Empire (27 BCE–476 CE), *2:* 305–306; *3:* 617–619
Romney, George, *3:* 528, 529, 530–531
Roosevelt, Franklin D., *1:* 64; *2:* 277, 407, 414
Roosevelt, Theodore, *1:* 135 (ill.); *2:* 399, 405; *3:* 710
Roper v. Simmons, 2: 285
Rose Parade, SeaWorld protests, *1:* 30,
Rowling, J.K., *1:* 175, 177, 182–183
Royal Society for the Prevention of Cruelty to Animals (RSPCA), *1:* 2–3
RSPCA (Royal Society for the Prevention of Cruelty to Animals), *1:* 2–3
Rubio, Marco, *1:* 115
Rudd, Kevin, *2:* 379
Runaway children, *3:* 645
Russia, *2:* 454–455, 455 (ill.). *See also* Soviet Union
Rustin, Bayard, *1:* 65–66
Ryan, Paul, *1:* 115; *2:* 260

S

Sacramento, CA, Black Panthers protest Mulford Act, *2:* 239–245, 243 (ill.)
Sacred Stone Camp, *2:* 367, 387–388
Sadler, Barry, *3:* 671
Salazar, Sonia, *1:* 81 (ill.)
Saleh, Ali Abdullah, *3:* 488–489
Salman bin Abdulaziz al Saud, King of Saudi Arabia, *3:* 717
Salovey, Peter, *1:* 200
Salt Acts, *2:* 341
Same-sex marriage, *2:* 430, 434, 438–439, 439 (ill.)
San Bernardino, CA, terrorist attack, *2:* 328
San Diego, CA, SeaWorld protest, *1:* 30
San Francisco Chronicle, 2: 245
Sanctions, *3:* 538
Sanders, Bernie, *1:* 229, 230; *2:* 426
Sandy Hook Elementary School mass shooting, *2:* 246–247
Sanger, Margaret, *3:* 558, 575
Santelli, Rick, *1:* 113
Sappho, *2:* 430
Sarsour, Linda, *3:* 728

Satrom, LeRoy, *3:* 674
Saudi Arabia
    Baladi campaign, *3:* 699, 714–718, 716 (ill.)
    women's rights, *3:* 714–715
Saudi Arabia. Shura Council, *3:* 716
Savage, Adam, *1:* 166–167
Save the Rhino, *1:* 21
Savio, Mario, *1:* 198
Schell, Paul, *1:* 214–215
Scheuer, Sandra, *3:* 675
Schmidt, Douglas, *2:* 444
Schmorell, Alexander, *3:* 593, 596
Scholl, Hans, *3:* 588, 592, 593, 596
Scholl, Sophie, *3:* 588, 592, 593, 593 (ill.), 595–596, 596
School segregation. *See also* Desegregation/Segregation
    Little Rock, AR, *1:* 47–52
    New Orleans, LA, *1:* 53
Schroeder, William, *3:* 675
Schwerner, Michael Henry, *1:* 58, 58 (ill.)
Schwimmer, Rosika, *3:* 660
Science Champions, *1:* 168
Scientific American, 1: 100
Scientists, as activists, *1:* 168
Scott, Elizabeth, *2:* 254–255
Sea level rise, *1:* 137, 146, 157–158. *See also* **Environment**
Seale, Bobby, *2:* 240, 242
Seaman, Elizabeth Cochrane, *2:* 278
Seattle, Washington, WTO protests, *1:* 209–216, 214 (ill.)
SeaWorld
    protests against, *1:* 25–31, 28, 30
    treatment of orcas, *1:* 26–27, 30–31
Secret Document of the Farmers of Xiaogang (1978), *1:* 105–111, 109 (ill.). *See also* **Economic discontent**
Seeds, genetically modified, *1:* 223
Seeger, Pete, *3:* 670
Segregation. *See* Desegregation/Segregation
Seim, Gavin, *2:* 254
Selbekk, Vebjørn, *1:* 185
Self-censorship, *1:* 184, 187
Semiautomatic weapons, *2:* 247
Seneca Falls Convention (1848), *3:* 696, 708, 708 (ill.)

Seneca Falls Convention (1848). Declaration of Sentiments, *3:* 708, 709 (ill.)
Sensenbrenner, James, Jr., *1:* 84–86, 87
Serfdom, *3:* 619–620
Service Employees International Union, *2:* 424
Sex reassignment surgery, *2:* 452–453
Sexual orientation, *2:* 429
Sexual predators, *2:* 459
Shanghai Pride Festival (2009), *2:* 452–458, 456 (ill.). *See also* **LGBTQ rights**
Shapi Township, Guangdong, China, *3:* 572
Sharia, *3:* 715, 718, 719
Sharpe, Samuel, *3:* 634, 635–637, 635 (ill.)
Sharpeville Massacre (1960), *3:* 534
Sharpton, Al, *3:* 539, 544, 546
Shekau, Abubaka, *3:* 722
Sheldrick (David) Wildlife Trust, *1:* 22
Shepard, Judy, *2:* 446, 450
Shepard, Matthew, *2:* 434, 446–447
    The Laramie Project, *2:* 456–457
    murder of, *2:* 445–446, 447
Shepard (Matthew) and James Byrd, Jr., Hate Crimes Prevention Act, *2:* 450, 451
Shepard (Matthew) Foundation, *2:* 447
Shook, Teresa, *3:* 726–727
Sicilia, Javier, *1:* 90, 91 (ill.), 92–93, 94
Sicilia, Juan Francisco, *1:* 92
Sidewalk counseling, *3:* 563
Sierra Club, *1:* 135, 213
Silent Spring (1962), *1:* 135
Singer, Peter, *1:* 3–4
Singh, Manmohar, *2:* 296
Singing Revolution (1988), *2:* 348
Single women, rights of, *3:* 693–695
Sisi, Abdel Fattah el-, *3:* 498
Sit-ins, *1:* 59–63; *2:* 256–257. *See also* Protests
    Democratic Congressional Representatives for Gun Control, *2:* 256–260, 259 (ill.)
    fast-food workers strikes, *2:* 425
    redwood trees, *1:* 152, 153 (ill.)
    University of California Berkeley, *1:* 198
Sitting Bull, *2:* 369
Skokie, Illinois, proposed neo-Nazi march, *1:* 188–189, 189 (ill.)
Slater, Amber, *2:* 242

GENERAL INDEX

Slave codes, *3:* 624
Slave rebellions, *3:* 623–624
    Christmas Rebellion/Baptist War (1831–1832), *3:* 634–638
    Louisiana Rebellion (German Coast), *3:* 623–628
    Malê Revolt of 1835, *3:* 626–627
    Turner's (Nat) rebellion (1831), *3:* 628–634, 629 (ill.)
Slave trade, *3:* 620–621, 621 (ill.)
    end of, *3:* 622
    triangular trade, *3:* 621
Slavery, *1:* 35, 36–37; *3:* 510–511, **617–649,** 619 (ill.), 621 (ill.), 629 (ill.), 633 (ill.), 635 (ill.), 639 (ill.), 640 (ill.), 642 (ill.), 644 (ill.), 647 (ill.).
    See also Abolition of slavery; Human trafficking
    Africa, *3:* 620–621
    American westward expansion, *3:* 638, 639–640
    ancient world, *3:* 617–619, 619 (ill.)
    Christmas Rebellion/Baptist War (1831–1832), *3:* 634–638, 635 (ill.)
    Fight to Stop Human Trafficking, *3:* 643–647, 644 (ill.)
    Harpers Ferry Raid (1859), *3:* 638–643, 642 (ill.)
    Louisiana Rebellion (German Coast) (1811), *3:* 623–628
    Malê Revolt of 1835, *3:* 626–627, 627 (ill.)
    Middle Ages, *3:* 619–620
    modern, *3:* 623
    Nat Turner's Rebellion/Anti-slavery petitions, *3:* 628–634, 629 (ill.). 633 (ill.)
    Native Americans, *3:* 624
    slave ships, *3:* 621, 621 (ill.)
    symbols of at Yale, *1:* 195, 196
Sleepy Lagoon murder, *3:* 520
Slovakia, *2:* 357–358
Smeal, Eleanor, *3:* 559–560
Smith, Molly, *2:* 247–249
Smith, Tommie, *3:* 516, 517 (ill.)
SNCC (Student Nonviolent Coordinating Committee), *1:* 57, 58
    Berkeley free speech movement, *1:* 198
    March on Washington, *1:* 65
    sit-ins, *1:* 60
Socialism, *3:* 587
Socialists, resistance to Nazis, *3:* 587–588

Society for Human Rights, *2:* 432
Solidarity movement, *2:* 356. *See also* **Labor rights**
Soroptimist International, *3:* 644 (ill.), 646–647
South Africa
    black consciousness movement, *3:* 532–533
    boycotts, *3:* 538
    brief history, *3:* 532–533
    HIV/AIDS drugs protests, *1:* 226–227, 227 (ill.)
    indigenous peoples, *3:* 532–533, 534
    racial discrimination, *3:* 513
    Soweto Uprising (1976), *3:* 530–539, 535 (ill.)
    student protests, *3:* 530–539, 535 (ill.)
    violence against blacks, *3:* 513
South America, *1:* 71, 72
South Carolina, Freedom Rides, *1:* 56
South Dakota
    AIM Occupation of Wounded Knee (1973), *2:* 367–375, 374 (ill.)
    Wounded Knee Massacre (1890), *2:* 369–370, 369 (ill.), 373
South Vietnam, *2:* 340 (ill.). *See also* Vietnam
Southern Christian Leadership Council, *1:* 65
Southern Poverty Law Center (SPLC), *2:* 446
Soviet Union. *See also* Russia
    book burning, *1:* 178
    break-up, *3:* 486
    control of Czechoslovakia, *2:* 353–354
    Estonian revolution, *2:* 348
    invasion of Czechoslovakia, *2:* 354 (ill.)
Soviet Union. Red Army, *2:* 354 (ill.)
Soweto Uprising (1976), *3:* 530–539, 535 (ill.). *See also* **Racial conflict**
    effects of, *3:* 538–539
    eyewitness account, *3:* 536–537
    spreading unrest, *3:* 537–538
Spain
    austerity measures, *1:* 117–118, 121
    Bilbao Anti-bullfighting Protest (2010), *1:* 12–18, 17 (ill.)
    15-M movement, *1:* 90, 116–122, 121 (ill.)
    Global Recession of 2008, *1:* 104–105, 116–117
Spanish colonies. *See also* Colonization
    independence movements, *2:* 338–339
    Puerto Rico, *2:* 343–344
    slave trade, *3:* 621
    slavery, *3:* 511

Spanish Socialist Workers' Party (PSOE), *1:* 120–121
Spanish-American War (1898), *2:* 338–339, 346
SPLC (Southern Poverty Law Center), *2:* 446
Sports, protests in, *3:* 516–517, 517 (ill.)
Spring of Life, *3:* 562, 564–565
    counterprotests, *3:* 565
    results of protest, *3:* 566–568
Springsteen, Bruce, *2:* 462
Stalingrad, Battle of (1943), *3:* 594–595, 609
Stand for Freedom, *3:* 647
Standing Rock Pipeline Protest (2016). *See* Dakota Access Pipeline (DAPL) Protest; **Indigenous peoples' rights**
    Dennis Banks, *2:* 390–391
    Native Americans, *2:* 367 (ill.)
Standing Rock Reservation, *2:* 369, 370, 384
Standing Rock Sioux, *2:* 384–385, 387–388, 388 (ill.). *See also* Native Americans
Stanton, Elizabeth Cady, *3:* 696, 697 (ill.), 708, 708 (ill.), 710
Starr, Edwin, *3:* 670
Stauffenberg, Claus von, *3:* 591
Steinem, Gloria, *3:* 560, 728
Sterilization, *3:* 549
Sting, *2:* 366, 383, 383 (ill.)
Stonewall Inn, *2:* 432, 436–437, 439, 441
Stonewall Riots (1969), *2:* 432–433, 435–441, 440 (ill.). *See also* **LGBTQ rights**
Stookey, N. Paul, *1:* 68
Stowe, Harriet Beecher, *3:* 631, 631 (ill.), 638
Strangeways Prison Riot (1990), *2:* 271
Street art, *1:* 212, 212 (ill.)
Strikes, *2:* 397. *See also* **Labor rights**; Protests
    cigar workers, *1:* 84
    coal miners, *2:* 410–411
    Delano Grape Strike and Boycott, *2:* 414–422
    equal pay for women, *3:* 728–729
    fast-food workers, *2:* 422–426, 424 (ill.)
    Flint strike against General Motors, *2:* 407–414, 412 (ill.)
    Gdansk Shipyard, Poland, *2:* 356–357, 357 (ill.)
    Kensington textile mill, *2:* 401–403
    legalization, *2:* 409
    McCormick Reaper Works, *2:* 418
    slaves, *3:* 634, 635–636
    University of California Berkeley, *1:* 199
Stroop, Jürgen, *3:* 605, 606
Student Armband Protest of Vietnam War (1965–1969), *3:* 663–668, 668 (ill.). *See also* Anti-war protests
Student Nonviolent Coordinating Committee (SNCC), *1:* 57, 58
    Berkeley free speech movement, *1:* 198
    March on Washington, *1:* 65
    sit-ins, *1:* 60
Student Protest at Kent State (1970), *3:* 669–676, 674 (ill.). *See also* Anti-war protests
    eyewitness account, *3:* 672–673
    wounded student, *3:* 674 (ill.)
Student protests. *See also* Protests
    counterprotests in Charlottesville, VA, *3:* 542
    Hong Kong, *3:* 500–501
    Kent State (1970), *3:* 669–676, 674 (ill.)
    Paris, France, *1:* 118–119, 119 (ill.)
    Soweto uprising, *3:* 530–539, 535 (ill.)
    Student Armband Protest of Vietnam War (1965–1969), *3:* 663–668, 668 (ill.)
    Vietnam War, *3:* 669–676
    White Rose movement, *3:* 588
The Suffragette, *3:* 705 (ill.)
Suffragettes. *See* Women's suffrage movement
Suffragists. *See* Women's suffrage movement
Summer of Mercy Protest (1991), *3:* 566–567
Sumner, Gordon, *2:* 366, 383, 383 (ill.)
Sun Yat-sen, *1:* 107
Supreme Court (United States). *See* United States. Supreme Court
Survivors, Armenian genocide, *2:* 299
Suu Kyi, Aung San, *3:* 502–503, 503 (ill.)
Sweden
    escape of Danish Jews to, *3:* 597, 601 (ill.)
    Melchior, Bent, escape to, *3:* 598–599
Sydney, Australia, aboriginal land rights protest, *2:* 375–379
Syria
    Arab Spring, *3:* 491–493, 492 (ill.)
    civil war, *2:* 319; *3:* 492–493, 720–721
Syrian refugees, *2:* 319, 321; *3:* 493, 720–724. *See also* Refugees

T

Tahrir Square protests (2011), *3:* 493–498, 494–495, 496 (ill.). *See also* **Political/Government uprisings**
Taigman, Kalman, *3:* 610
Taino (indigenous people), *2:* 343. *See also* Indigenous peoples
Taliban, *3:* 681, 719
Tariffs, *1:* 210
TARP (United States. Troubled Asset Relief Program), *1:* 112
Tax protests, *1:* 111–116
Tea Party movement, *1:* 103–104, 111–116, 114 (ill.)
    demonstration in Fort Myers, Florida, *1:* 114 (ill.)
    first events, *1:* 113–114
    membership statistics, *1:* 114–115
    mid-term elections of 2010, *1:* 115
Tema, Sophie Topsie, *3:* 536–537
Terauchi Masatake, *1:* 127, 127 (ill.)
Terra nullius, 2: 376
Terrorism, *1:* 190; *2:* 285
    animal rights, *1:* 4
    ecoterrorism, *1:* 11
    fears of, *2:* 310
    San Bernardino, California, *2:* 328
    Syria, *3:* 489
    United States, *2:* 326
    World Trade Center/Pentagon terror attack (2001), *3:* 677–680
Terrorist watch list, *2:* 257, 260
Testerman, Cabell, *2:* 410
Texas
    executions, *2:* 284
    Huey P. Newton Gun Club demonstrations, *2:* 244
    March to Abolish the Death Penalty, *2:* 287, 287 (ill.)
Textile mills, child labor, *2:* 400 (ill.)
Thebes, *3:* 469
Thomas, Jefferson, *1:* 50
Thoreau, Henry David, *1:* 133
350.org, *1:* 157, 161

Tiananmen Square protests, *3:* 473–478, 476 (ill.). *See also* **Political/Government uprisings**
    eyewitness account, *3:* 474–475
    origins, *3:* 473–474
    use of military force, *3:* 477–478
Tilikum, *1:* 5, 26, 27 (ill.), 31
Tillard, Violet, *3:* 703–704
Tiller, George, *3:* 566–567
Timberlake, Justin, *2:* 423
Times of India, 2: 296
Tinker, John, *3:* 664, 665, 668, 668 (ill.)
Tinker, Mary Beth, *3:* 664, 665, 668, 668 (ill.)
Tinker v. Des Moines Independent Community School District, 3: 657, 667–668
Title X, *3:* 577–578
Tlatelolco Massacre (1968), *1:* 94, 95. *See also* **Hispanic and Latino civil rights**
Tokyo Big March, *1:* 160
Tometi, Opal, *3:* 541
Torture, *3:* 686
Toxic chemical spills, Bhopal, India, *1:* 136
Toxic wastes
    fracking, *1:* 153–154
    Love Canal, *1:* 136, 143
Trafficking Victims Protection Act (TVPA), *3:* 646
Trail of Tears protest, *2:* 386–387
TransCanada, *1:* 140
Transgender people, *2:* 429, 435. *See also* LGBTQ people; Manning, Bradley/Chelsea
Transgender rights, *2:* 435. *See also* **LGBTQ rights**
    China, *2:* 452–453
    North Carolina, *2:* 458–464
Travers, Mary, *1:* 68
Treason, *2:* 285
Treaty of New Echota, *2:* 386
Treblinka
    closing of, *3:* 613–614
    deportations to, *3:* 604, 606
Treblinka Death Camp Revolt (1943), *3:* 607–614. *See also* **Resistance to Nazis**
Tree sitting, *1:* 152
Tresckow, Henning von, *3:* 591
Trial by jury, *2:* 265
Triangular trade, *3:* 621
Trick (music group), *1:* 30

Troubled Asset Relief Program (TARP), *1:* 112
Trump, Donald, *1:* 89, 115
    ban on transgender people in military, *2:* 435
    birth control and health insurance plans, *3:* 556
    Charlottesville protests, *3:* 543
    climate change policies, *1:* 165–166
    criticism of NFL protesters, *3:* 515
    Dakota Access Pipeline, *2:* 367, 385, 391
    election of 2016, *3:* 725–726
    immigration policy, *2:* 310
    Keystone XL project, *1:* 139, 144
    reproductive rights, *3:* 578
    supporters, *1:* 177 (ill.)
    women's protest marches, *3:* 724–731
Trump travel bans (2017). *See also* **Immigrant rights**
    airport protests, *2:* 330–331, 330 (ill.)
    countries excluded in first travel ban, *2:* 326 (ill.)
    demonstrations against, *2:* 330 (ill.)
    lawsuit against, *2:* 331–332
    Muslims, *2:* 325–326
    protests against, *2:* 325–332, 330 (ill.)
    worldwide protests, *2:* 331
Tubman, Harriet, *3:* 639 (ill.)
Tucson, AZ, mass shooting, *2:* 248
Tunisia
    Arab Spring, *2:* 318–319; *3:* 487–488
    democracy in, *3:* 493
Tunisian Revolution, *3:* 488, 495
Turkey
    American protests against, *2:* 302
    Armenian genocide denial, *2:* 300–301
Turner, Nat, *3:* 628–629, 629 (ill.)
Turner's (Nat) Rebellion (1831–1832), *3:* 628–634, 629 (ill.). *See also* **Slavery**
Turning Hawk, *2:* 373
Tuvalu, *1:* 147
TVPA (United States. Trafficking Victims Protection Act), *3:* 646
12th Street Riots, Detroit, MI, *3:* 524–530, 528 (ill.)
    aftermath, *3:* 529–530
    origins in "blind pig," *3:* 525
    Romney, George, interview, *3:* 530–531
"Twinkie defense," *2:* 444

U

UAW (United Auto Workers), *2:* 408, 409, 414
UCR (University of California, Riverside)
    animal experimentation, *1:* 7–8
    lab raid to protest animal testing, *1:* 7–11
UFW (United Farm Workers), *2:* 414–415, 420
Umbrella Revolution (2014), *3:* 498–505, 500 (ill.), 504 (ill.). *See also* **Political/Government uprisings**
Umpqua Community College, mass shootings, *2:* 251
Unauthorized immigration. *See* Undocumented immigrants
Uncle Tom's Cabin, *3:* 631, 638
Underground Railroad, *3:* 639
Undocumented immigrants, *1:* 74, 83–84; *2:* 325. *See also* Immigrants and immigration
UNFCCC (United Nations. Framework Convention on Climate Change), *1:* 137, 145
Union of Concerned Scientists, *1:* 168
Unitarians, *3:* 652
United Airlines Flight 93, *3:* 677
United Airlines Flight 175, *3:* 677, 678
United Auto Workers (UAW), *2:* 408, 409, 414
United Farm Workers of America, *1:* 78
United Farm Workers (UFW), *2:* 414–415, 420
United for Peace and Justice, *3:* 678–679
United Kingdom. *See also* British colonies
    abolition of slavery, *2:* 268; *3:* 637
    anti-fracking protesters, *1:* 155 (ill.)
    Easter Rebellion, *3:* 480–481
    exit from EU, *1:* 103–104, 122–129
    immigrants and immigration, *1:* 123, 124
    Industrial Revolution, *2:* 395, 395 (ill.)
    women's suffrage movement, *3:* 471–472, 697–698, 701–707
United Kingdom. Act to Prevent the Cruel and Improper Treatment of Cattle in the United Kingdom (1822), *1:* 2
United Kingdom. Cat and Mouse Act, *3:* 706
United Kingdom. Equal Suffrage Act, *3:* 707
United Kingdom. Health and Morals of Apprentices Act of 1802, *2:* 395

United Kingdom. Pease's Act, *1:* 2
United Kingdom. Prisoners (Temporary Discharge for Ill-Health) Act, *3:* 706
United Kingdom. Representation of the People Act, *3:* 706–707
United Kingdom. Slavery Abolition Act of 1833, *2:* 268; *3:* 637
United Nations
   abolition of slavery, *3:* 643
   environmental protection, *1:* 137
   human rights, *2:* 264, 268–269
   measurement of human development, *1:* 101–102
United Nations. Climate Change Conference, *1:* 144–145
United Nations. Framework Convention on Climate Change (UNFCCC), *1:* 137, 145
United Nations. Intergovernmental Panel on Climate Change (IPCC), *1:* 137, 148
United States. *See also* American Revolutionary War (1775–1783); United States Civil War (1861–1865); Specific states and cities
   abolition of slavery, *2:* 268; *3:* 633
   anti-gay laws, *2:* 432
   anti-war protests, *3:* 653–657
   attitudes about climate change, *1:* 164, 164 (ill.)
   book burning, *1:* 178
   child labor, *2:* 401
   civil rights movement, *3:* 472
   Day without Immigrants protests, *1:* 83–89
   free speech, *1:* 173–174
   gun control, *2:* 233–235
   gun ownership, *2:* 233–235, 235 (ill.)
   gun protests, *2:* 238–239
   hate crimes, *3:* 518 (ill.)
   hate groups, *3:* 518 (ill.)
   Hispanic and Latino population, *1:* 75–76
   immigrants and immigration, *1:* 74, 83–85; *2:* 306–309
   immigration policy, *1:* 83–85, 89; *2:* 416
   income inequality, *1:* 99–100
   labor laws, *2:* 397–398
   labor rights, *2:* 394
   migrant workers, *2:* 415
   presidential election of 2016, *3:* 725–726
   racial conflict, *3:* 515–518
   recession of 2008, *1:* 112–113
   sanctions against China, *3:* 478
   slavery, *3:* 622
   Tea Party movement, *1:* 103–104
   terrorism, *2:* 326
   treatment of Native Americans, *2:* 368–369
   undocumented immigrants, *1:* 74; *2:* 325
   westward expansion, *1:* 72–73
   women in early United States, *3:* 696
   women's rights movement, *3:* 696–698
   women's suffrage movement, *3:* 707–713
United States. American Recovery and Reinvestment Act (ARRA), *1:* 113
United States. Americans with Disabilities Act (ADA), *2:* 277, 280–283
United States. Animal Welfare Act of 1966, *1:* 3
United States. Army Corp of Engineers, *2:* 385, 389–390
United States. Bald and Golden Eagle Protection Act, *1:* 135
United States. Bill of Rights, *1:* 174; *2:* 267
United States. Brady Handgun Violence Prevention Act, *2:* 236–237, 253
United States. Centers for Disease Control and Prevention, *3:* 556
United States. Chinese Exclusion Act, *2:* 329, 416
United States. Civil Rights Act of 1957, *1:* 41
United States. Civil Rights Act of 1960, *1:* 41
United States. Civil Rights Act of 1964, *1:* 40, 41, 69
United States. Civil Rights Act of 1968, *1:* 40, 41
United States. Comprehensive Environmental Response, Compensation, and Liability Act (CERCLA), *1:* 143
United States. Comstock Act, *3:* 553, 575
United States. Congress. House of Representatives, *2:* 256–260, 259 (ill.)
United States. Congress. HR 4437, *1:* 83–85, 89
United States. Constitution. 1st Amendment, *1:* 174–175
United States. Constitution. 2nd Amendment, *2:* 237, 252, 254–255
United States. Constitution. 13th Amendment, *2:* 268; *3:* 622, 633
United States. Constitution. 14th Amendment, *1:* 46, 49; *3:* 709

United States. Constitution. 15th Amendment, *3:* 709–710
United States. Constitution. 19th Amendment, *3:* 698 (ill.), 708, 713
United States. Defense of Marriage Act, *2:* 438
United States. Department of Justice (DOJ), *2:* 463
United States. DREAM Act (Development, Relief, and Education for Alien Minors Act), *1:* 89
United States. Education for All Handicapped Children Act, *2:* 278
United States. Emergency Economic Stabilization Act of 2008, *1:* 112
United States. Endangered Species Act, *1:* 136
United States. Energy Information Administration (EIA), *1:* 155
United States. Environmental Protection Agency (EPA), *1:* 136
United States. Fair Housing Act of 1968, *1:* 40, 41
United States. Fair Labor Standards Act of 1938, *2:* 397–398, 407
United States. Federal Assault Weapons Ban, *2:* 234–235
United States. Federal Bureau of Investigation (FBI), *3:* 686–687, 725
United States. Firearms Owners' Protection Act, *2:* 234
United States. Freedom of Access to Clinic Entrances Act (FACE Act), *3:* 568
United States. Gun Control Act, *2:* 234
United States. Individuals with Disabilities Education Act (IDEA), *2:* 278
United States. Interstate Commerce Commission, *1:* 54–55, 57, 59
United States. Law Enforcement Officers Protection Act, *2:* 234
United States. Marine Mammal Protection Act, *1:* 136
United States. Matthew Shepard and James Byrd, Jr., Hate Crimes Prevention Act, *2:* 450, 451
United States. National Firearms Act, *2:* 234
United States. National Guard, *2:* 275, 389
United States. National Guard (Arkansas), *1:* 48, 50–52, 52 (ill.)
United States. National Guard (Michigan), *3:* 528, 528 (ill.), 531
United States. National Guard (Ohio), *3:* 674–675
United States. National Instant Criminal Background Check System, *2:* 253

United States. National Institutes of Health, *1:* 9–10
United States. National Labor Relations Act (Wagner Act), *2:* 397, 409
United States. National Oceanic and Atmospheric Administration (NOAA), *1:* 136
United States. National Park Service (NPS), *1:* 135
United States. No Taxpayer Funding for Abortion and Abortion Insurance Full Disclosure Act, *3:* 580
United States. Partial-Birth Abortion Act, *3:* 561
United States. Supreme Court
 abortion rights, *3:* 554
 death penalty, *2:* 285
 defining free speech, *1:* 175
 LGBTQ rights, *2:* 432
 marriage equality, *2:* 434, 438–439
 neo-Nazi march, *1:* 188–189
 right to free speech, *3:* 667–668
United States. Trafficking Victims Protection Act (TVPA), *3:* 646
United States. Troubled Asset Relief Program (TARP), *1:* 112
United States. Voting Rights Act of 1965, *1:* 40, 41, 58, 69
United States Civil War (1861–1865), *2:* 268. *See also* United States
 anti-war protests, *3:* 653–654
 impact on women's rights movement, *3:* 709–710
 military draft, *3:* 526
Universal Declaration of Human Rights (UDHR), *2:* 268–269, 290; *3:* 646
University of California, Berkeley, *1:* 176–177, 177 (ill.), 198–199, 199 (ill.)
 free speech movement (1964), *1:* 198–199, 199 (ill.)
 free speech rally, *1:* 176–177, 177 (ill.)
University of California, Riverside
 animal experimentation, *1:* 7–8
 lab raid to protest animal testing, *1:* 7–11
University of Maine. Basketball team, *2:* 460, 461 (ill.)
University of Munich, *3:* 588, 593, 595, 597
University of Pennsylvania. Head Injury Lab, *1:* 9
Untouchability, *2:* 292. *See also* Dalits
Uprising of 1967 (Detroit, MI), *3:* 524–530, 528 (ill.)
 aftermath, *3:* 529–530
 origins in "blind pig," *3:* 525
 Romney, George, interview, *3:* 530–531
Urbanization, *2:* 400

GENERAL INDEX

V

Van Buren, Martin, *2:* 387 (ill.)
Varna, *2:* 291
Velvet Divorce, *2:* 357–358
Velvet Revolution (1989), *2:* 341–342, 352–358. *See also* **Independence movements**
Venezuela, human rights protests, *2:* 269
Vera, Raul, *1:* 91 (ill.)
Vietnam
    independence movements, *2:* 339–340
    partition, *2:* 340 (ill.)
Vietnam War (1954–1975), *2:* 339–340; *3:* 664–665, 669–671
    anti-war protests, *3:* 655–656, 663–668, 669–676
    Nixon ends war, *3:* 676
    protest songs, *3:* 670–671
    student protests, *3:* 669–676
Villas Boas, Leonardo, *2:* 380–381
Villas Boas, Orlando, *2:* 380–381
Violence. *See also* Murder; Riots
    against African Americans, *1:* 38, 40, 56–57, 56 (ill.), 58, 62; *3:* 526–527
    against black South Africans, *3:* 513
    against cigar workers, *1:* 84
    against Dalits, *2:* 293–294, 297
    drug trade, *1:* 91–92
    against Iranian demonstrators, *3:* 490–491
    against Mexican students, *1:* 90, 94
    against Myanmar protesters, *3:* 502
    racial conflict, *3:* 512
    against Rohingya, *3:* 503
    against Tiananmen Square protesters, *3:* 477–478
    against women's health clinics, *3:* 558
    against WTO protesters, *1:* 215
Virginia
    anti-slavery petitions, *3:* 628–634
    Charlottesville Protests (2017), *3:* 542–543, 543 (ill.)
    debate over slavery, *3:* 628, 632
    Harpers Ferry Raid (1859), *3:* 638–643, 642 (ill.)
    Turner's (Nat) Rebellion (1831), *3:* 628–634, 629 (ill.)
Virginia Tech, mass shooting, *2:* 249
Virginia Yearly Meeting of the Society of Friends, *3:* 630
Vocal Majority Tour (2016), *2:* 248, 248 (ill.)
Votes for Women, 3: 703
Voting rights, *1:* 40, 58. *See also* Civil rights; Women's suffrage movement
Voting Rights Act of 1965, *1:* 40, 41, 58, 69

W

Wade, Henry, *3:* 576
Wagner Act, *2:* 397, 409
Walentynowicz, Anna, *2:* 356
Walesa, Lech, *2:* 356, 357 (ill.)
Walk for Freedom, *3:* 647
Walk Free Foundation, *3:* 623
Walkouts, Mexican American students, *1:* 77–82
Wall Street
    economic inequality, *1:* 218
    history, *1:* 217–218
    Occupy Wall Street movement (2011), *1:* 216–222
    opposition movements, *1:* 218
Walls, Carlotta, *1:* 50
Walter Reed Medical Center, *3:* 688–689, 689 (ill.)
War on drugs, Mexico, *1:* 91–95
War on Terror, *3:* 681–682
War protests, *3:* **651–692,** 656 (ill.), 660 (ill.), 667 (ill.), 668 (ill.), 671 (ill.), 674 (ill.), 679 (ill.), 682 (ill.), 686 (ill.)
    burning draft cards, *3:* 666–667, 667 (ill.)
    Candlelight Vigils against Invasion of Iraq (2003), *3:* 676–683, 682 (ill.)
    International Congress of Women (1915), *3:* 657–663, 660 (ill.)
    Manning, Chelsea, and WikiLeaks, *3:* 684–690, 686 (ill.)
    One Thousand Coffins Protest (2004), *3:* 678–679, 679 (ill.)
    protest songs, *3:* 670–671
    Student Armband Protest of Vietnam War (1965–1969), *3:* 663–668, 668 (ill.)
    Student Protest at Kent State (1970), *3:* 669–676, 674 (ill.)
Warren, Earl, *3:* 522–523
Warren, Elizabeth, *3:* 728

Warsaw, Poland
    anti-migrant protests, *2:* 323
    Polish resistance, *3:* 590 (ill.)
Warsaw Ghetto, *3:* 602–605
    creation of, *3:* 604
    deportations to death camps, *3:* 604–605
Warsaw Ghetto Uprising (1943), *3:* 590, 602–607, 606 (ill.). *See also* **Resistance to Nazis**
    end of the uprising, *3:* 606
    Willenberg, Samuel, *3:* 612
Washington, D.C.
    abolition of slavery, *3:* 633
    Capitol Crawl (1990), *2:* 276–284
    Forward on Climate rally (2013), *1:* 139–144, 142 (ill.)
    Justice for All March (2014), *3:* 515, 539–546, 545 (ill.)
    LGBTQ rights demonstrations, *2:* 433 (ill.)
    March for Gun Control (2013), *2:* 246–252
    March for Science (2017), *1:* 163–168, 165 (ill.)
    March for Women's Lives (1986), *3:* 556–561, 557 (ill.)
    Women's March on Washington (2017), *3:* 724–731, 730 (ill.)
    Women's Suffrage Protest at the White House (2017), *3:* 707–713, 712 (ill.)
Washington, D.C. Compensated Emancipation Act, *3:* 633, 633 (ill.)
Washington Post, 1: 141, 185; *3:* 688
Washington (state)
    background checks, *2:* 253–254
    WTO protests, *1:* 209–216, 214 (ill.)
Water pollution, *1:* 154
Watts Riots, *3:* 514 (ill.)
Weddington, Sarah, *3:* 576
Weiland, Hannah, *1:* 13
Weinberg, Jack, *1:* 198
West Virginia, Battle of Blair Mountain strike, *2:* 410–411
Westboro Baptist Church
    anti-gay protests, *2:* 449 (ill.), 451
    as hate group, *2:* 446
    protests of Matthew Shepard, *2:* 445–452
Westergaard, Kurt, *1:* 184–185, 187
Westwood, Vivienne, *1:* 13

WFL (Women's Freedom League), *3:* 703–704
Wheels of Justice March (1990), *2:* 282
When Abortion Was a Crime (1997), *3:* 552
Whistle-blowers, *3:* 684, 688
White, Dan, *2:* 441–442, 443–444
White, Micah, *1:* 219
White Night Riots (1979), *2:* 441–445, 444 (ill.). *See also* **LGBTQ rights**
White Rose Movement (1942–1943), *3:* 588, 592–597, 593 (ill.), 596 (ill.). *See also* **Resistance to Nazis**
    capture of leaders, *3:* 594–595
    methods, *3:* 594
    monument at University of Munich, *3:* 596 (ill.)
    origins, *3:* 593
White supremacists, *3:* 516–517, 542–543, 543. *See also* Race and racism
WHO (World Health Organization), *1:* 101; *3:* 550
Whole Women's Health v. Hellerstedt, *3:* 555
Wichita, KS, Summer of Mercy Protest, *3:* 566–567
WikiLeaks and, Manning, Bradley/Chelsea, *3:* 684–690, 686 (ill.)
Wilde, Oscar, *2:* 430
Wildfire (ship), *3:* 621 (ill.)
Wilkins, N.B., *2:* 329
Wilkins, Roy, *1:* 51
Will and Grace, *2:* 434
Willenberg, Samuel, *3:* 610, 611 (ill.), 612–613, 613 (ill.)
William Frantz Elementary School, *1:* 53
William III, King of England, *1:* 173
Willingham, Cameron Todd, *2:* 288
Wilson, Woodrow, *3:* 663, 710, 712
Wilson (Woodrow) High School, East LA, *1:* 81
Woman's Rights Convention (1848), *3:* 696, 708, 708 (ill.)
Woman's Rights Convention (1848). Declaration of Sentiments, *3:* 708, 709
Women's Equality Day, *3:* 713, 729
Women's Freedom League (WFL), *3:* 703–704
Women's health clinics, blocking access to, *3:* 557–558, 562–568, 566–567
Women's International League for Peace and Freedom, *3:* 661

GENERAL INDEX

Women's March on Washington (2017), *3:* 559, 724–731
   demonstrators, *3:* 730 (ill.)
   sister marches, *3:* 729–730
Women's Peace Congress (1915), *3:* 657–663, 660 (ill.)
   goals of, *3:* 661
   impact of, *3:* 661–663
   resolutions, *3:* 662
Women's rights, *3:* **693–732**, 697 (ill.), 698 (ill.), 704 (ill.), 705 (ill.), 708 (ill.), 709 (ill.), 712 (ill.), 716 (ill.), 719 (ill.), 723 (ill.), 729 (ill.), 730 (ill.).
   See also **Reproductive rights**
   Baladi campaign, *3:* 714–718, 716 (ill.)
   Bring Back Our Girls, *3:* 700–701, 722–723, 723 (ill.)
   British colonies, *3:* 693–695
   delayed by World War I, *3:* 658
   to education, *3:* 718–724
   Equal Rights Amendment, *3:* 558–559
   Hunger Strikes by Suffragettes in Prison, *3:* 701–707, 704 (ill.)
   Saudi Arabia, *3:* 714–715
   Seneca Falls Convention (1848), *3:* 696, 708, 708 (ill.)
   single v. married, *3:* 693–695
   21st century, *3:* 699–700
   Women's March on Washington (2017), *3:* 724–731, 730 (ill.)
   Women's Strike for Equality (1970), *3:* 728–729, 729 (ill.)
   Women's Suffrage Protest at the White House (1917), *3:* 707–713, 712 (ill.)
   Yousafzai, Malala, All-Girls School, *3:* 718–724
Women's Social and Political Union (WSPU), *3:* 703, 705
Women's Strike for Equality (1970), *3:* 728–729, 729 (ill.)
Women's suffrage movement, *3:* 696–698. *See also* Voting rights
   Derby Day Protest (1913), *3:* 705
   division over tactics, *3:* 703
   Hunger Strikes by Suffragettes in Prison, *3:* 701–707, 704 (ill.)
   impact of United States Civil War, *3:* 709–710
   impact of World War I (1914–1918), *3:* 710–711
   leaders, *3:* 697 (ill.)
   Saudi Arabia, *3:* 714–718
   United Kingdom, *3:* 471–472, 697–698, 701–707
   United States, *3:* 696–698, 707–713
Women's Suffrage Protest at the White House (1917), *3:* 707–713, 712 (ill.)
Woodrow Wilson High School, East LA, *1:* 81
Woolworth's, Greensboro, NC, *1:* 60
Work hours, *2:* 393
Workers. *See also* **Labor rights**
   farm, *1:* 75–76, 75 (ill.), 78–79; *2:* 416
   Fast-food Workers' Strike, *2:* 422–426, 424 (ill.)
   Filipino, *2:* 416, 418–419
   Mexican, *2:* 416, 418–419
   migrant, *2:* 415, 416
Workers' rights. *See* **Labor rights**
Working conditions
   Chinese workers, *2:* 398
   coal mining, *2:* 312
   farm workers, *2:* 416
   General Motors Co., *2:* 408–409
   labor laws, *2:* 397–398
   migrant workers, *2:* 416
World Bank, *2:* 381, 384
World Conservation Congress, *1:* 21
World Day against Trafficking in Persons, *3:* 647
World Economic Forum, *2:* 323
World Health Organization (WHO), *1:* 101; *3:* 550
World Trade Center terror attack (2001), *2:* 326; *3:* 677–680. *See also* Terrorism
World Trade Organization (WTO). Accountability Review Committee of Seattle, Washington, *1:* 215
World War I (1914–1918), *2:* 298
   anti-war efforts, *3:* 655
   impact on women's suffrage movement, *3:* 658, 710–711
World War II (1939–1945), *1:* 74; *3:* 585, 607, 655
   Battle of Stalingrad, *3:* 594–595
   Germany, *3:* 479–481
Wounded Knee, SD
   AIM occupation (1973), *2:* 364–365, 367–375, 374 (ill.)
   massacre (1890), *2:* 369–370, 373
Wright, Martha, *3:* 708
WSPU (Women's Social and Political Union), *3:* 703, 705

WTO (World Trade Organization), *1:* 205–206
    goals, *1:* 210–211
    protests in Seattle, Washington, *1:* 209–216
WTO (World Trade Organization). Accountability Review Committee of Seattle, Washington, *1:* 215
Wuchang Revolt (1911), *1:* 106
Wyoming
    anti-gay protests by WBC, *2:* 448, 449–451
    murder of Matthew Shepard, *2:* 445–446

X

Xiaogang, China, *1:* 103
    collective farms and communes, *1:* 108–110
    farmers' secret agreement, *1:* 105–111, 109 (ill.)
Xingu River, *2:* 379–381

Y

Yale University
    history, *1:* 195–196
    racial tensions, *1:* 196–199
    student protests on free speech, *1:* 194–201, 197 (ill.)
Yale University. Calhoun College, *1:* 195, 200
Yale University. Intercultural Affairs Council, *1:* 195, 197
Yarrow, Peter, *1:* 68
Ybor City Cigar Strike (1931), *1:* 84–85
Yemen, Arab Spring, *3:* 488–489
Yiannopoulos, Milo, *1:* 176
York County Prison Farm, *1:* 62
Young, Neil, *3:* 670
Young Turks, *2:* 298
Yousafzai, Malala, *3:* 700–701, 718–720, 719 (ill.), 720–721
Yousafzai, Malala, All-Girls School, *3:* 718–724

Z

Zhou Enlai, *1:* 108
Zimmerman, George, *3:* 540–544
ZOB (Jewish Combat Organization), *3:* 604–606, 605
Zoot Suit Riots (1943), *3:* 512, 512 (ill.), 518–524, 521 (ill.). *See also* **Racial conflict**
Zoot suits, *3:* 519–520
Zuccotti Park, *1:* 219